Lys de Bray's
Manual of Old~Fashioned Flowers

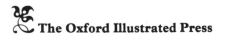The Oxford Illustrated Press

© Lys de Bray, 1984
Printed in England by **J.H. Haynes & Co Ltd,** Sparkford, Yeovil, Somerset.

ISBN 0 902280 91 0

The Oxford Illustrated Press, Sparkford, Yeovil, Somerset.

British Library Cataloguing in Publication Data

De Bray, Lys
   Lys de Bray's manual of old-fashioned flowers
   1. Flowers
   I. Title
   582.13   QX85.5
   ISBN 0–902280-91-0

Other books by Lys de Bray

The Wild Garden (Weidenfeld & Nicholson, 1978)
Midsummer Silver (Weidenfeld & Nicholson, 1980)
Fantastic Garlands (Blandford Press, 1982)
Cottage Garden Year (J.M. Dent, 1983)

CONTENTS

ACKNOWLEDGEMENTS

I want to thank all the people who gave me their flowers to paint for this book. I never cease to be surprised and humbly grateful for the helpfulness and kindness of not only my long-suffering friends and acquaintances but of complete strangers. The world of gardeners has some very good people in it who are as nice as their plants. The Marchioness of Salisbury graciously gave me permission to photograph her flowers in their beautiful setting of Cranborne, and Peter and Diana Chappell allowed me to do the same at their woodland garden, 'Spinners' in Hampshire.

It was lovely to have Rosemary back again to type some of the manuscript, and without Sue's regular Monday-morning miracle I should have been lost.

Producing a book like this is rather like producing a play – there's a great deal going on behind the scenes that the rest of the world can never know about, and this is where Hilary came in. She walked into the garden and offered to help, and she typed (from the hand-written manuscript) and tidied, and kept the filing baskets from overflowing, and did shopping, and vital sums (she can add, I cannot) and looked after the cats and the goldfish and the garden and the greenhouse, and sowed seeds that flowered on to these pages. And once, she even washed up. Without Hilary's dedication and conscientiousness, this book could not have been finished in time, and I'm sure that I don't deserve her.

My husband, Larry Blonstein, never ceases to encourage and support me, and his help is my strength.

Lys de Bray

Water-colour illustrations and photographs by Lys de Bray. The front cover photograph is of the author's cottage and garden.

Erratum
In the section of colour photos, for 'The ominously imposing *Acanthus mollis* ...' please read 'The sculpturally interesting flowers and foliage of *Acanthus spinosus* ...'

PLATES LIST

1. Amaryllidaceae

2. Boraginaceae

3. Campanulaceae

4. Caryophyllaceae

5. Convolvulaceae

6. Cruciferae

7. Labiatae

8. Leguminosae

9. Liliaceae

10. Malvaceae

11. Onagraceae

12. Papaveraceae

13. Primulaceae

14. Ranunculaceae

15. Scrophulariaceae

16. Violaceae

"How I hate modern gardens!" said St. Aldegonde. "What a horrid thing this is! One might as well have a mosaic pavement there. Give me cabbage-roses, sweet-peas, and wallflowers. That is my idea of a garden. Corisande's garden is the only sensible thing of the sort." ... As they entered it now, it seemed a blaze of roses and carnations, though one recognized in a moment the presence of the lily, the heliotrope, and the stock. Some white peacocks were basking on the southern wall.

Lord Beaconsfield: *Lothair*, 1869.

INTRODUCTION

Here is a gardening book with a difference – it will tell you not only how to grow those favourite old-fashioned flowers but where to get them. This has involved a great deal of pleasurable work among the catalogues to make sure that all the flowers in the book are obtainable as seeds, bulbs or plants. The history, myths, legends, folklore, mixed-up nomenclature and medical quackery are fascinating, and I hope that you will find them as interesting and amusing as I have done. The dates of introduction are sometimes quite surprising – plants that one thinks of as being quite old, like Clarkia and Chrysanthemums are not, whereas others such as Scilla, Cyclamen and the Muscari or Grape Hyacinth were grown by Gerard in his famous garden at High Holborn. Throughout the book the same names keep cropping up – Gerard, Parkinson, Pliny, Turner, Tradescant and others; these were the great gardeners of history, though they were philosophers, apothecaries or Professors of Botany as well. I have therefore included some very brief biographical notes which will be found in the appendices. These people had a great influence on garden history, and fortunately they made lists of the plants of their time, or they produced books or other works that were used as reference for centuries. Most of the plants in this book are exactly the same as when they were first discovered – surely a great comfort in this too-rapidly changing world. Fritillaries and Foxgloves, Sunflowers and Snowdrops, Marigolds and Madonna Lilies – these are just a few of the flowers that were grown in medieval gardens and are still unchanged by the passing years and the hybridisers.

When preparing the book, the first lists were far too long and there seemed to be too many plants which, though popular in earlier times are now no longer easily obtainable; this was a useful pointer as to which ones to leave out, Conversely, gardeners of some experience may find that I have not included certain species, and even a genus or two, and for this I apologise – there simply was not sufficient space. The history of the plants themselves, together with the notes on cultivation, seemed more important to me than producing a personal encyclopaedia.

There are no roses, woody climbers, flowering shrubs or trees, because it is hoped to produce a companion volume which will feature such old charmers as Honeysuckle and Heliotrope, Lavender and Lilac and all the many others.

Changing fashion is another reason why some of the original 'old' flowers are no longer in our gardens – there are fashions in gardening and in plants just as there are in other areas of life. When gardens were re-made to suit the times, the older (usually herbaceous) plants had to go, and the best known example of this is the carpet-bedding schemes of our Victorian ancestors. Thousands of plants (not always suitable sorts) were grown for their massed colour effects, to be planted out for the short season when 'the family' left their town houses to retreat to the country for the summer. When they returned to the cities in the autumn and the flowers were over, the beds and borders were often left empty until it was time to prepare them for the next year's display. So the herbaceous plants survived only by being planted in unwanted corners of the kitchen garden or as part of the 'picking flowers'. Some of them went home with the second gardener, and they were replanted in the comparative safety of a cottage garden among the fruit trees and the vegetables. The clergy usually remained quite untouched by garden fashions, and when the pendulum swung back again to an interest in the vanishing plants, it was often in the neglected gardens of country vicarages that such treasures as the double primroses or the old pinks were found.

The time scale of the book came naturally – it begins with Gerard's lists of his garden plants in 1596 and 1599, and ends with the outbreak of the First World War in 1914, which seemed a suitable date to close the pages of discovery: the days of the great English garden ended then in that twilight and transitional time of change.

Despite what visitors to this country say and think, because of the Gulf Stream we have an enviable climate for gardening. Our winters (though often too wet for the little alpine plants) are not too cold, and the snow, when it does come, is seldom deep, heavy or long-lasting as it is in certain northern zones of the United States. Our summers are not too hot, except once in a century or so, and therefore we can grow all the temperate-region plants. In a 'good' summer, our gardens are the best in the world, because for over four centuries plant collectors, both private and professional, have been bringing back the best and the newest discoveries from other lands.

The British people seem to have a natural aptitude for gardening and the care of plants, and all these reasons make a very good and solid foundation for a collection of those 'old-fashioned' flowers.

Lys de Bray

Wimborne, Dorset   March 1984.
ENGLAND.

ACANTHUS - Bear's Breeches. *(Acanthaceae).* In the fifth century BC the Greek sculptor Callimachos admired the handsome leaves of this stately plant; his stylised adaption of them can still be seen today at the top of Corinthian columns and elsewhere. In medieval times the plant was known to herbalists as Brank-Ursine, and two varieties only were grown, *A. mollis* and *A. spinosus.* Acanthus are mostly of mediterranean origin and are hardy in the south and south-western parts of the British Isles. They like a hot sheltered position and will grow larger and taller (sometimes inconveniently so) if planted with a south-facing wall for shelter and reflected warmth. The leaves (somewhat like those of a gigantic dandelion) vary in length and width according to type, with those of *A. spinosisimus* (a variety of *A. spinosus)* being particularly spiny. The roots of an established plant are huge, deep and tenacious, and Acanthus should only be moved when young or at its most dormant time, December to February. The inflorescence of *A. mollis* is very striking, with hooded flowers of white and purple interspersed with green bracts. The finest specimen I have ever seen was growing in a sheltered corner of Devon on an abandoned compost-heap; it was about ten feet wide and ten feet tall and was ominously imposing.

A. mollis (1548) grows to a height of about 5ft (150 cm) depending on soil and situation; a mature plant will be as wide as it is high, sending up spikes of white and purple tubular flowers with green bracts in July and August. A focal plant.

A. spinosus grows to 4ft (122cm) and has similarly coloured flowers in July and August. Its leaves are much more cut up and are spiny. Another focal perennial plant, but for a more sheltered border as it comes from Southern Europe.

Requirements: A warm and sheltered situation with well-drained soil. In a severe winter the leaves will be completely frosted and protection can be given to the roots beneath by mounding up the crown of the plant with ashes. *A. mollis* is the hardier of the two.

Cultivation: Division of the roots between December and February, or from seed sown in a greenhouse in March. Grow the seedlings on in the usual manner and plant out in large pots sunk in the ground in a cold frame for two years before planting out into permanent positions.

After flowering: Cut the flowering stems down as far as possible.

Uses: Excellent for large flower arrangements. In the garden mature plants present a handsome, sculptural appearance and they should be grown where this can be seen to advantage.

Seeds: Chiltern, Thomas Butcher, Thompson and Morgan, Unwins.

Plants: Most nurseries.

ACHILLEA - Yarrow. *(Compositae).* The wild plant, *A millefolium,* can sometimes be a troublesome weed of lawns but its descendents have now an established place in our borders. There are very many modern hybrids but they are not within the scope of this book. *A. ptarmica,* once called 'Sneezewort' or, more prettily 'Pearl Flower' is particularly charming because its small button-shaped flowers are so very white and long-lasting both in the border and when cut.

A. ageratum - Sweet Nancy. grows only 6-8ins high (15-20cms). Silver leaves and white flowers from July to September. Rock garden, border. A perennial plant from Greece.

A. millefolium 'rosea' - Yarrow. Grows to 18ins (46cm) with deep rose-pink flowers from June to September. Border. A European perennial plant.

A. ptarmica - Sneezewort, Pearl Flower. Grows to 2½ft (76cm) and has white flowers from June to September. Border. A European perennial plant.

A. taygetea (1640) grows from 18 – 30ins (46 – 76cm) has attractive silvery leaves and golden yellow flowers from July to September. Sunny, warm border. A perennial plant from the Levant.

A. tomentosa is mat-forming and grows to 9ins (23cm). It is well suited to the rock-garden where it needs good drainage. Bright yellow flowers from June to September. A perennial plant from Europe and N. Asia.

Requirements: All Achilleas like sunny, open situations and ordinary well-drained soil suits them well.

Cultivation: Division of roots in March.

Uses: Border and rock-garden subjects, most are good as cut flowers. The flower heads can be dried for winter decoration.

Seeds: Thomas Butcher, Chiltern, Dobie, Thompson and Morgan.

Plants: Most nurseries.

ACHIMENES - Hot-Water Plant, Cupid's Bower *(Gesneriaceae)*. The name Achimenes is derived from Cheimaino, to suffer from cold and this plant is, therefore, well named. It is not grown as much today as it needs a certain amount of care and a consistently regular temperature in order to do well, which was much more easily achieved in the days of cheap coal and cheaper labour. Its other name comes from those times, when the tubers were started into growth over the hot water pipes of the greenhouses and watered with warm water. *Achimenes longiflora* is the easiest of them to grow as it requires less heat than the others which do better when grown in Orchid-house conditions. The tubers should be started into growth in March or April in a temperature of 16°C (61°F). They should be covered with 1in (2.5cm) of a peat-based compost and may be planted quite closely together as they like to be crowded – 6 or 7 tubers to a 5-inch (12.5-cm) pot or 8 or 9 to a 6-inch (15-cm) pot. Water carefully to begin with, gradually giving more as the plants grow. They should have fortnightly feeds as soon as the flower buds form, and it may be found necessary to support the rather lax habit of the stems. The plants need shading from sun and ventilation and syringing in hot weather. After flowering they should be allowed to die down, watering less frequently. When the leaves have withered the pots should be put under the staging without disturbing the tubers, and should be kept in a dry temperature of 45 – 50° (114 – 122°F) for the winter.

A. longiflorus (1841) - Hot-Water Plant grows to about 1 foot (30.5cm) with gradually lengthening stems and (usually) violet blue flowers in July and August. A tender tuberous plant for the warm greenhouse or conservatory from Central America.

Requirements: *As described.*

Cultivation: The tubers will increase during the season but should be left in their pots until the following spring, then separated and grown on as described. Sow seed in a temperature of 20 – 25°C (68 – 78°F) from February to March. Press fine seeds lightly into moistened compost and do not cover. Put glass over box or pan and turn over each day until seedlings are growing well. Plant 3 or 4 to a pot and grow on.

Seed/Tubercles: Amand, Thomas Butcher, Chiltern, de Jager, Holtzhausen, Hortico, Kent County Nurseries, Suttons, Thompson and Morgan.

ACONITUM - Wolf's Bane, Monkshood *(Ranunculaceae)*. The tall, blue early-flowering Monkshood is one of the most interesting and one of the most deadly of our cottage-garden flowers. All of its parts are poisonous, even the pollen, and great care should be taken when handling the plant: it is not advisable to bring cut flowers into the house. However, Monkshood is very beautiful in the garden, and the long-lasting blue-purple flowers look very well when growing up through creamy yellow roses. The light green palmately-lobed leaves begin to appear very early in the year, often in Mid-January, when most other herbaceous plants are still fast asleep. Its name of 'Monkshood' is from a fancied resemblance to the cowled hood of a monk, and 'Wolf's Bane' is from the efficacious poison (Aconitine) that was used on arrowheads and in meat left out as bait for marauding wolf-packs of medieval Europe. Man used poison with brisk effectiveness in those times, though more to dispose of vermin than of his neighbour. The extract from the plant is still used by qualified homeopathic practitioners to alleviate the pain of sciatica, gout, arthritis, neuralgia and rheumatism. It was always considered to be a magic plant and was said to be one of the ingredients for the legendary 'flying ointment' that witches used. The nomenclature of this family is somewhat involved.

A. anglicum grows to a height of 3ft (91.5cm) and has lilac-blue flowers in May and June. Suitable for the border. An English perennial plant, long in cultivation.

A. Napellus - Monkshood. Grows to 3ft 6in (107cm) and has blue-purple flowers in July and August. Border. A perennial plant from Europe and Asia.

A. pyrenaicum. (1739) grows to a height of 2ft (61cm) and has yellow flowers in June. Border. A perennial from the Pyrenees.

Requirements: Good rich soil; Aconitums do quite well in semi-shade.

Propagation: Root division between October and January. (The earlier part of the winter is best.) *Or* sow seeds in March in a cold frame or unheated greenhouse.

Warning: Wear gloves at all times when handling this plant as it is very poisonous.

Seeds: Thomas Butcher, Chambers, Chiltern, Naturescape, Thompson and Morgan.

Plants/Rhizomes: Chambers, Beth Chatto, Goatchers, Hillier, Ingwersen, Kelways, Scotts.

AGAPANTHUS - African Lily *(Liliaceae).* Very handsome plants, well-suited to growing in tubs and containers as long as these are deep enough for the very large root-system. Agapanthus dislikes being disturbed and does not flower well the first year after being moved or divided. It is a greedy plant and relishes regular feeding with strained manure-water. The roots are exceptionally thick and fangy and should be divided with two garden forks placed back to back, at which time any perennial weeds such as Ground Elder can be removed and destroyed. When grown in tubs, which must be sufficiently large to accommodate the mature plant, it is better to take tub and all into a greenhouse for the winter, as severe frosts can penetrate the sides of the tub or damage the exposed roots on the surface. The tubs of Agapanthus should be placed below the greenhouse staging and kept on the dry side throughout the winter. They can be moved out when frost-danger is past, and by this time the flower-buds will be forming. Begin to water and feed them at this stage and the handsome and long-lasting flowers will have a head-start on garden-sited clumps. This is another group of plants where botanical nomenclature is unclear.

A. africanus syn. **umbellatus - African Lily** (1629). Grows 2 – 2½ft (61 – 76cm) with deep blue flowers. Sunny sheltered corner. A tender perennial plant from the Cape Peninsula.

Requirements: A sunny, sheltered border or large containers filled with an enriched compost. Agapanthus are generally hardy in the south and west of the British Isles, but plants that are established in the garden should be protected with ashes or bracken (this being longer-lasting than straw) before the winter.

Cultivation: Root division in March, or from ripened seed which will take about five years to flower. The plants may not be true to type.

Plants: Amand, Avon, Broadleigh, Beth Chatto, Hillier, St. Bridget.

AGERATUM *(Compositae).* A most useful edging and bedding plant whose flowers are almost guaranteed to last well in the garden. The name Ageratum comes from the Greek *a*, 'not', *geras* 'old', and providing the dead shaving-brush flower heads are snipped off when necessary the beautiful clear amethystine colour of the flowers will be a constant pleasure throughout the summer. This is an undemanding and easy plant and it should be planted thickly so that the unusual colour of the flowers is seen to best effect. Ageratum can be grown for winter flowering under glass if the seeds are sown in August. This is a plant that has been much hybridised and most well-known seedsmen stock several modern varieties which can be obtained in pink, mauve, blue or white or a mixture of these. The type species are almost unobtainable.

A. houstonianum (1822) grows from 5 – 12ins (12.5 – 30.5cm) with blue-mauve flowers from June until the frosts. A half-hardy annual plant from Mexico.

Requirements: Sun and moisture-retentive soil.

Cultivation: Sow seeds thinly in March at a constant temperature of 16 – 18°C (61 – 64°F). Prick out seedlings and harden off.

During and after flowering: Dead-head regularly.

Uses: As an edging plant.

Seeds: Most seedsmen.

ALCHEMILLA - Lady's Mantle *(Rosaceae).* Alchemilla is exceedingly easy to grow – in fact, one plant is all that is necessary to populate a garden. Once again it is the flower-arrangers who have taught us to appreciate this dainty-looking but sturdy plant that has sprays of tiny greenish yellow flowers that last for many weeks. The exquisite 'pleated' leaves are apparently circular and in wet weather each one holds a jewelled drop of rainwater, with smaller ones caught fast in the fringed edge surrounding each leaf. Alchemilla self-sows itself with tremendous prodigality, and after three years one plant can be as much as 3ft (91.5cm) across, forming a perfect circle of darker leaves edged with a petticoat-frill of flower sprays. Alchemilla should not be planted in the rock garden because it will smother other or less vigorous plants but it looks very well edging stone or brick paths and patios, as ground cover under roses and it does quite well in semi-shade though it prefers sunnier situations. In the middle ages the dew from the plant was carefully collected as one of the many strange ingredients essential to the preparation of the fabled Philosopher's Stone. This was a hypothetical substance that medieval alchemists believed would transmute all baser metals into gold. The arabic name for the plant was *Alkemelych* – the plant of the alchemists, later latinized into Alchemilla. In earlier times the plant was used medicinally as a wound herb and it had some reputation for restoring fading feminine beauty.

Alchemilla mollis - Lady's Mantle grows to 1ft (30.5cm) wide. Flowers from June to September. Plant as an edging plant for paving, or as ground cover. It can be invasive. A perennial from Asia Minor.

Requirements: A sunny position in almost any kind of soil.

Cultivation: Leave seed heads on adult plants and collect seed, or wait until spring and collect self-sown seedlings. Sow the seed in compost and germinate at a temperature of 15 – 21°C (60 – 70°F). Mature plants can be lifted and divided in early spring just before regrowth starts.

Uses: This is a useful background plant for flower arrangements and the flowers and leaves last well in water. It is equally useful as ground cover in sunny situations.

Plants: Most garden centres.

Seeds: Thompson and Morgan.

ALLIUM *(Liliaceae).* Alliums are almost as odoriferous as the Garlic, *A. sativum* (because of course they are sisters under the skin), when the leaves are touched or bruised. There are very many varieties but almost all of them need to be grown in sunny situations. Heights, colours and habits vary most interestingly from small and dainty rock-plants to tall and robust border giants, and if the soil in your garden suits them – in general, this needs to be light and free-draining – they will increase most obligingly. Many have exceedingly handsome flower-umbels that dry well for winter decoration. Some of the very large varieties may need staking for their own safety, and an example of this is *A. giganteum* which lives up to its name with 4-ft (122-cm) flower stems topped with dense spherical flower umbels. *A. moly* is a good border plant for a sunny position growing so well and so easily that it can almost be a nuisance, though a very attractive one, with its profusion of yellow flowers among light-green strap-shaped leaves. It is best trapped in a large rock-pocket of its own in a rockery, or a corner confined by concrete and then it cannot smother its near neighbours. After flowering all the aerial parts of this plant disappear completely, leaving apparently bare soil, so its position should be marked by the forgetful gardener. *A. siculum* is one of the most interesting of the Alliums, with nodding, bell-shaped flowers that are subtly shaded in green and salmon-red; later these turn into upright seed vessels that resemble the turreted castles of the Rhine. Preventive measures for all Alliums should be taken against the depredations of slugs.

A. albopilosum, syn. **Christofii** (1901) grows to 18in (46cm) with a large many-flowered (up to 80) umbel of metallic lilac flowers in June. Dries well. Border. A bulbous plant from Turkestan.

A. Backhousianum (1885) grows to 4ft (122cm) with a dense umbel of white flowers in June. Back of border. A bulbous plant from the Himalayas.

A. caeruleum syn. **A. azureum** (1830) grows to 2ft (61cm) with a globose head of sky-blue flowers in June and July. Border. A bulbous plant from Siberia and Turkestan.

A. cyaneum (1890) grows to 12in (30.5cm) with a scape of nodding blue flowers in August. Rockery or border. A bulbous plant from China.

A. giganteum grows to 4ft (122cm) with dense umbels 4in (10cm) across of bright mauve flowers in June. Needs staking. Border. A bulbous plant from the Himalayas.

A. karataviense (1878) grows only 6in (15cm). Handsome variegated leaves, blue-green with maroon markings. Large spherical umbels of iridescent star-shaped lilac flowers. Rockery. A bulbous plant from Turkestan.

A. flavum (1759) grows to 12in (30.5cm) with shining lemon-yellow flowers in July and August. Rockery. A bulbous plant from S. Europe and the Caucasus.

A. Moly. Probably the easiest to grow, 12in (30.5cm) high with hemispherical umbels of yellow flowers in June. Rockery, sunny border. A bulbous plant from the Mediterranean region.

A. narcissiflorum grows up to 12in (30.5cm) high with loose umbels of bright rose-pink flowers in July. Very beautiful. Rockery. A bulbous plant from the Alps and the Caucasus.

A. neapolitanum (1828) grows to 12in (30.5cm) and has snowy white flower umbels in May. Can be grown as a pot plant as it does not smell as much as some other members of this genus. Needs a sheltered position in the border if grown outside. A bulbous blant from the Mediterranean region.

A. Ostrowskianum (1883) grows to 12in (30.5cm). Grey-green leaves and a spherical umbel of mauve-pink flowers from June to August. Rockery. A bulbous plant from Turkestan.

A. roseum (1752) grows to 15in (38cm) with bright pink star-shaped flowers in June. Rockery. A bulbous plant from the Mediterranean region.

A. siculum grows to 3ft (91.5cm) with pendulous bells of salmon-pink and green flowers in May and June. Increases well, dried heads very unusual and early. Border. A bulbous plant from Sicily and Southern France.

A. triquetrum (1789) grows to 12in (30cm) high with nodding white bell-shaped flowers in May. Shady border, increases well. A bulbous plant from S. Europe.

Requirements: Mainly light, well-drained soils, sunny situations except for woodland species not named here.

Cultivation: Most of the Alliums are bulbs and are increased by offsets from

these. Plant the bulbs to a depth of from 3 or 4 times their own size. If
Alliums are to be grown from seed sow from October to April in a cold
greenhouse. Germination may take some time.
Uses: Excellent for flower arrangements and when dried for winter decoration.
Bulbs: Most bulb merchants.
Seeds: Chiltern, Thompson and Morgan.
Plants: Rock Garden Nursery.

ALSTROEMERIA *(Alstroemeriaceae,* formerly *Amaryllidaceae).* Alstroemerias
are a small genus of plants native to South America and are named after the
Baron Clas von Alstroemer, a friend of Linnaeus. Alstroemerias like to be
planted very deep at about 8 – 10ins (20.5 – 25.5cm) and will fail if grown
at the surface of the soil; they prefer to remain undisturbed for years so
their site should be chosen with some care. Ideally, these plants should be
grown facing south in a sheltered slightly sloping well-drained border with
some peat and sharp sand dug well in. Clay soils do not generally suit them.
The seedlings should be planted as they are, straight from the pot with no
thinning out or other root-disturbance; dig a deeper hole than would be
usual and plant the seedlings at the bottom of it, slowly earthing up the
stems as the plants grow. Feeding before the flowers form is advantageous
and well-rotted manure is best for this. Alstroemerias can be grown in large,
deep pots or containers, but these must be protected from winter frosts. The
stems of pot-grown plants are inclined to flop and will need staking; extreme
care should be taken so as not to damage the root system, and the canes
should be put into the pots or tubs when the final planting out is done. It
should be borne in mind that with Alstroemerias, germination can be
lengthy or sporadic, from 1 to 12 months being fairly normal.
A. aurantiaca - Peruvian Lily (1831). This is the hardiest variety. Grows to
36in (91.5cm) with orange flowers from June to August. Border. A
perennial plant from Chile.
A. pelegrina (1754) grows to 12in (30.5cm) with lilac-pink flowers spotted and
striped with purple. Flowers from June to August. There is a beautiful white
form, 'Alba' called 'Lily of the Incas'. Tubs and containers, sunny border.
A perennial plant from Chile.
Requirements: A south-facing border.
Cultivation: Soak seeds in warm water for 12 hours. Sow seeds *very* thinly (mix
with dry silver sand) into pots in a propagator at a temperature of 18 –
21°C (64 – 70°F) in March. When seedlings are large enough pot on into
larger, deeper pots.
Uses: Excellent as cut flowers.
Seeds: Thomas Butcher, Chiltern, Holtzhausen, Thompson and Morgan.
Plants: Notcutts, R.V. Roger Ltd, St. Bridget.

ALTHAEA - Hollyhock *(Malvaceae).* Of all the flowers associated with cottage
gardens the Hollyhock is perhaps the most evocative, being portrayed on
chocolate boxes, embroidered cushion-covers, tea-cosies and huckaback
guest-towels. However, this handsome plant – which can often grow tall
enough to peer in at the bedroom window – has survived all this pictorial
kitsch and still charms us as completely as ever.
    The Hollyhock has been in cultivation for over 500 years. Double
varieties, with flowers as frilled as a pincushion, can be grown just as easily,
but though these are very showy they are not as instantly recognisable as
the Hollyhock of our nursery fables. The plants are prone to 'Hollyhock
rust' and there is little to be done about this except to pick off the diseased
leaves as soon as the disfiguring marks are seen. Though Hollyhocks can
live for several years, if rust appears it is better to treat them as biennials,
or to move their planting position if this is practicable. Because they are so
large there is often only one place for them to be with advantage in the

average-sized garden, though changing the soil is sometimes efficaceous for a while. They thrive best in good garden soil enriched with decayed manure, which is why they did so well in the cottage gardens of old.

Unless there is a conveniently-situated wall for their support, staking is essential and 6-ft (1.85-m) stakes should be used which should be set in position at planting out time. The plants should be tied in as they grow or they will crash to the ground like factory chimneys during summer rainstorms. Though the seed should be sown as soon as it is ripe to be sure of germination, conversely, it can often remain viable for several years.

A. ficifolia - Antwerp Hollyhock (1597). Grows to 6ft (180cm) usually yellow or orange in June. Border. A short-lived perennial plant from Siberia.

A. rosea - Hollyhock (1573) grows to 8ft (240cm) and more, and the flowers can be white, cream, yellow, salmon, pink, rose, magenta, crimson and a very dark blackish red that is most striking. Flowers from June to August. Border. A short-lived perennial plant, probably from China.

Requirements: Good rich soil and a sunny position.

Cultivation: Space out large, flat seeds in trays or pots to obviate the need for first-size thinning, germinate at 10 − 15°C (50 − 60°F) if sown in March. Transfer into large pots and winter in a cold frame or sheltered corner until spring. Plant out in flowering position. Root cuttings can be taken − plant these in individual pots of sandy soil, keep shaded until growth shows.

After flowering: Cut down stems when seed has ripened.

Seeds: Bloms, Thomas Butcher, Chiltern, Suttons.

Plants: Bloms, Thomson and Morgan, The Weald Herbary.

ALYSSUM *(Cruciferae).* Once upon a time these plants had the reputation for calming anger, and their name is a derivation from *a*, 'not', and *lyssa*, 'rage' or 'madness'. There is much uncertainty as to which of the two species most commonly grown might have possessed this most remarkable power, though of the two it most likely is the yellow flowered 'Gold-Dust' or *Alyssum saxatile* which was known to both Gerard and Turner. The 'Alyssum' of those times was a certain cure for hydrophobia, and Lyte said that if the plant were "... presented only to the diseased person, without any internal or external application ...." it would act as a certain antidote to the bite of any mad dog. There are several plants in this genus that were called by the old country name of 'Madwort'. The two species that are most familiar are the grey-leaved, yellow-flowering perennial. *A. saxatile*, and *A. maritimum* the (usually) white-flowered annual used by the thousand as an effectively solid edging plant. This is Sweet Alyssum, so called because it has a rich, sweet scent that is most attractive to bees.

A. saxatile is, alas, grown only too often with that other member of the Cruciferae family, Aubrieta, whose rich colour-range of mauves and violets clashes most inharmoniously with the brilliant yellow of *A. saxatile*. This is a plant that has a tendency to straggle and clipping hard back after flowering helps to prevent this: it is also a good idea to sow half a box of seeds every two years or so to keep a succession of young and vigorous plants in readiness as replacements for those that have perished in the winter or that have ceased to flower well.

N.B. *A. maritimum* has now changed its name to *Lobularia maritima.*

A. saxatile (1710) grows to 9in (23cm) with bright yellow flowers in May and June. Grey leaves are attractive throughout the year. Rockery (can be too vigorous for small areas) or sunny dry walls where its yellow cushions can cascade freely. A perennial from E. Europe.

Lobularia maritima (formerly **A. maritimum) - Sweet Alyssum** grows to 6in (15cm) with a profusion of white, lilac or purple flowers throughout the summer. Borders, edging and in tubs and containers. An annual from Europe and W. Asia.

Requirements: *A. saxatile* needs sun and does best on banks or atop walls. *L. maritima* needs full sun and ordinary garden soil.

Cultivation: Sow *A. saxatile* seeds in March or April, grow on to flower following year. Sow seeds of *L. maritima* in February or March at a temperature of 10 – 13°C (50 – 55°F). Harden off before planting out.

During flowering: Dead-head *L. maritima*.

Uses: Wall, border and container plants.

Seeds: Bloms, Thomas Butcher, Chiltern, Dobie, Suttons, Thompson and Morgan, Unwins.

Plants: Most Nurseries.

AMARANTHUS *(Amaranthaceae)*. The plant most commonly grown is Love-Lies-Bleeding – *Amaranthus caudatus* – sometimes called Velvet Flower. Long, narrowing crimson tails dangle from amongst the attractive matching-veined pale green leaves; the 'tails' are made up of a multitude of petal-less flowers, and there is a green variety called 'Viridis' much beloved by flower-arrangers. The flower has a history of use and beauty – it was called 'Quihuicha' by the Aztecs who used the crimson ropes of its blossoms for ceremonial purposes and who ate its minute seeds by the ton. It looks best when grown where the trailing tassels can be seen to advantage, such as at the top of a low wall or in containers of a good size. It can grow to a height of some 3ft (91.5cm) and the ends of the flowers can sometimes be seen trailing sadly in summer mud, so it is a kindness to these showy and striking-looking flowers to grow them up high where they can be properly seen. It also helps if they can be lightly and invisibly staked from behind because the flower-tails absorb moisture during wet weather and make the plants lean drunkenly against each other for support. In the Victorian language of flowers, Love-Lies-Bleeding meant 'Hopeless, not heartless'. Gerard knew this plant as the 'Great Purple Flower-Gentle' though the name 'Flower-Gentle' was later given to the Celosia.

The other member of this family that was once more commonly grown was the Prince's Feather – *Amaranthus hypochondriacus* – a much taller 4- to 5-ft (122- to 152.5-cm) plant with similarly coloured but erect, tufted flower spikes.

A. caudatus - Love-Lies-Bleeding, Velvet Flower (1956) grows to 3ft (91.5cm) with long-lasting racemes of crimson flowers from July until the frosts. Site carefully, a raised position or tubs are very effective. An annual from the tropics.

A. hypochondriacus - Prince's Feather (1684). Taller, to 5ft (152cm) with erect crimson flower spikes from July until the frosts. Back of border. An annual from tropical America.

Requirements: A sunny situation and good garden soil; *A. caudatus* will do quite well in poor soil but will repay feeding with larger plants and longer tassels.

Cultivation: Sow seeds of these half-hardy annuals in March under glass, at a temperature of 15°C (59°F). Prick out seedlings and harden off in the usual way, plant out in May into soil that has been enriched by some well-rotted mature.

Uses: Both plants are very striking, though not beautiful. Both are good in large flower arrangements and last well in water. *A. caudatus* can be carefully dried and will retain its deep colour for some time.

Seeds: Thomas Butcher, Chiltern, Dobie, Kent County Nurseries, Suttons, Thompson and Morgan, Unwins.

AMARYLLIS - Belladonna Lily *(Amaryllidaceae)*. This is the sweet-scented Lily much beloved by the Victorians. The flowers appear on sturdy naked stems before the leaves which should be protected from late spring frosts. Amaryllis are not really happy as an outdoor plant in Britain, despite the bulb growers' protestations and are not successful for long except in Cornwall and the Scilly Isles. The only place that is suitable for them in the open is against a south-facing outside wall of a hot-house where the bulbs can receive the extra benefit of the warmth from the pipes within. Alas, such situations are rare. Amaryllis are more fragrant during the evenings and their scent would have formed part of the exotic and heavy sweetness to be found in the large hot-houses and conservatories of the wealthy Victorians. In their language of flowers the Belladonna Lily meant, romantically, 'silence' or 'hush'. Amaryllis are often confused with the rather similar Hippeastrums which can be induced to grow at almost any time of the year.

Amaryllis belladonna - Belladonna Lily (1712). Grows to 2ft 6in (76cm) and produces its (usually) pink and white flowers in August and September. Warm border or in tubs. A bulb from South Africa.

Requirements: An exceedingly sunny and sheltered situation: a compost of fibrous loam, sand and leaf-mould suits them best. Can be grown in containers or tubs in a warm greenhouse to be brought out in summer. The bulbs should be planted 8in (20.5cm) deep on a small pillow of sand in June or July: they can be planted less deeply in warmer areas. Protect the young leaves when they appear from spring frosts. The bulbs should be left undisturbed for some years.

Cultivation: When the leaves turn yellow in summer lift and divide the bulb-clumps, and replant immediately. Amaryllis can be grown from seed but will take 5 − 8 years to come into flower.

Uses: As late-summer tub-plants where their evening scent can be enjoyed, or as long-lasting cut flowers.

After flowering: Cut down stems.

Bulbs: Amand, Avon, Bloms, de Jager, Orpington.

Plants: Scotts.

ANAGALLIS (*Primulaceae*). This very pretty plant is not grown as often as it should be, possibly because it has to be treated as an annual. It is closely related to the native Scarlet Pimpernel whose other name is 'Poor Man's Weather Glass' from its habit of closing up at the onset of bad weather. *Anagallis linifolia* is the best known and it produces an abundance of brilliant gentian-blue flowers with red undersides throughout the summer.

Anagallis linifolia (1796), grows to a bushy shape 12in (30.5cm) high by 15in (38cm) across with blue flowers from June to September. Border or large rockery. A perennial plant of the W. Mediterranean, though treated as an annual.

Requirements: Ordinary soil in full sun. Re-pot in March if grown as a greenhouse plant. Treat as an annual.

Propagation: Sow seeds in March at a temperature of 16°C (61°F). Grow on in the usual way, harden off and plant out in May. If required as pot plants in winter, the seeds can be sown in July.

Uses: As a very colourful garden plant and in pots for winter flowers under glass.

Seeds: Thomas Butcher, Chiltern, Thompson and Morgan.

ANCHUSA (*Boraginaceae*). The name Anchusa is derived from the word *Anchousa*, meaning 'paint for the skin'. This was a harmless red dye found in the roots of a *A. tinctoria* (a synonym of *Alkanna tinctoria*) and used in classical Greece as a cosmetic. Much later on Gerard grew the plant in his famous garden and mentioned that French ladies of fashion painted their faces with the colour obtained from the roots; this was confirmed some two centuries later by Henry Phillips in 1829 who said that rouge made from this plant lasted for some days without rubbing off, being freshened by water, and does not "wither the skin so much as other kinds of rouge". The dye is found only in the outer skin or cortex of the root and in former times was used to give rich colour to inferior wines and to tint medicines. Pliny esteemed the plant and said "If a person who has chewed this plant should spit in the mouth of a venemous creature, he will kill it".

A. officinalis was the Bugloss of the old herbalists and this was reputed to be an effective cure for melancholia – when steeped in strong ale.

A. azurea, syn. **A. italica** (1810). Grows to 5ft (152.5cm) with a somewhat loose and rather flopping habit. A mature plant can be majestic when in full flower. This is the parent of most of the modern varieties such as 'Dropmore' (1905) deep blue, *grandiflora* (1900) deep blue, 'Opal' (1906) light blue. Large border. A perennial from the Caucasus.

A. capensis (1800). Grows to 18in (46cm) with indigo blue flowers from June to August. A half-hardy biennial for the border from South Africa.

A. tinctoria - Alkanet (1596) grows only to 6in (15cm) but spreads sideways. Deep blue flowers from June to August. Border or herb garden. A perennial from S. Europe.

Requirements: Anchusas need sunny positions in well-drained good garden soil. The taller *A. azurea* needs some support from twiggy sticks. *A. capensis* needs winter protection with cloches or it can be grown in large pots sunk in the ground which can be transferred to the greenhouse for the winter.

Cultivation: Sow seeds of *A. azurea* in March and grow on in the usual way. Root cuttings taken in January or February should be grown on in seed compost in a cold frame. Plant out in a temporary position for the first year and transfer to permanent situation in October. Sow seeds of *A. capensis* in open ground in April, thin out as necessary. These are treated as annuals. For biennial plants sow in June and thin out in the same way. Protect well in the winter.

After flowering: Cut down flowering stems by half to induce further bloom. Cut down stems altogether in autumn.

Uses: Anchusas do not generally last more than five minutes in water but their intensely blue flowers, a rare colour in the border, almost compensate for this. The flowers can be carefully dried to provide colour in potpourris.

Seeds: Thomas Butcher, Chiltern, Dobie, Thompson and Morgan.

Plants: Goatchers, Hillier, Kelways, Notcutts, Scotts, Sherrards.

ANDROSACE - Rock Jasmine *(Primulaceae).* Many of these charming little plants have been grown in the British Isles for over a hundred years. On the whole they are not the easiest of plants unless their exact requirements are met and in Britain this is very difficult because of our variable climate. Most members of the genus, though hardy, need protection from winter wet – it is this that kills them, because originally they come from the mountainous regions of the world where they can sleep the winters away beneath a coverlet of deep snow. A rock-garden with ledges that have specially constructed 'overhangs' is one way of protecting them, and this has the advantage of looking perfectly natural in the bleaker days of winter. The second method is to protect them with cloches, but the positioning of these in a rock garden is not always easy. The third way is to treat them as the alpines that they are and to house them in a conservatory or greenhouse devoted to these and other kindred plants. Alpines can become an obsession because they are such a challenge.

Androsaces are lovely little plants, generally forming neat hummocks or rosettes of leaves (often silvery) that flower abundantly when their situation is to their liking. Their charm lies also in their smallness and neatness and they are very suitable for troughs and sinks, as long as the drainage and soil-mix is right for them: a sink-garden is also more easily protected in winter. The genus has been divided into four sections of which only two are mentioned here because of the limitations of space. Group II *(the Chamaejasmes)* need light sandy soil containing limestone chips, and ideally, do best in moraine-like conditions in full sun. Group III *(the Aretas)* come from a higher altitude and often have wooly or hairy leaves. They need a 'rest period' which is difficult to simulate, and they must have perfect drainage.

A. alpina (1775) Group II. Grows only 1in (2.5cm) high with a spread of about

6in (15cm). It is best grown under glass. Pink flowers in June. A perennial from Switzerland.

A. carnea (1764) Group II. Grows to 3in (7.5cm) and spreads into a mat of elongated rosettes 6in (15cm) wide. Pink or white flowers with a yellow centre in June and July. Also best grown under glass. A perennial from Switzerland and the Pyrenees.

A. chamaejasme (1768) Group II. Grows to 2in (5cm) with white flowers in June. Slightly easier to grow. A perennial for the rock garden from the mountains of N. Europe.

A. helvetica (1775) Group III. Grows to 2in (5cm) with a spread of 6in (15cm). White flowers in April and May. Slightly easier to grow but still best in an alpine house. A perennial plant from Austria and Switzerland.

A. lanuginosa (1842). Group II. Grows to 1½in (3.8cm) wth trails of silvery leaves that spread to 18in (46cm). Pink flowers from June to October. Will grow well in the rock garden but needs protection in winter. A perennial from the Himalayas.

A. sarmentosa (1876) Group II. A trailing plant 4in (10cm) high with an ultimate spread of about 20in (51cm). Silvery green leaves and rose pink flowers from April to June. More tolerant of our climate than most other members of the genus. Sunny ledge in rock garden. A perennial from the Himalayas.

A. villosa (1790) Group II. Grows to 3in (7.5cm) and spreads to 10in (25.5cm) with neat silvery-white rosettes. Pink or white scented flowers in May and June. Its ideal situation is a sunny scree, or an alpine house. A perennial from the European Alps and Asia.

Requirements: A sunny, sheltered situation in well-drained soil or compost that has been especially mixed for each type. A properly constructed rock garden with ledges, overhangs and 'pockets' for the soil can provide this, and the plants look well when clothing the ledges and crevices. They always benefit from a 'collar' of chips or small pebbles to prevent rotting, and the surrounding soil can also be top-dressed with grit, chips or pebbles until the plants grow into the space.

Propagation: Group II. Produces runners: these can be gently detached in August and started off in damp sand. (Hold the parent plant firmly but gently while separating it from its offspring.) Keep cool until roots form. Group III can be treated similarly except that these need more care. If grown from seed this should be sown in January or February in a reliable seed compost. Place outside in a cold place so that the pans or trays can freeze for about two weeks, then return to the greenhouse and a temperature of 7°C (45°F). The seeds may not germinate during the first spring, so scatter grit on the surface of the pans or trays to prevent moss forming. Water from below. When the first true leaves form the seedlings can be potted on into a mix of three parts of leaf-mould to one of grit and kept in a cold frame for the summer, remembering still to water from the bottom. Top dress with grit. The seedlings can remain in the frame for the winter when watering should almost cease. When the small plants are finally planted out they may need to be protected from birds until their roots are established.

Seeds: Thompson and Morgan.

Plants: Broadwell, Hillier, Holden Clough, Ingwersen, Reginald Kaye, Potterton and Martin, Southcombe Gardens, Waterperry.

ANEMONE *(Ranunculaceae).* This is a large branch of a large family and it is interesting to discover that Anemones are cousins to the Buttercup, and therefore are closely related to Clematis, Delphiniums, Aquilegias, Hellebores and Aconites. Peonies are now a family on their own, *Paeoniaceae*, but until recently were also included in *Ranunculaceae*.

Anemone nemorosa is the native Windflower whose white or pink-tinged flowers open with the Bluebells and Primroses of the spring woodland.

Anemone blanda has leaves that closely resemble *A. nemorosa*, and these appear soon after Christmas, followed by brilliant blue daisy-shaped flowers in late winter and early spring. The flower buds form inconspicuously and it is one of spring's most charming surprises to be suddenly greeted with an unexpected burst of bright blue. Pink, white and mixed collections of rhizomes are available but the blue are always the most popular and can easily be obtained separately.

A. coronaria was known to Parkinson who wrote "The Anemones... so full of variety and so dainty, and so delightsome flowers, that the sight of them doth enforce an earnest longing desire in the minde of anyone to be a possessour of some of them at the least ..." A sentiment which is echoed today by many garden visitors to many other gardens, and not only about Anemones.

The original *A. coronaria* was found in countries bordering the Mediterranean and particularly in Palestine. During the time of the Crusades Umberto, Bishop of Pisa, instructed the ship-masters of the time to load their ships with soil instead of sand as ballast for the return journey. This sacred soil was then carefully spread on the Campo Santo at Pisa and in the following spring a myriad of scarlet flowers appeared as if by some miracle. The story is charming but it is a little spoiled by the knowledge that *A. coronaria* has always grown wild in parts of Italy. There is another tale of a Frenchman, M. Bachelier, who was a seventeenth century florist – a word that had a different meaning in those days (*see* Auricula.) M. Bachelier had some new and particularly fine varieties of Anemone much admired by his gardening friends. For years he had refused to give any of his precious plants to anyone until one day his garden was visited by a Councillor of Parliament who was practical as well as covetous. While strolling in the garden, this personage dropped his cloak, as if by accident, on the anemone bed. He had brought with him his servant and had given the fellow prior instructions which the man hastened to carry out. The cloak was gathered up together with some seeds of the anemones that adhered to the cloth. Today we are still doing more or less the same thing, though, alas, with less style – the cloak and servant have now been replaced by the plastic bag.

A. japonica is a graceful tall-growing flower of late summer with simple yet beautiful flowers of pink or white. It is actually a native of China but was introduced to Japan at an early date to be later discovered and described by a Doctor Andreas Cleyer in approximately 1684. It was very difficult for Europeans to penetrate the hinterland of either country in those days and their movements were very proscribed. Travellers or visitors were usually restricted to specific areas in the vicinity of certain ports and botanising was certainly not permitted. This early variety of *A. japonica* was later found by Robert Fortune growing wild among the native graves near Shanghai, and specimens were sent to England in 1844. *A. elegans* was produced and later on the original wild plant was found in the Chinese province of Hupeh: this plant was named *A. hupehensis*. Our beautiful late summer flower, therefore, should properly be called *A. hupehensis* x *elegans* though it seldom is.

A. pulsatilla – the Pasque flower – is now a rare wild flower in Britain though it was formerly found in great rippling sheets of silvery-purple on chalk and limestone downland. It is very beautiful, with its silky violet flowers and golden stamens and where found it has often been transplanted to gardens: this, together with the change in farming procedures has made the plant almost extinct in the wild. In former times the plant was used to dye hard-boiled eggs green at Easter, the name Pasque being derived from the M.E. 'Pasch', Easter, and the Hebrew 'Pasach', Passover. The two festivals are generally separated by only a few days.

A. blanda (1898) grows to 6ins (15cm) with blue, white or pink flowers in late winter and early spring. Sun, light rich soil. This plant aestivates so is good in the rockery where nearby summer-leafing plants can spread over its resting-place. A corm from E. Europe and the Taurus for rockeries, raised beds, edges of borders and in association with tulips (check flowering times). Massed plantings are the most effective.

A. coronaria (1596) grows 6 – 12in (15 – 30.5cm) high, white, red or blue flowers in March and April. Semi-shade, border. A tuber from S. Europe and Central Asia.

A. hupehensis (1908) grows $2\frac{1}{2}$ – 3ft (76 – 91.5cm) high, with pink or white flowers from August to October. Border. A perennial from China.

A. nemorosa - Windflower grows 6 – 8in (15 – 20cm) high, white flowers or sometimes with pink or deep rose-mauve reverse to petals. Deciduous woodland, orchards or wild garden. A perennial plant of Europe, Asia and N. America.

A. pulsatilla (see *Pulsatilla vulgaris*).

Requirements: *A. blanda* needs light, slightly sandy soil, well drained, and a warm, sunny position. *A. coronaria* will do in ordinary loam. *A. hupehensis* needs good garden soil, with some shade for part of the day. It hates disturbance and should only be moved in winter when dormant. *A. nemorosa* needs leaf-mould and the dappled shade of deciduous trees.

Propagation: Plant *A. blanda* corms as soon as available or sow seeds in August in boxes in a cold frame. Prick out into other boxes when large enough to handle. Transplant into a 'nursery area' for two years. Mark the place because the leaves disappear in late summer. *A. coronaria* has given rise to the modern de Caen and St. Brigid varieties. Treat as for *A. blanda*. Purchased corms can be induced to flower at almost any time of the year – the flowers come about three months after planting large corms. New corms should be planted every other year for a succession of good flowers as the old ones deteriorate. *A. hupehensis* Divide when essential – about once in four or five years, when the plant is dormant. *A. nemorosa* Plant the slender roots 2in (5cm) deep in humus-rich soil.

After flowering: Cut down flower stems of *A. hupehensis*.

Uses: As border, rock garden and wild garden subjects.

Seeds: Thomas Butcher, Chiltern, Dobie, Thompson and Morgan.

Corms: Amand, Avon, Bees, Broadleigh, Thomas Butcher, Hortico, Kelways, van Tubergen.

Plants: Most nurseries.

ANGELICA *(Umbelliferae)*. During the time of the great plagues which swept through Europe in the Middle Ages there was a legend about this plant which is said to be the origin of the beautiful name that it has had ever since. It was said that a very holy monk dreamed of an archangel who appeared to him in a vision, saying that this particular herb would cure the plague victims. For centuries, therefore, all parts of the plant were held in great esteem as a remedy for this and almost every other malady, and it was always included as a protective herb against evil spells and enchantments. Alternatively, it is known that John Tradescant the elder discovered Angelica when he visited Archangel in 1618 when accompanying Sir Dudley Digges on a diplomatic mission to Russia. Angelica is an exceedingly handsome plant, with its large light green leaves and huge, completely spherical umbels of matching light green flowers which are a great attraction to late-summer insects. The whole plant is pleasantly aromatic, generally flowering in the third year from sowing. The seeds should be allowed to dry on the plant unless the season is particularly wet, and should be sown immediately when ripe, in August or September, because they do not always remain viable if kept in the usual way until the following spring. The plant will not flower until the second and generally the third year, after which it will die. The candied or crystallized stems are used in the confectionery trade throughout the world and Angelica is an important flavouring for liqueurs, notably Vermouths and Chartreuse. If the leaves and stems are needed for culinary purposes the forming flower-stems can be cut away which will prolong the plant's life, though the same treatment would have to be repeated in the following year.

The leaves, stems and root are still used in homoeopathic medicine, though no part of the plant should be given to diabetics. If taken medicinally, infusions of Angelica are said to cause revulsion for spiritous liquors – though not for wine. Because this is a handsome and sculptural plant, it should be grown – where space permits – in groups of three or five and it looks particularly pleasing by the waterside. The leaves may be used as a 'sugar-saver' with tart fruit such as gooseberries, and as the stems are hollow they can be cut into short lengths to use as earwig traps among the Dahlias.

Angelica archangelica grows to 7ft (214cm) high with greenish yellow flowers that develop into handsome green seed-heads. Herb garden or by water. A biennial plant from N. Europe.

Requirements: humus-rich, moist (not wet) soil in sun.

Cultivation: Sow the large flat seeds on edge, into second-size pots in autumn and grow on in a cold frame for the winter. Plant out in late spring.

Uses: As a striking waterside feature plant. Dried seed-heads very ornamental: pick as soon as perfectly formed, otherwise seeds will begin to drop.

Seeds: John Chambers.

Plants: Beth Chatto, Ingwersen, Oak Cottage Herb Farm, Parkinson Herbs, Scotts, Sherrards, Stoke Lacy Herb Garden, The Weald Herbary.

ANTHEMIS - Chamomile *(Compositae)*. Chamomile is one of the plants that was so often featured in the flower-scattered lawns of medieval paintings. The quaint perspective employed by those early painters in no way detracts from the tranquil scenes of lute-playing, story-telling and flirting, where the blossomy sward seems to perfectly echo the flower-embroidered gowns of the ladies. Chamomile has been grown for centuries as a lawn plant because it can tolerate a reasonable amount of wear, and it was used to make 'turf' seats which must have been delicious to sit on – during dry weather. Shakespeare makes Falstaff say (in the first part of Henry IV) "... for though the chamomile, the more it is trodden on the faster it grows ..." which leads one to believe that there must have been many chamomile lawns in those days. The plant has an apple scent which becomes much stronger when it is bruised, sat or trodden upon and this is often the first indication of its presence. The clippings from the plants were mixed with the strewing herbs that once covered the floors of medieval homes, and this mixture of aromatic scents would, to some degree, have acted as a deterrent to insect life of the more noxious kind.

When the plants are thoroughly established they can be kept close by clipping (about twice a year) and they can even be mowed with the blades set in the highest position. A rotary mower can be set at 3in (7.5cm) from the ground, whereas the comfortable old-fashioned hand mower, with its pleasantly restful sound, can only be set at a maximum of 1½in (3.8cm) which is too low, as would be the modern electric hover-mowers. For a small lawn that should not receive too much wear, in spite of Falstaff's words, the plants should be set out at about 4 – 6in (10 – 15cm) apart and they will speedily join up when they have settled down. They should not be walked on initially as the roots must have a chance to become established. Single plants may be placed in spaces left in paving and patios, where they will give off a pleasant scent when stepped on.

The ancient Egyptians regarded the plant as a certain cure for the ague, and we are still drinking it today in the form of teas and tisanes. Chamomile was grown historically as a herb to cure or alleviate very many disorders, and it is becoming popular again because of the revival of interest in herbal medicine. The daisy-shaped flowers are most attractive and it is these that were used in former times to make the somewhat bitter-tasting Chamomile Tea which was considered to be an excellent cure for feminine hysteria and a remedy for recurring nightmares. Chamomile has long been known as an especially good rinse for naturally fair hair, to which it imparts a golden sheen.

In the garden Chamomile has been called 'The Plant Physician' because single specimens are said to be most effective in 'nursing' ailing or sickly plants back to health by their very proximity. *A. nobilis* will remain green in the hottest of summers and is useful in drought conditions.

Anthemis nobilis (now **Chamaemelum nobile**) - **Common or Roman Chamomile** grows to 6in (15cm) high, sometimes more, with white flowers from June to August. Herb gardens, lawns, as edging plants and in stone or flagged paths. A perennial herb of Europe.

Requirements: Sun, rich, well-drained soil.

Cultivation: Increased by division in spring or seeds sown in March. Prick out seedlings into individual pots, keep in cold frame for first winter. Set out in permanent positions in following May.

After flowering: Cut off flowering stems.

Uses: Small lawns and little-used paths, curatively and as a hair-rinse.

Plants: Beth Chatto, Cunnington, Hillier, Holden Clough, Oak Cottage Herb Farm, Stoke Lacy Herb Garden, The Weald Herbary.

Seeds: Thompson and Morgan.

ANTIRRHINUM - Snapdragon *(Scrophulariaceae)*. Children have always loved this familiar garden plant because of its mechanics. If the complex flowers are pinched at exactly the right place they will gape like half-friendly animals – hence its other names of 'Lion's Mouth or 'Dragon's Mouth'. Originally *Antirrhinum majus* came from Southern Europe and was introduced into our gardens, whence it escaped to naturalise itself comfortably on old walls and ruins and, much later, on old and undisturbed railway cuttings.

Pollinating insects may be able to enter the flowers in the usual way, but once inside they are not strong enough to escape except by eating their way out through the walls of the bloom: this is the explanation of the little round holes that quite often disfigure the flowers. In the language of flowers the Snapdragon represented 'Presumption' and in a book of the time the accompanying text ran as follows. "We have introduced them into our gardens on account of their beauty, but, frequently, like the presumptious, it is so importunate in spreading itself that we are obliged to banish it for ever ...". This extract refers, of course, to the wild variety which was a sturdy plant that settled down to colonise new territories as quickly as possible, being perfectly hardy in the southern parts of the British Isles. Then, in the middle of the nineteenth century the Snapdragon was noticed by the florists who never could leave well alone. It was cultivated, crossed, and cosseted and it is from those sometimes gargantuan varieties, some of which reached 7ft (213.5cm) in height that our modern bedding plants are derived. The plants often suffer from 'Antirrhinum rust' which appeared in the British Isles in 1933. This is an unsightly disease for which there is no real cure, and the only thing to do with afflicted plants (which will cease flowering in any case) is to destroy them. This is the main reason for treating these perennial plants as annuals. The flower-spikes should be cut off as soon as they are over and secondary ones will generally appear to prolong the flowering season.

The Antirrhinums of today have been divided into three main categories, according to height, and it is possible to have them as strong-growing back-of-the-border giants or neat and compact plants for edging flower beds or for growing in tubs and troughs.

Antirrhinums can be grown under glass for winter flowering. In which case sow the seed successively from July onwards in the same conditions as for normal early spring cultivation. Because it is the finest flowers that will be needed under these circumstances, the side shoots may be nipped off. The taller varieties may need staking in their pots, and the greenhouse temperature should not fall below a minimum of 4 – 7°C (39 – 45°F).

Antirrhinum majus - Snapdragon. Type plant grows to 4ft (122cm) with pink flowers from July until the frosts. Dry walls. A perennial plant of the Mediterranean region; the wild plant and the modern cultivar both have the same name.

Requirements: A sunny situation and rich, free-draining soil for modern counterparts.

Cultivation: Sow seed in February or March at a temperature of 16 – 18°C (61 – 64°F) in a compost of equal parts sand and moss peat. Water seeds in with fine rose on can or a mist-sprayer. Cover lightly with silver sand. When seedlings reach four-leaf stage water thereafter with very dilute liquid feed.

During and after flowering: Dead-head regularly.

Uses: As border, bedding, rock garden and container plants, according to height and type. As cut flowers.

Plants: Type plants unlikely to exist now, 'modern' varieties only.

Seeds: Most seedsmen.

AQUILEGIA - Columbine (*Ranunculaceae*). The wild Columbine was taken into our gardens in earliest times and it is still with us, virtually unchanged and as vigorous in its ability to survive as ever. This old-fashioned flower, sometimes called 'Granny-bonnets', has spurs that curl inwards towards the stalk, whereas the modern beauties of today have spurs that flick outward like a comet's tail, thus presenting a very different silhouette. The older varieties, whether single or double, are usually of one colour, being purple, mauve, lilac, deep rose, pink, pale pink and white, in contrast to the newer hybrids which are usually of two distinct colours. The original Columbine was named thus from its fancied resemblance to doves perched round a dish, from *columba*, a dove or pigeon. It is a plant that is often inherited with an old garden, as my own were, and it is impossible to get rid of the myriad seedlings that spring up year after year. Parkinson had the same problem in his day and though he grew several kinds and colours, including some double-flowered sorts he says "These double kinds doe give as good seede as the single kinds doe, which is not observed in many plants" and he goes on to say – "The rarer the flowers are, the more trouble to keepe: the ordinary sorts on the contrary part will not be lost, doe what one will." It is comforting to know that, over three centuries ago, he was experiencing exactly the same difficulties as the gardeners of today. Where the older and stronger kinds are grown together with the modern varieties it will be found impossible to keep the strain of these last pure.

In medieval times the Columbine was considered to have great therapeutic powers and was used almost indiscriminately to cure ailments ranging from measles to small-pox. Fortunately for invalids of later years the use of this plant in medicine has gradually died out, because it belongs to that large and generally unfriendly Ranunculaceae family.

In the garden, however, it is a delightful plant, coming into leaf very early in the year, where it helps to clothe the bare spring garden with its scalloped jade green leaves that are tinged with violet. Columbines can be easily transplanted in winter and set to grow in almost any 'difficult' corner – they seem to be indifferent as to their situation and will brighten up many problem places in the garden with their attractive foliage from which springs an abundance of tall flowering stems. The pale coloured kinds look particularly delicate and pleasing when growing up through ferns in a shaded area, under trees or along a woodland walk. The dried seed-heads are interestingly shaped and once emptied of their contents will last almost indefinitely. The seeds when crushed make an effective dusting powder to kill lice.

Division of the clumps of *A. vulgaris* is the only way to perpetuate a particular colour because the various shades in the garden will cross-pollinate, producing seed which is unlikely to be true. If the modern long-spurred varieties are grown in the same garden they should be kept well separated from *A. vulgaris* which has by far the most dominant characteristics: interesting hybrids will result in any case. Most of the species Aquilegias come true from seed, though germination is often slow: the seeds should be sown as soon as they are ripe and rattling in the seed-heads.

A. alpina (1731) grows to 12in (30.5cm) with blue or pale blue and white flowers in May. Rock garden. A perennial from Switzerland.

A. caerulea (1864) grows to 18in (46cm) with white-tinged blue and yellow flowers from April to July. Border. A perennial from the Rocky mountains of N. America.

A. flabellata (1887) grows to 10in (25.5cm) with white, violet and pink flowers from May to July. Rock garden. A perennial from Japan.

A. viridiflora (1790) grows to 18in (46cm) with scented green-black flowers in May. Rock garden. A perennial from Siberia to W. China.

A. vulgaris - Columbine, Granny-bonnets grows to 40x24in (102x61cm) in good soil and situation. Pink, mauve, violet and white flowers from May to July. Any situation. A European perennial.

Requirements: *A. vulgaris* grows anywhere, species and alpine types need sun or partly shaded situations.

Cultivation: Sow seeds in July or August in seed compost in a cold frame. Do not allow soil surface to dry out: prick out and grow on, plant out in spring in a nursery bed. Transfer to flowering positions in September.

After flowering: Cut down stems unless seeds or dried heads are wanted.

Uses: As cut flowers, border and rock plants: dried heads for winter decoration.

Seeds: John Chambers, Chiltern, Holden Clough, Holtzhausen, Thompson and Morgan.

Plants: Broadwell, Beth Chatto, Ingwersen, Washfield.

ARABIS *(Cruciferae)*. Arabis, sometimes called Rock-cress, seems almost always doomed to be planted with Aubrieta and *Alyssym saxatile* because all three flower at the same time. However, this plant, though sometimes scorned for its very 'ordinariness' can be used to great advantage when large areas of sunny bank and dry rocky wall need to be quickly covered. Arabis has neat, attractive grey-green leaves throughout the year which initially form equally neat hummocks and cushions, thickly covered with pure white scented flowers that attract over-wintering or early hatching butterflies; in addition the plant has a long flowering season from February until June. Once the plants are established they are inclined to grow vigorously and will surge all over their allotted space until the hard edges disappear under a soft green tide. To keep them tidy the skirts of the plants should be pegged down as necessary. The more delicate pink varieties make a charming contrast to blue spring flowers such as Forget-me-Nots, Iris, Grape Hyacinths, Bluebells or deep pink Tulips.

Arabis resents being moved once established. It is subject to several of the Cruciferae diseases such as Cabbage ring-spot which causes the leaves to develop unsightly yellow ring-like edges. *Dasyneura arabis* is the Arabis midge which lays its eggs in the central growing shoot, causing a gall, when the maggots develop. Several broods may hatch in one year and their presence is indicated by malformation and weak growth of the affected plant which should be rooted up and burnt. The maggots pupate in the soil below the plant so the ground should be disinfected, or if the infestation is light the plant can be dusted with nicotine dust.

A. albida (1798) grows to 9in (23cm) but may spread to 2ft (61cm) with racemes of scented white flowers from February to June. Dry walls, stone banks and as edging plants. Not for rockeries unless these are large. A perennial from SE Europe to Iran.

A. muralis syn. **A. rosea** (1832) grows to 12in (30.5cm) larger rose-mauve flowers from May to July. Walls or rocks, not as vigorous as *A. albida*. A perennial from SE Europe.

Requirements: A sunny position atop a wall or slope and room to spread.

Cultivation: Existing plants can be divided in September, or cuttings taken from non-flowering rosettes in July, put into a mix of equal parts of peat and sand in pots in a cold frame. Pot on and plant in spring. Sow seeds in March in a cold frame.

During and after flowering: Dead-head regularly.

Uses: As cover for large or rocky areas.

Plants: Most garden centres.

Seeds: Artiss, Chiltern, Suttons, Thompson and Morgan, Unwins.

ARCTOTIS *(Compositae)*. This is a group of daisy-flowered plants from South Africa, generally grown as annuals because they flower in the first year from seed. The flowers are particularly handsome, usually measuring some 3½in (9cm) across, with dark, metallic-seeming centres which may be black, brown or purple. The flowers do not open on dull days and they usually close in the late afternoon or when rain is imminent. They do well in tubs and windowboxes in sunny, sheltered positions. They need no special compost and any good garden soil will suit them. The young plants of *A. grandis* should be 'stopped' at a height of 5in (12.5cm) to encourage sideways growth.

A. acaulis grows to 9in (23cm) with yellow and copper-coloured flowers in July/August. Undersides of leaves woolly-white. Windowboxes, troughs, rockeries and edges of borders. A perennial from South Africa.

A. grandis - Blue-Eyed South African Daisy grows to 2ft (61cm) with large flowers in shades from white through cream, pale yellow and buff until the frosts. An annual from South Africa.

Requirements: A sunny and sheltered position.

Cultivation: Sow seeds in March at 18°F (64°F) covering lightly. Do not overwater seedlings.

During flowering: Dead-head.

Seeds: Thomas Butcher, Chiltern, Thompson and Morgan.

ARGEMONE *(Papaveraceae)*. These are beautiful flowers which deserve to be seen more often in our gardens because they are not difficult to grow. Their name of 'Argemone' is derived from the Greek Argema, meaning a small spot or growth on the cornea of the eye, because it was once thought that cataracts could be cured by the application of the bright yellow sap found in the stems and leaves of the plant. They have large, delicate Poppy-like flowers and strong-growing and handsome (though prickly) foliage. Argemones are best treated as annuals as they flower in the first year from seed and cannot withstand the winters of Northern Europe. The leaves of *A. grandiflora* are not as vicious-looking as those of *A. mexicana* and have an attractive silvery appearance from a distance because they have distinct white veins. *A. mexicana* is called the 'Devil's Fig' and 'Prickly Poppy' because of its prickly stem and spiny leaves or sometimes, inaccurately, the 'Golden Thistle of Peru'. Gerard knew it and wrote this passage about its spiny fruit which "doth much resemble a figge in shape and bignesse, but so full of sharpe and venomous prickles, that whosoever had one of them in his throte, doubtless it would send him packing either to heaven or hell". Argemones are sensitive to damage because of their succulent nature and should be grown first in small pots and then thinned out, rather than attempting to prick out the seedlings in the normal way.

A. grandiflora (1827) grows to 3ft (91.5cm) with clusters of 4in (10cm) white flowers in June and July. Border. A perennial from Mexico.

A. mexicana - Devil's Fig, Prickly Poppy (1592) grows to 2ft (61cm) with 3in (7.5cm) scented yellow or orange flowers from June to August. Border. A perennial from tropical Africa.

Requirements: Light soil and a sunny sheltered position.

Cultivation: Sow seeds very thinly in March at 18°C (64°F) in pots.

After flowering: Cut and dry seed heads of *A. mexicana* for winter decor.

Seeds: Chiltern, Thompson and Morgan.

ARISAEMA *(Araceae)*. The Aroids are a fascinating family of plants. In general the construction of the flowers is similar – they are insect traps, needing the services of flies or other insects that are attracted by the exciting and delicious (to the flies) smell emanating from the inflorescence when it is ready to be pollinated. The 'flowers' are usually massed on a central spadix or column, which may be club-shaped but is more usually cylindrical: this can be of varying length according to the species. The spadix is enveloped in a spathe or sheath which may be of a single colour but can have the most interesting reptilian-like spots and markings. The spathe of *A. griffithii* is purple, with veins and spots of a deeper violet, whereas some of the species of this family look – and smell – like decaying carrion, which is a positive banquet for all the flies of the neighbourhood.

A. griffithii (1875) grows to about 3ft (91.5cm) with purple flowers in late spring. Sheltered woodland garden. A perennial plant from India.

Requirements: Semi-shade, moist humus-rich soil.

Cultivation: Plant tubers 6in (15cm) deep in autumn. Propagation is by offsets, lift and replant in April.

Tubers: Avon, Broadleigh, de Jager.

ARISARUM *(Araceae)*. This particular member of the Aroid family is an amusing and interesting plant to grow because the brownish flowers resemble the rear end of a burrowing mouse, tail and all. *A. proboscidium* is a great favourite with children because in a well-established clump there will be a dozen or more of such 'mice' apparently frozen into temporary immobility by the presence of the observer. If it likes its situation and growing conditions the plant will colonise the surrounding area and after a few years it may even need to be checked. It likes a semi-shady situation where its rhizomes do not dry out, and these should be planted about 6in (15cm) deep to protect them from frost. The shining spear-shaped leaves appear early in the year, and the 'mice' from April until early June, according to the mildness of the spring. If this Arisarum is planted at the edge of a path the rhizomes will have a cool root-run beneath it, and the leaves may then be easily parted to see the flowers.

A. proboscidium - the 'Mouse-Plant'. Leaves grow to 8in (20.5cm) with brown-purple flowers from April to June. Shady rock-garden, wild garden or semi-shaded border. A perennial plant from Southern Europe.

Requirements: Moist but not wet soil, woodland or semi-shaded situation.

Propagation: By division in spring. Plant rhizomes about 6in (15cm) deep.

Plants: Avon, Broadleigh, Beth Chatto, Christian, Cunnington, Holden Clough, Ingwersen, Jackamoors, Reginald Kaye, Potterton and Martin, Alan C. Smith, Southcombe.

ARMERIA - Thrift, Sea-Pink *(Plumbaginaceae)*. Armeria, Thrift, Sea-Pink or Ladies' Cushions will always be affectionately remembered in the British Isles as the 'Threepenny Bit' plant by those adults who, as children, saved the heavy twelve-sided coin in their moneyboxes. In the sixteenth century Thrift was used as an edging plant for the elaborate knot gardens of that period, and Parkinson commented "This is an everlasting greene herbe, which many take to border their beds, and set their knots and trayles, and therein much delight, because it will grow thicke and bushie, and may be kept, being cut with a paire of Garden sheeres, in some good handsome manner and proportion for a time, and besides, in the Summer time send forth many short stalks of pleasant flowers, to decke up an house among other sweet herbes: Yet these inconveniences doe accompany it: it will not onely in a small time overgrow the knot or trayle in many places, by growing so thicke and bushie, that it will put out the forme of a knot in many places; but also much thereof will dye with the frosts and snowes in Winter, and with the drought in Summer, whereby many voide places will be sene in the knot, which doth much deforme it, and must therefore be yearely refreshed; the thickness also and bushing thereof doth hide and shelter snayles and other small noysome wormes so plentifully, that Gilloflowers, and other fine herbes and flowers being planted therein, are much spoyled by them, and cannot be helped without much industry and very great and daily attendance to destroy them."

Thrift is a wild plant of the seacliffs, forming heavy evergreen cushions of grassy leaves that hang from inaccessible ledges, firmly anchored by strong dark-brown roots. Though it can withstand the worst of wintry conditions when growing in its natural habitat, it often succumbs to winter wet when grown as a rock or wall plant inland. In summer each hummock of dark green leaves is covered with near round flower-heads on smooth stems, resembling an old-fashioned pincushion with its collection of glass-knobbed hat-pins.

Armeria maritima - Sea-pink, Thrift grows to 6in (15cm) with round pink flowerheads from May to July. Evergreen mats of dark green grassy leaves. Rockeries, wall-tops, edges of paths and borders. A European perennial.

Requirements: A sunny, free-draining position.

Propagation: Divide roots in spring: sow seeds in March in boxes of compost in a cold frame. Prick out seedlings into individual pots and grow on – do not overwater. Plant out in following spring.

During and after flowering: Dead-head.

Seeds: Thomas Butcher, Chiltern.

Plants: Most nurseries.

ARUM (Araceae). These fascinating plants are very similar in their construction, having evolved a practical method of pollination that explains their curious shape. The stalk of the 'flower' forms the central column, or spadix, which is enclosed or wrapped round by an urn-shaped spathe that may be differently proportioned according to the species. The female flowers are clustered round the base of the spadix, with a separate group of male flowers above them. Above these again, just where the neck of the urn or chamber is narrowest, there are several rows of downward-pointing hairs which are sterile flowers. When all is ready and ripe the spathe emits a distinctly unpleasant smell to attract small flying insects who creep past the hairs or bristles and fall into the chamber below. Here they are held prisoner for several days, unable to escape past the bristles because the plant has not finished with them yet. The insects have a relatively comfortable incarceration because the plant provides plenty of nourishment for its guests, and when the pollen ripens it is transferred to the female flowers by the insects, the barrier-hairs shrivel and become flaccid and the insects are at last able to leave. The spathe starts to wither almost immediately and the berries begin to form.

The wild Arum or Lords and Ladies – *Arum maculatum* of Northern Europe – is a typical example of this, and a handsome garden variety is *Arum italicum* var. *marmoratum* which is grown for its strikingly veined leaves that remain throughout the winter: frost certainly damages them but others grow up as replacements. This Arum needs a sheltered situation, and when grown against a background of evergreens it provides a patch of unusual vitality in the bare winter garden. The spathe is cream-coloured with a slightly darker spadix and as this Arum is completely dormant from midsummer onwards, its abode should be marked until the brilliant scarlet berries begin to appear in October together with the first of the new season's leaves. When established this Arum spreads quite rapidly, and it can be tried in various positions in the garden to see which suits it best. My own plants grow in two situations – the larger is in partial shade beneath the outstretched branches of an apple tree, and a smaller clump is in a sunnier position in a drier corner beneath a Laburnum. The clump in the shady border is the largest, the first to come into leaf again in the autumn and the first to produce berries. Other species formerly included in this family such as the Arum Lily – *Zantedeschia aethiopica* and the Dragon Arum – *Dracunculus vulgaris*, will be found on the appropriate pages, see index.

A. italicum marmoratum syn. **A. italicum pictum** grows to 18in (46cm) with handsomely veined leaves that appear in autumn and last through the winter. The spathe develops in spring and the red berries from bare earth in September and October. It is a European perennial, suitable for woodland areas or shady paths and borders.

Requirements: Sun or semi-shade, sheltered situation and good garden soil.

Cultivation: Plant the tubers about 6in (15cm) deep, or clumps can be divided in autumn when new growth starts.

Uses: Leaves for winter flower arrangements, plant for winter interest in the garden.

Warning: Prevent children from eating the poisonous berries.

Tubers: Avon, Broadleigh, Broadwell, Chappell, Beth Chatto, de Jager, Holden Clough, Ingwersen, Potterton and Martin, van Tubergen.

Plants: Robinsons, Sherrards, Treasures of Tenbury.

Seeds: Chiltern.

ARUNCUS - Goat's Beard *(Rosaceae).* This is an easy but imposing-looking plant to grow, with its creamy plumes of flowers above delicately dissected light-green leaves. In ideal conditions in a moist place beside the water's edge it will easily attain a height of 6ft and will spread accordingly. In dryer places it will do almost as well though it will not grow quite as tall. It is late coming into leaf in the spring, but grows exceedingly quickly once the soil warms up. Because this is such a splendid-looking plant it is worth taking some care in siting it, perhaps against a solid background of evergreens or conifers where its long-lasting flowers may be seen to advantage.

It can be split up during its dormant period, taking only the pieces from the outside edge of the plant and discarding the older centre-section. In some years it may be attacked by sawfly caterpillars which are quite capable of reducing the whole plant to an unsightly skeletal structure. A watch should be kept from May onwards for the first signs of these pests. If you see any holes begin to appear in the leaves examine the undersides of the leaves for eggs and tiny caterpillars, which hide there during the day. If the infestation is light the affected leaves should be picked off and burnt, but if this is not successful the plant should be sprayed fortnightly with Fenitrothion or Malathion. If the plant or plants are growing by a pond that is stocked with fish the spray cannot be used because the drift is poisonous, and the only thing to do is to cut off all the infested foliage, even if it means reducing an otherwise handsome plant to a clump of unseasonally bare stems. It will quickly throw up new shoots, even late in the summer. The autumn foliage is particularly pleasing, being a fine clear yellow which may last for some weeks. *Aruncus sylvester* was formerly known as *Spiraea aruncus,* and is very similar in appearance to the Astilbes which belong to the Saxifrage family.

Aruncus sylvester - Goat's Beard (1633) grows to a height of 6ft (1.85cm) and

more, with creamy plume-like flowers in June and July. It is a perennial
plant of the Northern Hemisphere. Waterside or moist border.
Requirements: Moist, rich soil in a partly shaded situation.
Cultivation: Divide existing plants in October, discarding exhausted centre of
plant.
Uses: As a sculptural waterside or foliage plant. For cut flowers and leaves. Seed
heads for winter decor.
After flowering: Cut flowering stems to ground level.
Seeds: Thompson and Morgan.
Plants: Bees, Bressingham, Beth Chatto, Cunnington, Goatchers, Holden
Clough, Jackamoors, Kelways, Notcutts, Scotts, Sherrards, Stapeley Water
Garden.

ASCLEPIAS - Milkweed, Butterfly-Weed *(Asclepiadaceae)*. This genus of
plants is named after Asclepius, the Greek God of healing, and the plant's
common name of Milkweed was given to them because most of the species
contain a milky latex (sometimes poisonous) in the hollow stems and leaf-
veins. *A. tuberosa* is the foodplant of the incredible Monarch butterfly,
which flies thousands of miles during its life-cycle and which very
occasionally gets carried across the Atlantic to the shores of Northern
Europe. Most of the species are somewhat tender because they come from
the warmer or tropical parts of the world. *A. tuberosa* can be grown from
seed in the usual way, but it is not one of the easiest of plants, and it has
requirements that must be met for even moderate success. It must be
planted in a sunny, sheltered spot, it likes sandy, peaty soil, and dislikes lime
and disturbance once and if it becomes established. It comes late into leaf
so its position should be marked during the winter, and care should be taken
not to damage the roots when weeding because the weeds will be up and
about before *A. tuberosa* has woken from its long winter sleep. One of the
handsomest, though again, not the easiest of the species is *A. curassavica*
which is best grown as a greenhouse subject, though its pot can be sunk
outside in a sheltered sunny border during the summer months. *A.
curassavica* has 'crowns' of bright orange-red flowers that are very striking.
It can be grown from seed and is well worth the extra trouble.
A. curassavica - Bloodflower, Milkweed (1692) grows to 3ft (91.5cm) with
brilliant orange-red and purple flowers from June to October. Best as a
greenhouse plant though very striking when placed outside. A half-hardy
perennial plant from Tropical America.
A. tuberosa - Butterfly-Weed (1690) grows to 2½ft (76cm) with bright orange
flowers from July to September. Sheltered border. A perennial plant from
Eastern N. America.
Requirements: Greenhouse for *A. curassavica* and a sheltered sunny border for
both, with lime-free soil for *A. tuberosa*.
Cultivation: Sow seeds of *A. curassavica* under glass at a temperature of 20° −
25°C (68° − 78°F). Grow on and plant in greenhouse border. Needs winter
temperature of 7 − 10°C (45 − 50°F). Sow seeds of *A. tuberosa* at a
temperature of 15°C (59°F). Grow on, harden off and transfer into nursery
bed. Move into final position in October or March.
Uses: As greenhouse plants and somewhat tender border subjects. Seed-heads very
ornamental.
Seeds: Suttons.
Plants: Bressingham, Beth Chatto, Hillier.

ASPHODELINE - Asphodel, King's Spear, Jacob's Rod *(Liliaceae)*.
Asphodels are flowers that are steeped in history, poetry and sombre legend.
In his poem *OEnone* Tennyson makes one see that Grecian glade with the
Three Graces, beautiful as the flowers they walked among ...
      "Then to the bower they came,

Naked they came to that smooth-swarded bower,
And at their feet the crocus brake like fire,
Violet, amaracus and asphodel,
Lotos and lilies:"

There is a certain amount of confusion between the similarly-named genera –
Asphodeline and *Asphodelus*, which in any case are closely related and also
look similar. The flowering stem of *Asphodeline lutea* is erect and leafy and
the leaves are furrowed and three-cornered or awl-shaped. The Asphodel
was sacred to Proserpine or Persephone, and was much used in funeral
garlands. It was believed that the shades of the dead walked in eternal
meadows of Asphodel, sipping the waters of oblivion, and in the Victorian
language of flowers those of the Asphodel meant "my regrets follow you to
the grave". Asphodels are not seen very often in our gardens today, but
there appears no real reason for this.

Asphodeline lutea - King's Spear (1596) grows to 4ft (122cm) with spikes of
fragrant yellow flowers in June. A perennial from the Mediterranean area.
Border.
Requirements: Ordinary soil and a sunny or partially shaded situation.
Cultivation: The roots can be increased by division in spring.
Uses: Border plants: seed-heads for winter decor.
After flowering: Cut down flowering stems.
Seeds: Thomas Butcher, Holtzhausen, Thompson and Morgan, Holzhausen.
Plants: Bressingham, Broadleigh, Beth Chatto, Hillier, Kelways, Scotts,
Sherrards, F. Toynbee Ltd.

ASPHODELUS - Asphodel *(Liliaceae).* The flowering stems of *Asphodelus
albus* are smooth and not as tall as those of *Asphodeline lutea* and the
flowers are white and come a little later in the year. It prefers a richer,
sandier soil.
this herbe in England but ones, for the herbe that the people calleth here
Affodil or Daffodil is a kind of Narcissus." It would seem that the Asphodel
and a white Narcissus had come from Europe at the same time and with the
same name, Affodil or Affodyl, which would be even more confusing for the
gardeners of those times. Turner solved this problem temporarily by calling
the Asphodel the 'Whyte Affodil' or 'Dutch daffodil' because he had also
seen it in gardens in Belgium. The roots of this plant were once important
enough to be eaten regularly both in ancient Greece and in the Middle Ages,
when they were called *Cibo Regia,* which means 'King's Food'. The Greeks
believed that the roots of Asphodel were particularly nourishing so they
were planted around the tombs of the dead in order to feed them in Hades,
and in his writings Homer says that Asphodels grew abundantly on the
banks of the river Styx.

Asphodelus albus - Asphodel (1596) grows to a height of 2ft (61cm) with grass-
like leaves and white flowers from May to June. Border. A perennial plant
from Southern Europe.
Requirements: A rich, sandy soil.
Cultivation: Divide the tuberous roots in spring or autumn.
After flowering: Cut down stems.
Plants: Kelways.

ASPIDISTRA *(Liliaceae).* Still the subject of jokes, this remarkably long-
suffering and good-natured plant is just about the most useful house-plant
available, and a mature specimen with many leaves is very expensive
nowadays and not always easy to obtain. In Victoria's reign the Aspidistra
was a cherished plant and had pride of place in bay-windows, on sideboards
and pedestals and in the middle of the parlour table; enshrined in its glazed
china pot it seemed to live forever, sometimes tenderly cared for but quite
often a neglected piece of living furniture. It was nicknamed 'The Cannon-

Ball Plant' because of its iron constitution, and it is beginning to come back
into fashion because of this and also because of the nostalgic trend to yester-
year. It is still as amiable as ever and will endure the conditions of aridity
caused by central heating which, together with gas fumes would quickly kill
most other plants. But if Aspidistras are watered well, fed regularly and
have their leaves washed free of dust they will respond with vigorous growth
and perhaps the curious little reddish-brown flowers will suddenly appear in
late summer, to sit quietly on the soil at the foot of the tall leaf-stalks.
Aspidistras can be stood out of doors in a partly shaded place during the
warmer summer months, but they must not be allowed to dry out. They
need firm potting, with a layer of broken earthenware shards at the bottom
of the pot, heavier soil above this and a good compost at the top for the root-
ball to grow into. They should be re-potted every third year or so, and
during the first year after this they need no food, but thereafter they can be
fed gradually with weak liquid manure. They should not be allowed to sit
in water.

A. lurida - Parlour Plant, Cannon-Ball Plant, Aspidistra (1822), grows to
20in (51cm) with inconspicuous reddish cup-shaped flowers occasionally in
August and September when the plant is healthy and well cared for. *(A.
lurida* var. *variegata* has striped green and white leaves.)

Requirements: House-temperature and a compost of good loam, leaf-mould and
sand in equal parts. Feeding once a month with weak liquid plant-food, re-
potting every third year.

Cultivation: Propagation is by division in spring.

Uses: Foliage plants for house or conservatory and indoor swimming-pools: a very
long-living perennial plant from China.

Plants: Florists and house-plant specialists. Fibrex, Oak Cottage Herb Farm,
Rochfords, R.V. Roger Ltd.

ASTER - Michaelmas Daisy *(Compositae)*. There is a certain amount of
confusion about the names of these two distinct genera of plant which often
begin flowering at the same time. The Michaelmas Daisy, a (usually) tall
autumn-flowering herbaceous perennial with blue, mauve, violet, white,
pink and carmine flowers is the true Aster, whereas the shorter annual
daisy-flowered plant producing larger pink, mauve, violet, white and cerise
flowers in late summer is the China Aster - *Callistephus* spp. The first
Michaelmas Daisy was brought from North America in 1633, and is thought
to be *A. Tradescantii* which is not generally grown now. Many species
Asters were discovered thereafter and introduced to gardeners and numbers
of hybrids have resulted. The Victorian craze for carpet-bedding was
responsible for the loss of many of the older varieties because Michaelmas
Daisies were but one of the many border subjects which were swept away to
make room for the even more labour-intensive displays of annuals that were
grown and planted by the thousand. Michaelmas Daisies should have good
soil to give of their best and they need to be divided up every two to three
years. At this time only the outer portion of the clump should be re-planted
– the centre is generally exhausted and should be discarded. They are
vigorous plants and will quickly exhaust the soil in which they grow, so a
good fertiliser is essential for them. The taller kinds may get damaged by the
heavy rains of autumn, and, while wet from these the stems can get broken
by seasonal gales. To prevent this they need to be staked as invisibly as
possible with strong but twiggy pea-sticks or prunings from garden trees
from which the leaves have been stripped. Placed in position early in the
season the flowering stems will grow up and hide the branches while being
supported by them. Canes and string are equally effective but are much
more visible. Michaelmas Daisies were so called because they began to
flower at Michaelmas, September 29th, but newer varieties can be had that
start to flower in July (alongside the confusing Callistephus) and continue,

weather permitting, until November. Michaelmas Daisies like a moist, rich soil and do well on heavy loam or even clay. If grown in a light, hot, free-draining situation they need manure in spring and mulching throughout the summer with grass-cuttings or other moisture-retentive material. In long periods of drought conditions they should not be allowed to dry out. Slugs are a great hazard to the growing shoots in late spring, and each gardener will have his own method of dealing with them. Mildew cannot always be eliminated, and early and regular spraying together with reasonable spacing between plants help to retard the unsightly whitened foliage caused by the fungus *Erysiphe cichoracearum* or Powdery Mildew. The Aster genus was limited at one time to 300 species, most of which had amoral tendencies. They hybridize with each other only too freely and the American botanist Asa Grey exclaimed "Never was there so rascally a genus, they reduce me to despair" and that opinion has been endorsed by taxonomists ever since.

Some gardeners inherit old gardens in which there are invasive clumps of tallish, mauvish Michaelmas Daisies of dubious parentage that flower until the frosts rime the small flowers into final and ephemeral beauty. These are often scorned and cast out – or into, the compost heap, but they can be very useful in winter flower arrangements, having accustomed themselves both to neglect and the soil of the garden where they continue to flower well into the winter months. They can be moved into less prominent positions, such as the wild garden or the back of the border where they will continue to give armfuls of flowers off and on until Christmas in some years. Curiously, they never seem to suffer from mildew. There is not sufficient space in this book to name all the species Asters and early hybrid varieties that may still be available. The genus has been divided into five sections: 1. *Amellus*, 2. *Cordifolius*, 3. *Ericoides*, 4. *Novae-angliae* and 5. *Novi-belgii*. Groups 1, 4 and 5 are the most generally grown. In gardens, propagation has to be by vegetative methods if the plant is to stay true to type.

A. Amellus frikartii (1596) grows to 2½ft (46cm) with lavender-purple flowers from July to October. Border.

A. novae-angliae 'Harrington's Pink' grows to 4ft (122cm) with clear pink flowers from September to October. A good butterfly plant. Border.

A. novi-belgii 'Blandie' grows to 4ft (122cm) with semi-double white flowers from September to October. Border.

A. novi-belgii 'Eventide' grows to 3ft (91.5cm) with violet-blue semi-double flowers from September to October.

A. novi-belgii 'Freda Ballard' grows to 3½ft (107cm) with deep rose flowers in September, Border.

A. spectabilis (1777) grows to 16in (40.5cm) with orange-centered blue flowers from August to October. Discovered in N. America. Border or edging.

A. Thompsonii nana grows to 18in (46cm) with light blue flowers from July to October. Border.

Requirements: Good, moisture-retentive soil, open situation.

Cultivation: Propagate by division in early spring every two or three years, *Novi-belgii* types annually. Stake tall kinds.

Uses: As border or rockery plants.

After flowering: Cut down stems.

Plants: Bressingham, Goatchers, Holden Clough, Kelways, Sherrards, F. Toynbee Ltd., Treasures of Tenbury.

ASTILBE *(Saxifragaceae).* Astilbes are graceful and colourful plants for the water's edge where possible, though they will grow elsewhere providing the soil is moist in summer. They do well in partial shade, providing pleasing contrast with their bronze-coloured spring foliage which many varieties still retain in maturity. The flowers are very similar, at first glance, to the feathery plumes of Aruncus but they are of a different family. Some varieties of Astilbe can be persuaded into early bloom (though for this a heated greenhouse is necessary) and they make colourful pot-plants. For forcing they should be potted up in autumn into 6-in (15-cm) pots, using a good rich compost. Plunge the pots in ashes or put into a cold frame for a month and then bring into a greenhouse with a minimum temperature of 10 – 13°C (50 – 55°F). Water well and gradually raise the temperature to 15°C (59°F). The Astilbes will come into leaf and flower very much earlier, as may a number of other plants in the greenhouse, and this should be taken into consideration.

About 70 years ago, early hybridists Lemoine and Arends were responsible for the large and beautiful section of 'modern' Astilbes, called *A x Arendsii* (though the species kinds may still sometimes be obtained by diligent searching in obscure nursery catalogues). Four species Astilbes were used as parents to obtain many named varieties still being grown today. They were – *A. astilbiodes, A. davidii, A. japonica* and *A. thunbergii.*

A x **Arendsii** (1907) has flowers in shades of pale salmon pink, rosy lilac, purple-pink, carmine, cream and white from June to August. The height and colours vary according to type, and some good kinds are 'Amethyst' – rosy-lilac, 3ft (91.5cm). 'Fanal' – dark red, bronze foliage, 2ft (61cm). 'Federsee' – rosy-red, 2ft 6ins (76cm). 'Dusseldorf' – salmon-pink, 2ft 6ins (76cm). 'Deutschland' – white, 2ft (61cm). 'Fire' – bright salmon-red, 2ft (61cm). 'Jo Ophurst' – ruby-red, 4ft (122cm). 'Rhineland' – pink (early) 2ft 6ins (76 cm).

All Astilbes are perennial plants originating from China, Japan, Korea, India and North America, and they thrive at pond or lake side and in moist borders: damp woodland and semi-shade suits them very well.

A. chinensis var **'pumila'** grows to 12in (30.5cm) with rose-purple flowers from August to September. Damp shade, rock garden.

Requirements: Deep, rich moist soil that does not dry out in hot spells, partial shade for some varieties.

Cultivation: By division in March. Mulch with manure or leaf-mould in April. Sow seeds in March, prick out and grow on. Keep in a nursery bed for first year, do not allow to dry out. Protect in a cold frame for first winter.

After flowering: Cut down stems unless needed for winter decor.

Uses: Beautiful waterside plants, or in large shady rockeries. As greenhouse subjects for early flowers: seed-heads for winter decor.

Plants: Bressingham, Chappell, Great Dixter, Hillier, Holden Clough, Kelways, Sherrards, St. Bridget, F. Toynbee Ltd, Treasures of Tenbury.

Seeds: Chiltern.

ASTRANTIA – Masterwort, Hattie's Pincushion, Melancholy Gentleman *(Umbelliferae).* A well-grown clump of Astrantia in a choice position is a pleasing sight, with its subtly interesting flowers of greenish white or pale pink that really do resemble a pincushion or a miniature posy. The leaves are interestingly shaped and there is a slightly more delicate variegated-leaved kind, *A. minor variegata* which is well worth taking trouble to establish in a suitable position where its pleasing cream and green foliage will show up to advantage. All Astrantias need deep, moist soil and partial shade, and they do well in woodland conditions (this does not mean the hungry, dry shade under a Laburnum or Flowering Cherry). The Reverend William Hanbury commented somewhat uncharitably on Astrantias, that "being flowers of no great beauty, the very worst part of the garden should be assigned to them". This is another plant that has been preserved by the flower-arrangers, who, by persistently requesting nurseries to stock the more uncommon plants have been at times almost their saviours. Astrantias are easy plants to establish, as long as their situation is not too dry for them, and though they belong to the huge *Umbelliferae* family they do not resemble the other members either in appearance or behaviour – most umbellifers having rampant tendencies that need checking.

A. major - Masterwort (1596) grows to 2ft (61cm) with delicate flowers of greenish white in May and June. Moist shady border, woodland or waterside. A perennial plant from Europe.

A. maxima (1804) grows to 2ft (61cm) with shining pale pink flowers in June. Var. 'Rubra' has deeper pink flowers. A perennial plant from the E. Caucasus for the shady border.

A minor (1686) smaller version of *A. major,* growing only to 9in (23cm). The variegated form *(A. minor variegata)* with cream-edged leaves does best in a sunnier position but requires the same moist soil. It is sometimes tender.

Requirements: Semi-shade, moist, rich soil.

Cultivation: by division in late autumn or spring.

Uses: Border, waterside and woodland plant. For flower arrangements.

After flowering: Cut flower stems to dry for winter decor. Mark position of plant as it disappears entirely in winter.

Plants: Most nurseries.

AUBRIETA *(Cruciferae).* Aubrieta was named after Claude Aubriet, the famous botanical artist who lived from 1668-1745. Aubrieta is usually pronounced 'Au-bree-sha' and is often mispronounced and mis-spelt 'Aubret-i-a'. His brilliantly executed and careful drawings show an appreciation and understanding of plant structure that was uncommon in those times, and an important book of the day *Institutiones rei herbariae* was illustrated with his engravings of plant dissections. The great botanist Tournefort took Aubriet with him on a journey to the Levant because, as he said, "It frets a man to see Fine Objects, and not to be able to take Draughts of them: for without this help of Drawing, 'tis impossible any account thereof should be perfectly intelligible".

Most of the flowers of this useful and easy plant are of a violet-to-lilac tone, though there are some modern varieties that are deep crimson or magenta, and a sloping, south-facing wall or bank covered with Aubrieta-cushions in all their hues is a sight to see. This is their natural situation for they are sun-loving rock plants from the hills and cliffs of the Mediterranean. However, they should not be used to fill up gaps in small rockeries because they will inevitably outgrow their allotted space: they do not take kindly to being moved or divided, except in autumn, and the best method of propagation is by layering and seed. If the long trailing stems are separated and layered, that is, pegged down firmly over pots of a compost consisting of sand and leafmould, they will root into the pots. Or if this is inconvenient, impractical or unsightly, the stems may be pegged down into the ground and a small mound of the same compost should be heaped over the pegged-down stem which will root into it; when this has taken place the rooted portions can be detached and potted up or replanted elsewhere. Put the new little plants in a somewhat shaded place for the summer. The nomenclature of the garden varieties differs widely from nursery to nursery because many hybrids have been bred with *A. deltoides* somewhere in their ancestry: some growers or nurserymen have used Latin names for their seedling crosses as though they are species, which they are not. However, good varietal names are as follows:- 'Dr. Mules', deep violet purple; 'Gurgedyke', bright purple; 'Henry Marshall', amethyst purple; 'Lilac Cascade', lilac; 'Red Carpet', deep red; 'Maurice Pritchard', light pink; 'Bob Sanders', red-purple.

Allow wall-plants freedom of growth to make their brilliantly-coloured cushions or curtains of bloom, but if Aubrieta is grown in the larger rockery it will need to be cut hard back after flowering.

A. deltoides - Aubrieta, forms large mats or hummocks about 4in (10cm) high of evergreen leaves with flowers in every shade of mauve, lavender and purple from March until June. A perennial plant from the Mediterranean area. Dry walls, rock banks, sunny borders, larger rockeries, cliffs.

Requirements: Full sun, plenty of growing space, well-drained good garden soil with lime.

Cultivation: Propagation is by layering because Aubrieta does not come true from seed and must be propagated vegetatively if named kinds are required. Spread out and peg down trailing stems, mound up with peat and sand or sand and leafmould and separate the 'new' plants when rooted. Divide established plants carefully in September. Sow seeds of named varieties in boxes of seed compost in a cold frame in March. Prick out and pot on individually and plunge into ground in a lightly shaded nursery area until autumn. Plant out into flowering position in September.

After flowering: Snip over wall plants with scissors to remove seed heads. Cut back rockery and border plants to manageable size.

Uses: For large rock gardens, dry walls, rock banks, wide sunny borders, paving and edging plants.

Seeds: Chiltern, Suttons, Kent, Thompson and Morgan.

Plants: Bressingham, Cunningham, Hillier, Ingwersen, Jackman's, Reginald Kaye, Kelways, St. Bridget, Trenear.

AURICULA - Bear's Ears *(Primulaceae).* Auriculas have had a particularly interesting garden history. For part of the late seventeenth century, all of the eighteenth and for the first half of the nineteenth century they were the most important florists' flower to be grown. By 'florist' I mean a specialist in flowers or a particular flower, not the florist in a flower-shop as we know the term today. Auriculas aroused the same turbulent passions among growers and fanciers as did the Tulip, and as with all fanciers, special terminology became common.

When the Flemish weavers were driven out of their own country by the persecutions of the Dukes of Alva, they came to England, late in the sixteenth century. The weavers settled in specific towns such as Rochdale, Middleton, Norwich and Ipswich. With them came the first Auriculas, which were very simple forms of what later became known as the 'Stage' or Show Auriculas. The colours that existed then bear different and charming names, redolent of the past, such as Oronge, Haire Colour, Murrey, Tawney, Ash, Dunne, Cinnamon and many others. Sir Thomas Hanmer describes and names some of these earlier flowers in his *Garden Book*, published in 1659. Other books of the period listed evocative Auricula names such as 'The Black Imperial', 'Ricketts' Sable', 'Mistris Buggs her fine Purple' and 'Mistris Austin's Scarlet', to name but a few from the very many that were being grown. Striped Auriculas were very highly prized, and changed hands at £20 each – a very great deal of money for one plant at that time. The stripes were probably caused by a non-debilitating disease, as in the Tulip, but the plants appeared healthy enough. There were many shows and competitions and the custom was to paint the pots green to "make a very pretty appearance on the stage". Square pots were preferred to round ones. The plants in their pots were arranged for the shows on staging, as they would be today, but the Auricula devotees went much further in their presentation. They invented the 'Auricula Theatre' and a description is as follows: "That place is termed a theatre, or buffet, where the Auriculas are placed when in flower. It is made of planks ... and covered with a high enough roof to give air to those upon the top tier. It is best to paint the back of a black colour, in order to make the colour of the flowers stand out well. Many fanciers have been at much trouble to make these theatres substantial and to lavish decoration upon them. They have painted at the back pictures which serve as ornaments to their gardens when the theatres are not staged with flowers. Fanciers are recommended to go and see the Auriculas in such theatres, between 20 April and 10 May."

At about the same time the edged Auricula came into being. Names and descriptions are fascinating: there was the green-edged 'Rule Arbiter', the white-edged 'Hortaine', the grey-edged 'Grimes Privateer' which can be exactly dated to 1785, another white-edged variety called 'Popplewell's Conqueror', and 'Wrigley's Northern Hero' which was green-edged. In addition to the growing range of colours, the Auricula was prized for its 'meal' or 'farina'. This was a delicate silver-white bloom or powdering, found on the leaves, stems and the backs of the petals, and careless handling or watering could mar the plant for that season.

Auriculas are not difficult to grow but they require certain conditions at different times of the year. They can be easily set in a rockery and left to get on with things, because, after all, they are originally the hardiest of Alpine plants. But for the perfect Show Auricula beloved by our great-grandfathers (this being the whole plant and not just the flower) they were kept in cold frames or cold greenhouses, which must have been the fore-runner of today's Alpine house. Auriculas do not mind the cold of winter but they do not like too much sun at flowering time. Therefore greenhouses with green blinds (or green painted panes) were used, or the plants were moved out of the sun's rays during the brightest part of the day (and moved back again in the evening). This preserved both the colour and the length of flowering time, though the shading was continued long after the flowers were over as Auriculas have a tendency to wither and shrivel in bright sunlight, or at least not to flower the following year. Double-flowered kinds were much prized, as were those with white 'eyes'. One of the most popular and well-named varieties was 'Dusty Miller' which can still be obtained today. This comes in many colours, but the flowers should be thickly coated with the characteristic 'meal'. All kinds of strange ingredients such as goose droppings and bullock's blood went into the secret compost recipes that the florists used. The Auricula became the recreation, or, more exactly, the obsession of the working man of the North. Faded photographs can still be seen of the weavers and miners at their Auricula society's meetings which were generally held in the large upper room or rooms of a convenient public house.

A summary of the conditions necessary to grow Show Auriculas follows: they need to be grown in a cold greenhouse or alpine house with good ventilation – the windows or doors should be left open throughout the year except in the most severe conditions. Humidity and wet are their enemies, and watering must be done with extreme care. If grown in frames, these should have good drainage and should face north from April until the end of August, when they should be turned round to face south for the other part of the year. During the coldest weather straw or bracken should be heaped against the sides of glass frames, and mats can be placed over the lights when the temperature is sub-normal for long periods. Light is essential to them so this can present a problem, and the protection should be transparent wherever possible.

Today's compost is not the witch's mixture of bygone times, but should consist of equal parts of loam, leaf-mould and well-rotted manure, in the proportions of a barrowful of each, together with half a bucket of sand, crushed oyster shell and bone-meal respectively. Re-potting is best done immediately after flowering. Dead leaves can be sharply tweaked out – they should come away without damaging the plant. The new pots should be quite clean and only one size up. Watering must be done with extreme care, not allowing any water to fall on the leaves, and much more should be given during the growing season. Auriculas do not come true from seed so the only way to be sure of propagating an existing variety truly is by offsets from the parent plant, which should be taken, using a clean, sharp knife, in June or when the plant has done flowering. Take only the offsets that have roots and these should be placed round the edge of a clean clay pot containing equal parts of sand, leaf-mould and sieved loam. Water sparingly, and keep

in a shaded frame until the new plants are well settled, then the normal
ventilation can be resumed.

Seeds sown in spring will germinate more quickly, though, like all the
Primulaceae family, the fresher the seed the more viable it is and therefore
seed can be sown as soon as ripe, in summer. The tiny seeds should be sown
thinly into lightly moistened soil-less seed compost and covered with a
dusting of the same (sieved) compost. A pane of glass should be placed over
the seed tray and placed in a warm greenhouse if sown in spring, and under
the staging in the shade if sown in summer. (Take precautions against slugs
and snails). Germination can take some time and in any case is sporadic, so
the tray should be kept for two seasons after sowing. When the seedlings are
large enough to handle they can be pricked off into individual pots of sandy
compost and may then be placed in a cold greenhouse or frame and kept
shaded during the summer months.

Auriculas are divided into five types: 1. Green-edged, with the petals
having a green border; 2. Grey-edged, where the edge is greyish or white
with a fine dusting of metal or farina; 3. White-edged, where the edge is
thickly powdered with farina, appearing silver-white; 4. Selfs – these have
a yellow central tube surrounded by a white eye: the remainder of the petals
are of one colour; 5. Fancy – these contain all other kinds. (See appendices
for the address of the Auricula society).

Primula Auricula - Show Auricula (1596). Leaves, stem and flowers lightly or
heavily dusted with meal or farina, according to type: very many colours.
Alpine house. A perennial plant, originally from the European Alps.

Primula x pubescens - Alpine Auricula, grows 4 – 6ins (10 – 15cm) high with
flowers in many colours in April and May. There is no farina on the flower;
use in the border or Alpine house. The oldest of the hybrid primulas in
cultivation.

Cultivation: For extended notes, see text. Outdoor plants need well-drained soil
and leafmould mixed with grit. They should be grown in a partially shaded
position.

Propagation: *See text.*

After flowering: Allow seed to set and ripen, sow as soon as ready (when
seedheads are dry).

Uses: For colour in the cold greenhouse. *P.* x *pubescens* for shaded rockeries and
borders.

Seeds: Suttons.

Plants: Bressingham, Broadwell, Beth Chatto, Holden Clough, Reginald Kaye,
Washfield.

BAPTISIA *(Leguminosae).* It is surprising that Baptisias are not grown more
often, because an established clump with its blue spires is an arresting sight
in a summer border. The elegant flower-spikes are of a particularly pleasing
and intense shade of blue, rather like aristocratic Lupins. The leaves are a
bright fresh green in early summer, making a perfect foil to the flowers;
large black seed-pods form in autumn which are most interesting in dried
winter arrangements. Baptisias require a certain amount of careful
nurturing but are worth the initial care needed to establish them. The hard
seeds should be soaked for 24 hours in warm water and then sown
individually in small peat pots in a propagator in March. When the
seedlings are large enough they can be removed from the propagator into
the warm greenhouse, and can be potted on without disturbance to the
roots. They can be hardened off in the usual way and they should then be
plunged in a nursery bed, still in their pots. In autumn they can then be
easily lifted and transferred to a cold frame, as it is the first winter which
causes most fatalities. They are deciduous, so their survival cannot be
checked until late spring. When they begin to shoot again they can be
planted out in their final positions, though some protection should be given

for the second winter, such as litter or ashes. Precautions should be taken against slugs.

Baptisia australis - False Indigo (1758) grows to 4ft (122cm) with spikes of blue flowers in June. Suitable for the border. A perennial plant from the E. United States.

Requirements: A sheltered sunny border and protection against frosts for the first few winters until well established.

Propagation: By division in spring or seed as described.

Uses: Border plant, for cut flowers and seed stalks for winter decor.

Plants: Bressingham, Hillier, Ingwersen, Scotts, Sherrards, Treasures of Tenbury.

Seeds: Chiltern, Thompson and Morgan.

BEGONIA *(Begoniaceae)*. Begonias are a large and interesting genus of tender and rather succulent plants grown for the beauty of their flowers and leaves; they are named after Michel Bégon (1638 – 1710) a French patron of botany. The handsome and often brilliantly coloured leaves of many Begonias have a recognisable characteristic – they are usually asymmetric, with one side much longer and larger than the other; this is particularly noticeable in the Rex Begonias. With a heated greenhouse or conservatory it is possible to have a profusion of colourful flowers throughout the year with a tremendous variety of shapes and shades and habits, and it is a curious fact that all this largesse of blossom arouses definite emotions in gardeners. Some admire and cherish their Begonias with total dedication, producing blooms of an almost unbelievable perfection, whilst others detest even the sight of them, as is sometimes the case with Orchids.

Begonias are divided into four sections: (1) Bulbous-rooted (2) Tuberous-rooted (3) Rhizomatous-rooted (4) Fibrous-rooted. The tuberous-rooted Begonias are probably the best-known of these, with flowers in a very great range of exotic colours and shapes. Some have a pendulous habit and are therefore excellent in hanging baskets or raised troughs and tubs where their beauty of form and colour can be seen to advantage from beneath. Some Begonias have flowers that resemble other flowers, and it is strange to see what is apparently a Carnation, a Cactus or a Camellia (with most uncharacteristic leaves) hanging from a basket. Tuberous Begonias are usually purchased in a dormant state and should be planted either on or in damp peat, hollow sides upward, in a warm greenhouse at a temperature of 13 – 15°C (55 – 60°F). Alternatively they can be started off in a cold frame in April, in trays of peat and sand, leaf-mould and sand or peat alone. They must be protected from slugs. They can be potted on, hardened off and planted out when all danger of the last frosts is past. In autumn they should be brought in to a cool greenhouse until the leaves turn yellow and natural leaf fall happens. Watering should gradually cease at this time. The tubers should be kept in peat for the winter at a temperature of not less than 7°C (45°F) and be watered occasionally to keep them from drying out.

The rhizomatous-rooted varieties are evergreen and often make excellent house-plants, though they will not tolerate gas fumes. Many of these, such as the large *B. rex* group are exceedingly handsome foliage plants, though they often bear flowers as well (usually pink) which are sometimes considered insignificant when compared to the varied shapes and brilliant colouration of the tuberous-rooted kinds.

Fibrous-rooted begonias such as *B. semperflorens* are the most useful of bedding plants, seemingly impervious to bad weather, with shining green or bronze leaves that set off the pink, white or red flowers. They bloom unceasingly until the frosts and should then be discarded, though they still look bright and vigorous and may be brought into the house for a while to give some extra colour to a collection of otherwise predominantly green house-plants.

Certain kinds of winter-flowering Begonias such as the Lorraine varieties (derived from *B. socotrana*, group 1) are raised each year from cuttings. The pruned-back plants should be encouraged into growth in March by raising the greenhouse temperature to 10 – 13°C (50 – 55°F). New shoots will then appear which can be severed and potted up separately in a compound of half peat and half sand. Put them in a propagator or where there is some form of bottom heat until they are well rooted. The greenhouse doors should be left open during hot weather and the plants should be shaded and syringed regularly at these times. Pot on as necessary and begin feeding a month after they are in their final pots. Pinch out the growing tips and turn the plants round regularly to keep the growth even and bushy. Some types may need canes for support, as they have fragile and easily-broken stems and leaves. Remove forming flower-buds until late October or mid November. A constant temperature of 10 – 15°C (50 – 55°F) should be maintained and draughts must not occur or the plants will signify their displeasure by shedding their flower buds. After flowering water less often but do not allow the plants to dry out completely. The leaves will turn yellow and the plants can be cut back to about 6in (15cm). Water sparingly and keep the temperature to 7°C (45°F). In March, repeat the process from the beginning.

Rhizomatous and fibrous-rooted Begonias for the greenhouse should be grown in 6 – 8in (15 – 20.5cm) pots. In the summer their part of the greenhouse should be shaded: they like humidity and they should be syringed frequently in hot spells. In the winter, very much less water should be given and the roots should be kept only slightly moist, with a minimum temperature of not less than 10°C (50°F) and slightly warmer, 13°C (55°F) for *B. rex*. Fortnightly feeds should be given during the summer months. Established plants should be re-potted in April.

In general, Begonia propagation is by vegetative methods as the progeny from seed cannot be counted on to remain true to type unless the parents have been hand-pollinated. The brilliantly-coloured flowers of today's tuberous Begonias are the result of much hybridisation and crossing and the original species are seldom seen or exceedingly difficult to obtain.

B. coccinea (1841) Fibrous. Grows to 6ft (185cm) with long-lasting pendulous coral pink flowers from May to October. For a large pot or the border of the warm greenhouse. A tender perennial from Brazil, parent of many of the modern hybrids.

B. Evensiana (1804) Tuberous. Grows to 2ft (61cm) with pink flowers in summer. A tender plant from Malaya, Japan and China for the cool greenhouse.

B. fuchsioides (1846) Fibrous. Grows to 3ft (91.5cm) with rich scarlet flowers in winter. A tender plant from Mexico for the warm greenhouse.

B. rex. (1858) Rhizomatous. The original plants are from Assam and are the parents of the large group of modern Rex Begonias, which are noted for their handsome and brilliantly coloured leaves. Pink flowers appear from June to September on mature and healthy plants. House-plants or for warm greenhouses or conservatories.

Requirements: Controlled warmth during periods of growth and also for the plants' resting times. Shading in summer for greenhouse or conservatory subjects by means of blinds, green paint or other overhead plants amenable to the temperature changes necessary for the Begonias. Syringing and humidity for certain kinds during hot spells, ventilation and syringing for others. Light soil which should be enriched for them before planting out in the garden or they can be watered with a liquid feed.

Cultivation: For notes on the growing of rhizomatous and fibrous-rooted Begonias for the greenhouse and garden, see main text. Seeds of named varieties of *B. semperflorens* can be sown in March. Begonia seeds are very small and should be thinly sown on a moistened sandy seed compost and left uncovered in a shaded place in the warm greenhouse (or propagator) at a temperature of 16°C (61°F).

Leaf-cuttings may be taken from the ornamental-leaves varieties in May or June. Select a mature and healthy leaf and make cuts in the veins on the underside and lay the leaf on a compost of leaf-mould or sand and peat. Weight the leaf down with clean pebbles, or pieces of earthenware crock, and shade until the growth comes at the cut veins, which can then be potted up when large enough.

Tuberous Begonias are increased by division of the tubers when the new growths are seen: take the cuttings in spring with a portion of the tuber still attached and plant in a compost of sand and leaf-mould in a propagator at a temperature of 18 – 21°C (64 – 70°F). When they have rooted pot them on individually in growing compost. A good growing compost for Begonias is made from 3 parts loam, 1 part leaf-mould or peat, 1 part sand and 1 part well-rotted manure.

Uses: Begonias are some of the most colourful plants for the greenhouse and conservatory, with a range of long-lasting flowers that can be planned to provide bloom throughout the year. In the garden they can be planted out in pots, troughs and hanging baskets, and are surprisingly resistant to inclement summer weather. Space should be allowed for normal traffic around them because of the fragility of the stems, leaves and flowers. The bedding varieties of *B. semperflorens* are excellent for massing where solid colour is required, and they will do well even in partial shade.

After flowering: Begonias need slightly different treatment according to their flowering period and type, and this should be taken into account when planning and purchasing.

Seeds: Chiltern, Thompson and Morgan.

Tubers, Rhizomes: Amand, Blackmore and Langdon, de Jager, Hillier.

BELLIS - Daisy *(Compositae)*. The double daisies of Elizabethan times are not the same as those of today but their flowers were as much appreciated then as ours are now. One of the old names for a daisy was the 'Measure of Love' because of the way that lovers use the flower petals to count when saying 'He loves me – He loves me not'. Poultices of daisy leaves were formerly used as field dressings on the battlefield to staunch bleeding wounds, and it is said that its name is derived from *Bellum*, 'War', because of this. But since the plant's name is also said to be from *'Bellus'*, meaning pretty, it would appear that opinions differ widely, which is often the case with plant nomenclature.

Because wild daisies grow everywhere in abundance unless physically removed, they are often particularly prolific in churchyards, whence comes the familiar phrase 'Pushing up the daisies' which signifies lying in one's grave beneath them. Double daisies are one of the archetypal cottage-garden flowers and are very easy to grow. They are best treated as biennials when grown from seed, rather than the perennials that they are, because in time they become less floriferous. When grown from seed they need no cossetting, being sown in the open in a nursery bed to be thinned out later and grown on through the summer. Initially the bed should be protected from birds and cats to give the seedlings a chance to grow; in September the small plants can be planted in their final flowering position.

Bellis perennis - Daisy. The garden variety has the same name as the wild flower and is originally derived from it. Older varieties are now lost, but many modern cultivars and hybrids exist such as 'Alice', 'Dresden China' (this does not seed), 'Pom-Pom', 'Goliath' and very many more.

Requirements: Ordinary garden soil and full sun.

Cultivation: Sow seed according to directions on the packet.

Uses: As edging plants, for troughs, windowboxes, spring bedding, borders and for cut flowers.

After flowering: Dead-head regularly.
Seeds: Most seedsmen. N.B. Seeds of the native wild daisy may now be obtained
for naturalising in the wild garden from Naturescape and John Chambers.
Plants: Garden centres and nurseries.

BERGENIA *(Saxifragaceae).* Bergenias were formerly called 'Megasea' and
children of all ages still call the plants 'Elephant's Ears' and 'Pig Squeak'.
They are one of the most useful plants possible for any kind of garden, being
so easy to grow that they were at one time rather despised as being too
ordinary. However, those plant-saviours, the flower-arrangers, brought
them back to favour because of their handsome leaves. Bergenias are
excellent everywhere and it is worth giving them a choice, sunny position,
perhaps where their fine leaves can clothe a low wall – they associate well
with stonework. Then they will reward the gardener with a profusion of
pink flowers in February when there is nothing else in the garden of such
size and abundance. Bergenias will grow equally well in shady corners,
where their leaves will act as excellent evergreen ground cover though they
will not flower as well. They will also grow in dry shade under trees and are
sculpturally handsome with ferns in damp rockeries or at the water's edge,
though they should not be planted in boggy ground. They are the garden
designer's standby for reliability and there are a number of colours and
hybrids now, though none are as free-flowering in the earliest, coldest days
of spring as the old variety *B. cordifolia,* whose fat pink panicles of flowers
often begin to bloom in December with a succession of flowers until March
in a favourable year. The leaves may be blackened by frosts in a hard winter
but established clumps recover quickly in the spring, and the dead leaves
can then be cut away.
B. cordifolia - Bergenia (1799) grows to about 1ft (30.5cm) with large green
leaves that are crimson beneath in winter. Flowers of pink, white, and
purplish pink appear in December until March, with intermittent ones
during the rest of the year. An excellent ground-cover plant, suitable for dry
walls, rockeries, under trees, in shade, as edging and in the border. An
evergreen perennial from Siberia.
B. crassifolia (1765) grows to about 1ft (30.5cm) with large leaves and pale pink
flowers in spring. For large rockeries, edging, border. An evergreen
perennial plant from Siberia.
B. purpurescens (1850) grows to 9in (23cm) with purple-pink flowers in June.
Rockeries, edging, borders, woodland. An evergreen perennial plant from
the Himalayas.
Requirements: Most Bergenias enjoy being in the sun and will flower better. Any
soil suits them, and almost any garden situation.
Cultivation: The heavy rootstocks can be divided in spring, taking care to detach
portions with roots attached. Leave the new plants in position until they
become overcrowded, then thin out.
Uses: As year-round ground cover and for cut flowers in early spring. Leaves for
arrangements, frost-killed flowers also.
After flowering: Cut stems down.
Plants: Most nurseries.

BRUNNERA *(Boraginaceae).* This is a small genus of plants, named after Samuel
Brunner, a Swiss botanist. The flowers look like a slightly larger Forget-me-
not and the leaves have the hispid feel and look of Comfrey. In maturity,
Brunneras have pleasing heart-shaped leaves that form large and handsome
clumps, with rather dainty sprays of bright blue flowers that associate well
with Bluebells, ferns and Aquilegia. Once established they will propagate
themselves readily by self-sown seedlings which will pop up almost
anywhere. Once these are recognised they can be transplanted back to the

family group because a massed planting always looks better than isolated specimens dotted about the garden.

B. macrophylla (1830) grows to 18in (46cm) high with panicles of blue flowers in May and June. A perennial from the Caucasus for the shady border or where woodland conditions exist.

Requirements: Leaf-mould and light, moisture-retentive woodland conditions.

Propagation: By division in October or March.

Uses: As a shady border plant.

Plants: Bressingham, Beth Chatto, Peter Chappell, Cunnington, Highfield, Hillier, Holden Clough, Kelways, Notcutts, Scotts, Sherrards, F. Toynbee Ltd., Treasures of Tenbury.

CALCEOLARIA - Slipper-flower *(Scrophulariaceae).* The plants' name of Calceolaria originates from the Latin word 'Calceolus' which means a little shoe; perhaps some of the early varieties resembled a medieval slipper even more than the exotically-shaped hybrids of today. Calceolarias were very popular in the nineteenth century when the vast bedding-out schemes required thousands of plants, all of a uniform height and appearance. It is curious that such an unusual flower was used in this way because the strange and interesting blooms are best seen when individual specimens are grown. Since most Calceolarias do not come true from seed it is certain that many of these earlier varieties are lost for ever. Many 'new' kinds were introduced from Mexico and South America by Benedict Roezl, an indefatigable plant collector of that period. He was able to get about in South America with a little more ease than was generally the case for this sometimes dangerous and often unappreciated profession, because the first railways were being built and the gradual improvement in the road systems there enabled his precious and bulky harvest to be transhipped to Europe in less time – and therefore with fewer fatalities than was generally the case.

Calceolarias are tender plants, usually treated as annuals and biennials when grown for bedding or for the house. The more delicate varieties make colourful greenhouse or conservatory subjects that are fascinating to children because of their strange pouched shape. There are many kinds of Calceolaria, from almost hardy to definitely delicate, and their requirements should be checked at the time of purchase. Some annual species can be sown direct into a prepared position in the garden to be thinned out later (precautions should be taken against slugs). Seeds of other varieties should be sown in July (fresh seed germinates more certainly). The seed compost should be moistened and allowed to drain and the tiny seeds should be pressed lightly in it and left uncovered, though the box or pan should be shaded and placed in a cold greenhouse or frame and grown on in the usual way in individual pots. During the winter they must be kept in frost-free conditions. If packeted seed is bought in winter or early spring, as is usually the case, then these seeds should be sown in a temperature of 18°C (64°F) and then grown on in the usual way. Aphis and white fly may be troublesome and regular spraying is beneficial, particularly beneath the leaves and on the soil surface of pots and in the frame.

C. biflora (1826) grows to 12in (30.5cm) with yellow flowers in July and August. Rock garden. A perennial plant from Chile, needing frost-free housing in winter, minimum temperature 7 – 10°C (45 – 50°F).

C. corymbosa (1822) grows to 18in (46cm) with yellow flowers, spotted purple, from May to October. Tender perennials from Chile for warm greenhouses, or containers outside during summer.

C. tenella (1873) grows only to 5in (12.5cm) with yellow flowers from June to August. A doubtfully hardy perennial from the Straits of Magellan. Best with some winter protection.

Requirements: A slightly acid, rich, moisture-retentive and light soil: warm greenhouse or propagator for most types being grown from seed: a constant temperature in winter for those varieties being grown on for the following year. Regular watering and spraying in summer, and shading for greenhouse subjects which must not be allowed to dry out in hot weather. Plenty of ventilation.

Cultivation: Packeted seeds may be grown as directed, but these are almost always modern hybrids and special varieties should be increased by cuttings taken at almost any time except in the winter.

Uses: As greenhouse, house and conservatory plants, for tubs, troughs, patios and window boxes.

Plants: Southcombe, Holden Clough, Ingwersen.

Seeds: Thomas Butcher, Holtzhausen, Thompson and Morgan for *C. biflora.*

CALENDULA - Marigold, Ruddles *(Compositae).* Marigolds are named for the *kalends* or *calendae* — the first day of the month, because these flowers are in bloom almost all the year round in old and undisturbed gardens. They are a favourite and easy plant that after a single generation in your garden will be there for ever, like unwanted relatives but much nicer. Straggling, single plants are something of a nuisance but if Marigolds are grown properly and planted out in a large bed all to themselves they can be a spectacular sight. Marigolds have useful medicinal virtues: a soothing ointment can be made from their aromatic leaves that will heal small wounds without a scar, the plant has antiseptic properties and it is a gentle cure for small warts. In earlier times there were many superstitions about Marigolds, all of them benevolent. A fourteenth century medical MS that can be seen in the Royal Library in Stockholm is full of praise for Marigolds or 'Goldes' as they were then called and adjures the reader to "look wyscely on the flower in the early morning it will protect you from feveres during that day". The dried petals may be safely used as a colourant for rice instead of saffron or turmeric, and were once widely sold for this practice.

It is best to start off with a good strain of seeds which will flower within a few months of sowing. In late summer, allow some of the seed heads to ripen and press the seeds into the soil: do not disturb the ground overmuch and early and very hardy seedlings will appear in spring. Alternatively, ripe seed can be saved and sown in a prepared nursery bed if the space for the Marigolds is still occupied by spring bedding plants and bulbs.

Calendula officinalis - Marigold (1593), sometimes grows to 2ft (61cm) with bright orange or yellow flowers from May until the frosts. A hardy annual from Southern Europe for the border.

Requirements: Full sun, ordinary soil and growing space.

Cultivation: Seeds can be sown in open ground in early spring and thinned out.

Uses: Medicinally, as border plants, as cut flowers and in the kitchen.

Seeds: Most seedsmen.

CALLISTEPHUS - China Aster *(Compositae).* The name means 'most beautiful crown' and this is the other aster, an annual plant that begins to flower in late summer just when the garden seems suddenly to look tired and a little jaded. Asters have been with us for a very long time, partly because they are easy flowers and partly because these last well in water. Some of the older named groups such as the Victoria, the Ostrich Plume, the Paeony and the Comet Asters are still being grown, though within these groups the varieties will not be the same now as they were in the eighteenth century when they were first introduced to the British Isles from China. Being shallow-rooted but rather hungry plants they appreciate a mulch of well-decayed manure, and will yield continuous flowers for cutting until the frosts. Asters should not be grown in the same place for two consecutive seasons, as they are liable to one or both of the two Aster diseases; Black Neck that causes the seedling stems to turn black, and Aster Wilt which produces a pinkish mould on the stems at soil level; the afflicted Asters should be burnt if either of these diseases is seen, and the soil should be sprayed with Bordeaux mixture.

Callistephus chinensis - China Aster. The species plant is seldom seen. Very many modern strains are grown; an annual from China for the border and cold greenhouse.

Requirements: Ordinary soil and an open situation.

Cultivation: Sow seeds at a temperature of 16°C (61°F) in March, grow on, harden off and plant out in late May or June: or sow in May or June and pot up for winter flowers in the greenhouse.

Uses: As border plants, cut flowers and pot plants under glass.

During and after flowering: Dead-head regularly.

Seeds: Most seedsmen.

CALTHA - Marsh Marigold, Kingcup *(Ranunculaceae)*. Marsh Marigolds seem to reflect the brilliance of the spring sunshine in their glossy yellow petals, and though they are a native wild plant they have always been a favourite with gardeners. The sudden explosion of flowers from their clustered, tight green buds is always a joyful surprise and the blooms last for many weeks. Marsh Marigolds will sow themselves around the edge of a garden pond very quickly so long as there is a sufficient depth of mud or moist soil for them to root into. In late summer the dark green leaves quietly disappear to be replaced by later-flowering waterside plants; when clearing or tidying the banks of the pond in winter or early spring it is sometimes difficult to remember exactly where the plants were growing in the previous season, because not a trace of them can be seen. Strangely enough, the double variety – *Caltha palustris* var. *'plena'* was known early in the seventeenth century and Parkinson had it in his garden, where it was yet another yellow-flowered plant that was called by the name of Batchelor's Buttons.

There is a lovely story of an acquisitive English gardener who knew of the existence of a particularly rare variety of this plant that grew only in the Vatican gardens. Arming himself with a cluster of female relatives to distract the keeper of the gardens, he used his umbrella to drag out some roots of the coveted plant, which was *Caltha polypetala*. This incident happened in the nineteenth century and the morals of some gardeners have not improved one iota in the intervening time.

Caltha palustris - Marsh Marigold, Kingcup grows to 2ft (61cm) with shining single yellow leaves from March to June. A European, Asian and N. American perennial water plant. *C. palustris flore plena* has double yellow flowers, is smaller and blooms earlier. There is a pleasing white kind, *C. palustris* var. 'Alba'.

Requirements: A boggy waterside situation in full sun.

Cultivation: By division in autumn or by seed sown in a moist compost in a frame in June. Transfer seedlings as soon as large enough to final position.

Uses: As a waterside plant.

Plants: Bressingham, Peter Chappell, Beth Chatto, Highland Water Garden, Holden Clough, Honeysome Aquatic Nursery, Kelways, Notcutts, Waverney Fish Farm, Wildwoods.

Seeds: Bennetts, John Chambers, Chiltern, Naturescape.

CAMPANULA - Bellflower *(Campanulaceae)*. This is a very large and always beautiful genus of flowers, with pygmy plants no higher than 2in (5cm) and seven-foot giants whose bells dangle above one's head. A favourite in old herbaceous borders is *Campanula Medium* – Canterbury Bells (called 'Coventry Bells' in former days) which has both single and double flowers: *C.* var. *calycanthema* is the 'Cup and Saucer' variety. *C. rapunculoides*, the Creeping Bellflower is a very easy plant, though precautions have to be taken against slugs just as the leaves are emerging from the ground in spring. It has rhizomatous roots and once it has settled in a garden it will increase vigorously, spreading very quickly – in some cases too much so. However, it is an attractive flower and is exceedingly useful in difficult places where other types of Campanula would refuse to grow, let alone flower. *C. lactiflora* is one of the giant campanulas, growing to a possible height of 6ft (183cm) or more. It can be cut down to about 8in (20.5cm) from the ground in May, if liked, as Gertrude Jekyll used to do with hers after observing the damage done to the plants by rabbits: the speedy regrowth of this type of Campanula to a sturdier form and bushier shape may in some cases be more useful. It is best not divided nor moved for several years after planting, however. *C. portenschlagiana* is a familiar sight to visitors to the West Country, where it can be seen dripping slowly down steps or clothing walls and crannies in paving. It is a sturdy plant, seeming to flourish in inhospitable chinks and cracks from which it pours forth an exuberant tide of crisp light green leaves and bright mauve bells.

   C. rotundifolia is the wild Harebell whose papery bells seem to ring with fairy music, inaudible to mortal ears. The roots of many of the Campanulas were cooked and eaten in former times and the leaves and flowers were used as gargles and lotions, though it is now known that the plant has no medicinal properties.

   One particular species, *C. pyramidalis,* the Chimney Bellflower, was so called because they were grown in large pots which were placed in the empty summer fireplaces; with it were ranged other plants, either sweet-smelling or colourful that made a pleasing summer display. This was fashionable for well over a hundred years, long enough to give the flower its common name.

   C. rapunculoides was grown as a salad vegetable in the Middle Ages and it must have had an addictive effect, because one remembers the tale of the peasant-woman who was expecting her first child after many years of waiting. But as in most pregnancies, she yearned for unobtainable delicacies, and in this case she craved for vegetables that she could see in the garden next to hers. There was a high wall round the garden which belonged to a witch. The young peasant woman became sick with desire for the fine salad vegetables that she could just see from her windows and refused to eat anything else, so she began to pine away. The anxious husband, fearful for the life of his wife and the child to come, risked climbing over the wall to steal the salad vegetables. All was well – the witch did not see him, and his wife was so happy that she began to eat normally again for a little while. But again the craving for the special vegetables overcame her, and once more she began to pine for them, refusing all other food. The husband climbed the wall once more – but this time the witch was waiting for him: in terror, the man promised to bring her his child when it was born, and in return the witch let him take what he wanted from the garden. The young wife gave birth to a fine girl, who was named Rapunzel, after the plant.

C. carpatica (1774) grows to 12in (30.5cm) with blue, mauve or white flowers from June to August. A variable perennial from the Carpathian mountains for the border or large rock garden.

C. portenschlagiana, syn. **C. muralis** grows only to 4in (10cm) with bright purple flowers in June and July. A carpeting plant for walls, rockeries, edging. A perennial from the mountains of S. Europe.

C. garganica (1832) grows to 6in (15cm) with prostrate 'branches' of white-centred flat blue flowers from May to September. A perennial from Italy for the rock garden, dry walls and paths. Likes sandy soil.

C. lactiflora (1814) grows to 6ft (183cm) with blue flowers from July to September. Back of border. A perennial from Caucasus.

C. Medium - Canterbury Bells (1597) grows to 4ft (122cm) though there are dwarf varieties, with pink, rose, carmine, white, mauve, blue and violet flowers from May to July. A biennial plant from S. Europe for the sunny border.

Campanula persicifolia grows to 3ft (91.5cm) with blue-mauve flowers in July and August. A variable European perennial, also from N. Africa and N. and W. Asia for the sunny border.

C. pyramidalis - Chimney Bellflower (1596), grows to 5ft (152.5cm) or 8ft (244cm) under glass. Two-tone blue-mauve flowers in July. A biennial from Europe for borders and containers.

C. rapunculoides - Creeping Bellflower, Bats-in-the-Belfry grows to 4ft (122cm) with creeping rhizomes and drooping mauve bells in June and July. Large borders, wild garden. A perennial from Europe. Spreads quickly.

C. rotundifolia - Harebell or Scottish Bluebell grows to 12in (61cm) with papery mauve bells from June to Aguust. A perennial wild plant of the N. hemisphere for the rockery or wild garden.

Requirements: For those mentioned, an open, sunny position in borders, rock gardens or containers. Well-drained soil with an annual mulch of well-rotted compost. Staking may be necessary for tall varieties unless they can be planted to grow up through open shrubs.

Cultivation: Sow seeds of annuals and biennials in September or March and grow on in a cold greenhouse. Biennials should be planted in nursery beds unless space for them already exists. Perennial varieties can be divided in autumn or spring.

Uses: Border or edging: rock plants, containers and for cut flowers.

After flowering: Cut down stems unless seeds are needed.

Plants: Most nurseries.

Seeds: John Chambers, Chiltern, Dobie, Naturescape, Suttons, Thompson and Morgan, Unwins.

CANNA - Indian Shot *(Cannaceae).* Cannas were beloved by the Victorians for their exotic appearance and their long-lasting flowers. There are still two main types of *C.* x *hybrida* that are grown today, the green-leaved and the purple or brown-leaved. Cannas are tender plants and need to be propagated and grown on in heat, which was, of course, no problem in the times when both coal and labour were cheap. These handsome plants were often used in complex bedding-out schemes, and still are today to a lesser degree in municipal parks and gardens. There is really no other plant quite like them for visual impact. Cannas flower late in the year, so they should be grown on safely under glass until the weather is settled and warm. The tropical appearance of their leaves is sufficient in the planting schemes until the flowers come later on, and they look well in pots near water.

They are greedy plants and must have a diet of real manure to do well. Greenhouse plants need a rich compost of equal parts of decayed cow manure and loam, with a little peat and sand added. They must be kept well watered during the growing season with weekly feeds of liquid manure until the flower buds appear. After flowering they should be allowed to die down and dry off until February in a minimum temperature of 10°C (50°F). In February the rhizomes should be replanted in fresh compost until they produce shoots. If specimen plants are needed the rhizome should be cut into segments, each with one shoot and some roots. These should be grown on in individual pots in a temperature of 16°C (61°F) and repotted again in April into large pots using a similar compost. Groups may be planted into large tubs, ready to go outside. If they are to remain in the greenhouse or conservatory the temperature should not fall below 13 – 16°C (55 – 61°F).

Plants outside should be brought in well before the frosts and temporarily planted in pots or boxes until they begin to dry off. The leaves, stems and roots should then be cut off and the rhizomes can be stored in damp peat or leaf-mould in a cool, frost-free place. The warm greenhouse is too warm, the rhizomes need to rest. Cannas can also be grown from seed, though they do not come true to type. *Canna indica* - Indian Shot (1570) grows to 5ft (152.5cm) with pink flowers and green leaves in August. A tender perennial rhizomatous plant from the W. Indies and C. and S. America for heated greenhouses, conservatories, summer bedding or tubs outside in a sheltered, sunny place.

C. x **hybrida** Very many varieties under this name with either green or dark leaves and red, yellow, orange or pink flowers in late summer.

Requirements: Frequent watering in the growing and flowering season, with weekly feeds of liquid manure. A sunny, sheltered bed outside if being used in a planting scheme. Careful storage in winter.

Cultivation: The hard seeds should be filed, nicked and soaked for 24 hours. Sow in February in a minimum temperature of 21°C (70°F) in a soil-less compost, grow on and begin feeding with very weak liquid manure. Pot on as for rhizomes. Germination is erratic and often lengthy.

Uses: As striking bedding, greenhouse and pot plants.

Seeds: Suttons, Thompson and Morgan, Chiltern.

Rhizomes: Amand, Thomas Butcher, Holtzhausen, Spalding.

CATANANCHE - Cupid's Dart *(Compositae)*. The origin of the plant's Latinised name is from the Greek *Katananke*, a strong incentive or to compel, because in ancient Greece women used it in love-potions – hence also its common name. Catananches have delicate blue-mauve daisy-flowers rather like Cornflowers that are very useful and long-lasting when cut. They dry well and can be kept for winter decor. Since they come from the warm shores of the Mediterranean, they cannot be completely relied upon for hardiness, but they are easily grown from seed. Gerard had it in his garden so it has been grown in these islands for over 400 years, yet it is not seen as often as might be expected.

C. caerulea - Cupid's Dart, Blue Cupidone (1596), grows to 3ft (91.5cm) with blue flowers in summer. A short-lived perennial from the W. Mediterranean for the border.

Requirements: Sunny, sheltered position.

Cultivation: Sow seeds in April for following year's flowers. Take root cuttings in March to propagate named varieties.

Uses: Border plants, cut flowers, winter decor.

Plants: Most nurseries.

Seeds: Chiltern, Sutton, Thompson and Morgan.

CENTAUREA - Cornflower, Bluebottle *(Compositae)*. The Cornflower is another plant of jumbled childhood memories that recall cottage gardens and cornfields for those of us old enough to remember. In its wild blue form it is still seen in botanic gardens but the flowers of today can be had in many colours. There was an early belief that in bad years the seed crop came up as Cornflowers instead of corn, and Turner said "About midsummer the chylder used to make garlandes of the floure – it groweth much amongst rye, wherefore I think that goode rye in an evell and unseasonable yere doth go out of kinde into this wede."

As anyone who has tried to pick them will know, the stems and leaves of Cornflowers and Knapweeds are very tough and the plant was formerly called 'Hurt-sickle' because it dulled the edges of the reaper's tools. The Centaury genus is named after the mythical centaur Chiron, half man and half horse, who used one of the plants to cure Hercules of a poisoned arrow wound. This particular genus is still used in homoeopathic medicine as a nervine, as a remedy for inflamed eyes, for insect bites and for cuts and grazes, thus bearing out the legend.

Centaurea cyanus - Cornflower, Bluebottle grows to 3ft (91.5cm) in the wild form (taller in cultivars) with blue, pink or white flowers from June to September. Border. A European annual.

C. moschata - Sweet Sultan (1629) grows to 2ft (61cm) with white, yellow, pink or purple flowers from June to September. An annual plant from the E. Mediterranean for the border.

C. macrocephala (1805) grows to 3ft (91.5cm) with light-green leaves and yellow 'thistle' flowers in June and July. Handsome brown buds are most attractive for winter decor. A perennial plant from the Caucasus for the border.

C. dealbata - Perennial Cornflower (1804) grows to 2ft (61cm) with purple or pink flowers in June and July. A perennial plant for the sunny border from the Caucasus.

Requirements: Ordinary garden soil and full sun.

Cultivation: Sow annual seeds in March, or autumn sowings produce larger, stronger plants. Divide perennial spp. in autumn or spring.

Uses: Border plants, as cut flowers.

During and after flowering: Keep dead-headed.

Seeds: Most seedsmen.

Plants Most nurseries.

CENTRANTHUS - Valerian *(Valerianceae).* This is that splendid mop-headed wall plant of Devon and Cornwall which is so characteristic of those areas, and expatriates like myself usually make sure that for reasons of sentiment we have it in our gardens. Valerian has many common names – Padstow Pride, Fowey Pride, Soldier's Pride, Pretty Betsy, Bouncing Bess, Setwall and so on. It is a plant that in maturity cannot be moved without rebuilding bank or wall from the bottom up. It is not a plant for any rockery, however large, and it can never be disciplined into tidy habits which is part of its charm. It flowers luxuriantly for the greater part of the summer and is a very good butterfly plant. The fluffy seeds will float on the wind for considerable distances and will populate walls, paths, cliffs and quarries for miles. A cliff covered in the many shading tones of rose-pink Valerian can almost be said to resemble a hanging garden, so beautiful is it.

The seeds should be sown when fresh if possible, in June and July, and some old mortar dust can be incorporated into the soil that they are sown in as they need no special compost. Do not allow the seedlings to get too large as they resent disturbance from the start. Plant into flowering positions, allowing plenty of room for growth. (This Valerian is not the medicinal Valerian which is *V. officinalis).*

Centranthus ruber, (syn. **Kentranthus ruber)** grows to 2ft 6ins (76cm) with scented flowers of pink, rose-crimson and white from May until September. As a strong-growing perennial plant from the Mediterranean, it is suitable for banks, walls and the wild garden.

Requirements: Full sun, a limey soil and growing room.

Cultivation: Allow seeds to germinate beneath parent plants where possible, or sow as described, or sow into crevices in walls, covering seed with some stiff soil or mud.

Uses: A wall cover for large areas; as a butterfly plant.

Plants: Waterperry, Bressingham, Goatchers, Nottcutts.

Seeds: Chiltern, John Chambers, Suttons.

CERASTIUM - Snow-in-Summer *(Caryophyllaceae).* Snow-in-Summer, when mature, well grown and in full bloom is a spectacular sight, though it should not be let loose in the average rockery. It has white-felted leaves throughout the year, but with spring re-growth these increase thickly and with the sparkling whiteness of the flower the whole plant is an excellent foil to darker-leaved herbaceous plants or shrubs, such as *Rhus cotinus coggygria* – the Smoke bush; *Rosa rubrifolia* with its blue-toned leaves; *Eucalyptus gunnii* if kept pruned down, the crimson foliage of *Weigela foliis purpureis* and *Berberis thunbergii atropurpurea;* Heathers of different colours, dark leaved Phormiums, not to mention other possible planting associations with blue, grey or yellow leaves. Cerastium has fallen into disrepute because of its invasive habits and its general willingness to grow in very poor soil, though it must have full sunlight to give of its best. It should be used as a carpeting plant, to drip down walls or as edging, and it is a plant for the laziest of gardeners – one needs to do nothing else other than to plant it, water it and then step back smartly before it swirls round your feet. Oddly enough, despite its reputation for rampant invasiveness, like all silver-leaved plants it may even need protection in winter. The poorer the soil, the whiter the leaves will become. It will be found that the main plant has many creeping underground stems which make division easy though this should be done at the right time.

Cerastium tomentosum - Snow-in-Summer (1648). Mat-forming with silver-white leaves and white flowers in June. A perennial plant from S. Europe for walls, banks and large areas needing ground cover.

Requirements: An open situation with average to poor soil.

Cultivation: Divide and replant immediately in March.

Uses: As ground cover, for dry walls and banks, *very* large rockeries and edging.

Plants: Bees, Hillier, Ingwersen, Ruth Thompson.

CHEIRANTHUS - Wallflower *(Cruciferae)*. There are a number of 'special' Wallflowers, but the ones most people associate with the name are *C. cheiri*, which are richly coloured and scent the air around in spring. Wallflowers get sadly mistreated at markets, nurseries, and garden centres, often being sold bare-rooted in bundles, or at best being kept in buckets of water in draughty passages. When planted after this it is no wonder that the poor things flop sadly for days, and it is a credit to their sturdiness that they survive and flower as sweetly as they always do. They are treated as biennials but in reality they are quite long-lived perennials, and if space permits a few plants should be set out in a sunny corner and left to grow to provide bowlfulls of flowers for the house. Another familiar wallflower of spring bedding is *C. x Allionii*, the Siberian Wallflower, whose flowers of a flat, bright orange should be carefully sited because of their colour.

Wallflowers are a fine example of the confusing plant nomenclature of the past: they were called by some 'Sweet William' because of their scent, and also 'Yellow Stock Gilliflower' – though the Stock Gilliflower was our present-day Stock (Matthiola) and the Geleflower, Gilofre or Gillofer was today's Carnation: Wallflowers were also called 'Heart's-Ease' to further complicate things because *Viola tricolor* is still called Heart's Ease today. They were even called 'Violet' which was another name for Honesty – and so on ...

But the word Cheiranthus means 'hand-flower' because bunches of the flowers were carried in processions and pageants, and this name they have not had to share.

There is a fourteenth-century tale about them which is as follows: Robert III of Scotland was to marry Elizabeth, daughter of the Earl of March. This would have been a fine match but as is the way of things she was in love with the son of a border chieftain who was probably younger and almost certainly handsomer. Her father locked her up in one of his castles to think things over, but her lover, Scott of Tushielaw, disguised himself as a minstrel so that he could sing under her window. His songs were cleverly made and told her how to escape from the castle, and Elizabeth plucked a spray of Wallflowers and dropped them at his feet as a sign that she had heard and understood. Young Scott arranged for the escape, and in her excitement at the prospect of an elopement and freedom, Elizabeth neglected to fix the rope-ladder securely and fell to her death. The young man was broken-hearted and left Scotland to travel through Europe as a minstrel, wearing a sprig of Wallflowers in his cap in memory of his love. Other minstrels, being in the business of romance, copied this, and ever since the Wallflower has meant 'Fidelity in Adversity' in the language of flowers.

C. cheiri - Wallflower grows to 2ft (61cm) in normal situations with flowers of red, crimson, orange, yellow, salmon, cream, pink, purple and white, from April to June. A European perennial, treated as a biennial for spring bedding, tubs and pots.

C. x Allionii - Siberian Wallflower (1846), grows to 12in (30.5cm) with bright orange flowers from April to June.

Requirements: Ordinary garden soil and a sunny, open position.

Cultivation: Sow seeds in May or June in boxes or a nursey bed. Thin out to 12in (30.5cm) apart and grow on until October. Transplant to flowering positions, taking up a ball of soil with each plant. In the spring pinch out the top flower buds to keep plant bushy.

Uses: As cut flowers, bedding and container plants and for naturalising on old walls.

During flowering: Cut off dead flower spikes.

Seeds: Most seedsmen.

Plants: Nurseries and Garden Centres.

CHIONODOXA - Glory of the Snow *(Liliaceae)*. The name is taken from *chion*, snow, *doxa*, glory, because in the wild the plants burst into bloom as the snow melts around them. Their existence was known in 1842 but they were not introduced to this country until 1877, when they were re-discovered, so to speak, by the members of a mountain-climbing expedition in Turkey. Surprisingly, the bulbs do quite well in the British Isles, though their soil must be well drained and their situation sunny – a rockery is particularly suited to them because drainage is more easily managed. The bulbs produce offsets which should be allowed to grow on for two or three years undisturbed.

C. gigantea, syn. **C. grandiflora,** grows up to 8in (20.5cm) with violet-blue flowers from February to April.

C. Luciliae (1877) grows to 6in (15cm) with blue flowers from February to March. A bulb from Crete and Asia Minor for the rock garden. There are pink and white flowered forms.

Requirements: A sunny sheltered shelf in a rock garden, or against a south wall.

Cultivation: Plant bulbs in autumn, 2 – 3in (5 – 7.5cm) deep. Thin out overcrowded bulbs when leaves die down.

Uses: Rock and border plants.

Bulbs: Avon, Bees, Broadleigh, Christian, Holden Clough, Ingwersen, Orpington, Potterton and Martin, Spalding, van Tubergen..

Seeds: Thomas Butcher.

CHRYSANTHEMUM *(Compositae)*. This is a very large genus with many familiar flower-faces. *Chrysanthemum maximum* is the Moon Daisy, Shasta Daisy or Marguerite, whose white flowers have always personified purity and wholesomeness. *C. Parthenium* or Feverfew is a short-lived perennial plant with aromatic, light-green leaves and small white flowers that have been used in herbal medicine for centuries. There is a golden-leaved variety, *C. Parthenium aurum* that was used for bedding-out purposes because of the unusual and constant colour of its leaves: the flowers would have been regularly nipped off by some early-rising gardener's boy.

Pyrethrums – *C. cinerariifolium* and *C. roseum* – are grown commercially as a source of non-toxic insect powder. The flowers are collected just as they open and dried naturally in the open air. When dry they are powdered, and this is used for dusting infested plants, or it can be used in liquid form. The powder *must* be fresh.

C. segetum the Corn Marigold was formerly a weed of cornfields, and the peasant farmers were heavily fined if 'Gold' was found growing in their fields. It has survived the persecution of centuries and is beginning to be grown in the wild garden as a colourful and historical annual. But by 'Chrysanthemum' most gardeners mean the shaggy-headed autumn-

flowering perennial that glorifies the garden border with a last splash of
defiant colour amid the frost-blackened stems of winter. This is said to be
C. sinensis x *morifolium* with all its diversity of descendants that are grown
throughout the year all over the world. It is known that in the East
Chrysanthemum culture was being carried on several hundred years before
the birth of Christ. The flower was originally cultivated in China where a
notable breeder there was so famous for his flowers that when he died, the
name of his native town was changed to Chu-hsien, the City of the
Chrysanthemums. The interest in the flower spread to Japan, and in the
year 797 the Chrysanthemum was made the personal emblem of the
Mikado. By then the flower had assumed a sacred position in Japan, with
its culture allowed only in the Imperial gardens and those of recognised
nobility. With all this history and tradition it is strange that the flower was
unknown in the British Isles until the end of the eighteenth century. But
from then on, seeds and plants were imported via the East India Company
– source of many a botanical treasure – and breeding programmes began
which, though interrupted by global warfare are still being carried on today.
There certainly are species Chrysanthemums still – *C. indicum* with its
small yellow flowers is a native plant of China and also Japan – but they
bear little resemblance to the incredible blooms known to the Japanese
which were the results of a thousand years of horticultural practice and
skill.

There are now six main groups of Chrysanthemum: 1. Incurved, with
firm florets or petals that form a perfect globe. 2. Reflexed, with the outer
petals curving outwards and the inner ones curving inwards. 3. The petals
curve inwards, but loosely and irregularly. 4. Anemone-flowered, single
types with tubular florets that form a firm cushion. 5. Pompoms, small-
flowered types originating from the Chusan daisy (discovered in 1846 by
Robert Fortune). 6. Singles, all other types having not more than 5 rows of
petals and a visible 'centre'.

All perennial Chrysanthemums should be propagated from cuttings, and
the time for this varies according to the type and purpose of the flowers. For
exhibitions, shows and pot plants, cuttings should be taken from November
to early May according to the group. Garden varieties should have the
ground prepared for them before they are planted, with plenty of organic
material worked into the soil, and with a dressing of fertiliser. 2 – 3in (5 –
7.5cm) cuttings should be taken in March which should be inserted into a
compost of equal parts of sand and peat. When the cuttings are well rooted
they can be put into a nursery bed to grow on, or they can be planted out
in the border and in both cases the soil should be prepared for them in
advance. Established clumps can be divided in March or April.

C. cinerariifolium syn. **Pyrethrum roseum** grows to 15in (38cm) with white
flowers in July and August. A perennial from the Caucasus and Persia. The
source of 'Pyrethrum' dusting powder.

C. maximum - Shasta Daisy or Marguerite grows to 3ft (91.5cm) with white
flowers in July and August. Suitable for the border. A perennial plant from
the Pyrenees.

C. Parthenium - Feverfew grows to 2ft (61cm) with aromatic foliage and white
flowers in July and August. Border, Herb-garden. A short-lived European
and Asian perennial.

C. roseum - Border Pyrethrum grows to 2½ft (76cm) with pink or red flowers
in July and August. A perennial from the Caucasus for the sunny border.

C. segetum - Corn Marigold grows to 18in (46cm) with yellow flowers from
June to August. An annual plant from W. Asia, N. Africa and Europe.
Border, wild garden.

C. morifolium. *See main text.*

Requirements: Border Chrysanthemums need an open situation, well drained,
fairly rich soil and staking when necessary. Take slug precautions in spring.

C. maximum needs an open, sunny position and may need staking. *C. Parthenium* will grow almost anywhere, in sun or semi-shade and in old walls and paving. *C. segetum* needs a sunny border.

Cultivation: See main text for *C. morifolium. C. maximum* can be divided in autumn or spring. *C. Parthenium* can be grown from seed sown as fresh as possible. Sow in open ground or shake seeds on to soil surrounding parent plants, do not disturb until April or May. Take up ball of soil with plant; *C. Parthenium* does not like being moved. *C. segetum* can be grown from seed, either sown in autumn or spring. Sow in flowering position, thin out as necessary.

Uses: As cut, pot and border plants. For shows and exhibitions.

Before, during and after flowering: Border Chrysanthemum plants should be reduced to six flowering stems if extra quality blooms are required. 'Stop' the growing tip of each stem at 8in (20.5cm) by late June. This forces the plant to produce lateral shoots, thus making a sturdier, bushier plant. Dead-head at flowering time. Leave the stems as winter protection to the roots until spring, then cut the old stems down to 6in (16cm) from soil level.

C. segatum – Plants: Ruth Thompson; Seeds: John Chambers, Chiltern.

C. Parthenium – Plants: Beth Chatto, Parkinson Herbs, Stoke Lacy Herbs, Ruth Thompson, The Weald Herbary; Seeds: Naturescape, Rock Garden Nursery.

C. maximum – Plants: Bees, Bloms, Bressingham, Beth Chatto, Goatchers, Hillier, Scotts, Ruth Thompson; Seeds: Thomas Butcher, Chiltern, Cunningham, R.V. Roger Ltd., Sherrards, F. Toynbee Ltd; Seeds: Thomas Butcher, Chiltern, Cunningham, R.V. Roger Ltd., Sherrards, F. Toynbee Ltd.

C. morifolium – Bloms, Collingwood, Orpington, Rileys, Harold Walker, Wells.

CINERARIA *(Compositae).* The name is taken from *Cinerea*, 'ash-coloured', because the grey bloom on the leaves resembles a light dusting of ash. The Cinerarias that brighten the florists' shops are mostly derived from *S. cruentus* of the Canary Islands, but there are several groups of garden Cinerarias known as Large-flowered, Stellata singles, Feltham Beauty strain, Intermediate, Multi-flora and Double-flowered. Cinerarias are generally treated as biennials and the best way of propagation is by seed from a reliable source (where the parentage is known). Cuttings usually produce rather weak plants with smaller flowers, as does seed saved from one's own one-variety plant.

Old varieties are now lost and a choice must be made from seeds or plants presently available. Many of the species have been transferred into the genus Senecio. Cinerarias for the greenhouse are grown from seed germinated in summer in a temperature of 13°C (55°F) and when the plants are large enough they should be pricked out into individual pots in an enriched compost, then transferred into a cold frame in a sheltered position. The lights can be removed, though the plants will need shading in hot spells. Move them back into the cool greenhouse in September or October, where the mean temperature should be a minimum of 8°C (46°F) until the flower buds form after which fortnightly liquid feeding should begin. The temperature is still important and should not exceed 16°C (61°F). Watering should be done carefully, as too much will cause the plants to collapse. Spring-sown seeds will flower in mid-winter, thus providing bright colour during the winter days; summer sowings flower a year later.

C. cruenta, syn. **S. cruentus** grows to 18in (46cm) with flowers in many colours. Flowering time will vary according to when seed is sown. A half-hardy greenhouse perennial, usually treated as a cool greenhouse biennial.

C. x hybrida. The name by which most Cinerarias are known.

Requirements: For greenhouse plants, see text for minimum winter temperatures. Garden plants need a sunny situation and liquid feeding.
Propagation: *See text,* set plants out in late May.
Uses: As winter colour and summer bedding.
After flowering: Discard plants.
Plants: Garden centres.
Seeds: Bloms, Chiltern, Suttons, Thompson and Morgan.

CLARKIA *(Oenotheraceae).* The original Clarkia was discovered by Captain Lewis and Captain William Clark in 1804 when they were sent by President Jefferson to find and map a route across North America and through the Rocky Mountains. Because the flower-shape of the original species plant was so different to those commonly grown at that time, it quickly became a favourite bedding-out plant, which seems to have been the undeserved fate of many of the new discoveries. Though the plant was first found in 1804 it was not introduced into Britain until 20 years later, in 1824, when the Royal Horticultural Society sent David Douglas to North America to find new plants. Plant-hunters led a perilous life – ten years after this particular trip, when exploring the Sandwich Islands for new species, Douglas had the misfortune to fall into one of the large pits which the natives used to capture wild cattle. Already in the pit was an angry young bull that gored the unfortunate plant-hunter to death.

The species plants are seldom grown now except in botanical gardens and have been superseded by the showier modern varieties. For interest's sake I have grown and painted the old species *C. elegans.*
C. elegans (1832) grows to 2ft (61cm) with pink flowers from June to September (modern varieties of *C. elegans* have flowers of pink, rose, crimson, white, salmon, scarlet and many intermediate shades).
Requirements: A sunny position and slightly acid soil.
Cultivation: Sow seeds *in situ* in March or September. Thin out; provide winter protection for autumn sown seedlings. Pot up for early spring flowers in the greenhouse.
Uses: Bedding plants and winter flowers under glass.
Seeds: Most seedsmen.

CLEOME - Spider Flower *(Capparidaceae).* Cleomes have unusual, whiskery-looking flowers that attract human curiosity and butterfly visitors in almost equal proportions. The strongly-scented flowers are massed at the top of the flowering stem, but are well protected by vicious spines that lurk spitefully beneath the leaves – the plant is well-named. Nevertheless, Cleomes are handsome and easy plants to grow for a sheltered position, needing no staking if their situation is out of the wind. Since they come from the West Indies the seeds need to be sown in the warm, in a temperature of 18°C (64°F). They will grow very quickly and can be hardened off in the usual way.
C. spinosa - Cleome, Spider Flower (1817) grows to 3ft (91.5cm) with massed pink and white flowers in July. A half-hardy annual from the W. Indies for the border.
Requirements: Sun, fairly rich, light soil and growing space.
Cultivation: Sow seeds in March in 18°C (64°F) grow on, harden off.
Uses: As border and cut flowers.
Seeds: Most seedsmen.

CLIVIA *(Amaryllidaceae).* The plant was named after a former Duchess of Northumberland whose maiden name was Clive, though they were and still are sometimes called by the ponderous name of Imantophyllums. The Victorians liked Clivias for their hothouses and conservatories because of their brilliantly coloured flowers and handsome dark green leaves.

Clivias are generally purchased either in flower – the most expensive way – or as resting crowns. The latter should be planted into 5in (12.5cm) pots in a compost of loam and leaf-mould, with a little charcoal to keep the mixture sweet, and a little bonemeal as a slow acting fertiliser. As soon as growth begins, plenty of water can be given and the long strap-shaped leaves should be regularly syringed. New leaves appear in summer on established plants to replace those that die off in winter. A minimum temperature of 16°C (61°F) should be maintained. Clivias can be potted on every second or third year or they can be top-dressed each spring with fresh compost until the roots completely fill the pot. They dislike disturbance so it may be found that the second method is better. Re-potting, when it eventually becomes a necessity, should be done in February. Clivias can be grown from seed, but its production weakens the plant.

C. miniata grows to 18in (46cm) with umbels of orange flowers from March until August. A bulbous plant from Natal for house, greenhouse or warm conservatory.

Requirements: Temperatures as described in text. Shaded greenhouse or conservatory, liquid feeding when buds show.

Cultivation: By offsets when repotting – division is difficult. From seed sown in individual pots in a temperature of 16°C (61°F).

After flowering: Cut off stems at base.

Uses: As handsome greenhouse and conservatory plants.

Crowns: de Jager.

Seeds: Holtzhausen.

COLCHICUM - Autumn Crocus, Naked Ladies, Naked Nannies *(Liliaceae).* The flower's name is taken from Colchis, an ancient city on the shores of the Black Sea. Legend has it that when Medea mixed a magic potion that would restore Aeson to youth, she accidentally spilled some drops on the ground and from these sprang the beautiful star-shaped flower called Colchicum.

Autumn Crocus should not be confused with the spring flowering Crocus, this belongs to a different botanical family, that of the Iris. To those gardeners lucky enough to persuade the Saffron Crocus – *Crocus sativus* – to flower, this is even more confusing because Saffron flowers in late summer and autumn – as do the Colchicums – though the Saffron is a true Crocus. However, it will be noticed that the Colchicums produce huge spinach-like leaves in spring which quietly vanish in summer: this is just as well because they are not at all attractive, though they must on no account be cut down. In September or October the Colchicum flowers suddenly appear like a conjuring trick out of apparently bare ground, so their position should either be marked or carefully remembered.

Colchicums have always been known to be poisonous plants, and at the time of Theophrastus they were eaten by sulky slaves who made themselves ill in this way to annoy their masters, knowing that the antidote to the slow-acting poison could be obtained easily, though repeat performances of this trick would have built up an accumulation of the drug in their bodies which would eventually have proved fatal. The plant contains the drug known as Colchicine which has been used medicinally since earliest times as a remedy for gout. The Ancient Egyptians knew and used it, and in seventeenth-century England it was prescribed for James I, flavoured with the powder from ground-up unburied skulls.

C. autumnale - Meadow Saffron has lilac flowers that grow to 6in (15cm) in autumn with tufts of leaves 10in (25.5cm) high in spring. A European corm for a large rockery or naturalising in grass.

C. luteum has flowers that grow to 4in (10cm) in February, with leaves that appear with the flowers and grow to 10 – 12in (25.5 – 30.5cm) afterwards.

A corm from Kashmir and the Himalayas for a sheltered sunny border or rockery.

C. speciosum - Autumn Crocus, has lilac-mauve flowers that grow to 6in (15cm) high in autumn. Leaves are 12 – 16in (30.5 – 40.5cm) high in spring. A corm from Asia for sunny borders and large rockeries or among autumn-colouring shrubs.

Requirements: Ordinary free-draining garden soil and a sunny position where the large leaves can die down naturally.

Cultivation: Plant corms 3 – 4in (7.5 – 10cm) deep and leave undisturbed. Divide in July when overcrowded and replant immediately. Protect leaves from slugs.

Uses: Large rockeries, among shrubs, sunny borders.

Warning: All Colchicums are poisonous.

Corms: Avon, Broadleigh, Christian, Holden Clough, Ingwersen, Reginald Kaye, Orpington, van Tubergen.

CONVALLARIA - Lily-of-the-Valley, May Lily *(Liliaceae).* Once upon a time the Lily-of-the-Valley grew wild in the British Isles. It is a plant of Northern Europe and in earlier times it was dedicated to Ostara, the Norse Goddess of the dawn. Medieval names were 'Our Lady's Tears' and, charmingly, 'Lily Constancy' from its Flower-language meaning of 'Return of Happiness'. The French name for the flower – 'Muguet du Bois, or Wood-Lily, became corrupted into the less than pretty word 'Mugget' and it is better to return to the sweetness of another name – 'Liriconfancie' which must have come from an early latinisation, *Lily convalle.* The plant has been grown for centuries for its perfume, and distilled Lily-of-the-Valley water was once considered so valuable that it was called Aqua Aurea and kept in gold or silver vessels. It is still a very important plant in the modern perfume industry.

Our ancestors went to a good deal of trouble when compounding their medications, and Gerard says "the floures of May Lilies put into a glass and set in a hill of ants, close stopped for the space of a moneth, and then taken out, therein you shall finde a liquor that appeaseth the paine and griefe of the gout, being outwardly applied: which is commended to be most excellent".

Lily-of-the-Valley flowers were used in love potions, which makes something of a change from the often unspeakable ingredients that went into some of them. In Germany, in the early part of the nineteenth century, the flowers were gathered by the thousand at Whitsuntide to decorate the churches. The perfume from so many flowers must have been quite wonderful, and near Hanover the woods were so carpeted with the plants that every year stalls, temporary huts and buildings were set up for Whit-Monday to provide food, drink and music for the townspeople who came out to make a holiday of it and to gather the flowers.

Pink and even 'red' kinds were grown as long ago as 1597 and there was even a striped purple and white variety, though this was not recorded until 1770. The leaves die down in late summer, though there is a certain amount of untidiness still to be seen where the plants have flowered.

Convallaria majalis - Lily-of-the-Valley grow to 8in (20.5cm) with scented white flowers in May. There is a pink variety. A rhizomatous European, Asian and N. American perennial for shady borders or woodland conditions.

Requirements: Convallaria need semi-shade, moist, humus-rich soil, and space to spread.

Cultivation: Plant the crowns in September or October. Cover to a depth of 2in (5cm). Sow seeds when ripe in seed compost in a frame, grow on for two years before planting out in final positions: or divide in autumn.

Warning: Red berries are very poisonous.

Uses: As cut flowers and for toilet preparations.

Crowns: Allwoods, Amand, Avon, Bloms, Broadleigh, Goatchers, Holden Clough, Jackman's, Notcutts, Scotts.
Seeds: Chiltern.

CONVOLVULUS - Life of Man *(Convolvulaceae)*. This distinctively-coloured flower has been known and grown for hundreds of years, being often painted by Dutch flower artists in the eighteenth and nineteenth centuries who included it as a colour contrast in their glorious but seasonally impossible mixtures of flowers, fruit and insects. *Convolvulus tricolor* is a plump little plant, growing no more than 1ft (30.5cm) in height, and covering itself with white-throated blue trumpets. Its little-used eighteenth century name was explained by the Reverend Hanbury (author of *A Complete Book of Planting and Gardening* published in 1770) who said "it has flower buds in the morning, which will be full-blown by noon, and withered up by night". The plant does well in poor soil, but it must always have a place in full sun. Small plants must be protected from slugs.
C. tricolor syn. **C. minor** (1629) grows to 1ft (30.5cm) with blue and white flowers from July to September. Shades of pink, rose, white and magenta are available in mixed modern varieties. A hardy annual from Sicily, Spain and Portugal for the border.
Requirements: Full sun, very ordinary soil.
Cultivation: Soak seeds for 12 hours, sow in seed compost in March in a warm greenhouse.
Uses: As border and container plants.
Seeds: Thomas Butcher, Chiltern, Dobie, Suttons, Unwins.

COREOPSIS - Tick-seed *(Compositae)*. The name Coreopsis is from the Greek *Koris*, a 'bug', and *opsis*, 'like', because the seeds look very like those insects. Coreopsis are fine, golden daisies for the border, with all the charm and simplicity that such flowers have. One of the earliest and most distinctive of this genus to be introduced is *C. verticillata*, which has feathery dark-green leaves and bright yellow flowers. It grows into a pleasing, low hummock, making a distinctive contrast to other border plants. It is not particularly long-lived with me, nor is it reliably hardy (it comes late into leaf) so steps should be taken in good time to ensure a succession of new plants. In earlier days *Coreopsis verticillata* was used as a dye plant for woollen goods, producing a good orange-red colour from the flowers as did *C. tinctoria*, sometimes now called *Calliopsis tinctoria*. (The annual species of Coreopsis are sometimes listed under *Calliopsis*). Most Coreopsis do well in areas of industrial pollution, hence their popularity at the turn of the century.
C. grandiflora (1826) grow to 18in (46cm) with yellow flowers from June to August. A perennial herbaceous plant from the S. United States for the sunny border.
C. lanceolata (1724) grows to 2ft (61cm) with yellow flowers from July to September. A perennial herbaceous plant from the E. United States for the sunny border.
C. tinctoria syn. **Calliopsis tinctoria** grows to 3ft (91.5cm) with yellow flowers from July to September. An annual plant from N. America for the open border. (Staking may be necessary).
C. verticillata (1780) grows to 2ft (61cm) with finely-cut dark green leaves and yellow flowers from July to September. A perennial herbaceous plant from the E. United States for the sunny border.
Requirements: An open position and ordinary garden soil.
Cultivation: Divide in autumn or spring or sow seeds in April in a nursery bed. Thin out and grow on. Transplant to flowering positions in October, protect from slugs.
Uses: As border and cut flowers.

During flowering: Dead-head.
Seeds: Suttons, most seedmen.
Plants: Bees, Bloms, Bressingham, Beth Chatto, Cunnington, Goatchers, Hillier, Holden Clough, Jackman's, Nottcutts, St. Bridget, F. Toynbee Ltd.

CORYDALIS *(Papaveraceae).* There are two well-known varieties of Corydalis – the weed of cornfield-edges and allotments with its pink flowers and delicate-looking trailing stems belying its suffocative ability, is *Fumaria officinalis*, a very close relative to *Corydalis lutea*, the Yellow Corydalis, whose delicate jade-green ferny leaves can be seen sprouting out of old walls and cracks in paving. The leaves can be most useful in early spring flower arrangements when a little lightness is required, and the flowers are attractive though not conspicuous individually. In midsummer they are very numerous and colourful, and can generally be found on the plant until very late in the autumn. Once *Corydalis lutea* is in the garden it is there to stay, as its seeds are swept or washed along the paths by autumn rains to spring up further along. It is quite charming when it has placed itself artistically in an otherwise bare wall, but it shares its wild cousin's invasive habits and must be sternly plucked out of situations reserved for better plants. It is a good thing to have for poor, damp corners as long as it receives a little sun at some time in the day – such plants are exceedingly useful in all gardens. It should not be planted or allowed to stay in paving-cracks because its somewhat glaucous leaves are too fragile to recover quickly from normal garden traffic.

C. *solida* is a charming plant for early spring, with a sudden cloud of pink-mauve flowers that are delicately interesting even from a distance, particularly at this time of the year. It likes a semi-shaded position in a rockery, but the leaves vanish without a trace after flowering so its position should be carefully marked.

C. lutea - Yellow Corydalis grows to 9in (23cm) or so with masses of yellow flowers successively from May until late summer, and odd ones at all times. A European perennial plant for walls and dull or difficult corners.

C. solida syn. **C. bulbosa** grows to 9in (23cm) with mauve-pink flowers from March to May. A European perennial plant for dry, semi-shaded rockeries and small borders.

Requirements: C. *lutea* grows anywhere, liking mortar dust. C. *solida* needs semi-shade and ordinary garden soil.
Cultivation: C. *lutea* will self-sow, C. *solida* can be divided after flowering.
Uses: Leaves of C. *lutea* excellent in flower arrangements. As rock plants.
Plants: Avon, Broadleigh, Christian, Holden Clough.

COSMOS - Cosmea *(Compositae).* The plant's Latin name is from the Greek word *kosmos*, 'beautiful'. Cosmeas are easy to grow and the seeds should be planted in a deeper tray than usual so that the growth of the seedlings is not slowed down too much before planting out, as they should be kept in the greenhouse until the statutory 'end of May' to avoid the late frosts. During this time they can grow surprisingly tall, hence the requirement for the deeper box.

In late summer the pink, carmine and magenta daisy-shaped flowers perch prettily on the feathery light green foliage which needs plenty of space. The plants like to grow closely together, and in this way they hook themselves into a flower-decked mass which generally needs no staking, though if the garden is an exposed one this is a different matter, and a discreet pea-stick or two will give support whilst being hidden completely by the exuberant greenery of the pinnatified foliage. Cosmea does better in a poor, light soil, as too rich a mixture makes the leaves too lush and delays the flowering time.

C. bipinnatus - Cosmos, Cosmea (1799), grows to 4ft (122cm) with pink, rose,

magenta, crimson and white flowers from August to September. A tall
border annual from Mexico.

Requirements: Light, rather poor soil and sun.

Cultivation: Sow seeds in February or March at a temperature of 16°C (61°F)
grow on and harden off.

Uses: As cut flowers and border plants.

During flowering: Dead-head.

Seeds: Most seedsmen.

CRINUM *(Amaryllidaceae).* Most Crinums are tender bulbs and it is when gazing
wistfully at a whole border of these grand plants all in flower in the gardens
of southern France that one remembers all the more the difficulties of the
sometimes stark and usually lengthy British winters. Crinums make
excellent greenhouse and conservatory plants, though they are best planted
in the greenhouse border to be left undisturbed. They need plenty of water
at growing time, liquid feeding, and if grown outside in the southern
counties of the British Isles a south-facing wall for reflected warmth. In
spring the new shoots should be well protected by litter; slugs will find
Crinums particularly succulent, so early counter-measures should be taken
against their depredations. If planted in pots in the greenhouse they should
be grown in a rich compost, with three of the large bulbs to a 10in (25.5cm)
pot. The pots may be stood outside in a sunny corner during the summer
months. There are very many varieties but not all of them can be obtained
easily.

C x powellii (1890) grows to 2ft (61cm) with 4ft (122cm) long leaves and pink
flowers from July to September. A fairly hardy bulb of hybrid origins for a
warm walled border, warm greenhouse or pot culture.

C. Moorei (1874) grows to 2ft (61cm) with many stems of pink and white flowers
from July to September. A tender bulb from S. Africa for greenhouse or pot
culture.

C. bulbispermum syn. **C. longifolium** (1752) grows to 18in (46cm) with white
flowers in September and October. More or less hardy bulb from S. Africa
for a walled border.

Requirements: A hot sheltered position, plenty of water during the growing
season and protection in winter for outdoor bulbs. Liquid feeding before and
during flowering.

Propagation: From offsets taken in March. Plant ovoid bulbs of *C.
bulbispermum* with tops just above soil surface.

Uses: As handsome container and greenhouse plants.

After flowering: Cut down stems.

Bulbs: Amand, Avon, Bressingham, de Jager, Hillier, Jackman's, Kelways,
Notcutts, Sherrards.

Plants: Sherrards, Stapeley Water Garden.

CROCOSMIA *(Iridaceae).* The names of Crocosmia and Montbretia are
indissolubly intertwined in most gardener's minds and they are as confusing
as an unsignposted crossroad. Many hybrids have been bred between
Crocosmia and *C. crocosmiiflora*, the garden Montbretia, and the botanical
nomenclature of these plants is blurred, particularly as varieties of Tritonia
are now included in the genus Crocosmia by some growers. The plants are
closely related, growing from small round corms and productin generally
tall sword-shaped leaves that are in themselves very handsome, providing a
definite accent in a border with mixed foliage shapes. This flower's name is
from the Greek work for *crocus,* 'saffron', *osme,* 'smell': the dried flowers
smell of saffron when soaked in warm water.

Crocosmias are not always hardy and this comes as something of a
surprise when one is used to the resilience of the ordinary Montbretia to
neglect which sometimes borders on cruelty. If these plants are to be grown

in colder areas it is as well to lift the corms, cut off the stems and hang them upside down so that any remaining moisture from the stalks can dry out. They should then be stored in a frost-free place for the winter, though it is difficult to balance the storage temperature so that they neither shrivel nor rot.

C. masonorum has flower stems that are 2½ft (76cm) high with upward-facing orange-red flowers in August and September, and handsome 'pleated' leaves. A hardy perennial from S. Africa for the large border.

C. Pottsii (1880) has a flowering stem 3 – 4ft (91.5 – 122cm) high with broad leaves and yellow and red flowers in August. A hardy perennial corm for the back of the border.

Requirements: Full sun and well-drained soil.

Cultivation: Plant corms in spring or autumn, depending on hardiness. Divide when overcrowded, either before growth starts in early spring or just after flowering.

After flowering: Cut down flowering stems unless needed.

Uses: As cut and border flowers. Dried stems for winter decor.

Corms: Amand, Avon, Broadleigh, Beth Chatto, de Jager, Goatchers, Hillier, Holden Clough, Kelways.

CROCUS *(Iridaceae).* The quickest way to tell the difference between a Crocus and a Colchicum is by the stamens – the Crocus has three and the Colchicum six. There are a number of species Crocus and very many hybrids of these which are mainly derived from *C. aureus* and *C. vernus.* The autumn flowering Crocus such as *C. byzantinus, C. speciosus* and *C. zonatus* are very welcome in our gardens, flowering as they often do so late in the year. However, bad weather or frosts or both can so damage the ephemeral beauty of the flowers that it is sometimes advisable to grow two sets of bulbs – one in the garden to take their chance with the weather and the other protected by being planted in pots in a frame cold greenhouse, or under cloches.

The offsets or small corms that grow at the sides of the parent should be left where they are for two or three seasons and then lifted and respaced just as the leaves are dying down. On no account should the leaves of Crocuses be knotted up into painfully tidy bunches because the plant needs its leaves to produce the food store within the bud below. It is better to plan the planting of the Crocus-corms well ahead, so that the new spring growth of other rock and border plants will gradually hide the yellowing leaves which do not disappear until June. Crocuses look charming in lawns when planted in groups of different colours, though it is as well to find out if those chosen all flower at the same time. For example, the old-fashioned *C. aureus* or Dutch Yellow usually flowers early, whereas the larger purple flowers of 'Remembrance' are often the last to bloom, and this makes a lawn planting look unfinished – it has no peak of glory, so to speak. The Crocus area of the lawn should not be mown until the leaves have quite turned yellow, though the grass can be clipped with shears in between the clumps to avoid a totally neglected look.

Almost any sunny situation suits Crocus, but their position needs to be marked or remembered exactly because subsequent weeding or border planting will have the effect of separating some of the corms from the main group. To achieve a natural effect when planting Crocuses in large numbers they should be thrown in handfuls on to the soil surfaces where they are to go, and then planted where they lie. Smaller collections among other spring flowers or in the rockery should be planted irregularly, but not too spread out. If the flowering position is needed for other plants the Crocuses should be carefully lifted with as much soil as possible and replanted in a sunny corner to finish their growing cycle. When the leaves wither they can then be lifted and stored, or dug up in August and replanted – if there is room

— in their spring flowering positions. August and early September is the right time to plant, and this early planting will produce better flowers.

Crocuses may be grown in pots for indoor flowers: the corms should be planted 5 or 6 to a 5-in (12.5-cm) pot in a good compost or sandy loam, leaf-mould and a little grit, and the pots buried to the rim in soil or ashes.

C. aureus - Dutch Yellow Crocus (before 1597) grows to 4in (10cm) with golden yellow flowers in February and March. A corm from E. Europe for borders, rockeries, lawns, open woodland, pots and troughs.

C. biflorus - Scotch Crocus grows to 4in (10cm) with white flowers flushed with silvery blue in February and March. A corm from the E. Mediterranean for situations similar to those for *C. aureus*.

C. byzantinus syn. **C. iridiflorus** (before 1629) grows to 4in (10cm) with lilac and purple flowers in October, (outer petals are longer). A corm for similar situations, from the E. Carpathians.

C. sativus - The Saffron Crocus grows to about 5in (12.5cm) high with veined purple flowers in September. Grown for commercial purposes and shy to flower in the UK, though formerly cultivated in Saffron Walden. Best grown in pots in a frame or cold greenhouse where corms can be well baked by the sun. Originally from the E. Mediterranean.

C. speciosus grows to 4in (10cm) with blue-veined flowers in September and October. A corm from Asia minor for the rock garden.

C. Tomasinianus grows to 3½in (9cm) with lavender to purple flowers in March. Increases well and quickly. A tiny corm from Dalmatia.

C. vernus flowers from February to April with a range of colours. This European species is 4in (10cm) tall and the varieties are 4 — 5in (10 — 12.5cm) in height. A corm for border and path edges, rockeries, wild garden, beneath deciduous trees, lawns, pots, troughs and window boxes.

C. zonatus syn. **kotschyanus** grows to 4in (10cm) with pale pink-lilac flowers in October. Similar planting as for *C. vernus*.

Requirements: Well-drained soil and a sunny situation with some shelter for early-flowering varieties.

Cultivation: Small offsets are generally produced by the 'parent' corm. When the leaves are dying down naturally established clumps can be lifted and the small new corms detached. The old corms may now be exhausted and can be discarded or planted in a wild garden or on a grass verge. New ones should be tidied by removing dead leaves, dead roots and shrivelled skin and they can then be sorted out into sizes. The larger ones will generally flower in the following year and the small ones can be grown on in 'nursery rows'. Plant all corms to 3 times their own depth.

After flowering: Do not cut off the leaves or tie into twists or bunches   corms need their leaves until they die away naturally.

Uses: For pot culture in winter and early spring and very many garden situations according to flowering times.

Corms: Avon, Bloms, Broadleigh, Christian, de Jager, Holden Clough, Ingwersen, Kelways, Orpington, Potterton and Martin.

CYCLAMEN *(Primulaceae)*. The plant takes its name from the Greek word *Kyklos*, 'circular', because of the spiral twisting peduncle or flower stem that plants the seed in the ground. In the Middle Ages the plant was known more for its medicinal properties than for its garden value and was used as a cure for baldness, it being recommended that the sufferer should "take this same wort and put it into the nostrils". It was also regarded as an infallible love charm, and as an aid to speedy childbirth. So effective was it thought to be that Gerard took the precaution of fencing in his collection of Cyclamen plants to prevent "... any good matron from accidentally stepping over them, thereby bringing about a miscarriage".

Most hardy Cyclamen have beautiful heart-shaped leaves, often symmetrically marked or marbled with silver and white. It is possible to have a succession of bloom and foliage throughout most of the year with different varieties following on. In many cases the flowers rise up out of bare ground and one must remember to prevent surrounding plants from encroaching during the Cyclamen's resting period. After the flowers are past the leaves appear, remaining for many months until it is time for their annual rest. Cyclamen corms are round, wrinkled and flattish, and are often very difficult to start into growth – indeed, it is often impossible to tell which way up to plant them, as top and bottom of a resting corm are almost identical. It is better to purchase container-grown plants, or get a reputable nursery to send the plants just after flowering. They will not like the move much but at least you will be able to plant them the right way up, and after a season in your garden they will have recovered. Cyclamen corms live for many years when their situation is to their liking and can attain a considerable size.

The hardy species Cyclamen have the most delicate flowers that look like frozen butterflies under the leafless branches of the November garden. The tender Cyclamen of the florist's shop is *C. persicum,* though the wild variety of this name is still obtainable: it has narrower petals than those of the modern hybrids.

C. cilicium (1872) Pale pink flowers in October and November, leaves with a silver zone. Roots from underside of corm. Only hardy in South-west counties, best grown in Alpine house. From Asia Minor.

C. coum Small bright carmine flowers from December to March. Roots from centre of underside of corm. Rockery or sheltered corner. From the Eastern Mediterranean area.

C. neapolitanum Rose pink flowers from August to November, before the leaves which have silver markings above. Roots from the upper part of corm. (Barely cover corm with soil when planting). For edges of shrubberies or shaded parts of the rockery. From S. Europe.

C. persicum (1731). (The original plant from the E. Mediterranean from which the modern plants are derived.) Scented pink flowers in March and April. Not truly hardy except in south-west areas.

Requirements: Cyclamen need well-drained humus-rich soil and benefit from a dusting of bonemeal after flowers and leaves have died. Semi-shaded woodland conditions suit them best. Sift a little peat into a shallow hole at planting and cover corms with 1in (2.5cm) of soil. Scatter leaf-mould over resting corms.

Cultivation: Obtain growing plants where possible. Cyclamen can be grown from fresh seed sown in summer or early autumn in pans of seed compost. Germinate in a shaded, well-ventilated cold frame. Prick out seedings when large enough into individual pots and overwinter in the frame. Plant out in flowering positions in spring or late summer according to type. Mice are partial to the seeds of mature plants.

Uses: Valuable for autumn and winter flowers in the garden. Long-lasting leaves often beautifully marked and a feature in themselves.

Corms: Most nurseries.

CYMBIDIUM *(Orchidaceae).* In the wild this kind of orchid is an epiphytic, but generally grown terrestrially when in cultivation – so one has the best of both of the Orchid worlds. Most are evergreen. The original species are still found in Malaysia, Australia, Ceylon, India and Japan. In the larger types the pseudobulbs are about 6in (15cm) high, sheathed by long narrow curved leaves. The flower stems rise from the base of the pseudobulb and can be erect, pendulous or arching, carrying as many as fifteen flowers which open from the bottom upwards or along the stem, and are very long lasting (8 – 10 weeks). The flowers are in almost any colour except blue.

Cymbidiums are one of the easiest of orchids to grow, needing cool or intermediate temperatures *(see* Orchid). They are easy to propagate – or, should I say, easier to propagate than most orchids and this has given rise to a tremendous number of hybrids and the species types are seldom grown now.

Cultivation: Begin with a mature small plant and one or two pseudobulbs. The mature plant is for beauty and general encouragement and the small fellows are there for you to see what you can do. Start the pseudobulbs in 4 – 5-in (10 – 12.5-cm) containers in a compost of one part loam, two parts osmunda fibre and one part sphagnum moss and a little bonemeal, with some charcoal for sweetness and broken crocks for drainage. Pot the pseudobulbs on every second year after flowering, and it will be found that the plants will grow very large and will need correspondingly large containers. They need shading in spring and summer, and a mean night temperature of 7 – 10°C (45 – 50°F) and 13 – 16°C (55 – 61°F) by day. Shading should be removed in winter. Water when the compost becomes dry. They need more ventilation than most orchids and can be stood outside the greenhouse in a sheltered shady place during warm summer weather. This will have the added advantage of getting rid of white fly which can spoil the appearance of the plant. Cymbidiums do not become dormant but need to rest after their flowering time which is generally December to May. When the new growth appear the Cymbidiums can be divided and re-potted, with a piece of new growth to each pot. Do not water for ten days after re-potting, but syringing the leaves is most beneficial. Rain water should be collected for your orchids.

Requirements: *See text.*
Orchid growers: Keith Andrew, Burnham.

DAHLIA *(Compositae).* The Dahlia is named after Dr. Andreas Dahl, a Swedish botanist who was a pupil of Linnaeus. The original plants were discovered in Mexico at the time of the Spanish Conquest (1519-24) and some of these early seeds were sent to Madrid in 1789, and from there the plant was introduced to the rest of Europe and the world. Initially it was hoped that the roots would be as useful as the potato, but, though edible, they were not palatable. Early Dahlia culture had to be carefully learned and many plants must have died, but so large and showy were the flowers that they became favourite Florists' (see introduction) flowers and in 1880 the Dahlia society was founded.

Species Dahlias are seldom grown except in botanic gardens, and the flowers that often dominate our later summer borders are all hybrid descendants of the original species plants – *D. pinnata, D. Coccinea* and *D. rosea* and they do not come true from seed. They must be propagated vegetatively to retain their characteristics and require certain conditions in order to do well. The soil should be dug over deeply and well-rotted manure should be incorporated in the autumn ready for the plants to be set out in June. Put in a stake or stakes at the time of planting, and never neglect tying the Dahlia stems as they are very brittle and easily damaged by summer rainstorms. When 6in (15cm) high, pinch out the top of the stem to encourage bushy growth. Dead-heading is very important as it prolongs the flowering time. When the frosts have killed off the aerial parts of the plant, the remains should be cut off and the roots lifted. Allow the soil on the roots to dry, and it can then be shaken or gently scraped off. The tuberous roots should be stored for the winter in a cool, dry, frost-free shed or garage. The tubers need to be checked every so often to see that no rotting is taking place; if this is found the affected part should be cut away with a clean knife. It may be advantageous to dust the tubers with copper-lime dust to prevent fungoid growth. In March the clump of roots or tubers should be placed in boxes and covered with a mixture of peat and sand with the crowns clear of the soil. The boxes should still be kept in the same frost-free place, but the soil mix should now be watered (do not allow any water to fall on the crown), and in a few weeks the 'eyes' on the tubers will swell. The clump of tubers can then be divided with a clean, sharp knife or they may be left as they are. You may end up with some very irregularly shaped bits but nobody but you and St Phocas (the patron saint of gardeners) will ever know. So long as each irregularly shaped bit has a healthy 'eye', this is all that matters. All the cut parts should be dusted with a fungicide such as flowers of sulphur. The tubers can be planted directly into the soil at a depth of 4 – 6in (10 – 15cm). If the weather and ground are too cold the tubers should be placed in large pots in a cuttings compost and kept in a frost-free conservatory or wherever there is a good light until the ground warms up. Late May is only just safe for planting out Dahlias – early June is better. Alternatively, cuttings may be taken in February from tubers that have been started into growth in a temperature of 15 – 18°C (59 – 64°F) during the previous month. When the cuttings are about 3in (7.5cm) long, cut them off about ½in (1.3cm) from the tuber leaving a stump from which other growths will arise. Take off the bottom leaves and dip the cuttings in hormone powder and put 3 or 4 round the edge of a clay pot in a mix of equal parts of peat, sterilised loam and sharp sand. Moisten and grow on in a temperature of 15 – 18°C (59 – 64°F). Do not allow the little plants to dry out and keep lightly shaded to begin with; this method is slower but will produce more plants.

Dahlias are divided into two main groups: Border Dahlias, which should be grown as previously described, and Bedding Dahlias which are grown from seed sown in a temperature of 16°C (61°F) in February. These should be grown on and protected from frost until it is possible to plant them out. These Dahlias benefit from liquid feeds and all kinds need plenty of water during dry spells.

Border Dahlias have been classified into the following groups: Class I: Single Dahlias, Class II: Anemone-flowered Dahlias, Class III: Collerette Dahlias, Class IV: Paeony-flowered Dahlias, Class V: Formal decorative Dahlias, Class VI: Informal decorative Dahlias, Class VII: Show Dahlias, Class VIII: Pompon Dahlias, Class IX: Cactus Dahlias, Class X: Semi-Cactus Dahlias, Class XI: Star Dahlias.

Requirements/Cultivation: *See text.*
After flowering: *See text.*
Uses: *See text.*

DELPHINIUM - Larkspur *(Ranunculaceae).* The name Delphinium evokes an instant picture of six-foot blue spires, but of course there are many uncommon species whose colours range from white through cream and yellow to the orange-scarlet of *D. nudicaule.* Young Delphinium plants are much esteemed by slugs and it is sometimes very difficult, in a wet spring, to prevent the plants from being entirely consumed. The old-fashioned method of ringing the plants with clinkers saved from the winter fires works as well as the more modern slug pellets or the less unsightly poisonous bran. Delphiniums are valued in the garden because they are the largest of the blue flowers which are the least numerous in the colour spectrum.

Delphiniums as we know them today are only just over a hundred years old, though it may seem that they are very much older because they feature so often in traditional pictures of country gardens. One of the earliest specialists in the country was James Kelway in 1859 with 16 different named varieties, folowed by Blackmore and Langdon in 1907. Because of the disruption caused by the First and Second World Wars, the plants that were being bred then are no longer obtainable, as to come true they needed to be propagated vegetatively or by means of carefully controlled seed production. It was the American plant breeders who produced the stately plants that are so much admired today, though there are not so many gardens with herbaceous borders that can accommodate their imposing

Plate 1

Amaryllidaceae:
Galanthus nivalis,
Nerine bowdenii,
Narcissus pseudonarcissus,
Narcissus poeticus.

Plate 2

Boraginaceae:
Pulmonaria officinalis,
Borago officinalis,
Omphalodes verna,
Myosotis sylvatica.

Plate 3

Campanulaceae:
Lobelia erinus,
Lobelia cardinalis,
Campanula Medium var. *calycanthema,*
Campanula persicifolia.

Plate 4

Caryophyllaceae:
Dianthus barbatus,
Lychnis coronaria,
Dianthus spp.

Plate 5

Convolvulaceae:
Convolvulus tricolor,
Pharbitis purpurea,
Ipomoea learii.

Plate 6

Cruciferae:
Lunaria biennis,
Cheiranthus,
Hesperis matronalis.

Plate 7

Labiatae:
Phlomis Samia,
Salvia patens,
Monarda didyma.

Plate 8

Leguminosae:
Baptisia australis,
Lupinus,
Lathyrus odoratus.

stature of about 8ft (2.44m) in good soil. There is a wonderful range of colours in the modern large-flowered hybrids – darkest blues, purples, crimson, royal blue, cream yellow, pink, sky-blue, gentian blue and silvery mauve, but these are almost all of recent origin and do not come within the scope of this book – though because they are so 'traditional' I am including the usual cultural notes.

Larkspur, *D. consolida* and *D. Ajacis* or Lark's heel as it was formerly called is a much older plant and was grown in sixteenth-century gardens as a wound-herb and for strengthening eyesight – "Nay, some say, that even the constant looking on them will have that effect: whence some hang up bunches of them in their chambers". It was also thought that the plant was a reliable antidote to poison.

D. Ajacis - Rocket Larkspur (about 1573) grows to 3ft (91.5cm) with blue, white or pink flowers from June to August. Border and as early colour in the greenhouse or conservatory. An annual from S. Europe.

D. consolida - Larkspur (before 1572) grows to 3ft (91.5cm) with dense spikes of blue, rose, purple or white flowers from June to August. An annual for the large border, from S. Europe.

D. grandiflorum. The true species is seldom seen, but it is the parent of most of the modern hybrids which are generally classified into two groups – the large-flowered, or Elatum varieties, and the Belladonna varieties.

D. nudicaule (1869) grows to 18in (46cm) with orange-red flowers from April to July. A short-lived perennial for the border or large rockery, from California.

Requirements: Large-flowered hybrids should have the soil enriched with decayed manure before planting; incorporate some lime at this time. Delphiniums need an open, sunny situation, sheltered from strong winds. Tall varieties should be securely staked. Water well while growing and during flowering season. Precautions should be taken against slugs.

Cultivation: For the large-flowered hybrids propagation is by division in March or April, or by seeds sown as soon as purchased because they do not remain viable if kept too long. 3 – 4in (7.5 – 10cm) basal cuttings may be taken in April. Cut off close to the rootstock, and put cuttings into a mix of equal parts of peat and sand in a cold frame. When they have rooted, plant out in rows to grow on for the summer, transplant to flowering place in September. Seeds of *D. Ajacis* and *D. consolida* should be sown thinly where they are to grow, either in September or March to April. Thin out when large enough. Delphiniums do not come true from garden seeds when mixed colours are grown together.

After flowering: Dead-head large-flowered perennials as necessary. Cut annuals back to a good leaf below flower-spike, and a secondary flush of bloom will occur in a good season. Cut back all perennials to ground level in autumn and mound with ashes.

Plants: Blackmore and Langdon, Bressingham, Highfield, Hillier, Holden Clough, Kelways, Robinsons, St. Bridget.

Seeds: Chiltern, Suttons, Thompson and Morgan, Unwins.

DIANELLA *(Liliaceae).* This is an uncommon evergreen plant that has panicles of small blue or white lily-like flowers according to the type. But it is the berries that are an excitement in the garden – these are like shining blue marbles and are most eye-catching in late summer. Dianellas can be grown in the Southern counties in a sheltered place in semi-shade, otherwise in a cold greenhouse or conservatory. They should be planted in a mixture of peat and loam and need no special care apart from protection in winter.

C. caerulea grows to 2ft (61cm) and has blue flowers in summer and brilliant blue berries in autumn. An unusual perennial for a specially sheltered corner or under glass from Australia.

D. revoluta (1823) grows to 2ft (61cm) with darker blue flowers in summer and paler blue berries. Needs same conditions as *D. caerulea*. A perennial from Tasmania.

D. tasmanica (1866) grows to 5ft (1.52m) with pale blue flowers and cylindrical blue berries in autumn. A perennial from Tasmania needing a sheltered corner or glass.

Requirements: A sheltered situation in semi-shade. Dianellas should be grown in a mix of peat and lime-free loam.

Cultivation: Plant in early summer or sow seeds under glass in spring. Grow on and prick out into pots in a partly shaded cold frame for first season.

Uses: A very striking plant for greenhouse or conservatory. Use berries for winter decoration.

Plants: Hillier, C J Marchant, Treasures of Tenbury.

Seeds: Chiltern.

DIANTHUS - Pink, Carnation, Gillyflower, Sweet William *(Caryophyllaceae)*. The name Dianthus comes from the Greek *Dios*, 'divine', and *anthos*, 'flower', given to it by Theophrastus because of its perfume and beauty. Pinks and Carnations have always been one of the most popular of flowers, particularly during the eighteenth and nineteenth centuries when there was a positive craze for Carnations. The flower shows of those times must have represented even more care and effort than they do today, because it was permitted to 'dress and lay out the flowers of Carnations and Pinks'. In 1826 or thereabouts, a barber called Christopher Nunn was famous for his prepared flowers and probably dressed more blooms than he did wigs, which were still being worn at that time. The preparation for the shows involved shearing off the petals to absolute symmetry, crooked and imperfect ones being removed and others teased or trained into their places; the finished flower would have looked as artificial as its wax counterpart did under glass.

At that time the Carnation was divided into two main categories – 'Bursters' and 'Whole Blowers' which were subdivided into Flames, Flakes, Bizarres, Piquettes or Picotees and Painted Ladies. The Bursters were known to produce flowers with split calyxes, a continuing fault even now, so much so that plastic calyx repairers or concealers may be purchased for those special occasions when a carnation has to look its best. During this period the carnation was grown mainly under glass because it was and still is a rather tender plant, liable to damage from cold wet winters and summer rainstorms. We know what these old types look like because there are exact descriptions for the show requirements, and there are reliable illustrations of them in a magazine called *The Florist* dated 1849 and 1850. When Parkinson wrote his great book in 1629 – *Paradisi in Sole Terrestris* he listed a number of Carnations whose names are redolent of the past. There was the Gray Hulo and the Red Hulo, the Striped Savadge and his companion the Blush Savadge, the Grimelo, the Greatest Granado and the Great Lombard Red. The name 'Gillyflower' has come down to us from similar-sounding words in several languages, all of them meaning a Clove. In the first century A.D. Pliny wrote about the Clove Carnation being discovered in Spain, and of its use by the Spaniards to spice their wines and the name of Sops-in-Wine for some kinds of Pink (though not the Carnation) – persisted for many hundreds of years.

The word Pink may have come from *Pinksten* which was the old German word for Pentecost (the flowers blooming the seventh Sunday after Easter). The word Pink or Pynke was eventually given to this member of the Dianthus family and the colour-name was taken from the plant, not the other way about; it is a comparatively recent word, not generally used as a fashion term before the end of the eighteenth century.

Early nomenclature has always been tangled because the comparative neatness of Linnaeus' binomial system had not been invented, and therefore it is not surprising to learn that the word Gillyflower (which is a pink) was at the same time used for Wallflowers (Cheiranthus) and even for Honesty (Lunaria). The old Gillyflowers, before they were generally known as Pinks, had delightful names such as the Lusty Gallant, the Ruffling Robin, Queen's Dainty, the Sad Pageant, John Whittie his Great Tawny and Master Tuggie's Princess. The Pink has strong associations with the Orient, being the subject of formal – though still very recognisable – design for ceramics and textiles in the sixteenth and seventeenth centuries. In the nineteenth century cultivation of the pink became an obsession with the colliers of Durham and Northumberland and also among the factory and foundry workers of Tyneside (Pinks are not fussy as to clean air and could stand a considerable amount of industrial pollution of the type that was common at that time). The weavers of Paisley, in Scotland, had a similar passion for Pinks and it was they who developed the first 'Laced' varieties (that is, Pinks with a contrasting edge to each petal which matched or toned with the central 'eye'). Sadly, though they had over a hundred varieties of Laced Pinks at Paisley, and also about the same number of Carnations, very few have survived. One of the oldest is Dad's Favourite which is white, laced with chocolate and with a dark eye; Earl of Essex, Inchmery, Messines Pink, Musgraves Pink, Sam Barlow, Red Emperor and White Ladies date from the last century or before. The one Pink that we can be certain of is 'Mrs Sinkins', a double white pink that is just over 100 years old. Like other well known personalities, it began life in a workhouse, being bred by the principal of the Slough Poor Law Institution who named it after his wife. Soon afterwards it was sold to a local grower who exhibited it at the Royal Horticultural Society in 1880, and today it can still be seen in the coat of arms of Slough.

Sweet Williams, *D. barbatus* were old garden favourites, but they have never been enthused about to the same extent, even though they were well known as early as 1533 when they were used in great quantities to plant a garden for Henry VIII at Hampton Court. Gerard liked them for themselves, and this famous quotation is an indication of his affection for the flowers. "These plants are not used either in meate or medecine, but esteemed for their beautie to decke up gardens, the bosomes of the beautifull, garlands and crowns for pleasure." Sweet Williams enjoyed a great popularity in Scotland and there were a number of growers; many shows and exhibitions were devoted particularly to them in the eighteenth and nineteenth centuries.

D. x allwoodii (1917) 'Modern'. A name usually given to the progeny developed by Montague Allwood from *D. caryophyllus* and *D. plumarius*. Very many kinds and colours. Included in this book because though they are not the actual descendants of the old Laced Pinks, they have been bred back to look like them.

D. alpinus (1751) grows to 4in (10cm), pink and purple flowers from June to August. Species not scented. A rockery perennial from the Austrian Alps.

D. barbatus - Sweet Williams (1573). Single or double scented flowers of many colours and heights, flowering in June and July. A biennial for massed planting in the border from S and E. Europe.

D. caryophyllus - Carnation. Very many types which vary from tender greenhouse kinds to hardy border annuals and perennials, usually scented. The wild ancestor of these came originally from S and W. France.

D. chinensis - Chinese or Indian Pink (1716). Many kinds, height varies according to type, flowers are in all shades of pink, red and crimson, often spotted, splashed or streaked with white or silver. Not always scented. An annual for edges of border or rockery from Eastern Asia.

D. deltoides - Maiden Pink forms a prostrate evergreen mat with bright scented flowers in shades of pink and red from June to Autumn. Useful as an edging, in sunny rockeries and dry walls.

D. gratianopolitanus (syn. **D. caesius**) - **Cheddar Pink** grows to 12ins (30.5cm), very fragrant pink flowers with fringed petals from May to July. A European perennial and now a protected rare wild flower of the British Isles. For edging and rock garden.

D. plumarius - **Pink** (1629). Similar to *D. gratianopolitanus* but with flower petals more deeply fringed. A perennial from S. Europe for the rock garden. One of the parents of the modern Pinks.

D. superbus (1596) grows to 2ft (61cm) with fragrant rosy-lilac flowers from June to September. A perennial for the sunny border from Europe, W. Asia and Japan.

Requirements: All pinks and border Carnations need a sunny open situation. Good drainage is essential, so add sharp sand if soil is heavy. Work in a small quantity of well-rotted farmyard manure or garden compost before planting both Pinks and Border Carnations. They do not do well on acid soils. Water new and young plants well during dry spells. Old plants benefit from a high-potash fertiliser in March, and both can have fortnightly feeds of dried blood just before and during flowering according to size – a dessertspoonful for young plants and two for older ones. Water well before feeding. 'Stop' young plants so that they form good clumps. Twiggy sticks can be used to support larger-flowering Border Carnations, though canes or special Carnation supports may be preferred. Bonemeal can be lightly raked in during September or October.

Cultivation: Propagation of Pinks is by seed and from cuttings. Sow seeds of species types from mid-April to July in a frame or cold greenhouse. Pot on in the usual way until plants are large enough to plant out. Do not set too deep in the ground. Take 4-in (10-cm) cuttings of non-flowering shoots from named or favourite plants in June to August and place in a mix of equal parts of peat, loam and sharp sand. Side shoots can be layered in July, severing layers after six weeks. Leave new plantlets *in situ* to establish own root system for a further three weeks before transplanting carefully. For border carnations the methods are similar, seed of named varieties can be sown in January or February in a minimum temperature of 15°C (59°F). When seeds have germinated, reduce temperature to 10°C (50°F). Pot on in the usual way and plant out in May. Staking of some kind is essential for Border Carnations and this should be done at the same time. For winter flowers under glass Carnations should be grown at a temperature of 10°C (50°F). For Sweet Williams, sow seed in open ground in summer, thin out, grow on and transplant to flowering positions in October.

During and after flowering: Dead-head Pinks unless seeds of species types are wanted. Keep large old plants free of blown leaves and litter which will collect around, under and among the leaves in winter. Carnations can be disbudded in June for larger blooms. New plants usually have a main stem with a crown bud and side shoots tipped with buds. Remove all other buds.

Uses: Carnations are excellent flowers for greenhouse and conservatory and are long-lasting cut and border flowers. Grey-leaved Pinks have excellent winter foliage.

Plants: Most nurseries.

Seeds: Allwoods, Artiss, Thomas Butcher, Chiltern, Dobie, Thompson and Morgan.

DICENTRA - Bleeding Heart, Seal Flower, Lady's Locket, Lyre Flower, Dutchman's Trousers *(Papaveraceae)*. It is odd to discover that this delicate-looking plant with its arching stems of dangling rose-pink flowers is a member of the Poppy family, sharing with them their general disinclination to be moved once established. It is also odd to find that such a romantically-named plant does not seem to be mentioned in the language of flowers, where one would expect to see it, but where the various vocabularies with their associated meanings often list horticultural curiosities which are barely recognisable today. Linnaeus named the plant from a dried specimen, having never seen it alive. He called it *Dielytra* meaning 'two-sheathed' – from the likeness of the flowers to the wingcases of some insects, and some early garden catalogues would have it listed under this name. It is a beautiful thing, with jade-green, glaucous, rather rue-like leaves and pendulous flowers of a particularly delicious pink that do indeed look like a row of heart-shaped lockets, or as I once read somewhere, a row of valentines pegged out to dry.

D. spectabilis was discovered in China round about 1810 and was then lost to cultivation for a while, being re-discovered by Robert Fortune on the island of Chusan. The plant became very popular as a graceful garden and greenhouse subject, so much so that it formed a main theme for wallpaper patterns of the times. Nowadays it is a slightly temperamental flower, or so I have found, seeming to need 'just so' conditions: but where it does well it is very beautiful indeed and worth any amount of cosseting. Another member of the genus from North America, *D. eximia*, is much hardier but nothing like as lovely. Dicentras have thick but fragile roots and dislike being disturbed, often sulking to death. *D. spectabilis* dies down and disappears completely after flowering, but as it looks perfect when grown in association with ferns, these will obligingly cover the bare patch by July.

D. eximia (1812) grows to 18in (46cm) with pink flowers from May to September. For the large rock garden in semi-shade. A perennial from the U.S.A.

D. formosa (1796) grows to 18in (46cm) with brighter green leaves and pink flowers in May and June. A perennial from west North America, for sun or partial shade.

D. spectabilis - Bleeding Heart (1816) grows to 24in (61cm) with delicate arching stems and dangling white-tipped pink flowers in May and June. A rather tender perennial for a sheltered, semi-shaded position from E. Asia and Japan.

Requirements: Well-drained soil enriched with well-rotted manure or compost, and a sheltered position for *D. spectabilis* protected from late frosts, strong winds and slugs.

Cultivation: Divide roots in autumn or early spring or sow seeds in March in seed compost at a temperature of 15°C (59°F). Grow on in the usual way and keep in a cold frame for a year before planting out.

Plants: Most nurseries.

Seeds: Thomas Butcher, Thompson and Morgan.

DICTAMNUS - Burning Bush, Dittany, Fraxinella *(Rutaceae).* At the right time of year this is a fascinating plant to show to the children, who are more impressed with the odd and the curious than the merely pretty. In summer, when the day has been hot and the air is dry, the old flowers give off an inflammable and volatile vapour which can be set alight with a match without harming the plant. This is always most effective just at dusk.

Some of the early books give the plant another name – 'Bastard Dittany' which is confusing, because the true Dittany is *Origanum dictamnus* or Dittany of Crete, appearing in the vocabularies of the language of flowers as meaning 'birth' whereas *Dictamnus fraxinella* quite naturally meant 'fire'. Both plants have a strong 'herby' fragrance but otherwise there is no similarity, and *O. dictamnus* has white-woolly leaves to further distinguish it.

One has to tiptoe carefully through the maze of plant nomenclature, because, just for fun and to further confuse things, there is an annual, columnar, bush-like plant called *Kochia scoparia trichophylla* that is also called by the name of Burning Bush. This would be a sad disappointment to the children, because the plant produces no vapour and therefore does not produce those magical Christmas-pudding flames. *D. fraxinella* is a pleasant plant for the scented garden and pot-pourris, because it smells of lemon-peel when the stems are rubbed and of the more aromatic balsam when they are bruised. Established plants should not be moved.

D. albus syn. **D. fraxinella - Burning Bush** grows to 18ins(46cms) with long racemes of white or mauve flowers in June and July. A perennial for the sunny border or herb garden from E. Europe or Asia.

Requirements: An open border and limy soil. Can be grown in acid soil by adding lime at 2-4oz (55-115g) per sq yd.

Propagation: Sow fresh seed outside in a drill in August and September. Thin seedlings and leave remainder to grow on for two years. Transplant carefully in spring.

After flowering: Cut stems down to ground level in October.

Uses: An interesting aromatic border-plant – site at path-edge. Star-shaped seed pods good for winter decor.

Seeds: Chiltern, Dobie, Thompson and Morgan.

Plants: Bressingham, Beth Chatto, Cunnington, Hillier, Holden Clough, Nottcuts, Scotts, Sherrards.

DIERAMA - Angel's Fishing Rods, Wand Flower *(Iridaceae)*. Dieramas should be sited in a sheltered, sunny place in the garden, preferably at the edge of a pool, where their dangling bell-shaped flowers can quiver continuously over the still water. They have tall, wiry stems that echo the slightest movements of breeze or passer-by. Dieramas are rather tender plants and hate disturbance, so once they are growing well do not move them – move the lawn or the path instead! They like to tuck their toes under cool flagstones, but as the clump will eventually grow large, the flagstones may have to be chipped away to accommodate their increasing girth. They will in time grow to large rushy clumps whose leaves are deceptively sharp-edged, so for all its beauty, this is not a plant for the path-edge, where in any case, its four or five-foot 'wands' would be damaged. Dieramas look well against rocks, though they are too large for the average small rockery, but in areas of good local stone it is worth building a tallish 'outcrop' (with a few extra soil pockets for smaller treasures) that looks as though it came naturally out of the ground. This can be very successful on sloping lawns. Many large-leaved things such as Bergenias seem to sit instantly into such a background and the choicer kinds of this useful plant can be grown. Another sun-lover with pleasing soft evergreen leaves is *Phlomis samia*. If these are grown together, choose the white flowered variety of Dierama. The rocks are an excellent reflector of warmth for the more doubtfully hardy plants and the more precious bulbs.

D. pulcherrimum - Wand Flower has flower stems up to 6ft (1.85m) with dangling magenta, white, violet or pale pink bell-shaped flowers in August and September. A rather tender bulbous plant for sheltered, sunny borders or pond side from S. Africa.

Requirements: Good well drained soil with added leaf-mould. Sunny, sheltered position. In cold areas protect with litter or bracken in winter.

Cultivation: Plant container-grown plants in springs or summer. Lift established plants in October, separate small offsets to increase stock, plant in nursery bed to grow on. In cold areas plant in pots sunk in frame to overwinter.

Uses: Excellent for waterside planting or the larger rockery.

Plants: Most nurseries.

DIGITALIS - Foxglove, Fairy Thimbles *(Scrophulariaceae)*. This familiar British wild flower is a handsome biennial for the larger border or semi shaded corner, especially if the white or paler pink varieties are grown in association with ferns. This is an amiable plant, quite happy growing atop the sunny stone walls of Southern Cornwall or in woodland shade throughout the British Isles. It also seems to thrive as a self-sown seedling right in the middle of paved paths, so it is as well to be able to recognise the seedling leaves because it can be easily moved when young.

The origin of the name Foxglove is charming – it is said that the bad fairies gave the flowers to the foxes to put on their paws so that they could creep silently up to their prey. In Norway the word for the flower is *Revbielde,* meaning Fox's Bell, so that he can have music as he wakes to hunt. Originally the plant was used by herbalists as a cure for anything from external ulcers to catarrh. It was not until the later part of the 18th century that the extract digitalin, which is used to stimulate the action of the heart was discovered. Today, the Foxglove is grown commercially, for as yet, no effective synthetic substance has been found. The leaves of second year plants are used just as the flowers are coming out, when it can be seen what the colour will be – darker-flowered plants contain more of the drug.

D. purpurea - Foxglove grows to about 7ft (2.75m) with spires of one-sided magenta, pink or white bells in July. (cultivated varieties have bells all the way round the stem, making them less graceful). A native biennial for large borders and woodland conditions in semi-shade.

D. ambigua syn. **D. grandiflora** (1566) grows to 3ft (91.5cm) with spires of yellow-brown bells in July and August. A perennial for the border from Europe and Asia.

D. lutea grows to 2ft (61cm) with yellow or white flowers from May to July. A European perennial for the border.

Requirements: Humus-rich soil that does not dry out and shelter from strong winds.

Cultivation: Sow the tiny seeds thinly in pans or boxes of seed compost in April or May, in cold frame or cold greenhouse. Prick out and grow on, transplant once only for best results, into individual pots or flowering positions.

After flowering: Cut down perennial flowering stems in October. *D. purpurea* often flowers a third year.

Seeds: John Chambers, Chiltern, Naturescape, Thompson and Morgan.

Plants: Bressingham, Beth Chatto, Cunnington, Holden Clough, Oak Cottage, Scotts, Stoke Lacy, Thompson and Morgan, The Weald Herbary.

DIMORPHOTHECA - African Daisy, Cape Marigold, Rain Marigold, Star of the Veldt *(Compositae).* Most of these Daisies are half-hardy, but are well worth the care that they need. These flowers close in damp or cloudy weather, and their subsequent opening is a surprise because the undersides of the petals are often of an inconspicuous colour. For example when the flowers of *D. ecklonis* suddenly begin to open, with their brilliant white petals and unflowerlike, scintillating, metallic blue centres, it is as if Pinocchio's Blue Fairy had just visited the garden. These plants, though perennial, are best treated as annuals unless space can be found for them in a sunny greenhouse or conservatory with a mean temperature of 7°C (45°F). Water very sparingly during winter. Cloches can be used and are often very successful in keeping the plants through a mild Northern European winter.

D. aurantiaca - Star of the Veldt (1774), grows to 18in (46cm) with bright orange flowers from June to September. A perennial for a hot, sunny border or large rockery from S. Africa. Reflected warmth from stone paths or nearby rocks suits the plant very well.

D. Ecklonis (1897) grows to 2ft (61cm) with pink or white flowers in July and August. A perennial for sunny borders or the large rockery from S. Africa.

D. pluvialis - Rain Daisy (1752), grows to 12in (30.5cm) has white flowers with brown centres tipped with metallic blue from June to August. An annual for a sunny border from S. Africa.

Requirements: Full sun and a sheltered position.

Cultivation: Sow seeds in compost at a temperature of 18°C (64°F). Prick out when large enough, grow on and harden off carefully. Seeds may be sown in large pots and thinned out to three per pot.

After flowering: Cut down stems in autumn if plants are to be kept for another year.

Uses: As vivid plants for edging a sunny border or as conservatory subjects.

Seeds: Thomas Butcher, Dobie, Unwins (hybrids).

Plants: Bloms, Hiller, Ramparts, Robinsons, St. Bridget, F. Toynbee Ltd.

DODECATHEON - Shooting Star, American Cowslip *(Primulaceae)*. Many of our garden flowers were discovered at an early date and brought from other countries to the British Isles as seed or plants. After a short time they would die, usually because their cultural requirements were not properly understood and they were often lost to cultivation for many more years. So it was with *Dodecatheon meadia* which was first discovered in 1704 by a plant collector called Bannister. This charming little member of the primrose family was sent to London to grow in the garden of the then Bishop of London, Dr. Compton. After a few years it had disappeared, but in 1744 it was rediscovered in America by John Bartrum, another plant collector. The plant was named Meadia, after the Presbyterian cleric Dr. R. Mead who was not a botanist, so Linnaeus renamed it *Dodecatheon* from the Greek *Dodeka*, twelve, and *Theoi*, 'Gods', because he "regarded the flowers in an umbel – about twelve – as so many little divinities". Other and later botanists have perhaps more realistically compared the flowering plant to a half-opened parasol. The Dodecatheons need specific woodland conditions – dappled shade and moist, humus-rich soil, and should be left undisturbed to form good-sized clumps.

D. Meadia - Shooting Star (1744), grows to 20in (51cm) with a many-flowered umbel of pink Cyclamen-like flowers from May to June. A perennial plant for a semi-shaded border from E. North America.

Requirements: Moist, fairly rich soil, semi-shade and a top-dressing of well-rotted manure in February.

Cultivation: Divide mature plants in autumn or sow seeds in March in a cold frame. Grow on and plant out in a shaded nursery bed for two years.

Plants: Avon, Broadleigh, Holden Clough, Jackamoor, Robinsons, Sherrards.

Seeds: Chiltern, Thompson and Morgan.

DORONICUM - Leopard's Bane *(Compositae)*. This is one of the earliest perennials to flower with any effect in the garden, its bright-yellow suns begin to smile as early as April and are always most welcome. In some gardens Doronicums grow into fine clumps in a few years, needing no special care. There has always been some confusion between this plant, *Doronicum pardalianches* and *Aconitum pardalianches* – the *pardalianches* meant 'Leopard strangler' which was an odd name for a European plant where no leopards existed. In earlier centuries the Arab physicians used Doronicum, which they called *Doronigi*, for all kinds of "cordiall medicines". The two plants were often confused, sometimes fatally. There was one effective way to tell them apart – and as Lyte said of the aconite "... if this harbe or root thereof, be layd by the Scorpion, then he shall lose his force and be astonied, until such time as he shall happen agayne to touch the leaves of white elebor, by vertue whereof he cometh to him selfe agayne". Scorpions are almost as scarce as leopards in Europe and this lack may be one reason for the confusion.

Slugs are very partial indeed to the leaves of Doronicums, as I have good reason to know, and will consume the whole plant if not prevented.

D. pardalianches - Great Leopard's Bane grows to 3ft (91.5cm) with yellow flowers from April to July. A vigorous perennial from Europe for the spring border.

D. plantagineum grows to 2ft (61cm) with yellow flowers in April. An easy perennial for a similar situation, from Europe. The old variety 'Miss Mason' is the one usually offered.

Requirements: An open situation and ordinary soil, do not allow to dry out in summer.

Cultivation: Divide established plants in October or spring.

During and after flowering: Dead-head regularly, cut stems down in late summer.

Plants: Bressingham, Holden Clough, Kelways, R.V. Roger Ltd, Scotts, Sherrards, St. Bridget.

DRABA *(Cruciferae).* A large genus of usually cushion-shaped plants, often grown in alpine houses, though many are very suited to a sunny rockery with made to measure drainage. Some Drabas may well need the protection of a sloping pane of glass in winter, or they may be left in their (clay) pots in the ground during the summer and taken into a cold, well ventilated greenhouse for the worst of the winter months. Many form a pleasing rosette of leaves and these can be easily divided up in August. Cuttings should be taken of non-flowering rosettes in July and put in pots of sharp sand in a cold frame. When rooted grow on in individual pots in a mixture of 2 parts potting compost to 1 of limestone grit. Keep in a well ventilated frame for a year.

D. aizoides grows to 4in (10cm) with yellow flowers in April. A perennial plant from the mountains of Central Europe for the sunny rockery or trough.

D. cinerea (1820) forms small neat tufts with white flowers in spring. A neat perennial from the Arctic for a sunny rockery, may need protection from the winter wet.

D. rigida forms a low cushion 6in (15cm) wide with yellow flowers in April. A tiny perennial from E. Europe for trough or sunny rockery.

D. violacea (1867) grows to 6in (15cm) with violet flowers in spring. A perennial from the Andes for a sunny rockery.

Requirements: Good drainage essential; grow in a mixture of loam and coarse sand. Keep roots moist before and during flowering, do not water top of 'cushion'.

Cultivation: *See main text.*

Uses: Trough, rockery and alpine house plants.

Plants: Broadwell, Beth Chatto, Cunnington, Holden Clough, Ingwersen, Potterton and Martin, Robinsons, F. Toynbee Ltd.

DRACOCEPHALUM *(Labiatae).* Dracocephalums are plants that are not often seen though they have been grown in gardens for several hundred years. When one reads something like this, one wonders – "where? and in whose garden?" and if the answer to this is not forthcoming from the wheelbarrow or the water-butt, then the thing to do is to grow them yourself or go to one of the botanic gardens and see them there. The name comes from the Greek. *Drakon*, 'dragon', and *Kephali*, 'head', because of the shape of the flowers which look like a refined sort of antirrhinum or a more definite Catmint. *(Phystostegia* is sometimes called Dragon's head in nursery catalogues). They are not difficult to grow, though they do not seem to survive a succession of cold wet winters. Most are perennial plants from Eastern Europe and Asia. Well-drained soil is essential and a situation in a semi-shaded border or rockery according to height and habit. Established plants can be divided in early spring or seed may be sown in a cold frame in March.

D. grandiflorum (1759) grows to 9in (23cm) with blue flowers in July. A perennial plant for the rock garden from Siberia.

D. Moldavica - Moldavian Balm (1596) grows to 18in (46cm) with blue or white flowers in July. An aromatic annual for the border from Siberia.

D. Ruyschianum (1699) grows to 2ft (61cm) with purple flowers in June. A European perennial for the border.

D. sibericum (1760) grows to 40in (102cm) with violet flowers in July. A perennial from E. Asia for the border. Protect from wet in winter.
Requirements: *See main text.*
Cultivation: *See main text.*
After flowering: Cut down stems.
Plants: Allwoods, Beth Chatto, Robinsons.
Seeds: Chiltern.

DRACUNCULUS - Dragon Arum *(Araceae)*. This is a very easy plant to grow, though perhaps only for the courageous collector of curiosities. It is a baleful-looking plant, with its huge dark-crimson spathe from which comes the most appalling stench. Once the spathe has unfurled it emits this odour to attract its pollinators, the bluebottles and other carrion flies, which get to it as fast as their wings can carry them. The construction of the flower is the same as in any Arum and once the flower has been effectively pollinated by its insect visitors – usually a maximum of three days – the livid purplish-red spathe withers quickly away, leaving the black spadix to dominate that part of the border for another day or two. Green berries then form which later turn to red and these fall to the ground when ripe to develop into the potato-shaped tuber. If the summer is cold and wet it will not flower, or the pale green spathe may form and grow quite large but may not open properly to change to the characteristic dark red. It is not a plant for the dainty gardener, though it has a considerable presence while it is growing because of the thick pale stems spotted with purple and the attractive light-green leaves.

The Dragon Arum needs a sheltered sunny wall to reflect warmth, and will start to send up its spotted stems in April. Once established it will spread all along that part of the border, and the young plants should be dug up as soon as they are recognised (or when their leaves die down in late summer) to be returned to the parent group, leaving sufficient room for their own development. It is very easy to spear the tubers with a winter fork, and so their part of the border should not be too thoroughly tidied.

D. vulgaris syn. **Arum dracunculus - Dragon Arum** grows to 3 ft (91.5cm) with 18in (46cm) maroon-black spathe in July. A tuberous perennial from the Mediterranean area for the base of a warm wall.
Requirements: Free draining soil and a south-facing wall.
Cultivation: Established clumps produce many small tubers which can be dug up when the foliage dies down.
After flowering: Cut off spadix if seeds are not wanted.
Tubers: Amand, Avon, Peter Chappell, Hillier.

DRYAS - Mountain Avens *(Rosaceae)*. Dryas is now a rare wild flower in the British Isles, seen only by the most intrepid of hill-climbing nature-lovers. It is a charming plant, with neat dark green oak-shaped leaves that are almost white beneath. It has eight-petalled white flowers with bright orange stamens, and a well-established clump on a sunny rockery in June is a lovely sight, and very gratifying when it is your own rockery. In the late summer fluffy seed heads develop like those of Traveller's Joy – *Clematis vitalba* and these can be sown as soon as ripe into a sandy compost in a cold frame; the seedlings can be grown on into individual pots sunk in the soil in the frame for a year before planting out; it will be two or three years before the little plants flower. Dryas hates to be moved once it has settled in, so it is not a plant for the dithering gardener who likes to have a game of General Post every year.

D. octopetala - Mountain Avens grows into an evergreen mat with white flowers in June and July followed by fluffy seed-heads in autumn. A European and N. American wild flower for a sunny rockery.
Requirements: Ordinary soil and full sun.

Cultivation: Take heel cuttings in March or August and put in damp sand in a cold frame. When rooted, transfer carefully into individual pots and grow on in seed compost. Plant out the following year.
Plants: Most nurseries.
Seeds: Chiltern.

ECHEVERIA *(Crassulaceae)*. The plant was named in honour of Atanasio Echeverria, one of the several botanical artists who co-operated in the production of the *Flora Mexicana* in 1858. Echeverias were very popular with the Victorians because of their neatness of shape and unusual pale colour; the succulent plants were planted out in gardens as mathematically-spaced edging plants or in tidy patterns round trees and bushes.

Echeverias are very easy to grow and their main requirement is to be handled as little as possible, because the delicate waxy bloom on their leaves is very easily damaged. They can be watered freely during the summer (in the mornings) but do not allow the water to fall on to the leaves. In the winter they need to be kept in the lightest and sunniest part of the greenhouse at a temperature of about 5°C (41°F) – which makes it very difficult for the gardener when he is allocating the winter quarters, since almost all the plants seem to need exactly the same conditions. During this time the plants get 'leggy'. Leave them until March, cut the tops off and allow to dry for a few days, then pot them up in a good seed compost. The rosette will root fairly quickly and the old stem, though unattractive, is still capable of child-bearing; it will send up new shoots which can be cut off when large enough and allowed to dry as before.

During the summer Echeverias look most attractive when planted at the edge of the larger rocks in a rockery, particularly if the stones echo or contrast pleasingly with the colour of the plants. Stems of long-lasting orange and yellow flowers will uncurl in late June, but they must be moved from their mountain home and brought into the safety of the greenhouse before October.
E. derenbergii grows to 3in (7.5cm) with yellow and orange flowers in June. A tender succulent perennial from Mexico for summer planting in trough or rockery.
Requirements: Full sun, ordinary soil and winter protection.
Cultivation: Sow seeds thinly in March at a temperature of 21°C (70°F). Propagate from leaves: detach fat, healthy leaves and lay on a damp, sandy compost. Keep sand just moist and temperature at 16°C (61°F) minimum. Tiny plants will appear, leave until large enough to handle. Pot plantlets in individual pots in same compost.
Plants: Abbey Brook, Whitestone.
Seeds: Thompson and Morgan.

ECHINACEA - Red or Purple Coneflower *(Compositae)*. This is a large and attractive plant, with fine rose-coloured daisy flowers and shining dark green leaves. It takes its name from *Echinos* 'hedgehog', because the scales of the receptacle (the top of the stem bearing the bracts and floral parts) are prickly. It blooms in late summer, and it is an unusual flower-colour at this time of the year, associating most pleasingly with most grey-leaved plants, and in particular, *Eucalyptus gunnii*, the Sweet Gum, which often has crimson-coloured old leaves among the blue-grey foliage that are the same tone as the Echinacea flowers. These are very long lasting and are rigid enough to withstand seasonal bad weather without suffering too much, if at all. Echinaceas are large, sturdy plants that will reach a height of about 4ft (122cm) and they should be allowed plenty of space in the late summer border, with such flowering companions as the larger Sedums, 'Autumn Joy', *Spectabile* and *purpurea*, the pink stars of *Schizostylis coccinea* 'Mrs Hegarty', the creamy pink-toned leaves of *Fuchsia magellanica* tricolour, with the little pink pokers of *Polygonum affine* and the oddity of Phystostegia. Early flowering Asters (Michaelmas Daisies) of appropriate heights and colours and a group of *Crocus speciosus* nearby will make a most interesting late summer group with much contrast of shape and form. The small plants are a little delicate and should be moved or planted in the spring because a cold wet winter can be fatal, as can slugs be to emerging leaves. Echinaceas are occasionally listed among Rudbeckias in some catalogues.

E. purpurea - Purple Coneflower (1799) grows to a bushy 4ft (122cm) with almost metallic rosy-mauve flowers from July to September. A very handsome and striking perennial from N. America for the middle or back of a large border.

Requirements: A sunny, open situation and deep, rich soil.

Cultivation: Divide established clumps in March or sow seeds in March at a temperature of 13°C (55°F). Grow on, plant out in a nursery row and move into final position in the following year.

During and after flowering: Dead-head regularly.

Plants: Bloms, Bressingham, Cunnington, Goatchers, Hillier, Jackman's, R.U. Roger Ltd, Sherrards, F.Toynbee Ltd.

Seeds: Thomas Butcher, Chiltern, Thompson and Morgan.

ECHINOPS - Globe Thistle *(Compositae).* A striking border plant whose metallic-looking spherical blue flower-heads are among the most useful and easily grown subjects for the flower arranger's winter collection. This is another plant named after *Echinos*, the hedgehog, this time because of the spiky sharpness of the flower-heads.

In the earlier part of the summer the leaves of most of the Echinops are very attractive, with pleasing tones of silver and blue and dark green. In some situations they can get a little coarse and therefore it may be as well to plant other perennials in front of them whose leaves remain attractive for the whole of the summer. Some suggestions are: *Achillea filipendula* (whose grey leaves and yellow flowers offer a pleasing contrast); *Aruncus sylvester,* Goat's Beard (delicate light green leaves which last throughout the season); the many varieties of *Phlox paniculata* (lavender and white would be most attractive), the feathery green tracery of Cosmea foliage with its tossing daisies; the grey flannel spikes of some of the Verbascums, and so on. There are many permutations, and a visit to the herbaceous border in the garden of the nearest stately home will provide many ideas and save one or two mistakes. Echinops are rigid plants that do not need staking, and in more open and windswept gardens they can provide some useful leeward shelter.

E. banaticus (1832) grows to 3ft (91.5cm) with silver stems and round prickly heads of blue flowers from June to August. A perennial plant for the sunny border from the Balkans.

E. Ritro - Globe Thistle (1570) grows to 4ft (122cm) with round, prickly heads of steel-blue flowers from June to August. A perennial for the sunny border from S. Europe.

E. sphaerocephalus grows to a noble 7ft (2.13m) with silvery grey flower heads in July and August. A perennial plant from S. Europe and W. Asia for a focal position or the back of the border, good in association with *Onopordon acanthium,* the Scotch Thistle.

Requirements: Ordinary soil and full sun.

Cultivation: Divide established clumps in early spring. Sow seeds in the ground in April, prick out and grow on in a nursery row and transplant when large enough in autumn, or best in spring.

Uses: Superb flower heads for winter arrangements, cut before flowers fade to prevent them disintegrating.

Plants: Bressingham, Beth Chatto, Goatchers, Kelways, Sherrards, Treasures of Tenbury.

Seeds: Thomas Butcher, Chiltern, Dobie, Suttons, Thompson and Morgan.

ECHIUM - Viper's Bugloss *(Boraginaceae).* To those familiar with the native Viper's Bugloss – *Echium vulgare* – the rarer and more tender species of this genus from the kinder climate of the Canary Islands are most interesting plants for warm garden corners in the southern part of the UK. Most are easily grown from seed, but must generally be treated as annuals because they grow too large to be moved under cover during the cold weather. If the winter is mild they may well survive, but this should not be counted on. All the Echiums are particularly good bee plants, so the apiarist (and the butterfly gardener) can easily grow a good patch of the biennial *E. vulgare* near the hives. The wild plant's name came from the resemblance of the seeds, or nutlets, to a viper's head, and according to Dioscorides and other Greek physicians, the plant was useful both to prevent and cure snake-bite. Later on in medieval times, the plant accumulated other virtues, being used to alleviate lumbago, as a cure for melancholia and to increase the natural flow of mother's milk.

E. plantagineum (1658). The species plant grows to 3ft (91.5cm) though (modern) dwarf varieties are most usually grown. White, pink, mauve, violet and blue flowers in July and August. An annual for the border from the Mediterranean region.

E. vulgare - Viper's Bugloss. A native wild flower with brilliant violet blue flowers from June to August. An annual or biennial for massing in the border.

Requirements: Well-drained soil in sunny position.

Cultivation: Sow seeds thinly in flowering position in April or in September. Thin out.

Uses: A bee and butterfly plant.

Seeds: Thomas Butcher, John Chambers, Chiltern, Thompson and Morgan.

ENDYMION - Bluebell, Wild Hyacinth *(Liliaceae).* The Bluebell has had its name changed several times by the indefatigable taxonomists, and in some books and catalogues it will be found under Scilla, and in others under Endymion. The garden variety of Bluebell is *Endymion hispanicus,* the Spanish Squill or Spanish Bluebell, and is taller and larger in its parts than the delightful wild flower that forms azure lakes beneath the catkins of the hazel coppices in spring. That Bluebell is *Endymion non-scripta* (more properly *Hyacinthoides non-scriptus* – there, you see what I mean?) though it may still be called *Scilla nutans* in some sources.

There is a legend about the beautiful youth Hyacinthus who was loved simultaneously by Apollo (the Sun-God) and Zephyrus, (god of the West Wind). Hyacinthus preferred Apollo which enraged the jealous Zephyrus, and one day, when Hyacinthus and Apollo were having a game of quoits, Zephyrus blew the heavy quoit out of course, accidentally killing the mortal Hyacinthus. Apollo was grief-stricken, and to mark his love for the dead youth he raised up a beautiful purple flower from the blood-soaked ground so that his sorrow should be known for evermore. The flower had symbols on it which resembled the Greek words *Ai, ai* – meaning 'woe'.

This marked variety of Bluebell or Wild Hyacinth grows in Greece but not northern Europe. Linnaeus gave the Northern European species the name of *non scriptus* ('not written-on'). Both kinds of Bluebell increase well. The flowers develop into papery brown bells containing rattling black seeds that should be collected as soon as ripe, usually about July. Sow them in a seed box, in a good mix of leaf-mould and sand and leave them out all winter. They don't need this coddling, but you will need to remember where they are, because when the seeds germinate and sprout they look exactly like grass, which you would ordinarily pull up. The seeds take a long time to germinate, so be patient. Leave the boxes under a sheltering shrub, where they can be subjected to frost and winter temperatures and a reasonable amount of rain. Just tweak out the weeds as you pass, because these will be stronger growing. Leave the tiny forming bulbs in the boxes until they are large enough to transplant, and remember that the leaves will vanish in June or July. When you plant them out, do not forget to mark the place. It should be remembered that the leaves of Bluebells (often the first of the bulbs to appear in late November) take six months or more to do their work of feeding the bulbs and then to disappear, and mature clumps are often composed of many deep and inaccessible bulbs which are gradually pulling themselves down, as all Bluebells do. The lax leaves do look obtrusive in midsummer, so think about their siting before you plant, and put summer-growing plants in front if you can. White flowers often appear among the blue varieties, and it is rather nice to dig these up and put them all together where the flowers will show up against a dark background. This is best done whilst the white flowers are still visible, it is cruel, the plant will not like it at all, but if you leave the job to do later, even if you mark each *stem*, it is one of the things that do not get done in midsummer. So do it while they are in their glory – they have short memories and will have forgiven you by next spring.

    E. non-scripta (now *Hyacinthoides non-scriptus*) prefers the dappled shade of deciduous trees or bushes and deep, humus-rich soil; though contrariwise, it seems quite happy in the wild state on sea-cliffs and slopes in Devon and Cornwall. *E. hispanicus* is an obliging plant and will do anywhere, though best in sun, and where its large rather untidy leaves will be hidden by later developing plants. Once planted it should be left alone to form its handsome clumps, though one can separate out the white and lilac colours to plant elsewhere as they are most useful for special effects.

E. hispanicus syns. **Scilla hispanica, E. hispanica, E. campanulatus - Spanish Squill, Spanish Bluebell** (1683), grows to 12in (30.5cm) with blue, white, pink and lilac flowers in May. An easy plant for spring borders and corners from Spain, Portugal and N. Africa.

E. non-scriptus (now Hyacinthoides non-scriptus) - English Bluebell, Wild Hyacinth and, incorrectly Harebell grows to 12in (30.5cm) with blue-purple or white flowers in May. Excellent for naturalising in light woodland, old orchards, on moist, sunny borders, or in semi-shaded corners. A native bulb, also of N & W. Europe.

Requirements: *E. hispanicus* does better in sunnier situations and is not fussy about soil. *H. non-scriptus* needs humus-rich soil and, generally, semi-shade.

Cultivation: The bulbs look like skinless potatoes with roots, to begin with. They have no protective skin and must not be allowed to dry out. Best purchased 'in the green' where possible and planted in flowering positions, 4-6in (10-15cm) deep and left to die down. Seeds may be sown as described, or in undisturbed corners where they will take from 4 to 6 years to come to flowering.

Bulbs: Avon, Broadleigh, Kelways.

Seeds: John Chambers, Chiltern, Naturescape, Thompson and Morgan.

EPIMEDIUM - Bishop's Hat, Barrenwort *(Berberidaceae).* When the rather dainty flowers are examined one can see how the plant got its common name – there is a pouch or spur at the back of the flower that resembles a medieval hood, though not necessarily an ecclesiastical one. Epimediums are most attractive plants, often used as ground cover, but their leaves are so pleasing that they should be planted in more conspicuous garden situations. Most of them bloom in April, with yellow, pink, white or red flowers – cut some of last year's leaves away so that they can be seen properly. Epimediums are almost evergreen, with veined, unevenly heart-shaped leaves on long, wiry stems. In the spring the new leaves are a delicate bronze-pink, and these later turn to a deep green with conspicuous veins of yellow or green. In autumn the leaves change to red or yellow and later to a more sombre chestnut brown, but they do not fall and this is another reason for planting them where one can see them properly, a large ledge half-way up the side of a shady rockery is ideal. Epimediums like a situation in dappled shade – they will endure full sun but the leaves have a scorched and unhappy look to them and the stems are shorter. The delicate flower sprays with pink, white or red appear from late March to July, often beneath the foliage, so they should be looked for at this time. They are an endearing and enduring plant, often surviving in spite of neglect and almost total suffocation by neighbouring vegetation, but they should not be put to this discomfort. Epimediums look well in association with stonework and small and delicate ferns.

E. grandiflorum (1980) grows to 15in (38cm) with yellow, rose, white or violet flowers in June. A rhizomatous perennial for partially shaded borders, large, shady rockeries and banks.

E. Perralderianum grows to 12in (30.5cm) with bright yellow flowers in June. Evergreen bronze-toned leaves. A rhizomatous perennial for similar planting from Algeria.

E. pinnatum (1849) grows to 12in (30.5cm) with yellow flowers from May to July. Evergreen leaves turn red in autumn. A rhizomatous perennial for similar garden situations from Persia.

E. x rubrum (about 1854) grows to 12in (30.5cm) with crimson flowers in May. Handsome leaves changing to yellow and orange in autumn. A rhizomatous perennial for similar garden planting.

Requirements: Good humus-rich soil and partial shade.
Cultivation: Divide rhizomatous roots in spring or autumn.
Uses: As foliage plants for semi-shade: leaves for decor.
Plants: Most nurseries.

ERANTHIS - Winter Aconite, New Year's Gift *(Ranunculaceae)*. This is a charming flower that is still occasionally seen in the wild. It is easily obtained from nurseries, but is not related, except distantly, to the poisonous Monkshood (Aconite, or *Aconitum* spp) though it belongs to the same large family of the Ranunculaceae. It has always been appreciated by gardeners for the earliness of its flowers, and Gerard speaks of it as "... coming foorth of the grounde in the dead time of winter, many times bearing the snow upon the heades of his leaves and flowers; yea, the colder the weather is and the deeper the snowe is, the fairer and larger is the flower; and the warmer that the weather is the lesser is the flower, and woorse coloured".

In early spring the flower stems back out of the ground, so to speak, trailing their transparent leaves behind them. By the next day they have straightened themselves up and adjusted their (by now) dark green ruffs, in which sit large buttercup-like flowers. These last for a considerable time, particularly if the weather is mild (I disagree with Gerard here). In snow and frosty periods the flowers do survive but soon become colourless and almost transparent. Eventually the show is over for another year and this it the time to buy the plants 'in the green' like Snowdrops. Purchased tubers are often dried up and may never break dormancy. The plants should be put in at the same soil depth and their position marked because after the leaves have withered it is very easy to forget their whereabouts. Where they do well they will cover a woodland slope with their glossy golden flowers, but in some gardens they just do not do. This may be because of a lack of water during the spring growing season. If there is a cold dry spring, judicious watering with rainwater may produce more flowers the following year.

E. hyemalis - Winter Aconite grows to 4in (10cm) with yellow flowers in February, sometimes earlier in mild winters. A tuber from W. Europe for partially shaded places beneath deciduous trees.

Requirements: Humus-rich soil in a sheltered position.
Cultivation: Plant tubers 1in (2.5cm) deep and as early as possible. Lift and
divide overcrowded groups after flowering. Replant as soon as possible.
Tubers: Avon, Bees, Broadleigh, Ingwersen, Kelways, Stassen, van Tubergen.

EREMURUS - Foxtail Lily *(Liliaceae)*. These majestic plants are one of the
handsomest sights in a garden, with their enormous, floriferous 'pokers' in
shades from white through cream, yellow, buff, deep apricot and copper.
The tallest of them is *E. robustus* which can attain a height of 9-10ft
(2.75-3.05m) with a 4ft (1.22m) spike of flowers in an elegant shade of
creamy copper. Such tremendous plants need to be planned for during the
previous year, and their neighbours-to-be should be carefully considered so
that there is a harmonious group. They look well against the background of
an evergreen hedge such as yew or holly. They have long, bent strap-shaped
leaves that form into large clumps very early in the summer, and which die
away as soon as the plant has sent up its stout flower stem. This leaves a
decided gap in the border just at midsummer, so it is as well to grow a lax,
floppy plant of some appropriate colour that can be allowed – even urged
– to fall forward into the space. Gertrude Jekyll used *Clematis* and
Gypsophila for the purpose, and there are a number of tall-growing later
summer herbaceous plants such as *Solidago* – Golden Rod, *Rudbeckia* and
Helianthus that can be relied on to shoot up quite quickly from July
onwards: these can be planted in front of the Eremurus. Soapwort,
Saponaria officinalis is a guaranteed 'flopper' though not tall-growing. The
planting of the Eremurus 'crowns' has to be done unhurriedly and with
care. On arrival, check that they are not damaged, and if they are, make a
fuss because these are expensive plants. The roots radiate from a central
tuber-like brittle wheel-hub, and this should be set 6in (15cm) deep in the
ground, sitting on a cushion of sandy grit. Mix up the surrounding soil with
the same grit (before you plant the Eremurus) and cover with more of the
same. They need to be planted in an open sunny place in well-drained rich,
sandy soil that has been manured the season before. When setting the crown
in the ground place a cane (as a guide) between the roots where the stake
is to go, so as not to do any damage subsequently. Eremurus should be
protected with bracken or litter for the winter and should be mulched with
well-rotted manure in spring, as such large plants have large appetites to
match. The manure should not be allowed to lie over the central part of the
crown. If the plants have established themselves it will be seen that new
crowns have formed. These can be gently eased apart at the end of the
season, uncovering them as carefully as one would an archaeological
treasure. They should be replanted immediately.
E. Bungei (1885) grows to 3ft (91.5cm) with yellow flowers in June. A medium
height perennial plant from Iran for the large sunny border.
E. Elwesii (1897) grows to 9ft (2.75m) with clustering pink flowers in May. A tall
perennial of uncertain origin for the large border, or grouped at a focal
point.
E. himalaicus grows to 8ft (244cm) with spires of white flowers in May. Another
handsome perennial from the Himalayas for the larger garden.
E. robustus (1874) grows to 10ft (305cm) with copper-cream flower-spikes in
May and June. An enormous perennial plant from Turkestan for a big
border. It may need support in unsheltered gardens.
Requirements: Eremurus should be planted in sunny borders facing South-West
so as to avoid early-morning sun, they develop very quickly in spring and
may need sheltering from late frosts. Other herbaceous plants nearby are
generally sufficient protection, but listen to the weather forecasts and be
prepared.
Cultivation: For main points see text. Only the extra tall kinds need staking. Set
new plants out in September, and specify an early September delivery when

ordering. Seed can be sown as soon as ripe, or in March. It should be stratified (a fortnight in the freezing compartment of the fridge) and should be sown at a temperature of 15°C (59°F). Grow the seedlings on in very large pots for two seasons so as to avoid damaging the fragile roots. Seedlings generally take about six years to flower and germination of all seed is lengthy and erratic.

Plants: Amand, Bloms, Bressingham, Hillier, Ingwersen, Orpington, van Tubergen.
Seeds: Chiltern, Thompson and Morgan.

ERIGERON - Summer Starwort, Fleabane *(Compositae).* The Erigerons are a pleasant group of plants, the most rampant and enduring of them being often seen as a cascade of mauve daisies spilling over dry stone walls, rock banks and cliffs in the West Country coastal areas. It is an attractively evergreen plant eminently suited to this kind of home, as it seems to need little or no attention, its long, strong roots finding moisture deep within the wall or bank. It is not regarded as anything special by its owners, who are so used to its presence that they have ceased to see it: they will casually give you a generous armful of it when asked. This accommodating plant is usually a variety of *E. glaucus,* spreading rapidly once established into huge mats of pleasant greyish leaves. The modern hybrids have larger, brighter flowers in shades of mauve, violet, lavender, pink, yellow and orange, but these often need just-so conditions and have not the enduring tenacity of *E. glaucus;* the mauve, blue and violet kinds are hardier than the pink sorts.

Most of the genus comes from N. America, including a charmless weedy cousin called *E. conyza* syn. *E. canadensis,* the Canadian Fleabane. This was accidentally introduced into the UK in the seventeenth century inside a stuffed bird. When the bird was eventually cast out on to a rubbish heap it disintegrated and the stuffing (containing the seeds of *E. conyza)* blew away and began to populate its new home.

E. aurantiacus (1879) grows from 9-12in (23-30.5cm) with bright orange-yellow flowers from June to August. A perennial plant for the rock garden, sunny border or path edge from Turkestan.
E. glaucus (1812) grows to 12in (30.5cm) or lower, depending on site. Mauve to purple flowers in July and September. Glaucous (or green in gardens) evergreen leaves. A very vigorous perennial plant from W-N. America, not for small rockeries. Suitable for banks, dry walls and other stony places in sun. Does well in coastal gardens.
E. macranthus grows to 2ft (61cm) with blue flowers in July and August. A hardy perennial evergreen for the sunny border from the Rocky Mountains of the USA.
E. speciosus grows to 18in (46cm) with purple flowers from July to August. A vigorous perennial from N. America for the sunny border.
E. mucronatus grows to 6in (15cm) with small and dainty white daisies with pink or purple on the reverse. It flowers from June to September and is charming in rock crevices, paving, large rockeries or walls. Hates being moved but will spread and self-sow once established. Top growth may be frost-damaged in hard winters. A perennial from Mexico.
Requirements: A sunny site and well-drained soil. Some tolerate poor soils well.
Cultivation: Divide in early spring or sow seeds in March in a cold frame. Prick out and grow on in a nursery bed. Transfer to flowering positions in autumn, or best in spring.
Uses: Pleasing in association with stonework, and as cut flowers.
During and after flowering: Dead-head to prolong flowering.
Plants: Artiss, Hillier, Ingwersen, Reginald Kaye, Robinsons, Sherrards, Waterperry.
Seeds: Chiltern, Suttons.

ERYNGIUM - Sea Holly *(Umbelliferae).* These stiffly rigid plants, often with shiningly metallic-looking flowers are most interesting in the garden and afterwards as 'drieds' for winter flower arrangements. Four of them were known to our Elizabethan ancestors, and a fifth our native *E. maritimum,* was particularly popular because its thick roots were candied with the new (and expensive) sugar and orange-flower water to make comfits, or sweets. These sweets had a particularly erotic symbolism, being thought to have aphrodisiac effects − Gerard said of the roots "... condited and preserved with sugar ... are exceedingly good to be given to old and aged people that are consumed and withered with age, and which want natural moisture; they are also good for other sorts of people that have no delight, nourishing and restoring the aged and amending the defects of nature in the yoonger". The sweets were still being enjoyed at the end of the nineteenth century. The roots − uncandied − were also considered to be very good for such natural disasters as the bites of serpents, broken bones, quartan agues (distinguished by a paroxysm every fourth day) and thorns in the flesh.

Sea Holly grows in certain places along British beaches, but do not be (illegally) tempted to try and dig it up to put it in the garden − its roots will defeat you because they reach clear through to Australia. It is, in any case, a miffy thing, disliking the averageness of garden soil: after all, it is a wild plant and has been used to the free-draining beach sand and pebbles and it will not compromise. But it may be easily grown from seed in a mixture of equal parts of peat and sand − sow the seeds in John Innes seed compost in a cold frame in the summer. When large enough to handle, prick out the seedlings into individual pots. Plant out in October or spring, and mark the place with a cane as the young plants will disappear for the winter. They are high on the list of the slug's dietary delights, so take precautions. Older plants are safer, they will have developed iron-hard stems that are slug-proof. Or almost.

E. alpinum (1577) grows to 2ft (61cm) with the upper part of the plant and its flowers turning blue. A European perennial for a sunny border needing better soil than the other Eryngiums.

E. amethystinum (1648) grows to 2ft (61cm) with spiny leaves and heads of amethyst flowers from July onwards. A European perennial plant for a hot sunny border.

E. giganteum 'Miss Willmot's Ghost' (1820) grows to 4ft (122cm) with blue-toned stems and leaves tinged with ivory. Silver-blue flower-heads in August. Though not the tallest of the variety it is one of the handsomest. Miss Ellen Willmott, the famous Edwardian lady gardener, used to scatter a few of the seeds when she visited other gardens. They would subsequently appear, to surprise the owners − or so the story goes. In those days, with gardeners available everywhere, it is unlikely that a thistly-looking seedling would have escaped to grow to maturity. But it is a nice story.

E. maritimum - Sea Holly grows to 18in (46cm) with veined, leathery pale green leaves and pale blue flower-heads from July. A native wild flower (now becoming scarce) for a sunny border.

E. plenum (1596) grows to 3ft (91.5cm) with dark blue stems and flowers in July. An Eastern European perennial for a sunny corner.

Requirements: Free-draining sandy soil and full sun.

Cultivation: Take root cuttings in February and insert in a compost of equal parts of sand and peat and put in a cold frame. When rooted, pot on or set in a nursery row, remembering that the roots will grow large and long. It is better to keep them in large pots sunk in the ground if they are to stay for some time.

During and after flowering: For winter arrangements, cut stems before flowers are finished. Cut stem to ground after flowering.

Plants: Beth Chatto, Goatchers, Highfield, Hillier, Holden Clough, Ingwersen, Potterton and Martin, Scotts, Sherrards.

Seeds: Thomas Butcher, Chiltern, Thompson and Morgan

ERYTHRONIUM - Dog's Tooth Violet *(Liliaceae).* There are several kinds of Erythronium but one in particular, *E. dens-canis* seems to have given its name to the whole genus. 'Dens-canis' is Latin for Dog's Tooth (from the shape of the bulb) and Erythros is Greek for red, which is the colour of the European flowers. The American varieties usually have yellow flowers so one has to keep a clear head and a good memory in all this maze of classical derivation, most of which is comfortingly logical. However, when it comes to common names, the following tortuous explanation will make your head spin. The descriptive word 'violet' was used for many medieval flowers and this must have been dreadfully confusing for gardeners of those times. For example, Honesty *(Lunaria biennis)* was called 'Viola Lunaria major', the Snowdrop *(Galanthus nivalis)* was 'Viola alba' in 1542 though it later became the 'The Bulbous Violet': the Canterbury Bell *(Campanula Medium)* was 'Viola Mariana' and the Lupin' *(Lupinus* spp.) was 'Great Spanish Violet'. So the Erythronium was just another such 'Violet'.

Erythroniums have dainty flowers like small lilies with usually mottled leaves: they look best when planted in groups. In Gerard's time they were thought to be similar to a group of Orchids called the Satyrion (Satyrium) which was reputed to have aphrodisiac powers. Parkinson had Erythroniums in several of the European shades and had just received an American specimen. He says "Wee have had from Virginia a roote sent unto us, that wee might well iujge by the forme and colour thereof, being dry, to be either the roote of this, or of an Orchis, which the naturall people holde not onely to be singular to procure lust, but hold it as a secret, loth to reveale it" The Russians didn't tip-toe about wondering what effect it would have on their libidos, they were still making a nourishing soup out of Erythronium bulbs as late as the eighteenth century.

Erythroniums need a light rich soil and a mixture of loam and peat suits them well. They prefer a semi-shaded situation and once planted the bulbs should be covered with sand and top-dressed with new soil after flowering.

E. albidum (1824) grows to 9in (23cm) with white flowers in April and May. The bulb forms burrowing stolons and will not flower until it reaches the correct depth. A bulb for partial shade, from Central N. America.

E. americanum (about 1665) grows to 8in (20.5cm) with yellow flowers in April and May. A bulb for similar situations, from E. North America.

E. Dens-canis - Dog's Tooth Violet (1596) grows to 6in (15cm) with purple-pink flowers in April and May. A bulb for partial shade from Asia, Japan and Europe.

E. Hendersonii (1887) grows to 8in (20.5cm) with lilac flowers in April. A bulb from Oregon, USA for a shaded place.

Requirements: Erythroniums need moisture-retentive but not wet soil and a north-facing slope or rockery suits them well.

Cultivation: Plant bulbs 3in (7.5cm) deep and leave undisturbed. They may be planted deeper in humus-rich leaf-mould to prevent them from drying out. Only move just after flowering, as the leaves die down. Offsets will form when the plants are happy.

Bulbs: Avon, Bloms, Broadleigh, Christian, de Jager, Ingwersen, Jackamoors.

Plants: Rock Garden Nursery.

ESCHSCHOLZIA - Californian Poppy *(Papaveraceae).* Lovely gay flowers, so easy to grow. Often they will come back if left to themselves next year, though not in such numbers. If they look right where they are, then scatter some more seed at the end of the season. The plants will last in bloom until the frosts so there is plenty of time to decide whether you like the tangled mass of pale green leaves and bright flowers that sprawls so comfortably all over the Irises. These are poppies of a kind, with the familiar orange-coloured flower being the best known and the strongest-growing. The French call them 'Bonnets-qui-tombent' because of the green 'nightcap' that neatly covers the new flowers like a candle-snuffer. Californian Poppies have always been popular flowers, right back to the time of their discovery in California by the conquering Spaniards, who called the flower 'Copa de Ora' – Cup of Gold, so the land that it grew in became the Golden West because of the miles and miles of brilliant orange flowers.

The first seeds were sent to Britain by Archibald Menzies in 1792, and the first flowers were grown at Kew at that time. Thereafter nothing was heard of the plant. It reappeared in 1815 and was named after a member of an expedition led by the Russian botanist Kotzebus, who travelled round the world on an extended plant-collecting trip. The member of the expedition was Dr. Johann Friedrich Eschscholz, whose name and that of the flower have been mis-spelled ever since. By 1833 it was a popular annual and later its common and so much easier name of Californian Poppy was extensively used in advertising Brilliantine for smart young working men, with a perfume of the same name for their girls. I remember seeing it in Woolworths in 1936, along with a much naughtier 'perfume' called 'Evening in Paris' by Bourjois. Both promised untold excitements to the would-be wearers. Times change, names change, but the promise is still there and still being successfully marketed. A hair oil is still made from the plant by the Spanish-speaking Californians who fry it in oil and add perfume to the result. The product is reputedly excellent for hair growth.

Californian Poppies grow to 18in (46cm) and sometimes taller, depending on soil and conditions, and they form a mass of attractive light green foliage that is rather inclined to lean on neighbouring plants. The quickly-growing Californian poppies will cover earlier-blooming plants very tidily, and they flower continuously until the frosts. Californian poppies do not transplant successfully (few poppies do) and if the place for them is occupied temporarily, as it so often is in the small garden, the Poppies can be grown on in 5in (12.5cm) pots and transferred with as little root disturbance as possible when their flowering site is ready. They are not long-lasting in water, though very colourful for a one-off occasion. Pick flowers as well as buds, to open later.

E. californica - Californian Poppy (1790) grows to 18in (46cm) with bright orange-yellow flowers successively from June until the frosts. Good in hot positions with poor soil, along with dwarf Nasturtiums. An annual from N. America, it needs a sunny border. The flowers close in wet or dull weather.

Requirements: Full sun and sandy soils.

Cultivation: Sow thinly where plants are to flower and thin out later, or as described in text. Sow successively for a longer flowering season, make last sowings in August or September for next year's flowers.

Seeds: Thomas Butcher, Chiltern, Suttons, Thompson and Morgan.

EUCOMIS - Pineapple Plant *(Liliaceae)*. The plant gets its proper name from *Eukomes*, beautiful-headed', from the crown of leaves above the flower spike, rather like a Crown Imperial. This is an interesting though not loveable species, as the plant is pollinated by flies of the nastier kind and therefore the opening star-shaped flowers reek of carrion.

Eucomis have been popular for well over a hundred years and are not difficult to grow. They are handsome patio plants when planted three bulbs to a large and ornamental pot, and remain interesting throughout the summer and autumn until it is time to take the pot into a warm greenhouse or conservatory for their dormant winter period. The leaves will die off and should be tidied away. No water, or only a very little should be given until the livid purple-spotted snout of the emerging plant begins to show in early spring. Re-potting should be done after flowering, into rich light soil and as soon as the bulb begins to grow away, fortnightly feeds of weak liquid manure can be given. Offsets are produced that can be seen as flowerless stems growing up beside the parent bulb. They should be gently detached when the plant dies down. The pot or pots can stand outside in a sheltered sunny place from June onwards. The bulbs may be successfully grown in the ground in South Devon and Cornwall, planted 6in (15cm) deep and well covered with litter during the winter. The changing appearances of the pineapple-shaped inflorescence is a source of interest and curiosity, though there will undoubtedly be comments from the faint-hearted when the flowers begin to open, but it's your garden, after all.

E. bicolor (1878) grows to 18in (46cm) with purple-edged green flowers that give off a powerful odour. This attracts flies, so be prepared for this. A tender bulb from Natal for pots in the greenhouse, conservatory or in the open.

Requirements: *See text.*
Cultivation: *See text.*
Bulbs: Amand, Avon, de Jager, Dobie.

EUPATORIUM - Hemp Agrimony, Raspberries & Cream, Holy Rope, Joe-Pye Weed *(Compositae).* The wild plant *E. cannabinum* is a tall, bushy plant of country lanes and damp ditches, where it grows very tall. Like many other European wild flowers it had medicinal virtues attributed to it so that John Pechey, in his *Compleat Herbal* of 1694 says "... 'tis epatick and Vulnerary. 'Tis chiefly used for an ill habit of Body; for Catarrhs, and Coughs; for Obstructions of Urine, and the Courses. It cures the Jaundice". Culpeper thought along the same lines and, though not much used nowadays, the plant contains a volatile oil that acts on the kidneys. Homeopaths use a tincture of the plant for influenza and feverish chills, and a hot tisane or infusion of the dried leaves gives relief at the onset of colds and catarrh. Several tropical varieties contain valuable medicinal properties. It is too large for the average plot, but its soft, brushy-looking lavender-pink flower heads look well in the wild garden and at the water's edge. There is an even larger and taller species *E. purpureum* which has darker flowers and which associates well with the native plant if there is the space for them. The leaves of the Eupatoriums are very like those of *Cannabis sativa*, the Indian Hemp, hence its Latin and common names.

E. cannabinum - Hemp Agrimony grows to 5ft (1.5m) with soft rose-lilac flowers from July to September. A large perennial plant from Europe and Asia, suitable for the wild garden, waterside, and quarry garden.

E. purpureum - Purple Joe-Pye Weed (1640) grows to 10ft (3m) with darker pink flowers from August to October. An even larger perennial from N. America for similar positions.

Requirements: Eupatoriums thrive best in damp conditions and full sun but will do almost as well in the border, though they will be smaller.
Cultivation: Divide mature plants in autumn or spring. Sow seeds in March in the open, thin out later.
Plants: Beth Chatto, Hillier.
Seeds: John Chambers, Chiltern.

EUPHORBIA *(Euphorbiaceae).* This is a huge genus with many plants that do not appear to be related at all. An example of this is the well-known Poinsettia, *E. pulcherrima* which is totally different at first – and second – glance to the plum-pudding shape of the succulent *E. obesa* that looks just like a firmly-stuffed pincushion topped with artificial flowers. In this huge family there are annuals, shrubs, climbers, succulents, viciously spined 'cacti' and even trees.

Most of the herbaceous Euphorbias are recognisable as such, having similar 'flowers' to the native Woodspurge *E. amygdaloides*. Almost all Euphorbias exude a milky latex when their stems are cut or otherwise damaged, and this is poisonous in some of the tropical varieties: it is highly irritant to sensitive skins, and must not be allowed to get into the eyes. As well as looking different, Euphorbias *are* different, with a unique form of inflorescence. This consists of five bracts that look like a normal calyx, a central female flower with a long-stalked ovary, surrounded by one or several male flowers each reduced to one stamen. This arrangement forms the often insignificant centre to the 'flower' and is called a cyathium. A typical example of this is *E. pulcherrima,* the Poinsettia, whose scarlet, pink or white 'petals' are in reality bracts.

Many of the European Euphorbias are the handsomest of plants, doing well in poor soils so long as the site is sunny. It is interesting, if space permits, to have a part of the garden devoted entirely to Euphorbias – there are so many of them, with differently coloured inflorescences, heights, habits and life-spans. Most of these were introduced more recently than the time-scale of this book, and so will not be described. Others, sometimes surprisingly, are classed as shrubs, like the Poinsettia, and are not included for that reason.

Their name of 'Spurge' is the same as 'purge' and in former times the sap was used for this medieval purpose. The native British Caper Spurge, *E. lathyrus* (which looks as though it has been designed by a structural engineer) was grown in monastery gardens for this purpose, and the seeds were often used as a substitute for pickled capers instead of the spiny Mediterranean shrub *Capparis spinosa.* Both uses were and are exceedingly dangerous. *E. lathyrus* is often called 'The Mole Plant' because its presence in the garden or orchard was thought to repel moles. Opinions differ as to its effectiveness, but as I grow *E. lathyrys* and have no moles – at present – I am prejudiced in the Euphorbia's favour while my lawns remain smooth and free of bumps. An old legend tells us that the plant had the power to open locks and release bolts and bars, and for this purpose it was much sought after in bygone times. One of the ways to obtain it was to seal the entrance to a woodpecker's nest. The unfortunate bird would fly away to find a piece of Caper Spurge which would magically release the obstruction. The bird would drop the plant as soon as its nest was freed, and the cunning watcher had merely to pick it up.

The Euphorbia's name was given to the genus by the learned king Juba II of Numibia and Mauretania (c. 52 BC – c. AD 24) who wrote a treatise on the known uses of the Spurge genus. He named them after his physician who was called Euphorbus.

E. heterophylla - Mexican Fire, Fire on the Mountain, Annual Poinsettia (1889) grows to 3ft (91.5cm) with scarlet bracts from July-September. An annual plant for the sunny border from both the Americas.

E. lathyrus - Caper Spurge, Mole plant grows to 3ft (91.5cm) with horizontally growing white-veined glaucous leaves that make it an unusually sculptural plant when grown in small groups. Green seeds and bracts in summer. Usually grown for its general appearance rather than the inflorescence. A European biennial for strategic places. (Ripe seed pods explode on hot days, flinging seed to considerable distances.)

E. marginata - Button-hole Flower, Snow on the the Mountain (1811), grows to 2ft (61cm) with attractive white-edged leaves. Inflorescence has white bracts. An annual from N. America for a sunny place.

Requirements: The hardy Euphorbias need sunny sites and do well in poor soil where leaf colour is better. They should never be moved when established.

Cultivation: Sow seeds of annual and biennial kinds in March or April in flowering positions, thin out. Sow seeds of perennial kinds in pots in a cold frame. When large enough prick out into nursery bed or individual pots. Shade bed, and keep pots sunk in ground. Plant in final position in autumn or best in spring in cold areas.

Seeds: Chiltern, Thomas Butcher, Naturescape, Suttons, Thompson and Morgan.

Plants: Ingwersen, Oak Cottage Herb Farm, Sherrards.

FOENICULUM - Fennel *(Umbelliferae).* Though generally classed as a herb, Fennel is included here because many people are now appreciating it as a foliage plant in the border. It has great beauty of form and foliage for many months of the year, and the heavy dews of autumn make it a thing of magical loveliness because one knows that in an hour the frosting of dewdrops will be gone. It has been used for hundreds of years for both medicinal and culinary purposes, and a sprig laid along a fish lends a delicacy only to be found by using the fresh plant. Fennel can be used to flavour cheese dishes, and is the main constituent in babies' Gripe water. It was always a magical plant, powerfully protective, and was put up over doorways on Midsummer's Eve to keep off evil spirits.

   Root, stem and leaves were used as a vegetable in Southern Europe, and at one time the Catholic poor used to eat Fennel on fast-days to assuage the craving for food. It has always had a certain reputation as a slimming agent, and in 1650 William Coles wrote in his book *Nature's Paradise* that "... both the seeds, leaves and root of our Garden Fennel are much used in drinks and broths for those that are grown fat, to abate their unweildiness and cause them to grow more gaunt and lank". The plant can grow to about 6 or 7ft (1.85-2.15m) in good soil, and its softly diffuse foliage makes an excellent smoky foil to the more positive outlines in the border. Once Fennel has been allowed to flower and seed, it will begin popping up everywhere, particularly in the paths.

   The stems should be cut down in late autumn, after the seeds have ripened, and in January it will be seen that feathery green fluffs are beginning to form. This is the time to move or divide the huge root. Seeds should be sown out of doors in March in shallow drills, thinned out and grown on. A small stock of spare plants should be kept by, because one spring the feathery green fluffs will not be there – Fennel is not a long-lived plant. There is a pleasing bronze-leaved variety that is equally useful in the kitchen and even more beautiful in the garden. The yellow flowers can be accented by planting yellow summer flowering daisy-type flowers in front of the Fennel – there are many of these, Heleniums, annual Helianthus and Coreopsis, and Evening Primrose and Achillea have different flower shapes and tones of yellow.

F. vulgare - Fennel grows to 6ft (1.85m) with diffuse green or bronze foliage in summer and yellow flowers in July and August. An early introduction from S. Europe.

Requirements: Almost any soil in full sun.

Cultivation: Sow seeds as described, or divide in spring.

After flowering: Cut down stems in November, seed ripens very late.

Plants: Most herb gardens.

Seeds: Most seedsmen.

FRITILLARIA - Fritillary *(Liliaceae).* The name of this genus comes from *Fritullus,* a 'dice-box', because of the shape of the flowers. Fritillaries of many kinds have been grown in gardens for over 400 years, most of them remaining unchanged in appearance during all this time. The most well-known is *F. imperialis,* the Crown Imperial, with its hanging bells of yellow or reddish orange. Curiously, there has never been a white variety but no doubt the hybridists will get to it in time. This is an astonishing plant – tall, stiff and stately, and out of place in a freezing English garden in early spring. The flowers are strong-smelling, to put it politely, and some people think this is unpleasant, but it is as violets when compared to the Dragon Arum.

   There are several legends about the flower – one is that it was once white and bloomed in the garden of Gethsemane. All the other flowers bowed their heads in sympathy, all, that is, except the Crown Imperial which remained stiffly upright. When gently rebuked by Our Lord, it bent its head and blushed crimson with shame, and tears dropped from its flowers. The 'tears' have been there ever since: in reality they are drops of nectar which do not fall even when the flower is shaken. Another story is of a Persian Queen who was wrongly accused of infidelity by her husband. An angel turned her into a Fritillary that still weeps in sadness.

The Crown Imperial has huge scaly bulbs with a hollow centre. They should be deeply planted on their sides in a warm, sunny border, on a cushion of sharp sand for drainage. They need not be disturbed for many years, though they do not flower well and continuously in all gardens. The bulbs are poisonous.

The Snake's Head Fritillary – *F. meleagris* – a dainty, viperish-looking plant with snake-like flower buds in a range of sombre shadowed colours. All are chequered, even the white ones, and this unusual petal colouration is rare in the plant world. The name 'meleagris' means a guinea-fowl. This little flower is very particular as to where it grows, liking moist, humus-rich soil and semi-shade. It will grow in grass, increasing by self-sown seed, but in most gardens fresh bulbs will need to be planted every few years to keep the group from dwindling away. I have found that if you plant one of anything, particularly if it is rare and expensive (this is why you only plant one) it often dies. Plant three, and two will survive. Plant eleven and they hold their own; plant two dozen and they begin to increase. Such is the cussedness of the vegetable world. So the moral of beautiful bulbs is, never plant one. Go without something inessential like new saucepans or a holiday, and put the cats on a starvation diet (which will encourage them to stir themselves to catch mice that are eating the bonemeal in the shed) but never plant one of anything. Unless, perhaps, it's a Wellingtonia.

Some of the common names for *F. meleagris* are not kind ones – Snake-flower, Toad's heads, Widow-veil, Sullen Lady, Madam Ugly, Dead Men's Bells, Death Bell, Widow Wail and the Drooping Bell of Sodom. Perhaps our forefathers were right to worry about this flower because it is now known that *F. meleagris* yields a poison called imperialine.

F. imperialis - Crown Imperial (before 1590) grows to 4ft (122cm) with darkly spotted stems and yellow *(F. imperialis lutea)* or reddish *(F. imperialis rubra)* bell-shaped flowers in March and April. A bulb from the W. Himalaya for a sunny border. Does well in heavy soil.

F. meleagris - Snake's head Fritillary grows to 15in (38cm) with chequered flowers in shades of maroon, purple mauve, pink, slaty grey, cream and white. A European bulb for a lightly shaded place, it does particularly well in grass.

F. recurva (1870) grows to 3ft (91.5cm) with red and yellow flowers in spring. A bulb from California for a sunny border.

Requirements: All Fritillaries need good soil and most need sun and a sheltered situation.

Cultivation: *See text* for *F. imperialis* and *F. meleagris*. Do not disturb bulbs that are flowering well.

After flowering: Cut down flowering stems when leaves turn yellow.

Bulbs: Amand, Avon, Bees, Broadleigh, Christian, de Jager, Ingwersen, Kelways, Orpington, Potterton and Martin, Stassen, van Tubergen.

GAILLARDIA - Blanket Flower *(Compositae)*. The Gaillardia was named after Gaillard de Marentonneau, a French magistrate who was an amateur botanist. One of the parents of the modern hybrids is *G. aristata* which is still grown today. It is a slightly tender plant, needing good drainage and a sunny position, but its large, jolly-coloured flowers have a long season of bloom which truly earns them a place in the sun. The annual *G. pulchella* has hairier grey-green leaves which may have given rise to the plant's common name of Blanket Flower, or it might have been that a mass of the flowers in bloom with their banded petals of red and yellow looked like the patterns on a brightly coloured Indian blanket. (One of the modern varieties is appropriately called 'Indian Chief'.)

Gaillardias are particularly good in hot weather, and withstand drought conditions well – it is the winter wet of Northern Europe that they cannot bear. Since these American daisies are not really hardy, cuttings should be taken from the perennial varieties in late summer and over-wintered in a cold frame to be planted out in late spring. Seeds of perennial kinds may be sown out of doors in May or June, or under glass in February or March at a temperature of 15°C (59°F). These latter will flower the same year, the ones in open ground should be protected by cloches during the winter months except in the extreme South-West.

G. aristata (1812) grows to 3ft (91.5cm) with yellow or yellow and red flowers from June to November. A tender perennial from W. North America for the sunny border.

G. pulchella (1787) grows to 18in (46cm) with (usually) yellow flowers from July to October. A perennial, usually grown as an annual, from Central N. America for a sunny border.

Requirements: Light, well-drained soil and protection in winter. Twiggy sticks to support taller growing kinds.

Cultivation: *See text.*

During and after flowering: Dead-head, cut down stems in autumn.

Uses: Good in hot corners. As cut flowers.

Plants: Hillier, Holden Clough, Scotts.

GALANTHUS - Snowdrop *(Amaryllidaceae)*. Harbinger of spring that it is, the Snowdrop is often the first of the spring flowering bulbs to come out in the garden. It has some very fine forms though these are surprisingly expensive per bulb and therefore it is often better to have a great many of *G. nivalis* (the 'ordinary' kind – which are sold in tens or fifties, and save a special and very visible place for the more precious varieties. The Snowdrop was first grown in monastery gardens because of its association with Candlemas Day (February 2nd) and the Feast of the Purification of the Virgin. On this day, the statues of the Virgin Mary were removed from the altars and Snowdrops were left in the empty places. Another tale is told of the departure of Adam and Eve from the Garden of Eden. Snow was falling and the cold and unhappy pair were cheered by an angel who took pity on them, telling them that though it was winter, spring would soon follow. The angel touched the falling snowflakes and they were instantly changed into Snowdrops.

When taking walks in the wilder parts of the country in early spring it is infuriating to see the gardens or orchards of ruined farmhouses fairly spilling over with these flowers – growing so closely together that they surge over walls and come up through cracks in concrete paths. Where they like to grow they do well, and seem to like to grow undisturbed, in spite of what the gardening books say; we are constantly being exhorted to divide, split and feed, but when one has just seen an acre or so of spring woodland totally covered with Snowdrops (neglected and un-managed) then it makes one think.

When bringing Snowdrops into the house, try standing the first bowlful on a circular mirror with a bevalled edge but no frame. This will reflect most charmingly the inside of the bell which is seldom seen. The Snowdrop has learned to survive by retaining day-time warmth within its bell, and the night temperature (just before dawn) is sometimes two degrees warmer inside the flower.

The name Galanthus comes from *gala*, 'milk', and *anthos*, 'flower'. The more special kinds of Snowdrop need particular situations in the garden, whereas *G. nivalis* will do just about anywhere, as long as your soil suits it and you can refrain from fiddling about with it. It is a determined little plant altogether, with a mind of its own and will flower in its own time too; it will not tolerate attempts at forcing. Snowdrops do not mind other things near them as long as the leaves of these later plants do not cover the fading Snowdrop foliage until after April.

G. byzantinus (1893) grows to 8in (20.5cm) with larger flowers from November to January. A fine bulb from Broussa for the partially shaded rockery.

G. Elwesii (1875) grows to 10in (25.5cm) with double green markings in the inner petals. Flowers from January to February. A bulb from Asia Minor for a special site.

G. nivalis - Snowdrop average height 8in (20.5cm). Flowers of variable size according to locality, from February to March. A bulb for massed planting in deciduous shrubberies, light woodland, orchards, lawn-edges, or places where it will not be disturbed.

Requirements: Good rich, moisture-retentive soil on the heavy side; partial shade.

Cultivation: Snowdrop clumps can be carefully divided after flowering, replant immediately to same depth. Do leave clumps undisturbed for as long as possible; plant bulbs early in autumn, (end August not too soon) or acquire 'in the green' after flowering and plant immediately.

Bulbs: Amand, Avon, Helen Ballard, Bees, Broadleigh, Ingwersen, Kelways, Potterton and Martin, Stassen, van Tubergen.

GALEGA - Goat's Rue, French Lilac (*Leguminosae*). The name comes from Gala, 'milk', because the plant was fed to livestock in the belief that it was particularly effective in increasing the milk yield; this has since been proved to be true.

Goat's Rue is an unusual plant to grow as a good-sized clump at the back or middle of the border, depending on the height of the other plants. Galega grows to 2½ft (76cm) but seen as a mass of flowers and foliage (consisting of at least three plants) it is most attractive, with bright green leaves and unusual, somewhat Lupin-like, lilac flowers. It has interesting cousins like Woad (*Isatis tinctoria*), used by the ancient Britons to paint themselves and their possessions blue and indigo, and an American plant *G. toxicana* that was once used to catch fish. This plant was bruised and thrown into still water, where it had an intoxicating effect on the fish who would rise to the surface in an insensible state to be easily collected. If grown on the banks of certain rivers in England, unethical non-fishing persons could put it to good use – think of all that time saved.

In the Middle Ages it was used medicinally to alleviate fevers and like many plants at that time was thought to cure or at least to lessen the dreadful symptons of the various plagues; in Germany it was called Pestilenzkraut.

Galega has rosy-lilac flowers and is the best to grow in a mixed border; the white form is inclined to look like a larger Melilot unless it is deliberately grown as a group and set against a dark background. It is a good 'flopper' for concealing earlier-flowering plants after their season of bloom.

G. officinalis - Goat's Rue (1568) grows to 2½ft (76cm) with spikes of rose-lilac pea-flowers in June and July. Var. 'Alba' is taller and has white flowers. A vigorous perennial from S. Europe and Asia Minor for a large sunny border or the wilder parts of the garden.

Requirements: A sunny situation and light, free-draining soil. Provide twiggy sticks for support.

Cultivation: Sow seeds in April in a nursery bed and grow on, plant out in flowering positions in the following spring. Roots may be divided in spring.

After flowering: Cut flower stems down.

Plants: Oak Cottage, St. Bridget, Stoke Lacy, Weald Herbary.

Seeds: Chiltern.

GALTONIA - Summer Hyacinth *(Liliaceae)*. The Galtonia was named after Sir Francis Galton, (1822-1911) who travelled extensively in S.W. Africa. In addition to writing about his travels, he advocated finger-printing as a method of identification. Not really like a Hyacinth, Galtonias are taller and looser in form. If anything, they look like giant white Bluebells. A little used name is Spire Lily, which is slightly more appropriate. These are summer flowering bulbs whose stems rise to a height of 4ft (122cm) in good soil. They should be planted in groups of seven or nine or they will not show up against the ebullience of the summer borders as well as they deserve to. Slugs adore the emerging leaves and it is difficult to preserve the plants from their nightly devastations. I have grown the bulbs on in large pots to be carefully transplanted with as much soil as possible, and this works well, as far as protection goes, but the stems do not grow as tall as they might in a less pest infested garden. But better shorter Galtonias than no Galtonias at all – this is often the reason that people say "the bulbs just didn't come up!" The bulbs in question probably did, but a passing gastropod will have observed this new and succulent morsel and will have consumed it joyfully. Once the growing tip has gone the more special bulbs are inclined to give up.

The bulbs should be planted at least 6ins (15cm) deep in spring, grouping them together in uneven numbers. The leaves can grow to 2ft (61cm) but the bulbs can be randomly planted and the flower stems have more impact when they are seen as if naturally crowding together.

G. candicans - Summer Hyacinth grows to 4ft (122cm) with spires of pure white scented bells from July to September. A bulb from S. Africa for the sunny border.

Requirements: A situation that is sheltered from strong winds, light rich soil.

Cultivation: *See text.*

After flowering: Cut down stems.

Uses: Late summer border plants, beautiful as tall cut flowers.

Bulbs: Amand, Avon, Beth Chatto, Bloms, Broadleigh, Peter Chappell, de Jager, Goatchers.

GAURA *(Oenotheraceae)*. This is an exquisite, love-at-first sight border plant, though difficult to define why. The individual flowers are nothing special, it is just the overall effect of a mass of them. Once you have it you will have to defend it from your gardening friends whose morals (when it comes to plant acquiring) are often surprisingly lax. Gauras are rarely offered at nurseries, and are therefore best grown from seed.

G. Lindheimeri (1850) grows to 4ft (1.22m) with spikes of pink-toned white flowers from July until the frosts. A perennial plant from Texas for a sheltered border.

Requirements: Sun, ordinary soil and protection with litter in winter.

Uses: As an unusual border subject and as even more unusual cut flowers.

Cultivation: Sow seeds in spring in boxes of John Innes seed compost in a warm greenhouse and grow on in the usual way, transferring seedlings into individual pots. Keep in frame for first winter and plant out in final position in second year after frosts.

Seeds: Chiltern.

GAZANIA - Treasure Flower *(Compositae)*. Gazanias are one of the brightest-coloured of the sun-loving daisies, with firm, brilliant flowers in almost neon shades of orange and yellow which seem all the brighter when seen against their contrasting greyish leaves. It is thought that Gazanias were named after Theodore of Gaza who translated the works of the Greek philosopher Theophrastus into Latin. Though they are perennials in their native S. Africa, they have to be grown as annuals in Northern Europe though if there is space they can be lifted and overwintered in a greenhouse that is warm and dry – they are not happy in humidity.

Gazanias close in late afternoon and in any case do not open in wet weather, but their showy colours, enhanced by a black zone, more than make up for this. They are easily propagated from side shoots taken from the base of the plant and put in pots of sand to root. Take these cuttings in July, and grow on in a cold frame for the winter; or best in a greenhouse at a mean temperature of 7 - 10°C (45 - 50°F). Harden off and plant out in June. They have attractive leaves, silver beneath, and a compact habit of growth which makes them pleasing rockery plants, particularly if they can be planted to tumble naturally over the edge of a miniature declivity. Since their colour range is from bright to brilliant, their neighbours can be easily eclipsed and this also should be taken into consideration when siting them. Grow things above, below and on each side, that will not suffer from the proximity of these dazzlers. The stonework, if large and substantial, is an excellent natural foil for them, but so is a paved path, with Eschscholzias, a white flowered Campanula, some Gypsophila and the grey-mauve of Catmint nearby to cool things down a little. Species plants are still found occasionally but most Gazanias are hybrid plants best grown from seed sown in January or February at a temperature of 16°C (61°F) and treated as half-hardy annuals.

Plants: *See text*
Seeds: Thomas Butcher, Thompson and Morgan.

GENTIANA - Gentian *(Gentianaceae).* The Gentian is named after Gentius, King of Illyrica (more or less where Yugoslavia is now) who is said to have discovered the medicinal value of these plants. In South America, Gentians are usually red, whereas in Europe they are almost always the characteristically intense blue, with the exception (there is always an exception in the plant world) of *G. lutea,* which is yellow. All Gentians have a bitter property which has a tonic quality in medicine and which is used as a flavouring. Gentian root was used, with other herbs, for brewing before the introduction of hops. *G. lutea* is the most important of the Gentians and it is one of the largest of the species, with a yard-long tap-root. This is still used medicinally today as a tonic, to relieve dyspepsia, to alleviate the effects of jaundice and to reduce feverish temperatures. It has strong antiseptic properties. The plant is tall and stately, with yellow flowers in whorls at the top of the 4-ft (122-cm) stems. Many virtues have been attributed to the plant in Culpeper's time, and he says that it "... comforts the heart and preserves it against faintings and swoonings: The powder of the dry roots helps the biting of mad dogs and venomous beasts. The herb steeped in wine, and the wine drank, refreshes such as be over-weary with traveling, and grow lame in their joints, either by cold or evil lodgings: it helps stitches, and gripping pains in the sides: is an excellent remedy for such as are bruised by falls ... when Kine are bitten on the udder by any venomous beast, do but stroke the place with the decoction of any of these and it will instantly heal them."

Gentians are not easy, but of all flowers they are worth the trouble to get their growing conditions right. In the wild they are upland and mountain flowers, enjoying hot, scree conditions and a covering of snow in winter. Cold, therefore, does not worry them. The Willow Gentian, *G. asclepiadea,* is one of the easiest if the soil is permanently damp and lightly shaded, and the wild *G. pneumonanthe* likes nothing better and wetter than a warm, sunny bog (one has only to look at its name). It closes quickly, often permanently, in dull weather, refusing altogether to open again. *G. sino-ornata* needs an acid soil, ideally a compost of sand, leaf-mould and peat. It must not be allowed to dry out in the spring and early summer. Gentians do not like the drip from trees, though they appreciate their shade during the middle of the day. *G. acaulis* needs an open sunny position, but again, it should not be allowed to dry out during the growing season. It likes a covering of grit over the roots, and may even move itself by degrees to a nearby gravel path. Gentians do better in the more northern parts of the British Isles, because the temperature is cooler and wetter. It is comforting to read that even in the sixteenth century gardeners had just as much difficulty in establishing Gentians as we do today, and many and various were the composts that were tried in order to persuade them to flourish and flower. In the Language of Flowers, *G. lutea* meant 'ingratitude' because it nearly always died in spite of every care and attention. *G. acaulis* will usually grow for you but flowering is another thing – it may form a little patch of exquisite and purest blue in the rockery soon after you plant it there and then may never flower again. If it is possible to see the Gentians in flower before purchasing them then this is the thing to do.

The European types flower in spring and the Asiatic kinds in autumn. They are fairly easily grown from seed and may take to you and your garden better this way. It is important to obtain fresh, ripe seed: sow this in boxes or pans of a peat-based compost in October and put the pans in the freezing compartment of a domestic fridge for a short time to aid germination. Leave in a cold frame for the winter. When the seedlings do germinate, prick out when large enough and grow on. Pot up in individual pots of John Innes No. 1 and leave plunged in the ground in the frame until it is time to plant them out, usually in September. Once planted, do not disturb them. The blue Gentians have a fascination for most, if not all gardeners, because of their wonderful colour and, more realistically, because they are difficult to grow.

G. acaulis syn. **G. gentianella** grows to 3in (7.5cm) and may spread beautifully for 1ft (46cm) with intensely blue trumpets in May and June, when it has the right conditions. A perennial from Europe for the rockery (must not be limestone).

G. asclepiadea - Willow Gentian, Swallow-wort (1629) grows to 2ft (61cm) and has arching leaf stems with blue trumpets in July and August. Needs a semi-shaded moist situation. A European perennial for light woodland, streamside and shaded borders.

G. farreri is of prostrate habit with 8-in (20.5-cm) flower stems. Sky blue flowers from August to October. Tolerates lime. A perennial from N.W. China and Tibet for the rockery.

G. lutea - Yellow Gentian grows to 6ft (1.85m) with yellow flowers in July and August. A European perennial for partly shaded border with moisture-retentive soil. Do not try to move when established.

G. septemfida grows to 12in (30.5cm) with blue flowers in July and August. A variable perennial from W. Asia for the edge of the border or rockery.

G. sino-ornata grows to 6in (15cm) and spreads to 15in (38cm). Blue flowers in September and November. Does well in acid soil. A perennial from W. China and Tibet for a place in a semi-shaded rockery.

Requirements: *See text.*
Cultivation: *See text.*
Plants: Most nurseries.
Seeds: Chambers, Chiltern, Kent County Nurseries.

GERANIUM - Crane's Bill *(Geraniaceae).* These are the perennial herbaceous plants that are such a feature of summer borders. The many-coloured flowers seen in pots, troughs, hanging baskets and dripping from balconies in Europe are Pelargoniums. Geraniums are delightful plants, absolutely no trouble and increasing gently and politely over the years. When half their circumference starts to cover about four feet of lawn it is time to divide them up in early spring, but until then they need no attention. Some varieties grow very quickly in early summer, and will engulf their slower-thinking neighbours if not prevented, but this is an excellent thing in some cases because it means that all the Daffodil leaves vanish opportunely under a tide of very attractive foliage. Geranium leaves are always pleasing – they vary in size, colour and texture, but most of the larger ones can be used with good effect in flower arrangements, especially *G. endressii* and the pale green aromatic ones of *G. macrorrhizum*.

The blue Geraniums are truly beautiful, even as the flowers die – when the last petals are ready to fall they all fall together, making a pool of upside-down sky on the grass.

In Viking times a blue-grey dye was extracted from one of the blue flowered kinds – it is not known which of the two natives it was – *G. pratense* or *G. sylvaticum* – though it was more likely to have been the latter, as this is a plant of the Northern British Isles whose range does extend as far as Iceland. The colour was described as 'fittest for fighting heroes' and one can imagine the Vikings coming up out of the cold sea, clad in garments of the same colour that soon would be dyed again, this time to crimson.

The Meadow Crane's Bill *G. pratense* was called by an old name – 'Odin's Grace' or 'Odin's Favour' so perhaps it was this flower that was used to colour the raiment of the sea-wolves from the North. The French called the flower 'Bassinettes' because it was bowl-shaped, and in Somerset it is still occasionally called 'Blue Basins' which is almost the same thing. It would be interesting to know the story behind the Wiltshire name of 'Loving Andrews'.

G.phaeum is an evergreen plant, unlike most of the family, with tiny flowers of an unusual blackish red. This is a rare flower-colour and this Geranium is a most obliging soul, growing quite happily in the rather dry shade beneath deciduous trees. It must be said that it will grow better in full sun, but it does well under my greedy Laburnum which in turn is overshadowed by a gigantic Philadelphus. It must have some direct sunlight for part of the day but is impervious to drip.

G.sanguinem is a prostrate, bright magenta-flowered plant, looking delightful when creeping among the graceful leaves and flowers of the blue *Iris siberica* – both are in flower at the same time.

G. Endressii grows to 12in (30.5cm) with a circumference of about a yard (0.95m) when mature. It has dark, almost evergreen leaves and pink flowers from May to August. A handsome circular plant throughout the winter, a perennial from the Pyrenees for the border and large rockery. Does quite well in partial shade.

G. ibericum now more correctly **G. x magnificum** (1802) grows to 24in (61cm) with intense violet-blue flowers in July and August. A perennial from the Caucasus for the spring border.

G. macrorrhizum (1576) grows to a lax 18in (46cm) with large easily-broken aromatic stems and roots. Pink, red or mauve flowers from May to July. A perennial from S. Europe for the border and in semi-shade.

G. phaeum - Mourning Widow, Dusky Crane's Bill grows to 18in (46cm) with blackish crimson flowers in May and June. A native evergreen perennial for the border and in light shade.

G. sanguineum - Bloody Crane's Bill. A scrambling, trailing prostrate plant with magenta or white flowers from June to September. A native perennial plant for rockeries, walls, banks and border-edges. Quite happy in sandy soil.

G. tuberosum (1596) grows to 9in (23cm) with purple-pink flowers in May. A tuberous-rooted perennial from Afghanistan for a sunny border or large rockery.

Requirements: Most Geraniums need to be planted in full sun. Any soil suits them, but they do better if it is light and free-draining.

Cultivation: Divide established clumps in early spring. Sow seeds in August in a cold frame, prick out into boxes for the winter and transplant into nursery rows for the summer. Move into final positions in the following spring. Protect small plants from slugs.

After flowering: Not essential, but the stems and leaves of vigorous border varieties such as *G.endressii* can be sheared off to encourage a second flush of flowers and a neat new crop of leaves for the autumn and winter.

Uses: Excellent border and rockery plants according to size. Leaves of many varieties good for arrangements.

Plants: Most nurseries.

Seeds: Chambers, Chiltern.

GERBERA - Transvaal Daisy *(Compositae).* Gerberas were named after Traugott Gerber, a German naturalist who travelled widely in Russia. The species plants are mostly found in S. Africa, and have huge daisy-shaped flowers about 5in (12.5cm) across in shades of orange-scarlet. They are not hardy except in the most westerly parts of the British Isles and should be grown in pots which can be sunk in the ground or stood out in a sunny summer corner. They can be very successfully grown in a greenhouse or conservatory. The seeds should be sown in February or March at a temperature of 16 - 18°C (61 - 64°F) in an ordinary seed compost. When large enough, prick off and grow on into larger pots of John Innes No. 2 if the Gerberas are to remain in these, or into temporary pots if they are to be planted in the ground. Harden off and plant out for the summer, where they will need a situation at the base of a warm south-facing wall. They will make an amazing display when grown well. If they are to be overwintered they should be lifted and brought into a warm greenhouse with a mean temperature of 5 - 7°C (41 - 45°F). Water very sparingly. Re-pot in spring into a similar compost if the plants are to stay in their pots.

G. jamesonii - Barberton Daisy (1887) grows to 15in (38cm) with huge orange-scarlet flowers from May to August. A tender perennial from the Transvaal for a sheltered sunny border or large pots on a patio. This is a good place for them because they are so strikingly large and bright that they do not generally associate well with the gentler tonalities of the herbaceous border.

Requirements: *See text.*

Cultivation: *See text.*

Uses: As superb cut or out-door pot plants.

Seeds: Chiltern, Suttons, Thompson and Morgan.

GEUM *(Rosaceae).* This is one of the few herbaceous members of the great family of roses. Geums are easy, undemanding plants that have single or semi-double flowers with waved petals in shades of yellow, orange and true scarlet. The plants come from various parts of the world and are rather prone to hybridise when they meet, so if more plants of named varieties are wanted then they should be propagated vegetatively.

G.chiloense, formerly *G.quellyon*, is one of the parents of most of the border plants that are grown today. Geums seem not to have made much of an impact on the garden scene, perhaps because when space is limited they are not definitely different enough. But as they have such a long flowering season, can be chosen to blend or contrast with their neighbours and are so very easy and undemanding, they should be seen more often. They need to be planted in a group of three or more plants of the same colour, and then you will be glad that you gave them house-room. One of the quieter species is *G.rivale* which has nodding tomato-coloured flowers like small Columbines: it grows very well in shade and is evergreen, though it likes best to be at the edge of water or to be planted where the soil is permanently moist. It will get along quite well in the ordinary border, so it is a very good ground-coverer. If you are plagued as I am with its cousin the weedy *G.urbanum*, you may have to wait until both flower to sort out which is which because the leaves are rather similar. *G.urbanum* has small yellow flowers and seed-capsules with determined hooks to them. All the Geum genus roots are aromatic to some degree, and were formerly dried and powdered to be used as moth and vermin repellants.

G. chiloense (1826) is not often seen and has been superseded by the more 'modern' cultivars: 'Mrs Bradshaw' is one such fine old lady of about 80 years of age with excellent red flowers. Most of these hybrids grow to about 2ft (61cm) and should be planted in a sunny border.

G. rivale - Water Avens grows to 1ft (30.5cm) (lower in dry conditions) with evergreen leaves and reddish flowers in May and June. A native perennial for shaded borders and pond sides.

G. montanum grows to 12in (30.5cm) with silver leaves and yellow flowers from May to July, followed by fluffy seed heads. A European perennial for the damper rock garden.

Requirements: Ordinary soil in sunny border and rock garden situations except for *G. rivale.*

Cultivation: Sow seeds of named varieties at a temperature of 15 - 20°C (60 - 68°F) in January/February, or February/March in a cold frame. Prick out and grow on in a nursery bed. Set out in autumn in southern areas and spring in northern counties. Divide established plants in spring.

Uses: As cut, border and rockery plants.

Plants: Most nurseries.

Seeds: Thomas Butcher, Chiltern, Dobie, Suttons, Thompson and Morgan.

GILIA *(Polemoniaceae).* These are flowers that are not often seen and as the annual kinds are very easy to grow it is worth trying some in the garden next year. They are named after Philipp Salvador Gil, an eighteenth-century Spanish botanist. Two of the blue-flowered sorts such as *G.capitata* – Queen Anne's Thimbles, and *G.achilleifolia*, are particularly pretty when grown in a dense mass so that the small flowers trail through surrounding plants. Seed can be sown in March where the plants are to flower, and thinned out later, or the seed can be sown in September in a cold frame. The seedlings are delicate and easily broken, so if the seed is sown thinly in boxes it should be grown on undisturbed and a rectangle of well-grown seedlings and compost – or several rectangles – can be planted out as it is in the border.

G. achilleifolia syn. **G. abrotanifolia** (1833) grows to 2ft (61cm) with pale blue clusters of flowers in July and August. A delicate and unusual annual from S. California for a sunny border.

G. capitata - Queen Anne's Thimbles (1826) grows to 2ft (61cm) with dense heads of blue flowers from June to September. An annual from California for a sunny border.

G. tricolor - Bird's Eye (1833) grows to 2½ft (76cm) with pale violet flowers with a maroon zone at the base. An annual from California for the border.

Requirements: Full sun and a rich sandy soil.

Cultivation: *See text.*

Uses: For massing in borders and as cut flowers.

Seed: Thomas Butcher, Chiltern, Dobie, Thompson and Morgan.

GLADIOLUS *(Iridaceae).* The Gladiolus is one of the most handsome summer flowering corms and is deservedly popular because it is so easy to grow. The smaller-flowered species kinds have been known to gardeners for many hundreds of years, though they were mostly grown for medicinal purposes. The large flowered modern hybrids do not come within the scope of this book. The earliest record of Gladioli being grown is in Henry Lyte's *Nievve Herball* and in 1597 Gerard had two European kinds – *G.communis* and *G.segatum* in his garden. He considered the Gladiolus very useful to make a poultice that would draw out splinters. Gradually more kinds were introduced – in 1604 *G.imbricatum* had been discovered and by 1629

Parkinson was growing *G.byzantinus* which is still obtainable. Almost all of the Gladioli came from S. Africa and most of the early flowers were pink, cerise, red or white. A trickle of new kinds found their way to Europe as South Africa was explored more thoroughly, and in 1745 the sweet-scented *G.tristis* was found in Natal. This had pale yellow flowers and was one of the first of this colour to be discovered. In 1904 Sir F. Fox designed and built the bridge over the Zambesi at Victoria Falls and the yellow-flowered *G.primulinus* was discovered growing in the spray of the thundering waters of the Victoria Falls. Though Gladioli are sun-lovers, this variety had developed hooded petals to protect its floral parts from the drenching spray. This characteristic and the new yellow-to-orange colour were seized upon by the hybridists to add the variety of shape and form which has resulted in the larger modern flowers.

Prepare the ground for Gladioli in the autumn before, well-rotted manure should be spread on the surface in October and dug in, and in March or April bonemeal should be scattered over the soil at a rate of 3oz (85g) to the square yard (0.84 square metre). Plant the corms 6in (15cm) deep in free draining soil, and 4in (10cm) deep in heavy soil and in the latter case sit them on a pillow of sharp sand for drainage. Put in a stake at this time suitable to the ultimate size of the plant (to serve as a reminder of its whereabouts as well). The more delicate species Gladioli do not need staking. Stakes are never attractive, but they can be painted green, or bamboo canes can be used and either is better than a Gladioli in full bloom face down in the mud after a summer rainstorm. Owing to man's interference they are heavy plants and need a little help. After the flowers are over cut off the spike, leaving some leaves at the base of the stem to feed the new corms. When the foliage turns yellow the corms should be carefully lifted (about mid-October) and the stem cut off ½in (1.3cm) above the old corm. Arrange them in a single layer in an airy place so that the soil can dry, then clean each one. The exhausted flowering corm can be broken away from the cluster of new corms, separating the large ones from the small 'cormlets' or 'spawn': label and store them in a dry airy place for the winter, such as the top of the wardrobe in the spare bedroom. The smaller species types appreciate leaf-mould and should not be allowed to dry out during the summer.

G. byzantinus (1629) grows to 2ft (61cm) with magenta-purple flowers in June. Hardier than most and can be left in the ground in southern counties.

G. communis (1596) grows to 2ft (61cm) with pink or white flowers from May to July. A corm from the Mediterranean region.

G. imbricatus (1820) grows to 2ft (61cm) with purple flowers from June to July. A corm from Eastern Europe.

Requirements: *See text.*

Cultivation: *See text.*

Corms of species Gladioli: Amand, Avon, Broadwell, Holden Clough, Ingwersen, Kelways, Orpington, van Tubergen.

GLOXINIA - See **Sinningia** *(Gesneriaceae).*

GODETIA - Farewell to Spring, Summer's Darling *(Onagraceae).* The original Godetia was named after C. H. Godet (1797-1879) a long-lived Swiss botanist. The present-day plants have been derived from *G.amoena*, *G.whitneyi* and others. *G.grandiflora* was discovered in 1867 and has given rise to a separate sst of smaller modern flowers. These are so easy to grow that they are included in children's seed packets, and when they come up they always look just like a posy of flowers all ready to put into a vase. Godetias can be grown to flower as pot plants in the greenhouse or conservatory where their bright satin flowers remain cheerfully pretty for two months or more. For these winter flowers, sow seeds in September under glass and grow on in the usual way, transplanting into 5-in (12.5-cm) pots of John Innes No. 1. For next year's flowers in the garden, seeds can be sown in September in the open ground and the young plants protected with cloches through the winter. Slugs absolutely adore the seedlings. Normal sowings in the spring can be made either under glass in February or March, or in April in the flowering position, to be thinned out later. From this it will be seen that the Godetia is a most useful and good-natured plant. The modern hybrids are hardly recognisable as Godetias, and unfortunately they are usually the only seeds that can be obtained. When a flower has a shape that typifies it, it is annoying to see pictures and excitable descriptions in the catalogues, which say 'Anemone-flowered, Peony-flowered, Lily-flowered, Cactus-flowered and so on, and when the thing comes up it is not recognisable as anything in particular.

G. grandiflora syn **G. amoena whitneyi - Godetia** grows to 15in (38cm) with rose-purple flowers from June to August. An annual plant from W. North America for the border.

Requirements: Full sun and a moisture-retentive soil.

Cultivation: *See main text.*

Uses: As border, cut and pot plants.

Seeds: Chiltern: most seedsmen for modern varieties.

GYPSOPHILA - Baby's Breath, Chalk Plant *(Caryophyllaceae)*. No garden should be without this useful but ethereal plant. It acts as a frame, a foil, a background and as contrast to almost everything else and there is no other plant like it. A mature plant in full flower is a sight to see and was always much used in old-fashioned herbaceous borders.

G. *paniculata* produces a positive cloud of tiny pink or white flowers (it is related to the Dianthus, but is, alas, scentless) and established plants should not be moved. The ultimate spread of the plant should be considered when planting, as a full-blown Gypsophila can be about 4ft (122cm) wide and this must be allowed for.

The name Gypsophila comes from *Gypsos,* gypsum, and *philos,* loving. (The small rockery plant G. *repens* grows well on gypsum rocks.) In the Language of Flowers Gypsophila is not mentioned at all, which is surprising, because G. *paniculata* was introduced in 1759 and must have been well-known. Friendship was personified by the Acacia or Ivy, early friendship was the blue Periwinkle, true friendship by the Oakleaved Geranium and unchanging friendship by the *Arbor vitae.* It has occurred to me that both donor and recipient, when using this floral language, would have had to have had a considerable knowledge of plants of all kinds or the most unfortunate mistakes would have happened and lover's tiffs might have widened into chasms as wide and deep as Colorado.

G. elegans (1828) grows to 20in (51cm) with much branched panicles of pink or white flowers from May to September. An annual from Asia Minor for the sunny border.

G. paniculata - Gypsophila, Baby's Breath (1759), grows to 4ft (122cm) with large panicles of tiny white or pink flowers from June to August. A perennial from Eastern Europe and Siberia for the large border.

G. repens syn. **G. prostrata** (1774) grows only to 6in (15cm), forming a trailing mat of grey-green leaves with pink flowers from June to August. A delightful cascading plant for the sunny rockery from the European Alps.

Requirements: Full sun and for border flowers dry soil (Gypsophila dislikes acid soils). Twiggy sticks as 'invisible' supports for G. *paniculata.*

Cultivation: Some broken and powdered brick rubble mixed in with the soil will be appreciated; sow annual seeds thinly in March and grow on and thin out in the usual way. Sow perennial seeds in boxes of John Innes No. 1 in March, grow on and plant out in nursery rows or large pots. Set out in the following spring. Take lateral non-flowering cuttings from G. *repens* in

May, put in a sand and peat mix to root. Grow on in John Innes No. 1.
Uses: No flower-arranger or florist can be without a row of *G. paniculata.* Even in death it may be used as a misty brown cloud in winter arrangements.
Plants: Most nurseries.
Seeds: Thomas Butcher, Chiltern, Dobie, Suttons, Thompson and Morgan.

HEDYCHIUM - Ginger Lily *(Zingiberaceae).* Hedychiums are all very sweet scented and are very easy to grow, providing you do what they want you to do. They are so vigorous when they become established that their roots often burst the pot. The plant's name comes from *Hedys,* 'sweet', and *chion,* 'snow', as one of the first plants to be introduced in 1791 was the Sweet Scented Garland Flower or the Ginger Lily, which had white flowers.

H. gardnerianum is fairly easy to obtain and is perfectly happy outside in hot summers. It makes a very handsome (shaded) patio plant producing imposing spikes of tubular creamy-yellow flowers with bright red stamens. The plant will grow to about 5 or 6ft (1.60 or 1.85m) and will need a large pot – and a conservatory to match if the summer is a cold, wet one. Hedychiums should be planted in a compost of loam, sharp sand and well-rotted manure, and when they begin to grow they should have fortnightly liquid feeds and will need to be watered three times a day in hot weather. After the flowers are over the stems should be cut down unless the unusual scarlet seeds are wanted for winter decor. When the plant begins to die down it should be allowed to rest in the winter and should be kept in the same way as Cannas.

H. gardnerianum - Ginger Lily (1819) grows to 6ft (1.85m) with handsome ridged, leathery leaves. Spikes of scented yellow flowers from August to September. A tender rhizomatous plant from N. India for a greenhouse, border or as a handsome pot plant for conservatories or patio.
Requirements: *See text.*
Cultivation: *See text.*
Plants: Amand, de Jager, Holtzhausen, Treasures of Tenbury.

HELENIUM - Sneezeweed *(Compositae).* These are flowers that are named for the sun, and in ancient Greece they were called 'Helenion'. The central disk sits on the petals like the hub of a wagon-wheel, and this is one quick way to tell them from the Helianthemums whose central disk seems to nest *in* and not on the petals. One cannot go by colour because some Heleniums are as yellow as the yellowest of Sunflowers. However, the shape of the Helenium petals is more of a wedge than those of the Sunflowers which are pointed, or nearly so. Heleniums are one of the most useful of the late summer perennials, flowering on and on with no temperament or special care needed except to dead-head them at intervals. The colours are bright and therefore they should be placed with care, as they can look ordinary and even vulgar if they are put next to the wrong-coloured neighbours. The red-to-mahogany shades are pleasing and make a change from a too-much yellow garden in August. Do not put the yellow kinds within earshot of the pink and mauve China Asters – *Callistephus,* or the pink Phloxes and the magenta Loosestrife – *Lythrum salicaria,* or the atonality will be deafening. Instead, choose white flowers of almost any shape except Daisies, or the different primrose yellow of Evening Primrose *Oenoethera* spp. with the grey flannel leaves of *Stachys lanata* in front. Dahlias are good with Heleniums, having even more flamboyance, but colours and heights and shapes should be carefully worked out beforehand – cream, soft orange, apricot and bronze are good colours to look for.

The original species – *H.autumnale* – is not generally grown now, having been superseded by all the modern hybrids.
H. autumnale - Helenium (1729) grows to 6ft (1.85m) with bright yellow flowers from August to October. A hardy and vigorous perennial from E. United States for a large sunny border.

Requirements: Full sun, ordinary soil and subtle staking.
Cultivation: Divide and replant roots every three years.
During and after flowering: Dead-head, cut down stems in late autumn.
Plants: Most nurseries sell modern varieties now. These are shorter in height and more suited to smaller gardens.

HELIANTHUS - Sunflower *(Compositae)*. These flowers take their name from *Helios,* 'the sun' and *anthos,* 'flower'. The most familiar is the huge *H. annuus,* whose shaggy yellow heads are often tall enough to peer in at the bedroom window — though they never do, as they are too polite, preferring always to gaze at the sun rather than at any goings-on behind them. They turn solemnly to face the east and the rising sun (though not all at once, there is always one straggler in the platoon). Then through the day they follow the sun's progress through the sky until they are looking to the west to catch the last of the light. Each night they turn again to the east. I find it a comforting state of affairs and am glad that nothing has ever happened to prevent this daily traverse — one would not wish to have neurotic sunflowers. These friendly giants are most useful to mankind, being grown for their oily seeds. What is left from the oil-making process is very nourishing for stock generally and poultry in particular. These tall, heavy fellows should be staked from the word go with real stakes made of two-by-two (paint them dark green to make them less conspicuous), not fragile canes, in case some of them try to beat the world's tallest Sunflower record. When there is a row of them it will be noticed that they never manage to achieve a uniform height, and that is also part of their charm. They are fun for children because they grow so quickly.
H. annuus - Sunflower (1596) grows to 12ft (3.7m) with huge yellow flowers up to 16in (40.5cm) across, from July to September. An annual from W. United States for a south-facing wall or fence.
Requirements: Full sun, any soil, but they will grow taller in richer ground. Feed regularly if you are after a record.
Cultivation: Sow large seeds where required to grow, allow 3ft (91.5cm) between plants. Stake at this time. Water regularly in hot weather.
Seeds: All seedsmen.

HELICHRYSUM - Everlasting Flower, Straw Flower, Immortelle *(Compositae)*. There are many forms and shapes of 'everlastings' and all are attractive in the garden and even more so indoors in the dark days of winter. Some of this interesting and varied genus are shrubs, but there are some annual kinds that are easily grown and several tender perennials that are well worth looking after during the winter, because of the subtlety and variety of their leaf-forms and colours.
    H. bracteatum is the Immortelle, an appropriate name that suited the purpose for which it was grown. In the early nineteenth century the flowers were made into funeral wreaths and this became quite an industry in the South of France. Helichrysums are charming and very effective flowers — providing they are thrown away each spring when you sow the seeds of the next batch. They need a light, well-drained soil in full sun. Seeds should be sown under glass in February at a temperature of 18°C (64°F). Grow on in the usual way and plant out in late May. If the flowers are wanted for decoration and arrangements, cut them when they are quite dry in mid-afternoon and before they are fully open. Tie in bunches and hang upside down in a ventilated room until they are really dry. Drying in sunlight makes them brittle, so to keep them flexible hang away from bright light. Begin doing this as soon as the flowers come into bloom — bad summer weather prevents them opening evenly and damages the flowers. Do not wait until the end of the season.
H. bellidioides - Everlasting Daisy grows only to 3in (7.5cm) with white

'everlasting' flowers from May onwards. A tender perennial for the rockery from New Zealand needing protection in winter.

H. bracteatum - Immortelle (1799) grows to 4ft (122cm) with orange, pink or yellow flowers from July onwards. A half-hardy annual from Australia for the border and afterwards.

Requirements: *See text.*

Cultivation: *See text.* Shoots of *H.bellidioides* can be detached in summer and placed in peat and sand to root in a cold frame. Grow on and leave in frame for first winter.

Uses: As everlasting flowers for many purposes.

Seeds: Bloms, Thomas Butcher, Chiltern, Dobie, Suttons, Thompson and Morgan.

Plants: Hillier, Holden Clough, Reginald Kaye.

HELLEBORUS - Lenten Rose, Christmas Rose, Bear's Foot *(Ranunculaceae).* The Hellebores inspire gratitude in the gardener because they flower so early and so lengthily in the year. Many of the flowers look like other-coloured buttercups, often with a tinge or a tone of green or purple, with firm strong 'petals' that remain attractive for many months. These 'petals' are sepals and this why they have the strength to withstand the cruelty of the elements at this time in the year.

In previous centuries the Hellebore was believed to be a cure for insanity. This dates from the legend of the Greek goat-herd, Melampus, who noticed how his goats behaved after eating the plant; later on he used this knowledge to cure the mad daughters of King Argus – some said by giving them the milk from the goats who had been fed on Hellebore, and in other versions of the story, by doses of the plant followed by cold baths in a fountain. Since all parts of all Hellebores are poisonous I do marvel at the constitutions of those ancient Greeks.

The beautiful Christmas Rose *H. niger* is a slow to establish, but very long lived plant. It seldom flowers at Christmas these days but the calendar change in 1752, with its loss of ten days *(see* Introduction) may have a little to do with this. It is known from tree-rings that the summers were much hotter in previous centuries. Christmas Roses were once planted very close to cottage doorways to stop evil spirits from entering. There is an old nativity play that features a peasant girl called Madelon who came with the shepherds to see the infant Jesus; being very poor she had nothing to give Him, not even a flower, because of course, it was winter – even in Bethlehem. But an angel heard her weeping and appeared to her, leading her outside into the cold night. Touching the bare earth, he made the Christmas Rose appear and blossom, and Madelon was able to gather the pure white flowers to give to the Holy Child. I hope that she gave some to Mary, too.

H. niger is sometimes called the black Hellebore because its root is dark. It appreciates feeding after flowering, and a cloche over its head from November onwards. The Lenten Rose is *H. orientalis,* which flowers from January onwards. The flowers come in a fine range of subtle colours from greenish white through soft dull rose, crimson to wine-purple. These are easy plants, appreciating a mulch of leaf-mould and bonemeal when the flowers have finally gone. *(H. atrorubens* disappears completely, but only for a short rest). The strong, stiff leaves remain throughout the year in Southern England. It should have the shade of other plants in front of it and over its head, though it needs to be remembered about in Midsummer in case it gets smothered.

H. foetidus is a curious spiky, claw-leaved plant with the previous season's dark green leaves below the new, lighter-coloured foliage, forming three tiers of green when the flowers appear. Its name is unkindly translated as the Stinking Hellebore, not much more kindly as the Setterwort, but livable with as Bear's Foot, which its rather cross-looking leaves could be said to resemble – at a pinch.

H. corsicus is the only sun-lover, eventually growing into huge plants whose spiny-edged thick-leaved flower stems spend the summer lying down. It is a handsome plant, needing a great deal of space in maturity, but well worth growing in a focal spot.

H. foetidus - **Stinking Hellebore, Setterwort, Bear's Foot,** grows to 2ft (61cm) with purple-edged green 'flowers' from February onwards, lasting some months in the garden. A European short-lived perennial for the shady border.

H. niger - **Christmas Rose** (16th century). Grows to 18in (46cm) with white flowers from December onwards. A perennial plant from Central Europe for a sheltered corner in sun or partial shade. Protect open flowers with a cloche or pane of glass in winter, and feed with well-decayed manure and leaf-mould in March. Do not disturb once planted.

H. orientalis (1839) - **Lenten Rose** (1839) grows to 2ft (61cm) with flowers in shades of greenish white, pink and maroon from January onwards. A perennial from Greece and Asia Minor for the edge of a shrubbery or a semi-shaded corner.

Requirements: Deep, rich soil and a sheltered position. Feed during early summer.

Cultivation: All dislike disturbance. If this is unavoidable, divide or lift *H. atrorubens* in October, *H. niger* and *H. orientalis* in March or April. Ripe seeds can be sown in June or July in boxes of sandy soil in a shaded cold frame. Prick out into a shaded nursery bed and grow on – protect with tunnel cloches the first winter. They will flower in the third or fourth year. *H. orientalis* hybridises very readily with its cousins of a different colour and the seedlings will not come true.

Uses: As a superb winter flower of a substantial habit. *H. orientalis* is not good for picking.

Plants: Most nurseries.

HEMEROCALLIS - **Day Lily, Daylily** *(Liliaceae)*. The plant takes its name from *Hemera,* 'a day' and *Kallos* 'beauty' – each of a Day Lily's flowers lasts only for one day. These plants seemed to go out of style for a while, and I can remember several people who had rooted them out of their gardens because they 'took up so much room'. Now they appear to be back, such is the fickleness of flower-fashion, though in the process *H. fulva* is getting very hard to find. Day Lilies need to be undisturbed for a few years to give of their best, and need little or no attention. The most familiar kind is – or was – *H. fulva* which has the characteristic orange-copper flowers. It was known in China many centuries ago as The Plant of Forgetfulness because it had the reputation of curing sorrow by means of forgetfulness. The Reverend William Hanbury (1725 – 78) of Church Langton in Leicestershire, thought that it had a rather 'bad' colour, but he grew it, apparently for quirky amusement, and I quote "... The stamina are large, and possessed of much copper-coloured farina, which is emitted from the antherae in great plenty of being touched, and has often afforded much merriment to the Gardner, who causing the flowers to be smelt to by the unknowing ones, the farina has discharged itself in such plenty over their faces, as to stain them of a copper colour." The flowers and buds were formerly eaten as a delicacy in the Far East.

The young leaves of Day Lilies are beginning to be appreciated in the garden for their colour – a sharp, light green – and their form. Those of *H. Dumortierii* are even more attractive, being narrower, but one is apt to forget them after the flowers are over until you find yourself constantly tripping over them – they are about 30in (76cm) long by the end of the summer and will flop over their neighbours and suffocate them if allowed so to do. As it is the earliest to flower it is forgiven, but after the third year, when the clumps are bigger and the leaves even further out, longer, and more abundant, one has to take the drastic action of shearing off the leaves immediately after flowering. They will look reproachfully appalling for a few weeks but will soon send up new shoots which will be respectable for the rest of the year.

H. Dumortierii (1832) grows to 18in (46cm) with scented daintier flowers and dark purple-brown buds in May and June. Leaves light green and 25 – 30in (63.5 – 76cm) long. A perennial from Japan for a sunny border.

H. flava (1570) grows to 3ft (91.5cm) with scented yellow flowers from May to July. A perennial from the Far East (probably China) for a sunny position.

H. fulva - Day Lily (1576) grows to 3ft (91.5cm) with orange flowers from June to August. A rhizomatous plant from Japan. It does not seed and has been propogated vegetatively for hundreds of years. A sunny place in the border suits it.

H. middendorfii (1866) Grows to 2ft (61cm) with orange-yellow flowers in June. A perennial from Japan and Siberia for a sunny corner.

Requirements: Almost any kind of soil, but best if moisture-retentive. Leave undisturbed. Mulch with well-decayed manure in early spring.

Cultivation: Divide roots in early spring.

Uses: Handsome border plants, leaves usually a good feature.

Plants: Hillier, F. Toynbee Ltd.

HEPATICA - Liverwort *(Ranunculaceae).* People are sometimes put off even looking at this lovely thing by the unfortunate name of Liverwort, given to it many centuries ago. The name Hepatica comes from *Hepar* 'the liver', because according to the Doctrine of Signatures, the plant had great curative properties. It has been used in medicine for many years, but has such a gentle action that other more effective plants were used instead. The name Liverwort is more generally associated with the frilly green growth found in shaded, wet areas and in the tops of old established flower-pots in the greenhouse.

The Hepatica is an exquisite plant, growing in semi-shade, with blue flowers in early spring. For these three reasons, no garden with shady areas should be without it (some catalogues and growers still list it under Anemone).

H. triloba syn. **H. nobilis** grows to 4in (10cm) but spreads to about 12in (30.5cm) with blue flowers from February to April. A charming plant from many areas of the N. hemisphere for the shady rockery on limestone.

Requirements: Rich, moisture-retentive humus-rich soil and semi-shade.

Cultivation: Divide roots in August or September

Plants: Avon, Beth Chatto, Cunnington, Hillier, Holden Clough, Ingwersen, Jackamoors, Reginald Kaye, Washfield Nursery.

HESPERIS - Dame's Violet, Sweet Rocket *(Cruciferae).* This old-fashioned plant is not easy to find in nurseries and is not often seen in gardens, though it is easy to grow and most rewarding to have. Its name comes from the Greek word *Hesperos* 'evening', and its pale lilac flowers (sometimes a deeper mauve-to-violet and sometimes white) are most sweetly scented, but only in the evenings and at night because they are moth-pollinated. Sweet Rocket looks rather like a white or pale-coloured Honesty, but is a perennial plant. It flowers at the same time as *Aconitum anglicum* and the blue spires with the mass of light-coloured flowers are very pleasing. The leaves are evergreen and therefore there will be no gap in the flower bed during the winter. It does not mind a situation in dappled shade, though you may find that it will edge towards the sun. It self-sows once established, and it is well to keep the young plants, because Hesperis is sometimes a short-lived perennial and may not survive a bad winter. There is a double variety which is even harder to get and this is also short-lived. It was the favourite flower of Marie Antoinette, and when she was imprisoned in sordid conditions, the gaoler's wife brought her posies of Sweet Rocket, Pinks and Tuberoses, an act of kindness for which she herself was imprisoned.

H. tristis was grown in Elizabethan times and called 'Melancholy Gentleman' – another example of the confusion of common names. This plant is now difficult to find.

H. matronalis - Sweet Rocket, Dame's Violet (before 1562), grows to 4ft (122cm) with scented white, lilac, mauve or violet flowers from June to August. A vigorous perennial for a sunny or partly shaded border from S.Europe to Siberia.

H. tristis (1629) grows to 18in (46cm) with scented creamy-white flowers in May and June. A biennial from E. Europe for a sunny border.

Requirements: Any soil

Cultivation: Collect seed as soon as ripe and sow in boxes in a cold frame, and scatter some around the plants as well. Grow on and prick out into nursery rows, set out in the following year.

Uses: For the wild garden, in shrubberies, as a cut flower and for pot-pourri.

Seeds: Thomas Butcher, Chiltern, Dobie, Stoke Lacey, Thompson and Morgan.

Plants: Oak Cottage, The Weald Herbary.

HEUCHERA - Alum Root, Coral Flower *(Saxifragaceae)*. One of the most useful and dainty flowers for semi-shaded borders, where it can be planted as a thick froth of tiny scarlet flowers to provide colour for months. The plant was named after Johann Heinrich Heucher (1677 – 1747) who was a professor of medicine at Wittenburg. The evergreen leaves are most attractive when it is not in bloom and the plants will gradually increase in size and attractiveness. Winter frosts and Anno Domini cause them to 'heave' and the temptation to push them back into the ground is strong, but resist it. Instead, build up a little cushion of compost for them to sit on, or lift and divide them in March or April, though this is best done in September.

The plant was discovered in Mexico by a Dr. Murray and when brought to the British Isles Heucheras became instantly popular. The species plant is seldom grown now, as the cultivars are much brighter. The plant called Heucherella is a hybrid between Heuchera and Tiarella. Heucheras may be grown from seed sown in boxes in March or April in a cold frame. Grow on in the usual way and plant out in a nursery bed. Set out in final position in October or spring. Garden seed will not come true if several varieties are grown.

H. sanguinea - Coral Bells, (1882) grown to 18in (46cm) with panicles of small red flowers from June to September. An excellent edging plant from Mexico for borders in sun or partial shade.

Requirements: Good, moisture-retentive soil.

Cultivation: *See text.*

Uses: As edging or rockery plants and as cut flowers.

Plants: Artiss, Bees, Goatchers, Hillier, Holden Clough, Scotts, St. Bridget.

Seeds: Thomas Butcher, Chiltern, Thompson and Morgan, Suttons.

HIPPEASTRUM *(Amaryllidaceae)*. Their name comes from *Hippeus* a 'horseman', and *astron* 'a star', and it is not known why the flowers are so called. Hippeastrums are easily confused with Amaryllis and are often sold as such, but seen side by side, they are quite different. The Hippeastrum has larger, flatter flowers with wider petals and nowadays it comes in a great range of colours. The species bulbs were mostly discovered in the nineteenth century in South America, except for *H. reginae* which was found in Mexico in 1725, and *H. reticulatum,* discovered much earlier in Brazil in 1677.

The flowers cross-pollinate only too easily if several kinds are being grown in a greenhouse where bees have access, therefore if true seed is wanted the anthers should be removed, bees kept out or the plants separated, which last is a most irritating arrangement. If you have several Hippeastrums they make a better show if they are all glorious together. They make handsome house plants, though these are almost always the modern hybrids, which are sold all ready packaged. Seeds should be sown 1in (2.5cm) apart in a temperature of $16 - 18°C$ ($61 - 64°F$) and kept shaded until germination has taken place.

Grow on in the same temperature into larger pots successively, waiting until the roots fill the pot before transplanting to a larger size. Do not let the plants get dry, and feed with weak liquid manure once a week during the growing season. Flowers should form in the third year from sowing. Purchased bulbs should be grown in a temperature of $13 - 16°C$ ($55 - 61°F$) in a 5-inch (12.5cm) pot of John Innes No.2, leaving the top half of the bulb uncovered. Water from the base until the growth begins – the flower stems may appear before or just after the leaves. Water more often and begin weekly feeds. After the flowers are over, the leaves will continue to grow and should be regularly syringed, and the watering and feeding should continue as regularly until the leaves begin to turn yellow. Gradually cease watering until the leaves have withered and then stop altogether for three months – this is the bulb's essential resting period. Repot when starting into growth and use a size larger pot if necessary. Offsets will often form, these will be exactly the same as the parent. The flowers will last longer in a cooler room or conservatory.

Requirements: *As text.*
Cultivation: *As text.*
Uses: As handsome greenhouse, conservatory and house plants.
Seeds: Chiltern (hybrids).
Bulbs: Amand.

HOSTA - Funkia, Plantain Lily *(Liliaceae).* Though this plant and all its varieties was formerly called the Funkia or Plantain Lily, it is now known by its proper name of Hosta, after Nicholas Thomas Host (1761 – 1834) a Viennese physician. The flowers are attractive, especially the white sorts, but it is for the handsome leaves that the plant is known and grown. These are deeply veined and come in many shades, from almost blue or yellow to striped green and white. The plants like semi-shade and moisture and therefore they are immensely useful and attractive in shady walks, town gardens, courtyards, shaded patios and light woodland, and look particularly pleasing when grown at the edge of water, Slugs like all these places, and will make a disaster area of the leaves, and where these pests are numerous it is exceedingly difficult to keep the plants in a pristine condition except by waging total war on the gastropod population. I have found that the only way I can keep my Hostas looking respectable – and not like old lace curtains – is to grow them in something high, like the old chimney-pot from the cottage here. This is almost 3ft (91.5cm) tall, and has a rich brown glaze. The broken end has been planted deep in the ground and the whole thing filled with soil, and it now has *H. fortunei marginata* 'alba' growing well out of the top, a bit like Struwwelpeter's hair, only much prettier. The slugs seldom trouble to climb all the way up the chimney and the Hosta is increasing in size and beauty.

Hostas are the most good-natured of plants, and very long-lived. They can even be moved in full sail, as it were, providing a good ball of soil is taken up with them. If you have just one large clump and need another, you can go to the back of a plant and take a wedge out of it, like a slice of Cheddar cheese, though you will need a sharp spade. Do the deed with one quick slash each time – ineffectual cuts will damage the poor plant. This should be done in early spring before the leaves appear. Many Hostas turn a pleasing soft golden yellow in autumn, and these leaves can be used as background in seasonal arrangements.

The nomenclature is very confused (no two reliable sources can agree) partly because of new introductions, and cultivars. Some come true from seed and some do not, and where there is a fine plant it is best increased vegetatively as described. The permutations and crosses on these and more that are available are innumerable, but almost all are pleasing. Try to see a good collection before choosing.

H. Fortunei (1876) grows to about 18in (46cm) with local flowers in July and grey-green leaves. A handsome plant from Japan for patio, courtyard, shaded border, waterside and anywhere else where shapely and sculptural foliage is needed.

H. lancifolia (1829) grows to 2ft (61cm) with lilac flowers from July to September. A perennial from Japan with long, narrow green leaves for similar planting.

H. plantaginea (1830) grows to 20in (51cm) with fragrant white flowers in August and glossy, heart-shaped yellow-green leaves. A perennial from China and Japan for similar places.

H. Sieboldiana syn. **H. glauca** grows to 24in (61cm) with greenish white flowers in August and mid-green leaves. A perennial from Japan for shady places.

H. ventricosa (1790) grows to 3ft (91.5cm) with violet mauve flowers in July. A large plant from E. Asia for a focal position in a shaded place.

Requirements: Hostas need rich, moisture-retentive well-manured soil. Top dressings of peat, leaf-mould and well-rotted compost should be given in spring. The leaf colouration of plants in shade, particularly the variegated kinds, is usually much better. Protect from slugs and snails.

Cultivation: Divide or split off as described.

Uses: As superb foliage plants for greenhouse and conservatories (where they can be well protected from slugs), edges of lawns, shrubberies, waterside, woodland, shady garden borders, large shaded rockeries and North-facing borders.

Plants: Scotts, Chappell, Goatcher, Highfield, Kelways, Holden Clough, Robinsons, Notcutts.

IBERIS - Candytuft, Billy Come Home Soon *(Cruciferae)*. Candytuft is from Candia, or Crete, and both the gay annual and the smart perennial plant with its dark evergreen leaves and starch-white blooms are favourite old cottage-garden flowers, rather scorned by proper gardeners who are inclined to despise plants that are so untemperamental and challengeless. Because of this agreeable trait the perennial *I. sempervirens* is as much a part of spring bedding as Aubrieta and Alyssum. Candytuft is an old plant and the ancient Egyptians used the seed as mustard, and when it was brought to the British Isles it was known as Candy Mustard – Gerard was given a plant and knew it as Candy thlaspie "... Candie Mustard excelleth all the rest for the decking up of gardens and houses, as also for that it goeth beyond the rest in his 'physicall vertues' ... It is reckoned a chief among those Simples, with which Mithridate and treacle is made, and is mixed in counterpoysons and such like compositions." Parkinson disagreed with all this "... Candie, or Spanish Tufts, is not so sharp biting in taste as some of the other thlaspies are, and therefore is not to be used in medicines, where Thlaspe* should be, in the stead thereof.

*There is a small group of the Cruciferae family whose generic name begins with Thlaspi – e.g. *Thlaspi arvense,* Field Penny Cress, *Thlaspi Alpestre,* Alpine Penny Cress, etc. The annual Candytuft is easily grown from seed sown in open ground when the plants are to flower. They will often re-sow themselves from year to year. Slugs like the seedlings very much. The perennial *I. sempervirens* is increased by cuttings from non-flowering shoots taken after flowering is over and placed in peat and sand to root. Grow on and overwinter in a cold frame.

I. gibraltarica (1793) grows to 12in (30.5cm) with lilac to pink flowers in May and June. A nearly hardy perennial from Gibralta for a sunny rockery.

I. sempervirens - Candytuft (1731) grows to 12in (30.5cm) with white flowers in spring. A perennial for sunny walls, rocks and edging.

I. umbellata - Candytuft (1596, probably earlier) grows to 12in (30.5cm) with scented flowers in all shades of pink, red, purple and white in spring and summer. An annual for a sunny border.

Requirements: Full sun and any soil.

Cultivation: Sow seed of *I. umbellata* in September and successively in March, April and May to extend flowering time. Leave seed heads in border for seed to fall.

Uses: As wall, rock, border, trough and cut flowers. Green seed heads for arrangements.

Seed: Thomas Butcher, Chiltern, Dobie, Kent County Nurseries, Thompson and Morgan.

Plants: Artiss, Cunnington, Goatchers, Hillier, Holden Clough, Hortico, Ingwersen, Sherrards, St. Bridget, F. Toynbee Ltd., Waterperry, The Weald Herbary.

IMPATIENS - Busy Lizzie, Touch-me-not *(Balsaminaceae).*The name Impatiens means 'impatient' – from the elasticity of the ripe seed pod which explodes suddenly when touched. This is another flower that suits many situations though not always happily. I have seen unbelievably huge plants, about 6ft (1.85m) in diameter, contented in the tropical heat of the hothouses at the Jardin des Plantes in Paris where they were growing by the water's edge; I have also seen sad, attenuated little things that live on office windowsills and filing cabinets. It is difficult to believe that these are one and the same with the cheerful half-hardy bedding plant that brightens up the shady parts of the garden with an unceasing succession of gaily-coloured flowers. Impatiens are quite marvellous for shady borders if you can protect the young plants from slugs. The flowers come in quick succession, and the plants get larger and larger, and the whole show goes on well into October until the first frost. They are no trouble at all, but appreciate a liquid feed, if you remember, and all they need is plenty of watering.

The native Balsam, once called *Impatiens noli-me-tangere* – Touch-me-not, has yellow flowers and explosive seeds, as does the tall, pink-flowered Himalayan Balsam, *I. glandulifera*. Of the yellow-flowered Balsam, James Justice (1698 – 1763) said that "... it was preserved only by the Curious, for the Diversion it affords to Persons who handle its seed-vessels when ripe ..." which "... will soon skippe out of the heads, if they be but a little hardly pressed between the fingers".

I. glandulifera had not been found then, it was discovered in India in 1839 and has now made itself most comfortable in many of our damp ditches, canals and slow streamsides. This one is easier to find or grow from seed and the explosive seed-vessels are great fun for children.

I. sultanii loves moisture, and with careful nurturing and regular feeding it will gobble up everything that you give it and will puff itself up to be a houseplant to be proud of. The eminent botanist Sir J.D. Hooker began a study of the Balsam family at the age of 92, which must have been very interesting because it took him nine years to complete. He appears to have taken against the genus in general during this work, because he called *I. glandulifera* "deceiptful above all plants and desperately wicked".

Seeds of the annual plants can be sown in a warm greenhouse in spring and grown on and hardened off in the usual way. *I. glandulifera* will usually sow itself, but if you really want this one, it is better to sow it in a box in a cold frame. Seeds of *L. sultanii* can be sown in March in a temperature of 16 – 18°C (61 – 64°F). Grow on and plant in individual pots of John Innes No. 2 if plants are for greenhouse or indoor use. Pinch out the growing tips to keep plants bushy. Keep shaded in the greenhouse and out of strong sunlight in the house. Give liquid food once a week. When the plants begin to straggle, take 3 – 4inch (7.5 – 10cm) cuttings and put in a mix of sand and peat to root at a temperature of 16°C (61°F).

I. Balsamina - Balsam (1596) grows to 2ft (61cm) with (in the species) pink flowers from June to September. A half-hardy annual from India, Malaya and China for pots and bedding. (Do not pinch out growing tips).

I. glandulifera syn. **I. Roylei - Himalayan Balsam, Policeman's Helmet** (1839) grows to 6ft (1.85m) or more with handsome dark green leaves and pink flowers from August to September. A determined annual from India for damp gardens and waterside. Will grow in ordinary garden soil but not as tall.

I. Sultanii - Busy Lizzie (1896) grows to 2ft (61cm) or larger with orange, white, pink, crimson and purple flowers from April to October. A very useful, eternal-flowering half hardy perennial from Zanzibar for the house or partially shaded borders.

Requirements: *See text.*

Cultivation: As described. Seeds of species types not easy to find, modern cultivars most generally offered.

Uses: Excellent as cut, pot, trough and border flowers for a very long flowering season.

Seeds: (Modern varieties) Thomas Butcher, Chiltern, Dobie, Suttons, Thompson and Morgan.

INCARVILLEA *(Bignoniaceae).* Named after Pierre d'Incarville (1706 – 57) a French missionary who corresponded with the great botanist Bernard de Jussieu. These handsome plants are quite happy in a sheltered, sunny border in the Southern parts of the British Isles, though their crowns should be protected by litter in November. They form very large roots when established and have pleasing fern-like leaves above which rise the exotic-looking pink flowers. As the leaves vanish for the winter, the plant's whereabouts should be marked with a cane to prevent them from being spiked by a carelessly wielded fork. They should be mulched with rich compost and this can be heaped up above them for extra protection. Since the compost is usually a different colour from the surrounding soil, this will help to mark the position of the plants for some time. Though it is possible to divide the roots, this is difficult because they are very hard; it is easier to sow seeds in boxes in a warm greenhouse during the summer, where the seedlings can be grown on in the usual way. The young plants can be moved out to a cold frame when large enough and should stay there for the winter.

I. Delavayi (1893) grows to 2ft (61cm) with pink Gloxinia-like flowers before the leaves. A semi-tender perennial tuberous rooted plant from W. China and Tibet for a sheltered, sunny place.

I. grandiflora (1898) grows to 12in (30.5cm) with cerise flowers from May to July. A smaller perennial with rounded leaves from W. China, for a sheltered sunny border.

Requirements: Rich, free-draining soil and a sunny site.

Cultivation: *See text.*

Seeds: Thomas Butcher, Dobie, Chiltern, Suttons, Thompson and Morgan.

Plants/Tubers: Amand, Avon, Bees, Bloms, Beth Chatto, de Jager, Dobie, Hillier, Holden Clough, Jackman's, Kelways, Robinsons, St. Bridget.

INULA - Elecampane *(Compositae).* A large and ornamental plant with historical associations. It can form part of an authentic collection of herbal plants, because it was used medicinally in former times (and still is, to a lesser degree) and the roots when candied were used for sweetmeats. They had healthier sweets in those days. Pliny said of the root "... being chewed fasting, doth fasten the teeth" and he recommended that "... no day should pass without eating some of the roots of Enula, considered to help digestion and cause mirth". It sounds an altogether jolly sort of plant to have, providing your garden is large enough, because it will grow to a height of 5ft (1.75m) with a similar girth; at least, mine does, though the reference books give less height and therefore so will I at the end of this piece, in case you are disappointed. It has huge and handsome grey-green leaves, each about 2ft (61cm) long that will effectively suffocate all else nearby. The plant produces tall stems of large yellow daisies which rise up in August or September (the yellow-flower season). Butterflies absolutely love these and will gorge until they fall sideways in a state of blissful repletion.

The plant was used as a diuretic, a tonic, an expectorant, an antiseptic and for many other ills. It is still used with other herbs as a cough-cure, for respiratory difficulties, catarrh, asthma and bronchitis. The list of ailments that it cured or alleviated is very considerable and reads as follows: "shortness of breath, a remedy against counterpoysons and the bitings of serpents and for them that are bursten, cramps, convulsions, to warm a cold, windy stomach, to cure putrid and pestilential fevers, and even the plague: to quicken the sight of the eyes, destroy worms in the stomach, to fasten loose teeth and keep them from putrefaction, for spitting of blood, gout, sciatica [Galen knew about this and said 'it is good for passions of the hucklebone called sciatica'] ruptures, scabs, itch, putrid sores and cankers, and to cleanse the skin of the face or other parts from any morphew, spots or blemishes." What a recommendation for any one plant!

The huge leaves decay floppily in autumn and should be cut off when dead, or for tidiness' sake, as they die. Nothing visible remains of the vast, fangy roots until in late spring attractive silver-green spikes appear and the Inula is back. It likes damp soil and full sun.

I. helenium - Elecampane grows to 4ft (122cm) with large, yellow daisy flowers in August and September. A vigorous European perennial plant for a damp corner in a sunny border. Will do in normal garden soil but will not be as lusty.

Requirements: Best in rich, moisture-retentive soil in sun or partial shade, or ordinary garden soil.

Cultivation: Divide roots in early spring.

Uses: A fine sculptural plant for late summer. In the herb garden.

Plants: Beth Chatto, Hillier, Oak Cottage, Parkinson Herbs, Stoke Lacy, Weald Herbary.

IPOMOEA - Morning Glory *(Convolvulaceae)*. Closely related to our own strong-growing, aptly named Bindweed this genus of plants has varieties that have very brightly coloured flowers, often of an intense and beautiful blue. The Morning Glory is so called because it opens its parasols soon after sunrise (I got up early one summer's day especially to watch it wake up). The brilliant blue circular flowers live only for a few hours and collapse and shrivel just after mid-day. The plant continues to give a succession of these daily blue moons until late in the summer, and does even better with liquid feeds. It looks quite lovely in hanging baskets in company with pink or white pelargoniums, twining down and round and back on itself with flower-studded stems. Recently it was thought that the seeds caused hallucinations when chewed, and for a time they were not obtainable while tests were carried out. However, the seeds are now known to be quite harmless. For gardeners plagued with its cousin, the Bindweed, formerly called *Convolvulus sepium* but now renamed *Calystegia sepium*, there is an effective if drastic remedy. Introduce pigs to the garden, because they are supposed to be very fond of the pernicious roots. Alas, pigs are not deft gardeners, and the experiment might not be worth the devastation they would inevitably cause. Such is the perversity of all living creatures, the pigs would probably take a fancy to the Delphiniums or the Peonies (perhaps fatal when consumed in pig-sized quantities?) and would then expire in the middle of the border in a welter of crushed and broken stems, with the jeering Bindweed left quite untouched. The hard seeds of Ipomoea should be soaked in warm water for 24 hours, then sown in individual peat pots, or in threes in larger pots in any good seed compost. The compost should be sprayed weekly with a copper fungicide, and more seeds should be sown than are needed, to allow for damping off. The individually-sown pots can be put straight into larger pots of the same compost when the seedlings are large enough, and given a thin cane. Try to keep the pots well separated in the greenhouse or conservatory as each waving tip of the plants will search out its own kind and grow into an inextricable tangle which it is not possible to sort out later without breaking off too much. They should not be planted out before the end of the frosts, and are quite difficult to cope with in a winter-packed greenhouse because of their speedy growth and loving ways.

I. caerulea now **Pharbitis purpurea-rubra** - **Morning Glory** grows to 8ft (2.55m) with circular blue flowers from July to September. A half-hardy perennial, (grown as an annual), from Mexico, needing full sun. For hanging baskets, trellis, posts and pergolas, and in association with pink, white or cream roses.

I. learii syn. **Pharbitis learii** - **The Blue Dawn Flower, Railway Creeper, Porter's Joy** (1839). An evergreen climber, grown as an annual or tender short-lived perennial in the Northern Hemisphere. It has exquisitely blue trumpets fading to magenta each day from June to October. A quick growing plant from Tropical America for a sheltered patio trellis or pergola outside in Devon and Cornwall, warm greenhouse elsewhere or as an annual.

Requirements: Full sun, does well in poor soil, amazingly well in better.

Cultivation: Sow soaked seeds in compost at a temperature of 15 − 18°C (59 − 64°F). Harden off, plant out in May.

Uses: *See text.*

During flowering: Dead-head, but not essential.

Seeds: Bloms, Thomas Butcher, Chiltern, Dobie, Kent County Nurseries, Suttons, Unwins.

IRIS *(Iridaceae).* The goddess Iris was the daughter of Thaumus and Electra, and was messenger to Juno. To facilitate her journeys between heaven and earth Iris used the rainbow, and it is fitting that these flowers of every shade in the spectrum are named after her, as is the iris of the eye with which we see their colours and everything else besides.

There is not sufficient space in this book to more than touch on a few of these always beautiful flowers. One of the easiest to grow and the most familiar is *I. pseudacorus,* the Yellow Flag, a native British Iris which, though a water or bog plant will also grow perfectly well in a flower bed, except that it will not be as tall − just as well, perhaps, when the plant can achieve 6ft (1.85m) in ideal conditions. *I. foetidissima* is another native plant that should be grown by everyone who does any kind of flower arranging, however simple. It has dark, evergreen leaves, which form large, handsome clumps in the dry shade under deciduous trees, and for this reason it is very useful in the garden, especially in winter. Its flowers are nothing to speak of, less to look at and fleeting in their stay, but the berries are another matter. In October the seed-heads split to reveal their bright orange contents that remain in the garden through the winter − if allowed, or much more likely they will remain through the winter indoors in someone's vase and it may not be yours. Infusions of the plant, unkindly called the Stinking Iris, were mixed with ale and drunk as a purge, and this plant would have had its place in a medieval herb garden. The plant does not smell at all unpleasant, just a faint whiff of cold roast beef when the leaves are crushed.

It is possible to have Irises in bloom for much of the year, and even when they are not in flower their leaves are attractive.

The leaves of the Siberian Irises have a more delicate look and are different in colour, being a light, fresh green and curving gracefully outwards. Large, established clumps gradually form a symmetrical circle with an empty space in the middle, this is perfectly all right as long as you have the room because the whole thing will occupy about 4ft (122cm) of border, and in late summer the leaves get tired and lie down to the detriment of their neighbours. The roots can be split up in early spring, but if the mature clump is such a glorious sight when in full bloom, with a succession of delicate flowers in shades of blue and violet, it should be left as long as possible. When it begins to produce less bloom, then that is the time to sort it out with a spade. Each segment of the circle will eventually make a similar-sized plant, and so it goes on. Where is one to put them all in a small garden?

The little early flowering species Iris, such as *I. danfordiae* and *I. reticulata* are a great joy in the rockery. *I. xiphium* is the 'florist's' Iris of hospital bouquets, and can be grown for winter colour in the greenhouse, as can the easy Dutch Iris which is a hybrid form of *I. xiphium*. *I. laevigata* likes to grow in 6-in (15-cm) of water, and *I. Kaempferi* likes shallower water or the moister soil a little higher up the bank. *I. chrysographes* likes moist soil but not wet feet. *I. stylosa,* now called *I. unguicularis,* is an easy but determinedly temperamental treasure to acquire, but worth its whims. You will need patience with *I. unguicularis.* Put in three of the evergreen plants in a sunny corner against a south wall where they can cook, or the side of a greenhouse will do very nicely, or an extra large shelf in the rockery where there is a good big rock behind them. Then forget them for a few years, and one January you may be rewarded by the first flowers. All they need is the warmest, driest spot in the garden, ordinary soil on the poor side, and nobody to interfere with them. Move them about and they will retaliate by not flowering for a further two years. But they really are worth it – the flowers can be picked in bud to open indoors in the dreariest, darkest days of winter. The most familiar kinds of all are the German Irises, with their stiff, grey-green flat fans of leaves that make such essential planting accents in a good herbaceous border. This species has given rise to most of the modern hybrids grown today.

Irises have been divided into eleven sections as follows: (1) Apogon (2) Evensia: (3) Pogoniris (4) Onocyclus: (5) Regelia (6) Pseudoevensia (7) Pardanthopsis (8) Nepalensis (9) Juno (10) Xiphion (11) Gynandriris. Here is a small selection of the most familiar Irises.

I. chrysographes Group 3 (1911) grows to 18in (46cm) with flowers in shades of blue and violet in June. A rhizomatous perennial for moist soil in sun or part shade, from Szechwan and Yunnan. Does well in acid soil.

I. Danfordiae Group 10 (1890) grows to 1ft (30.5cm) with yellow flowers before the leaves in January and February. A bulbous iris from the Cicilian Taurus for a sunny rockery. Any good soil.

I. foetidissima Group 3 - The Stinking Iris or Gladdon grows to 2ft (61cm) with dark evergreen leaves and dull purplish-yellow flowers briefly in June. Orange berries, excellent for winter colour and decor. Any soil, good under trees. Does very well in calcareous areas.

I. germanica Group 3. Long in cultivation and the parent of many of the garden Irises of today. Flowers from May to June. A rhizome whose origins are not known, for the sunny border. Rhizomes should be planted facing one way and on the top of the soil. Try to protect young leaves from slugs.

I. Kaempferi Group 1 (1857) grows to 2ft (61cm) with flowers of various colours in June and July. A rhizomatous perennial from Japan for the waterside, plants like to grow in water during summer and where the water level is below the rhizomes in winter.

I. laevigata Group 1 grows to 2ft (61cm) with blue flowers in June and July. A rhizomatous plant from Japan for a similar garden site.

I. pseudacorus (Group 1) Yellow Flag grows to 4ft (122cm) with yellow flowers in May. A vigorous native rhizomatous perennial for the pool. Grows in shallow water or in ordinary soil in full sun, where it must be watered regularly.

I. pumila Group 3 (1596) grows to 5in (12.5cm) with almost stemless flowers in various colours in April. A rhizomatous perennial from Europe and Asia Minor needing full sun. Plant with rhizomes partly exposed. Limy soil suits them well.

I. reticulata Group 10 grows to 1ft (30.5cm) with violet-purple flowers in February and March. A bulbous plant from the Caucasus for the sunny rockery. Protect from slugs.

I. xiphioides Group 10 - English Iris (1570) grows to 20in (51cm) with flowers in shades of blue in June and July. A bulbous plant from the Pyrenees for a sunny border or greenhouse culture.

I. unguicularis syn. **I. stylosa Group 1** Grows to 20in (51cm), flower stem shorter. Blue or lilac flowers from November to March. A treasure for a warm, sheltered place from Algeria. Rhizomes should be planted in poor gravelly soil in a sunny place and not disturbed.

I. Xiphium syn. **I. hispanica Group 10 - Spanish Iris** (1596) grows to 2ft (61cm) with flowers in shades of blue, yellow and white in May and June. (This has been crossed with other species in the group to produce the Dutch Iris). A bulbous plant from S. France to Portugal for the sunny border and any soil.

When purchasing Irises, check their soil requirements and flowering times. It is possible to have them in bloom from late October through to August and the long flowering season is the reason for Iris gardens which are interesting for most of the year.

Requirements: See text and cultivation notes. Requirements vary considerably according to type.

Cultivation: For the rhizomatous bearded Irises – plant rhizomes in a sunny place in light, rich free-draining limy soil. Wet winters are not good for them, and for special plants cloches are the only solution. Established clumps can be divided after flowering, each piece should have one or two strong leaf-fans. Discard centre of clump. In autumn, cut leaves down by half to prevent wind from rocking them.

I. pseudacorous and I. laevigata do well at pool margins.

I. Kaempferi needs feeding, which is not possible when grown in water, therefore it should be planted in a suitably enriched boggy area beside the pool. It dislikes lime. It does not come true from seed and has to be propagated vegetatively if more of the same are wanted. Divide the clumps immediately after flowering while the leaves are still growing. *I. Kaempferi* (mixtures) can be easily grown from seed, grow these in the normal way but in a shady place. This Iris can be grown in deeply dug rich garden soil and kept very well watered if no wet margin is available. It is greedier than it is thirsty.

For *I. chrysographes* and *I. siberica,* plant rhizomes 1in (2.5cm) deep in rich garden soil in a sunny place, or near a pond with naturally damp soil. In spring, top-dress with well-rotted manure and peat or compost and avoid damaging the surface roots. Cut up the large hollow centred plants into pieces after the foliage begins to die, or in spring.

For *I. reticulata* plant bulbs in a very well drained soil in the rockery. They do not like heavy soils. After flowering give a liquid feed once a month for three months.

For *I. Xiphioides* (Spanish, Dutch and English Irises)

Top left: Pink *Aquilegia vulgaris* against the softness of *Ballota pseudodictamnus.*

Top middle: The intricate form of *Astrantia major* with the simpler leaves of Bergenia.

Top right: The brilliant blue of Anchusa set off by *Viola* x *wittrockiana.*

Right: Grass and stone are a good foil for *Allium moly.*

Below left: Steps are softened by flowers such as *Geranium Endressii* and Montbretia.

Below right: Culinary Chives *(Allium Schoenoprasum)* and *Oxalis floribunda.*

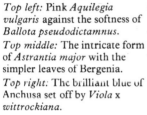

Top left: The plumes of *Aruncus sylvester* show up well against the surrounding shrubs.
Above left: Campanula carpatica, Tanacetum densum Amani and *Origanum vulgare* 'Aureum'.
Above right: The beautiful contrast of white-flowered *Centranthus ruber* with red roses.
Below left: Polygonum affine with *Campanula poscharskyana* in the background.
Below right: The delicate flowers and leaves of *Dicentra formosa*.

Above left: Campanula poscharskyana, Alchemilla mollis, and *Chrysanthemum parthenium* look charming with *Tropaeolum majus.*

Above right: Hesperis matronalis growing happily with *Aconitum anglicum.*

Right: Geranium phaeum and Montbretia planted for their foliage as well as their flowers.

Below left: Irises amidst a froth of Heuchera.

Below middle: Iris Kaempferi and *Geranium Endressii.*

Below right: The 'ominously imposing' *Acanthus mollis* with *Bergenia cordifolia* in front.

Above left: Doronicum pardalianches lights up the statue in its dark setting of yew.

Above, top right: Meconopsis cambrica and Potentilla fruticosa flower together for many months.

Above right: Limnanthes douglasii at the pond side with Alchemilla mollis and ferns.

Below: Lilium monadelphum szovitsianum shows up well against a blue-flowered Hebe.

Above left: Papaver orientale needs plenty of space – seen here with pink roses.

Top right: This handsome urn needs formal planting: Pclargoniums and *Begonia semperflorens.*

Below left: Thousands of pansies *Viola* x *wittrockiana* make a charming border.

Below right: Paeonia officionalis and Dianthus are colour matched beside brick paving.

Above: Inspired planting of *Papaver orientale* in the sunlit centre of a woodland glade.

Below left: Woodland subjects such as *Hyacinthoides non-scriptus, Polygonatum multiflorum* and ferns associate naturally with old apple trees.

Below right: Colour contrast of various Astilbes set against *Salix repens argentea.*

Above left: Viola cornuta flowers for months with the more modern Heuchera 'Palace Purple'.
Above top right: The bright colours of Candelabra primulas associating perfectly with ferns.
Above right: The silver silhouette of *Stachys lanata* against dark-leaved shrubs.
Below left: The tall spires of *Althaea rosea* soar happily against the traditional thatched roof.
Below right: Chrysanthenum maximum is set amongst Artemisias, *Curtonus paniculata* and *Cornus alba* 'Elegantissima'.
Below bottom right: The sharp shapes of *Phlomis samia* softened by *Alchemilla mollis*.

Above: The dry stone wall makes a natural setting for Helianthemum, Dimorphotheca, *Halimiocistus sahuccii*, Dianthus, *Penstemon barbatus* with white peonies, climbing roses and Delphiniums behind.

Below: A typical herbaceous border including *Nepeta gigantea, Viola cornuta*, Dianthus, *Viola cornuta purpurea, Geranium Endressii*, Delphiniums, Lupins and *Lavatera arborea*.

Plant English Irises 4 – 6in (10 – 15cm) deep in rich, moisture-retentive soil.

Plant Dutch Irises in good light soil in a sunny place, protect winter leaves of established clumps with cloches. They may be grown in pots under glass. Plant Spanish Iris in dry soil in a warm corner, lift bulbs after leaves have died down and store until September.

After flowering: Cut off seed heads unless seed is required, or seed heads for winter decor *(I. pseudacorus* is most attractive).

Rhizomes and Bulbs: Most nurseries.

Seeds of native varieties: Chambers, Chiltern, Naturescape.

IXIA - African Corn-Lily *(Iridaceae).* The plant's name of Ixia was given to it by Theophrastus: it means 'bird-lime', alluding to the sticky sap. Not really hardy in this country naturally, Ixias are best grown in pots and plunged in the ground out of doors during a hot summer. They are pretty, dainty flowers, particularly the species *I. viridiflora,* with its black-centred, blue-green flowers. Alas, this variety, being the least vigorous, is the hardest to grow, as is often the way with so many of the more interesting and unusual plants. To grow Ixias in pots for winter flowers, place five or six corms in a 5-in (12.5-cm) pot or twelve in an 8-in (20.5-cm) pot using John Innes No. 2 or a mixture of one part of leaf-mould, three parts of fibrous peat and two parts silver sand. Cover with 1in (2.5cm) of the compost and water once. Do not water again until the little green spears appear and keep in a temperature of 4 – 7°C (39 – 45°F). Never over-water. After they have flowered, cut off the flower-head below the last bloom, leaving the stem. When the leaves are dead, lay the pots on their sides in the greenhouse on a shelf or staging in full sunlight, or in a cold frame, so that they can be thoroughly baked. In September they can be shaken out of their pots and sorted out, detaching any offsets and re-potted as before. If grown in the ground outside, in spite of what the catalogues say, they are not reliably hardy because of having to endure the wetness of the Northern European winters. Seeds may be sown in pans or boxes in a frame in the autumn and brought into a greenhouse with a similar temperature as that for growing the mature corms. They should be grown on for a year, allowing the small corms to bake as previously described.

I. viridiflora (1780) grows to 12in (30.5cm) with black-centred blue green flowers in May and June. An unusual corm from S. Africa for pot culture.

Requirements: *See text.*

Cultivation: *See text.*

Uses: As very unusual cut and greenhouse flowers.

Corms: Amand, Bees, de Jager.

Seeds: Chiltern.

KIRENGESHOMA *(Saxifragaceae).* The name is taken from the Japanese *Ki* 'yellow', *rengeshoma,* the native name for a member of the Ranunculaceae family – *Anemonopsis macrophylla.* I cannot see what this has to do with Kirengeshoma, and would rather not be confused by the knowledge, but there it is.

Kirengeshoma is a beautiful plant, though a little exacting in its requirements. It is quite hardy and should be grown more often, as all it needs is moist leaf-mould and a sunny position in a sheltered place. It has nodding bell-shaped flowers late in the year, and the shape and elegant habit of the plant make it particularly welcome in the garden at that time. Seed should be sown in March in a cold frame and grown on in the usual way (germination is slow and takes from one to ten months).

K. palmata (1891) grows to 4ft (122cm) with handsome leaves and yellow flowers in September and October. A perennial from Japan for a sheltered place with some shade.

Requirements: *See text.*
Cultivation: *See text.*
Plants: Bressingham, Peter Chappell, Hillier, Notcutts, Scotts, Sherrards, Treasures of Tenbury.
Seeds: Chiltern.

KNIPHOFIA - Red Hot Pokers, Torch Lily *(Liliaceae).* The species was named after Johann Hieronymus Kniphof (1704 – 63) a professor of medicine who produced a great work called the *Herbarium Vivum* in 1764. There were twelve folio volumes with 1200 illustrations, produced in conjunction with a printer called Funke who set up an establishment especially for the project. The folios are very valuable because they contain hand-coloured examples of nature-printing. The plants that were to be used for the illustrations were dried and then held over candle smoke until blackened all over. They were then placed carefully between two pieces of soft paper and smoothed down with a bone and the impression of the veins and main features of the soot-impregnated plants was transferred to the paper. The printer's office was required because printer's ink was used instead of soot. Of course the plants would have disintegrated quite quickly, and therefore other, similar plants had to be ready; also, the blackening process was tedious and time consuming.

Kniphofias are assertive plants with stiff spikes of red or yellow flowers. They do well in Cornwall and South Devon, but even the hardiest are apt to disappear if the winter is colder and wetter than usual.

Ideally, they should be planted at the top of an incline, or some steps, so that when in full bloom they make a fine picture with the sky as background. They need light, rich soil that has been well manured, and they should not be moved once – and if – they have become established. (They were formerly called Tritomas, which is much easier to spell: it is mostly the modern hybrids that are offered for sale now.)

K. uvaria - Red Hot Poker (1707) grows to 9ft (2.75m), with 'pokers' that change from coral to red to orange and then to yellowish green in August and September. A perennial from S. Africa for a sheltered garden.
K. caulescens (1862) grows to 5ft (1.75m) with red flowers changing to salmon then to greenish white in September. A perennial from S. Africa with handsome glaucous foliage to grow as a group in a focal position.
Requirements: Dig a hole large enough to take the spread roots, water well until established. Tie up the leaves into a bunch for winter protection, and cover over all with litter, especially in Northern counties.
Propagation: Established plants can be divided in spring. Seeds can be sown of species types or of mixed hybrids, and should be sown thinly in the open ground in April. Protect from slugs, and grow on in the usual way.
Plants: Notcutts, Chappell, Bressingham, Beth Chatto.
Seeds: Chiltern.

LACHENALIA - Cape Cowslip *(Liliaceae).* These plants have recently become popular again – they were once grown much more in the days of the great greenhouses and conservatories. Lachenalias are named after Werner de la Chenal (1736 – 1800) a professor of botany at Basel in Switzerland. They are very suitable for a cooler greenhouse or conservatory, needing only sufficient heat to keep out the frost. Some of them look like rather exotic bluebells in shape, with red, yellow or orange bell-shaped flowers. The bulbs should be planted in 5-in (12.5-cm) pots of John Innes No. 2, cover bulbs lightly with the compost and grow on in a temperature of 10 – 13°C (50 – 55°F) in a good light and with plenty of ventilation. In other words, a conservatory with an outer door is a very good place for them, as long as the minimum temperature is generally maintained. Water pot and bulbs thoroughly once after potting and then wait for the shoots to appear. Water carefully until the flowers form and then more freely while they last, giving fortnightly feeds of weak liquid manure. When the flowers have faded, decrease watering until the leaves turn yellow. Stop watering and allow bulbs to rest in pots until the following August. Shake out of pots, re-pot in fresh compost.

L. mutabilis (1825) grows to 8in (20.5cm) with blue flowers in February. A bulb from S. Africa for greenhouse, conservatory and hanging baskets.

L. Nelsonii syn. **L. aloides** grows to 12in (30.5cm) with spotted leaves and green, red and yellow flowers in January and February. A bulb from S. Africa for similar planting.

L. pendula syn. **L. bulbifera** grows to 10in (25.5cm) with purple, green and red flowers in April, for similar planting.

Requirements: *See text.*

Cultivation: *See text.*

Bulbs: Amand, Avon, Bloms, Orpington, Potterton and Martin.

LAMIUM Galeobdolon *(Labiatae)*. Most of these useful plants make excellent ground cover, particularly *L. galeobdolon* whose name has been changed to the even more difficult to pronounce *Lamiastrum galeobdolon*. This rose by any other name is a fine carpeter for the dry soil under large shrubs like Lilac, Weigela, Forsythia, Kerria, Chaenomeles, Prunus etc., whose greedy roots will take all the nourishment from the soil and whose leaves prevent the rain from reaching it in the summer. In these conditions, few plants are happy, few, that is, except *L. galeobdolon*, which, left to itself will clothe the whole area with its very attractive silver-splashed leaves. In the spring there are spikes of pleasant creamy-yellow flowers which are a bonus in such situations. But after a while this plant will begin to extend its territories and will climb into the nearest Hydrangea or small Viburnum when your back is turned, covering them over completely so that they look like bumps under a bedspread. It is not difficult to get rid of but you will have to be ruthless and keep a sterner eye on it in the future.

L. maculatum is a useful edging plant with a silver stripe down the centre of each leaf. It makes a good edging plant and has no territorial acquisitiveness.

L. Galeobdolon var. **'variegatum'** - **The Yellow Archangel** grows to 18in (46cm) and will spread over an entire garden if allowed. Invasive but very useful ground cover plant. Yellow flowers in spring.

L. maculatum grows to 9in (23cm) with pink flowers in May. An edging plant or gap-filler for a large rockery in partial shade.

Requirements: Any soil. *L. galeobdolon* will grow in shade.

Cultivation: *L. galeobdolon* spreads by runners – capture a few at any time of the year and loop two or three of the stoloniferous tufts into a bunch and plant them together. (They look more of a plant this way). They in turn will make runners. A root forms at each node to send up yet another plant and if you look you will see it forming. Cuttings can be pushed into (watered) ground and pegged down with a hairpin, and they will start to grow in all but the hottest weather.

Plants: Most nurseries.

LATHYRUS - Sweet Pea *(Leguminosae)*. Everything has been said that can be said about the charm of the Sweet Pea and its legendary scent, and as the Reverend W.T. Hutchins said at the Bi-Centenary Sweet Pea Exhibition at the Crystal Palace "... The Sweet Pea has a keel that was meant to seek all shores; it has wings that were meant to fly across all continents; it has a standard which is friendly to all nations; and it has a fragrance like the universal gospel, yea, a sweet prophecy of welcome everywhere that has been abundantly fulfilled." The words are as redolent of the times as is the flower itself, and there is no need to describe it here.

The first Sweet Peas came from Sicily and a description of them was included in the *Hortus Catholicus,* published by Father Franciscus Cupani in 1697. He sent seeds to Dr. Robert Uvedale, a collector of plants who was Headmaster of the Grammar School at Enfield. The next appearance of the Sweet Pea was as an illustration in *Twelve Months of Flowers* in 1730. Seeds of the plant had been on sale for about eight years, but they were of a plant described as being of a red and blue colour. In 1754 there were known to be three such sorts – purple, white and the 'Painted Lady' and the scent is always mentioned in the descriptions. By the beginning of the nineteenth century there were five colours, and but one more by 1837. The first attempts to breed other colours came around 1855 when Colonel Trevor Clarke of Daventry began trying to produce a blue Sweet Pea, (and both British and American growers are still trying). In 1870 Henry Eckford began to breed from the flowers that were available (still no more than about 15 distinct sorts) and by 1900, at the great Bi-Centenary Sweet Pea Exhibition there were 264 varieties on show, 115 being the results of Eckford's work. The Sweet Pea had begun to change and was beginning to look like the flower we know today, with four flowers to a stem instead of two, new colours and new shapes. After that the Sweet Pea became a very fashionable flower much beloved by Edwardians. It was said that no dinner-table, no wedding, no bouquet and no buttonhole was complete without the Sweet Pea.

Growing good plants requires a certain amount of planning. It is not difficult, but it must be done thoroughly or the Sweet Pea will feel cheated and will not flower as vigorously. Limy soil is best, though they will do quite well in other well-drained loams. The ground needs to be trenched or double-dug in the autumn, putting a good thick layer of well-decayed manure in the bottom spit. Soak the seeds for 12 hours and sow in boxes in a temperature of 16°C (61°F) in March (or sow in individual pots). Grow on and transplant into separate pots, pinching out top growth at 4in (10cm). Harden off properly and plant in prepared ground in early May. Set out in rows against wires or trellis (the Victorians called them 'rissels') and keep well watered. A feed of weak liquid manure once a week is very good for them. Pick them as hard as they flower and this will encourage yet more bloom.

The old kinds have been superseded by hundreds of modern varieties, but it is still possible to get seeds of the 'Old-Fashioned' kind from Chiltern. These have undistinguished flowers – see the illustration – but their perfume makes that of a modern Sweet Pea seem diluted by comparison.

L. latifolius grows to 10ft (3.05m) with rose-mauve flowers from June to September (the white form is lovely). A European perennial plant for scrambling over lavender hedges, sharing a rose pergola, climbing a trellis, festooning a wire fence or creeping through a lax-growing shrub.

L. odoratus - Sweet Pea (1700) grows to 6ft (1.85m) with flowers of many colours throughout the summer. An annual plant from Sicily that can be grown against walls or fences as well as in the kitchen garden for picking.

Requirements: Full sun and alkaline soil, though this last is not essential. Do not attempt to move *L. latifolius* once established.

Cultivation: As described. In spells of hot weather, dig a 6-in (15-cm) trench each side of the row of Sweet Peas and fill with water each morning and evening.

Seeds: Most seedsmen for modern varieties. Chiltern, Thomas Butcher, Dobie.

Plants: *(L. latifolius)* Boltons, Thomas Butcher, Chambers, Chiltern, Dobie, Hillier, Naturescape, Thompson and Morgan, Trenear, Unwins.

LAVATERA - Mallow *(Malvaceae).* Lavatera was named after the brothers Lavater, two eighteenth-century Swiss physicians and naturalists. This plant always looks like an established perennial when in bloom because of its substantial form and the size of the flowers, but it is a fast-growing annual which is ideal for filling those gaps that sometimes appear when you have been doing a bit of space-juggling. Its shining pink or white flowers are very beautiful. The seeds should be sown in April (or in September if possible) in the flowering position, which should be sunny and sheltered. Seedlings can be thinned out later, and the plant will seed itself about if it likes your garden.

L. trimestris (1633) grows to 6ft (1.85m) with large pink or white flowers from July to September. An annual plant from the Mediterrian region for a sunny sheltered position.

Requirements: Any soil, full sun.
Cultivation: *See text.*
Seeds: Most seedsmen.

LEONTOPODIUM - Edelweiss *(Compositae).* The name of this plant comes from *Leont* 'lion', *podion* 'foot', from the fancied resemblance of the flower head to a lion's foot, which try as I may I cannot agree with, it looks more like a starfish. Much loved by the Swiss, the emblematical pictures of Edelweiss have appeared on everything from china cats to cuckoo-clocks. It is a pretty flower and looks very appropriate on rockeries but as it is a true alpine it hates damp which collects and remains on its soft woolly leaves. It is worth protecting with a pane of glass in winter, or it may be grown in a pot and 'planted' in the rockery, pot and all, for the summer. Seeds can be sown in a compost of 2 parts John Innes No. 1 and 1 part grit in a cold frame in spring. Grow on and plant seedlings in individual pots. Keep in frame until the following spring.

L. alpinum - Edelweiss (1776) grows to 8in (20.5cm) with white flowers surrounded by the petal-like bracts in June and July. A European alpine perennial for a sunny rock garden or alpine house.

Requirements: Sandy, gritty soil.
Cultivation: *See text.*
Plants: Bees, Bressingham, Broadwell, Cunnington, Goatchers, Hillier, Holden Clough, Hortico, Ingwersen, Reginald Kaye, F. Toynbee Ltd., The Weald Herbary.
Seeds: Thomas Butcher, Chiltern, Holtzhausen, Kent County Nurseries, Suttons, Thompson and Morgan.

LEUCOJUM - Snowflake, Loddon Lily *(Amaryllidaceae).* There is a considerable difference between Snowflakes and Snowdrops. Snowflakes have large bulbs and shining leaves and a larger, different flower whose petals are all the same length, unlike the Snowdrop. Snowflakes seen from some way off look just like their name – a snowflake frozen in mid-air because the pedicel that supports the plant is invisible at a distance. There are three kinds – *L. vernum,* the spring-flowering Snowflake, blooming with the Snowdrops in the spring, *L. aestivum,* the Summer Snowflake, with longer leaves and taller stems, flowering just as *L. vernum* ceases and very much less choosy about its requirements. *L. autumnale* has delicate pale pink flowers in early Autumn. *A. aestivum* had two other common names – Early Summer Fooles and Summer Sottekins (from the Dutch). In the wild state this plant prefers to grow by streamsides and its seeds have built-in buoyancy tanks so that they can float safely away to colonise new territory. The Greek word *Leukoion* means 'white violet' – perhaps because the flower is scented: this is yet another 'violet' flower.

L. aestivum - Summer Snowflake grows to 18in (46cm) with white bells in April and May. A European bulb from Majorca for a partially shaded corner with moist soil.

L. autumnale - Autumn Snowflake (1629) grows to 10in (25.5cm) with palest pink flowers from July to September. A bulb from N. Africa for a sunny corner or in the rockery. Protect emerging leaves from slugs.

L. vernum - Spring Snowflake (1569) grows to 8in (20.5cm) with white flowers in February and March. A bulb from Central Europe for moist soil and semi-shade. Protect leaves and flowers from slugs.

Requirements: *L. vernum* needs moist, humid-rich soil and partial shade. *L. aestivum* needs the same and *L. autumnale* needs ordinary free-draining soil and a sunny situation.

Cultivation: Get bulbs in as soon as available or buy them 'in the green' when in season. *L. vernum* and *L. aestivum* should be planted 3 – 4in (7.5 – 10cm) deep and *L. autumnale* 2in (5cm) deep. Leave undisturbed if doing well until bulbs become congested, then lift and separate when leaves die down.

Bulbs: Amand, Avon, Bloms, Broadleigh, Holden Clough, Ingwersen, Orpington, Potterton and Martin, van Tubergen.

LEWISIA *(Portulacaceae).* The plants were named after Captain Meriwether Lewis (1774-1809) of the Lewis and Clark expedition across the United States of America (see Clarkia). Lewisias are beautiful little rockery plants for the warmest and most sheltered place in the garden. They are not truly hardy, disliking the temperature changes of the British Isles, and, of course, the wetness. The best way to keep them is to plant them in a pot that can accommodate their large roots and can then be kept in a cold frame for the winter or a well-ventilated cold greenhouse and brought out in spring to grow on through the summer. They should have a deep collar of chippings around their necks to protect them, and their soil should be rich and well-drained, with the addition of more of the chippings. They are quite greedy plants and need some well-decayed manure at the bottom of their pot or pots. During the growing season water carefully in dry weather, but keep drier once flowering is over. This is best achieved with a pane of glass on wire legs. The plants will make offsets which can be detached in June and planted in peat and sand in a cold frame to root. When they have rooted, put them in individual pots of John Innes No. 3 and put back in the frame for the winter. Protect plants from slugs in spring.

L. oppositaefolia (1887) grows to 6in (15cm) with pale pink or white flowers in summer. A tender perennial from California for rockery or alpine house.

L. rediviva - Bitter Root (1826) grows to 3in (7.5cm) with pink or white flowers in June. A tender perennial from the W. United States.

Requirements: *See text.*

Cultivation: *See text.*

Plants: Broadwell, Hillier, Holden Clough, Ingwersen, Reginald Kaye, Robinsons.

LIATRIS - Blazing Star, Gayfeather *(Compositae).* Liatris have very unusual plumy flowers that everyone stops to look at when they are in bloom. Some of the varieties are quite tall and bushy and the flowers make an arresting and very different display. The different kinds need different conditions. If they stay two or three years in one spot in your garden, producing nothing but healthy-looking leaves, then move them to a totally different site. Maybe they just wanted a different view, and often this does the trick. Bees appreciate their late summer flowers. Most prefer rich, free-draining soils and a mulch of well-decayed manure in spring. Those planted in hotter, dryer situations need watering well during hot weather. The plants vanish during the winter, so their position should be remembered or marked. Seeds can be sown in March under glass and grown on in the usual way. Set out in nursery rows and leave for a year before transplanting 18 months after sowing.

L. spicata (1732) grows to 2ft (61cm) with purple flowers in September. A stout perennial from the Eastern USA for a moist place in sun.

L. callilepsis grows to 3ft (91.5cm) with foot-long flower spikes from July to September. A perennial from the U.S. for poor, dry soils.

L. pycnostachya grows to 5ft (1.52cm) with pale purple flower spikes in August and September. Grow as a biennial. From Central U.S. Best in dry soils in full sun.
Plants: Most nurseries.
Seeds: Thomas Butcher, Chiltern, Suttons.

LIBERTIA *(Iridaceae)*. Libertias take some years to get established and until then they are just clumps of Iris-like leaves in the border. But when they finally get settled and put their minds to it they are most interesting, with tall stems of long-lasting three-petalled white flowers. The Libertia was named after Marie A. Libert (1782 – 1865), a Belgian authority on liverworts. Libertias should be planted in a very sunny and sheltered place in the garden; free-draining neutral soil suits mine very well, as it flowers lustily in summer. It is recommended that it likes a peaty soil, but as mine is doing well enough at time of writing this I would not wish to upset its rhythms. The large tuft of evergreen leaves should be covered over in protracted cold weather. More northern counties will need to take this precaution in any case.
L. formosa (1837) grows to 16in (40.5cm) with clustered white flowers in May. A perennial from Chile for a hot, sheltered position.
L. grandiflora - Libertia (1876) grows to 3ft (91.5cm) with white flowers in June and July. A tender perennial rhizomatous perennial with evergreen leaves from New Zealand for a sheltered sunny border.
Plants: Bressingham, Broadleigh, Beth Chatto, Holden Clough, Ingwersen, Notcutts, Thompson and Morgan, Treasures of Tenbury.
Seeds: Thompson and Morgan.

LIGULARIA *(Compositae)*. This handsome plant, formerly *Senecio clivorum* is more correctly *Ligularia dentata* syn. *Ligularia clivorum.* It has most interesting heart-shaped green leaves that are crimson-purple beneath, with matching branched stems and brilliant orange-yellow daisies about 3 – 4in (7.5 – 10cm) across. The plant should be grown in semi-shade or its leaves will droop, and it really needs damp soil. Slugs are very partial to its foliage and will quickly spoil the whole plant, so take precautions. *Ligularia przewalskii* (formerly *S. przewalskii)* has large jagged very green leaves and these also wilt if the plant is grown in ordinary soil and a sunny position. Tall black stems carry spikes of raggedy yellow daisies, which makes a very striking colour contrast and a group of the plants always arouses notice and admiration. Both plants can be increased by division in the spring, and both should be grown in moist soil and partial shade.
L. dentata syn. **L. clivorum** (1900) grows to 4ft (122cm) with purple stems and purple undersides to the leaves. Orange daisies in July and August. A perennial from N. China and Japan for a moist or waterside position.
L. przewalskii syn. **L. stenocephala - The Rocket.** Grows to 5ft (1.52m) with black stems and spikes of yellow flowers in July. A perennial from China for a moist or waterside position.
Requirements: *See text.*
Cultivation: *See text.* Seeds may be sown in spring and grown on in the usual way. The seedlings will need protection from slugs.
Plants: Most nurseries.
Seeds: Chiltern, Thompson and Morgan.

LILIUM - Lily *(Liliaceae)* Lilies are found throughout the world and all of them are beautiful. They have been cultivated for centuries, particularly the pure white Madonna Lily, *Lilium candidum,* which is not so easy to grow as it seemed to be in former years. It is one of the few lilies that likes to be planted in full sun, with the nose of the bulb above, or only just below the surface of the soil. Rosettes of leaves will appear in late autumn and these will remain throughout the winter − it is also one of the few lilies that have winter foliage. Paintings of Madonna Lilies go back through history and one of the most famous is a sketch by Leonardo da Vinci (c.1479) that is owned by Her Majesty Queen Elizabeth II. A much earlier representation is to be seen at Amnisos, near Knossos, whose date is round about 1550 B.C. This is a pleasing painting that would translate with no changes at all into a stylised modern design. The Madonna Lily was and still is the symbol of the purity of the Virgin Mary, and more recently the flowers are associated with cottage gardens, together with roses, honeysuckle and hollyhocks. Madonna Lilies prefer an alkaline soil and the bulbs should be given a bed of coarse sand to sit on for drainage, with more of the same laid on the soil surface to discourage slugs.

Most lilies should be planted with their bulbs in partial shade but so that they can grow to the sun. Almost all of them are scented, in one way or another, and some most oppressively so. You really get your money's worth with a lily-bulb. *Lilium regale* is one of the easiest to grow, with perfumed pink trumpets in summer. It is a fairly recent newcomer, but is very popular because it will tolerate more neglect than most lilies, and it can be grown easily from seed to flower in about three years. A fine and often overpoweringly scented and floriferous lily is *Lilium auratum*, the Golden-rayed Lily of Japan. This can reach 8ft (2.4m) in an ideal situation. In almost any soil it will flower the first year, with yellow-striped white trumpets flecked with purple spots in August and September. It can have as many as 30 huge flowers (though this is exceptional) on each stem and this, because of the size of each flower is such a visual feast that it makes your senses reel.

Lilies should be bought from a reputable grower and not a garden centre. The bulbs damage easily, being (generally) composed of thick, fleshy scales which can be broken off only too easily. The bulbs dry out very quickly and become dessicated if they are exposed to the drying action of air – as I know to my own sorrow. Ideally, they should be collected in person from the growers at the right time of year, which can be different for the various types. Most bulbs are imported nowadays, and one cannot tell if they are healthy or not – Lilies for all their beauty are a race of disease-prone bug-carriers (though everyone loves them despite this) that need the utmost care in growing conditions if they are to increase in your garden.

It will be noticed when consulting the lily-lists that many of the species names are, to put it charitably, inharmonious when linked with such beautiful flowers. In many cases, the lilies were named after the men who discovered them, often at extraordinary discomfort and even danger: in several cases plant hunters have lost their lives quite literally in the field in finding the parents of the garden flowers that we often take for granted. Ernest Henry Wilson (1876 – 1930) was one such plant collector, and a brief account of his travails when searching for one species is as follows. In 1910 Wilson was in China, looking for plants and in particular a beautiful new lily that grew in the Min Valley. There were roads of a sort by then, but he had to travel from Ichang to Cheng-tu (in Szechwan) and since no road existed that would take him directly to his destination, he and his party walked the 200 miles in 22 days to Sung-pan. This was an important trade-route, passing through deep gorges and alongside roaring rapids, with perpendicular cliffs or steep slopes always beside the track. The Min river wound through deep defiles, where the cliffs were of a slippery shale that was unsafe after heavy rain. This was where his lily grew and as he wanted to collect 6000 bulbs for the American market he was determined to endure the discomforts and privations in order to fulfil his instructions. While at Sung-pan he arranged for the lilies to be dug up, carefully packed and shipped to America in the following October. After making these arrange-ments he began the return journey to Cheng-tu, but was caught in an avalanche that swept him down the hill-side, still in his sedan chair.

Struggling out of the wreckage of this, a tumbling rock hit his leg, breaking it in two places. Though in great pain he directed his men to carry him up to the track and make a splint from the legs of his camera tripod. While this was being done, a mule train came along, and there was no room for it to pass; it could not stop because the cliffs were so dangerous, and so it had to proceed. Wilson's men laid him across the path and signalled to the train to walk over his prostrate body. Nearly 50 mules stepped over him, carrying their loads, and not one animal touched him. After that terrifying experience he was taken to Cheng-tu, though by this time the leg had become infected and for six weeks he faced the possibility of amputation, because the bones refused to knit. However, after three months the leg had healed partially, and he was able to start the long voyage back to America. There the limb was broken again and re-set in aseptic hospital conditions, and the leg mended well, though he walked with a limp for the rest of his life. The 6000 lily bulbs arrived safely, and *Lilium regale* is often as beautiful in our gardens as it once was in its home in a distant river valley in China.

There are many thousands of lilies and their hybrid descendants, and the following collection is representative of the species types that can still be obtained quite easily.

Some Lilies for ordinary garden soils: *L. candidum* (white); *L. chalcedonicum* (scarlet); *L. henryi* (orange-yellow); *L. martagon* (purplish-pink); *L. pyrenaicum* (acid-yellow with black spots); *L. regale* (pink); *L. tigrinum* (orange with black spots).

Lilies for 'woodland' conditions (gardens with leaf-mould, moisture retentive soil and partial shade): *L. auratum* (white with gold stripe); *L. Brownii* (cream inside, chocolate brown outside); *L. canadense* (yellow to pale red); *L. Parryi* (pale yellow); *L. superbum* (orange to crimson with maroon spots).

Lilies for calcareous or chalky soil: *L. candidum* (white); *L. hansonii* (orange-yellow with brown spots); *L. pumilum* (bright scarlet); *L. regale* (pink); *L. monadelphium* (deep yellow, shading to red).

Lilies for open woodland: *L. giganteum* (white, tinged green); *L. japonicum* (pink); *L. Humboldtii* (reddish orange); *L. cordatum* (white with yellow streaks and purple markings)

L. auratum - The Golden-rayed Lily of Japan (1862) grows to 8ft (2.4m), having ivory flowers with a central band of yellow and many raised dark purple spots. 20 or more scented flowers on a stem in August and September. Plant stem-rooting bulbs 6 – 8in (15 – 20.5cm) deep. For partially shaded conditions, needs leaf-mould.

L. Brownii (1835) grows to 4ft (122cm) having large chocolate flowers with cream interiors in July. Plant 4 – 6in (10 – 15cm) deep in humus-rich soil. A bulb from S. China.

L. canadense - Canada Lily (1620) grows to 5ft (1.52m) with bright yellow to pale red flowers spotted on lower petals, in July. Plant 4 – 6in (10 – 15cm) deep in woodland conditions. A bulb from Canada.

L. candidum - The Madonna Lily (Long cultivated) grows to 5ft (2.4m) with scented pure white flowers in June – July. Plant in slightly calcareous soil 2in (5cm) deep in August, in a sunny position. Do not then disturb. A bulb from the E. Mediterranean.

L. chalcedonicum (about 1600) grows to 4ft (122cm) with bright scarlet flowers in July. Plant 4 – 6in (10 – 15cm) deep in good soil in the border. Benefits from leaf-mould. A bulb from Greece.

L. cordatum (1876) grows to 6ft (1.85m) with yellow-streaked white flowers with purple marks. Plant 8in (20.5cm) deep in woodland conditions. A bulb from Japan.

L. giganteum syn. **Cardiocrinum giganteum** (1852) grows to 10ft (3.05m) with huge green-tinged white trumpets in July and August. Monocarpic. (Dies

after flowering but leaves small offsets to grow on). Plant huge bulbs just
below soil level in woodland conditions, benefits from an annual mulch of
compost. Water in dry spells. From the Himalaya.

L. Hansonii (1870) grows to 4ft (122cm) with fragrant orange yellow flowers in
June and July. A basal-rooting bulb from Siberia and Japan.

L. Humboldtii (1872) grows to 5ft (1.52m) with reddish-orange flowers in July.
Plant 6in (15cm) deep. A bulb from California.

L. japonicum (1876) grows to 3ft (91.5cm) with fragrant pink flowers in June
and July. Plant 6 – 9in (15 – 23cm) deep in a sheltered shady position. A
stem-rooting bulb from Japan.

L. martagon - Martagon Lily (1596) grows to 4ft (122cm) with spotted pink-
mauve 'turk's cap' flowers in June and July. This one smells. A European
and Asian bulb, plant 4in (10cm) deep.

L. monadelphum (1804) grows to 5ft (1.52m) with fragrant, deep yellow shaded
red flowers in July. A stem-rooting bulb from the N. Caucasus. Plant 4 – 5in
(10 – 12.5cm) deep. Lime tolerant. Grow in partial shade.

L. Parryi (1879) grows to 4ft (122cm) with pale yellow flowers in July. Plant 6in
(15cm) deep in woodland conditions. A bulb from S. California.

L. pumilum syn. **tenuifolium** (1816) grows to 4in (10cm) with bright red flowers
in June. A stem-rooting bulb from E. China and Siberia for ordinary soil in
full sun.

L. pyrenaicum - Pyrenean Lily (1596) grows to 3ft (91.5cm) with black-spotted
acid yellow flowers in June. (This one smells, too). Plant bulbs 5in (12.5cm)
deep in ordinary soil. Lime tolerant.

L. regale - The Regal Lily (1903) grows to 6ft (1.85m) with fragrant pink and
white flowers in July. A stem-rooting bulb from Szechwan. Plant 6 – 9in (15
– 23cm) deep in full sun and ordinary soil.

L. superbum grows to 7ft (2.14m) with purple-spotted orange-crimson flowers.
Plant 7in (18cm) deep in woodland conditions, do not allow to dry out in
summer. A stem-rotting bulb from Eastern N. America.

L. tigrinum - Tiger Lily (1804) grows to 6ft (1.85m) with black spotted orange
flowers in August and September. A bulb from China, Japan and Korea,
producing stem bulbils that can be detached to grow on. These will
eventually become flowering size bulbs. Plant 6in (15cm) deep in lime-free
soil in full sun.

Requirements: *See text,* but check before purchasing lilies to see if you have the
right kind of soil for them. When they arrive and seem dry, restore them by
leaving overnight in moist (not wet) peat.

Cultivation: Some lilies produce offsets, many can be grown from seed and take
from 5 – 7 years to come to flowering. In a mixed garden collection the
seedlings will not be true.

Bulbs: Amand, Bees, Bloms, Broadleigh, Thomas Butcher, de Jager, Kelways, St.
Bridget, van Tubergen.

Seeds: Suttons, Chiltern.

LIMNANTHES - Poached Egg Flower *(Limnanthaceae).* The proper name of
this charming flower comes from *Limne,* marsh, *anthos,* flower because it
likes wet soil. If your soil suits it you will have it for ever. The white petals
have a bright yellow zone in the middle hence the common name. Sadly, it
is an annual which makes one appreciate it the more because there is always
the slight worry, round about December, that it may not reappear in your
garden. Seed is easily obtained and sown from March to May where the
plants are to flower. The very characteristic seedlings with their light green
leaves will soon appear and can be thinned out as necessary. It is a good bee
flower.

Limnanthes douglasii - Poached Egg Flower (1833) grows to 6in (15cm) with
white and yellow flowers in early summer. *Limnanthes* is an annual from
California.

Requirements: Prefers damp soil in full sun.
Cultivation: *See text.*
Seeds: Thomas Butcher, Chiltern, Dobie, Suttons, Thompson and Morgan.

LIMONIUM - Pink Pokers, Statice, Sea Lavender *(Plumbaginaceae).* The name of the plant comes from *liemon*, a meadow, from its habit of flowering in salt marshes. Most of these plants have flowers that have 'everlasting' qualities, and there are several distinct shapes which make a mixed collection of them very useful for flower arrangements. A familiar variety is Sea Lavender, or *Limonium vulgare* which likes to grow in those inaccessible coastal mud flats, where it forms a positive field of colour. *L. suworowii*, which looks like a collection of melting pokers frozen in anguish, is beloved by flower arrangers because it combines flowing lines with useful rigidity. *L. latifolium* takes a little while to come into its own from seed but produces a cloud of tiny, long-lasting lilac flowers, which hang suspended in the garden for many weeks. Even as the colour fades to soft bracken-brown, it is still useful as a 'filler' in the vases because it retains its shape and colour. *L. sinuatum* is the best known of all and is grown as an 'everlasting' producing pink, mauve, blue, salmon and white flowers. It can be grown to flower under glass in early spring. Sow seeds in August and pot up seedlings in September into 5-in (12.5-cm) pots of John Innes No. 1. Keep in a greenhouse or conservatory with a mean winter temperature of 8°C (46°F). If grown for use as dried flowers, the stems should be cut when the flowers are half open: they should be bunched and tied to hang upside down in an airy place to dry, out of direct sunlight.
L. latifolium (1791) grows to 18in (46cm) with a much branched cloud of tiny lilac flowers from May to July. A perennial from Russia for a focal position in full sun.
L. sinuatum (1629) grows to 18in (46cm) with many coloured flowers from July to September. A perennial (grown as an annual) from the Mediterranean region for a sunny border.
L. Suworowii - Pink Pokers (1833) grows to 18in (46cm) with contorted pink flower stems in August. An annual from W. Turkestan for a sunny border.
Requirements: Ordinary well-drained garden soil and a sunny position.
Cultivation: Sow seeds thinly in seed compost in March under glass at a temperature of 13-16°C (55-61°F). Prick out and grow on in the usual way, plant out end of May. Sow perennial sorts in the same way but set out in nursery rows. Plant out in the following year.
Uses: As very long-lasting garden flowers and even longer-lasting dried ones.
Seeds: Thomas Butcher, Chiltern, Thompson and Morgan.
Plants: Cunnington, Hillier, Jackman's, Scotts, Sherrards, St. Bridget, F.Toynbee Ltd.

LINARIA - Toadflax *(Scrophulariaceae).* Linarias of all kinds look like smaller, daintier Antirrhinums and are most useful and attractive in rock gardens. They are not long-lived plants and some younger replacements should be kept by, either grown from cuttings or from seed.
The wild *L. cymbalaria*, the Ivy-leaved Toadflax has been moved into another family now, together with the rest of its common names – Kenilworth Ivy (it was formerly planted on artificial ruins by the Victorians), Mother of Thousands, Penny Leaf and Penny Wort. This is a very pretty little wall plant, with mauve flowers and most attractive evergreen leaves, that have a succulent appearance. After flowering the stem curves down and 'plants' the ripe seed into a convenient crack. There is a white variety that is worth searching for. Many people now buy flower seeds and sow them in appropriate – or inappropriate – places in the wild. Those that come up are often not the 'right' plants for the area which worries the botanists. But this sort of thing has been going on for many years, and early

in the nineteenth century *L. cymbalaria* (at that time thought to be an introduction to the British Isles) was discovered growing on some rocks at Barmouth in Merionethshire. This made the botanical fraternity think that the plant was actually a native after all, and then a Mr Dovaston rather smugly revealed "... that several years ago in one of my numerous tours through that and other mountainous regions, I carried a box of seeds of this beautiful, gracious and tenacious plant, which I distributed in appropriate places on rocks, ruins, churches, castles and bridges, where I have since beheld it thriving in tresses and festoons to my fullest satisfaction". Mr Dovaston was probably influenced by the fact that "in Italy there is nothing more common than it on Mud-walls, old Ruins, and upon Rocks."

L. alpina is a hardy alpine that looks best perched on the edge of its own pocket in a rockery. *L. maroccana* is a gay annual which makes a fine splash of colour either in a border, in tubs or in a rockery. Grow the plants closely together for the best effect.

L. Cymbalaria now **Cymbalaria muralis - Ivy-leaved Toadflax** etc. grows to 2in (5cm) or even less, but hangs in curtains from old walls or creeps in cracks with mauve flowers from May to September. A European perennial for dry stone walls. Too vigorous for a rockery. White forms are *L. albiflora* and *L. albo-compacta*.

L. alpina - Alpine Toadflax grows to 6in (15cm) with blue-violet flowers from June to August. A compact plant from the European Alps for a sunny rockery.

L. Maroccana - Fairy Flax (1872) grows to 12in (30.5cm) with flowers of many colours in June. An annual from Morocco for low flower beds, pots or large rockeries.

Requirements: All Linarias prefer sunny positions; *C. muralis* looks charming on stone walls and ripe seeds can be inserted into old mortar with a little soil or a tuft of turf to help things.

Cultivation: Sow seeds in boxes in February or March and grow on in the usual way. Plant out in May. Sow seeds of *L. alpina* in flowering position in April and thin out later. Take basal cuttings from *L. alpina* in May, inserting them in sand and peat to root. Transfer into pots of John Innes No. 1 and keep in a cold frame. Plant out in September in warm areas and the following spring in Northern counties.

Seeds: Thomas Butcher, Chiltern, Thompson and Morgan, Unwins.

Plants: Hillier, Ingwersen, Reginald Kaye, Robinsons, Sherrards, Treasures of Tenbury.

LINUM - Flax *(Linaceae)*. Flax is one of the oldest plants to be used in man's service. Long before the Egyptians wrapped their dead in the linen made from *L. usitatissimum*, the plant was being used by prehistoric man. It is almost impossible to believe that this fragile-looking little plant with its delicate blue flowers has such a great history. It was and is used to make linen, cord, canvas, lamp-wicks, bow-strings, fishing nets, linoleum, linseed oil, paint, varnish, cattle cake, printer's ink and medicines. There is a delightful tradition from old Bohemia that if seven year old children dance among the flax flowers, they will become beautiful. Medicinally the action of this plant is very powerful. It is still used as a poultice for deep-seated inflammation and it alleviates pain. It is used in cough medicines and linseed tea is good for colds, with the addition of honey and lemon juice. Mixed with lime water it was used for burns and scalds, and has been used as a laxative. Cage birds eat a mixture of seeds, and linseed is usually part of their diet: and the plant is found in the veterinary pharmacopoeia. The perennial varieties of Flax dislike cold and wet, and *L. narbonense* dies back in winter. *L. perenne* isn't, really. Both can be easily grown from seed, and a large patch is better than a small one both from the point of view of the impact of the beautiful blue flowers of *L. narbonense*, and the fact that the more plants there are the more likelihood there is that they may set seed. This can be collected as soon as ripe and sown in boxes of seed compost in a cold frame: or the seeds can be sown in the open ground, or saved until the following spring. The seedlings of perennial sorts do not generally flower in the first year.

L. narbonense (1759) grows to 2ft (61cm) with very blue flowers from May to July. A short-lived perennial from S. Europe for the sunny border.

L. perenne grows to 18in (46cm) with paler blue flowers in June and July. A European perennial for a sunny border.

L. usitatissimum - Flax grows to 18in (46cm) with pale blue flowers in June and July. A historic annual for a sunny corner in the herb garden or border.

Requirements: A very warm sunny border and ordinary free-draining soil.

Cultivation: *See text.*

Uses: As border plants, grown thickly, and in association with Pinks or Evening Primrose.

Seeds: Thomas Butcher, Chiltern, Dobie, Goatchers, Thompson and Morgan.

Plants: Most nurseries.

LIRIOPE *(Liliaceae)* The plant was named after the nymph Liriope. The evergreen perennial plants look interesting through the winter because their leaves are a good green, and even more so when they produce their spikes of bead-like flowers in later summer. They like a sandy soil. Liriopes do not always flower, and if they remain for more than two years in a green sulk then move them to a different and better place if there is one available. Their flowers are so interesting that it is worth having a bit of a general post in order to make them happy.

L. muscari grows to 15in (38cm) with dense tufts of shining evergreen strap-shaped leaves. Spikes of mauve flowers from August to October. A rather tender perennial from China and Japan for a very sunny border.

Requirements: *See text.* Dislikes lime.

Cultivation: Divide in early spring.

Plants: Broadleigh, Beth Chatto, Hillier, Kelways, Notcutts, Sherrards, South-combe Gardens, Treasures of Tenbury.

LOBELIA *(Campanulaceae)*. Lobelias were named after Matthias de L'obel 1538-1616, a botanist and physician to James I. The best known of the genus is *L. Erinus*, the edging and hanging basket plant whose blue flowers are so abundant throughout the summer, whatever the weather. One of the handsomest is *L. cardinalis* which has dark red leaves and brilliant scarlet flowers. This is an elegant plant that should be grown in a group, and oddly enough, it is perfectly happy in the pond – happier, in fact, because it will reach a height of 5ft (1.52m) and can even be left there for the winter providing the pot is 9in (23cm) below water level as it is not reliably hardy. Queen Henrietta Maria of France said that its colour reminded her of a cardinal's stockings. *L. fulgens* is very similar in appearance to *L. cardinalis* but its flowers and leaves are slightly downy: it goes on flowering later in the year and it is taller. There is often confusion because there are hybrids between it, *L. cardinalis* and *L. syphilitica*, the latter being a blue flowered species that has been known in English gardens since 1665. Linnaeus gave the plant this unfortunate name because he had heard that it was used by the Red Indians to cure venereal diseases. The secret of the preparation of the plant for this purpose was purchased from the Indians but nothing came of it, and the plant has to bear this mortification for ever.

L. cardinalis - Cardinal Flower (1626) grows to 2ft (61cm) with scarlet flowers in July and August (vars. with purple foliage). A tender perennial from N. America for the border and in ponds. Protect in winter or lift and grow on in a large pot in a greenhouse.

L. Erinus - Blue Lobelia (1752) grows to 6in (15cm) with blue, pink or white flowers throughout the summer. An annual from S. Africa for massed plantings, edging, pots, troughs and hanging baskets.

L. fulgens (1809) grows to 3ft (91.5cm) with scarlet flowers from May to September. A tender perennial from Mexico for the border or ponds.

L. syphilitica (1665) grows to 2ft (61cm) with light blue flowers in autumn. A hardier perennial from the E. United States, for the damp border or pond side in sun.

Requirements: The annual Lobelia is a half-hardy plant and the perennial kinds are tender. These can be lifted and kept in a warm greenhouse for the winter or left in a deeper part of the pond. Feed all of them, particularly *L. cardinalis.*

Cultivation: Protect perennial species with litter. In later spring the various 'rosettes' can be separated and grown on until established. Plant out when all danger of frost is past. Sow seeds of annuals in February thinly in seed compost in a temperature of 16°-18°C (61-64°F) and grow on in the usual way.

After flowering: Cut off central flower stems to encourage the others.

Seeds: Thomas Butcher, Chiltern, Dobies, Suttons, Thompson and Morgan, Unwins.

Plants: (perennial species) Most nurseries.

LOBULARIA - See **Alyssum** *(Cruciferae).*

LUNARIA - **Honesty, Penny-flower, Moonwort** *(Cruciferae).* The name is taken from *Luna,* the moon, because of the shape and colour of the seeds. There is a little confusion between this plant and the Moonwort fern *Botrychium lunaria* which had the magical power of making horses cast their shoes. Honesty had quite a range of names in olden times – Judaspence, White Sattin, Silverplate, Shillings, Money-in-both-pockets and Pennies-in-a-purse. The nicest reason for its name of Honesty is that the shining middle membrane (called the replum) is quite transparent when the other two are rubbed away. There is an old saying *In cruce salus* 'Health is in the Cross' which alludes to the fact that all the Cruciferae family are wholesome to eat, and it is said that Honesty will not grow in the garden of a dishonest person.

L. biennis syn. **L. annua** - **Honesty** (1595) grows to 3ft (91.5cm) with mauve-magenta flowers from May to July. A biennial plant from Sweden for anywhere in the garden. Does well in semi-shade and good for 'poor' corners.

Requirements: Any soil, sun or semi-shade.

Cultivation: Sow seeds when ripe in flowering position. Thin out as early as possible.

After flowering: Pick seed stems on a dry day in autumn, hang upside down in an airy place to dry. Carefully rub away outer membrane to reveal silver replum.

Seeds: Most seedsmen.

LUPINUS - **Lupin, Lupine** *(Leguminae).* The name comes from *lupus,* a wolf, because the ancient Greeks believed that Lupins devoured the goodness in the soil and left it infertile. In actuality the annual kind *L. luteus* has been used to improve sandy soil in S. Europe because of its ability to take nitrogen from the air and leave the soil richer. This useful characteristic is shared by most of the family, particularly Clover which is often ploughed in as green manure. Parkinson said that Lupin seeds would "scoure and cleanse the skin from spots, morphew, blew markes and other discolourings thereof" and an ointment made from them was still being used in the eighteenth century by ladies to "smooth the face, soften the features and make the few charms they possess a little powerful". The parti-coloured lupins of today are very late comers to the herbaceous border, being bred by a George Russell, a jobbing gardener aged 60, who began to specialise in the breeding of lupins at the time of the coronation of King George V of England in 1911. The splendid flowers that are grown today are derived from his devoted work to this genus, but they were not exhibited until 1937 – another coronation year. Most of the modern kinds are crosses and recrosses from *L. polyphyllus*.

L. polyphyllus (1826) grows to 5ft (1.52cm) with silky leaves and flower spikes in cream, yellow, blue, red and purple in May and June. A perennial from W. North America for the sunny border

Requirements: Lupins prefer neutral to acid soil. Protect emerging leaves from slugs.

Cultivation: Sow seed in March, grow on and prick out into a nursery bed. Move to flowering positions in October, take off first year's flower spikes as they form.

During and after flowering: Cut off flowered stems to encourage secondary flower spikes.

Plants: Hillier, Holden Clough.

Seeds: Most seedsmen.

LYCHNIS - Rose Campion, Jerusalem Cross *(Caryophyllaceae)*. Rose Campion or *Lychnis coronaria* has silver grey leaves and stems and bright magenta flowers. It is short-lived perennial, valuable in the winter garden because of its permanent silver hummocks. The down on the leaves was once used to make lampwicks. It has always been a popular garden flower from the fourteenth century onward, several old names that are not used now are Gardener's Delight, Gardener's Eie, and Bloody William. *L. chalcedonica* was called the Jerusalem Cross because it was introduced into the British Isles at the time of the crusades, and it has this name in most of the European languages. It was called the 'Fioure of Constantinople' in 1578, though it came originally from Russia. In 1597 it was being grown in gardens and had several common names – Nonesuch, Campion of Constantinople and Flower of Bristow, probably given to it because of a popular dye colour that was made at Bristol called Bristowe or Bristol red. Other names were Scarlet Lightning, Knight's Cross and (particularly charming) Bridget-in-her-Bravery. *L. chalcedonica's* flowers are very red and care must be taken in its siting, or its colour will clash with almost everything else except equally hot reds and oranges. Plant it with yellow flowers such as *Lysimachia punctata*, Nasturtiums to creep between its toes, white Shasta Daisies, and cool it down with blue and grey-leaved edging plants.

L. chalcedonica - Jerusalem Cross, Maltese Cross (1593) grows to 3ft (91.5cm) with bright scarlet flowers in July-August. A perennial for a sunny border from E. Russia.

L. Coronaria - Rose Campion (1596) grows to 30in (76cm) with magenta flowers, silver-hairy, ever-grey leaves and stems. Flowers from July to August. A short-lived perennial from S. Europe for the sunny border. Small new plants make very attractive edging plants before they flower.

Requirements: *L. coronaria* does best in full sun and light soil. *L. chalcedonica* needs full sun and ordinary soil, does well in damp gardens.

Cultivation: Grow *L. coronaria* from seed sown in February in John Innes No. 1. Grow on and plant out in flowering position. *L. chalcedonica:* sow seeds in March or as soon as ripe and grow on in a nursery row, or divide established clumps in early spring.

After flowering: Cut down stems of *L. chalcedonica*.

Seeds: Thomas Butcher, Chiltern, Suttons, Thompson and Morgan, Unwins.

Plants: Most nurseries.

LYSIMACHIA - Yellow Loosestrife, Creeping Jenny *(Primulaceae)*. Although it is difficult to relate both these flowers with their very different heights and habits to the Primrose, they share the same botanical characteristics. Creeping Jenny is a delightful little plant, though not so little sideways, only upwards. It lives up to its name of Meadow Runagates, and its other names of Herb Twopence and Moneywort relate to its almost round coin-like leaves. It is a most useful plant for clothing rocky areas, though not rockeries. It has a yellow leaved variety – *L. nummularia aurea* which is even prettier when creeping over grey stone, though it needs to grow in sun. Creeping Jenny was once used medicinally as a wound herb though it is now known that it has no curative powers.

The other derivation of the plant's name is from Lysimachus, King of Thrace (on the shores of the Black Sea) who discovered the plant's supposed medicinal value. Its taller cousin, the Yellow Loosestrife (no relation whatever to Purple Loosestrife – see *Lythrum salicaria)* is a very pleasant and easy-going flower. It will grow almost anywhere, and is unfussy as to soil though it does best of all in a sunny damp ditch. Its common name is an old one, given to it in the belief that it would quieten savage beasts and more particularly that it had a special virtue "... in appeasing the strife and unruliness which falleth out among oxen at the plough, if it be put about their yokes". Yellow Loosestrife is disliked by gnats and flies, and the plant was burnt indoors so that the smoke would clear the room of these noisome insects. The rhizomatous roots can be easily split up in autumn or early spring and small rosettes of leaves will rise up from each piece. It lasts long in flower and should not, as it often is, be scorned because it is so easy and troublefree to grow and because it does have something of a wander-lust. Its whorls of bright golden-yellow flowers are very distinctive in shape and are therefore most useful in contrast to other plants.

L. nummularia - Creeping Jenny, Moneywort. Prostrate with evergreen stoloniferous stems and bright yellow flowers in June and July. A European perennial, excellent as ground cover by the waterside, in hanging baskets, and trailing down walls and banks. This plant will grow in ordinary dry soil as well.

L. punctata - Yellow Loosestrife (1820) grows to 2ft (61cm) with yellow flowers from June to August. A perennial from Asia Minor for boggy pond margins, but seems to do just as well in ordinary border soil. Can be invasive, but always a pleasure.

Requirements: *As text.*

Cultivation: *L. nummularia* does not set seed, but can be easily propagated by detaching the runners in April or September and replanting or potting immediately. For *L. punctata* see text.

After flowering: Cut down *L. punctata* in late autumn.

Plants: Most nurseries.

LYTHRUM - Purple Loosestrife *(Lythraceae).* The name *Lythrum* comes from *Lythron,* black blood, from the flower colour of some of the species, though this is overdoing it, I feel. This plant is not related to the Yellow Loosestrife. There are several colours including a very definite magenta that is sometimes difficult to integrate into a harmonious late summer colour scheme (which has to include all the shades of yellow) but the pinks and carmines are softer and all blend together. They are excellently floriferous at this time in the garden year, and much later, in October, the leaves turn to a good yellow which lasts for some weeks and can be quite a feature. If grown with its toes in mud the Purple Loosestrife will reach 8ft (2.4m) (at least, mine does) but its normal height is about 5ft (1.52m). It seeds itself about very readily, and the seedlings appear to be quite content to live in a path, (where their roots are cool beneath the stones) but they must be moved as soon as recognised or their stems will become woody and almost impossible to dislodge. One has to be firm with this plant or your pool will be full of it and a little of its colour goes a long way. Plant with *Polygonum amplexicaule atrosanguineum* – both like the same conditions. The plant has been used medicinally for dysentery, diseases of the liver, quinsy and for external treatment to wounds and sores.

L. Salicaria - Purple Loosestrife grows to an average height of 5ft (1.52m) more in damp soil, with magenta or pink flower spikes from June to September. A perennial from the north temperate region, also Australia, for pond-edge or the back of a border.

Requirements: Sun, any soil.

Cultivation: Divide in spring – plants are late coming into leaf. Sow seeds in April in a cold frame and grow on, prick out and plant in a nursery bed.

Uses: As adaptable border or water-side plants with a long flowering season.

After flowering: Cut down stems after leaves have fallen.

Plants: Bressingham, Beth Chatto, Cunnington, Goatchers, Hillier, Holden Clough, Honeysome Aquatic Nursery, Notcutts, Scotts, Sherrards, Waveney Fish Farm.

Seeds: Thomas Butcher, Chiltern.

MACLEAYA - Plume Poppy *(Papaveraceae).* This is the least Poppy-like of Poppies but it is a fine plant to grow because of the shapely and beautiful jade-green leaves, that have coral-coloured veins and stems and silver green undersides, which show when the wind blows. The plant was named after Alexander Macleay (1762-1848), the Secretary of the Linnaean Society, who later became the Colonial Secretary for New South Wales. The Plume Poppy is excellent for a tall back-of-the border plant, or against shrubs. When it has settled down it will be found that it may be invasive, but by that time all your friends will have fallen in love with the leaves so there will be no lack of homes for pieces of the wandering orange roots. The crown of the plant should be well protected with litter for the winter, or the early emerging orange coloured shoots will be badly blackened by frost. Many nurseries list this under 'Bocconia'.

M. cordata syn. **Bocconia cordata** (1795) grows to 10ft (3.05m) with panicles of tiny buff flowers from June to August. A spreading perennial from China and Japan for a large border or any focal position. Grow this for the leaves.

Requirements: Any soil, sun or partial shade.

Cultivation: Lift and divide roots in autumn or early spring.

After flowering: Cut down stems.

Uses: As superb foliage plant.

Plants: Bressingham, Goatchers, Hillier, Jackman's, Kelways, Nottcutts, Scotts, Stoke Lacy Herb Garden, F. Toynbee Ltd.

MALCOLMIA - Virginia Stock, Virginian Stock *(Cruciferae).* This plant needs to be grown in masses or in drifts to have any effect and to make the most of its daytime fragrance. It is best to mix the seed with that of the Night Scented Stock – *Matthiola bicornis* so as to have substance as well as scent. Oddly enough Virginia Stock comes from the Mediterranean area and has nothing to do with the United States. The Latin name was changed from *Cheiranthus maritima* to *Malcolmia maritima* to honour an eighteenth century nurserymen, William Malcolm, who lived in Kensington; several rather dainty suggestions as to the common name have been put forward, such as that of Mrs Loudon, the energetic Victorian lady gardener who said that it might be "a corruption of Virgin's Stock, the easiness of its culture rendering it fit for young girls".

Maeterlinck was even more fanciful and described the flowers thus "The Virginia Stock, arch and demure in her gown of Jaconet, like the little serving maids of Dordrecht and Leyden, washes the borders of the beds with innocence".

M. maritima grows to 10in (25.5cm) with pink, mauve, lilac, rose, red and white

flowers in the summer. A hardy annual from the S. Mediterranean region for massing in a border, in troughs and pots and edge of patios.
Requirements: Any soil. Protect seedlings from slugs.
Cultivation: Sow thinly in flowering position and thin out if necessary. Flowers will appear in four weeks and will last successively for eight weeks.
Seeds: Most seedsmen.

MALVA - Mallow *(Malvaceae)*. These flowers are similar to the Common Mallow, *Malva sylvestris*, though they have more delicacy and the plants do not have the sprawling habit of the wild plant. Most are very good on poor soils which is a very useful asset. *M. moschata*, the Musk Mallow (named because of the musky smell given off by the crushed leaves) is very free-flowering with very attractive dissected leaves – the white flowered form is lovely and has an equally long flowering season. The Marsh Mallow *(A. officinalis)* was originally used to make the sweets that we still eat today, though, alas, those of the present day have nothing of the plant except the name.
M. Alcea (1797) grows to 4ft (122cm) with light green leaves: mauve pink flowers from July to October. A perennial from Italy for a sunny place in very ordinary soil.
M. moschata - Musk Mallow grows to 2½ft (76cm) with attractive finely cut leaves and pink or white flowers from June to September. A European perennial for a sunny place – the pink form is charming in front of Delphiniums.
Requirements: Sun, any soil including poor gravel.
Cultivation: Sow seeds in March or April in a cold greenhouse or frame. Grow on and plant out in a nursery row. Move to flowering position in Autumn or Spring.
Seeds: Chiltern, Dobie, Thompson and Morgan.
Plants: Beth Chatto, Holden Clough, Hillier, Southcombe.

MATTHIOLA - Stock, Night-Scented Stock *(Cruciferae)*. The plants were named after Pierandrea Mattioli, 1500-77, an Italian physician and botanist. Not a plant to grow for its looks, the Night-Scented Stock seems to droop in a languid way during the daytime, with exhausted-looking half-open washy lilac flowers. But, come the evening, the plants perk up and the flowers open and give out their sweet scent and they are really worth having, if you can plant them in masses where their evening perfume will be most noticeable. The cottage-garden stock is *M. incana*, and most gardeners will be familiar with the term 'Ten Week Stock'. This is an annual plant with many present-day subdivisions, flowering some ten weeks after sowing. The second group is the (annual) perpetual flowering Stock, which continues to flower throughout the summer.

A third group, the Brompton Stocks are grown as biennials, and were named by the firm of London and Wise whose nurseries were at Brompton. In Elizabethan times they were called Stock-Gilliflowers and were much cultivated, with many growing instructions being exchanged between gardeners. One of the most sensible came from John Hill in 1757 who said "the seeds saved from these plants will not fail to produce the Gardener many double and fine Flowers, but the best method is to exchange them annually with some person of Integrity at a Distance".

Stock seeds were even used medicinally, but only, as Jane Loudon said "certain Empiricks and Quacksalvers about love and lust matters, which for modestie I omit". The plants must have been very sturdy to have survived the folllowing treatment recommended by the Reverend Henry Stevenson in the eighteenth century " ... Stock Gilliflowers are raised commonly of Seed sown in April at Full Moon ... When they are 3 or 4 Inches high, take them all up, and throw some Sand upon the Bed to render it poorer; then plant them again, at a convenient Distance; this do for three full Moons to make them grow low; those that run up are in Danger of being killed in the Winter ... Often removing them does not only contribute to their Worth, but Duration. Let it be once a Month, if not at the full Moon."

M. bicornis - Night Scented Stock grows to 12in (30.5cm) with limp stems of night-fragrant lilac flowers in summer. An annual from Greece for planting near garden seats or under windows, or with other flowers in patio pots.

M. incana - Stock (1731) grows to various heights according to type with single or double purple flowers. Modern varieties come in all colours except blue.

Requirements: Stocks will grow in any soil but do better in slightly alkaline (chalk) areas. Ignoring the advice of the Reverend Stevenson, Stocks do better in richer soil in which some well decayed manure has been incorporated. In cold areas biennial plants may need cloches, and give a little ($\frac{1}{2}$ teasp) dried blood to each plant in the spring.

Cultivation: Sow seeds of *M. bicornis* thinly where they are to flower and protect seedlings from slugs. Sow seeds of annuals in March at a temperature of 13-15°C (55-59°F). Grow on and harden off. Sow biennials in a frame or in nursery rows, grow on and protect during winter.

Uses: As sweetly scented cut flowers and border annuals of a traditional type.

Seeds: Most seedsmen.

Plants: of *M. incana*, wild Stock: Southcombe.

MECONOPSIS - Poppy *(Papaveraceae).* The Welsh Poppy is *Meconopsis cambrica* which is a very graceful little plant that looks charming in the rockery and among ferns. It will usually seed itself about the garden and the seedlings can be collected as soon as recognised, to be planted as a group. *Meconopsis betonicifolia* is the exquisite Blue Poppy, whose flowers are among the most beautiful that a gardener can grow. It was first seen in 1886 by a French missionary Jean Marie Delavay, who sent specimens back to France to be named *M betonicifolia* by the botanist Franchet. Later the flower was seen in bloom by Lt. Colonel F. M. Bailey in 1913 whilst exploring the largely unmapped border between India and Tibet. Though he was everything else but a botanist (a soldier, surveyor, diplomat and secret agent) he must have been struck by the celestial beauty of the flowers, because he preserved some specimens in his pocket book. Later (in 1924) the poppy was again discovered by Kingdon-Ward who gathered a pound of seed. It is from these seeds that almost all the present day *Meconopsis* have come, but this part of the story is outside the time-scale of my book.

M. cambrica - Welsh Poppy grows to 12in (30.5cm) with yellow flowers from June to September. An unfussy European and Asian perennial for shady rock gardens, dry walls and moist places, or in full sun.

M. grandis (1895) grows to 24in (61cm) with blue or purple flowers in May and June. A perennial from Nepal, Sikkim and Tibet for a semi-shaded place.

Requirements: Meconopsis need light, rich soil that is moist but free draining and dry in winter. Most of them are monocarpic.

Propagation: Sow seed as soon as ripe, prick off as soon as large enough and grow on in boxes in a conservatory, cold frame or greenhouse until spring.

Plants: Peter Chappell, Holden Clough, Ingwersen, Potterton and Martin, St. Bridget, F. Toynbee Ltd, Treasures of Tenbury.

Seeds: Thomas Butcher, Chiltern, Dobie, Naturescape, Thompson and Morgan, Unwins.

MESEMBRYANTHEMUM - Kaffir Fig, Hottentot Fig, Livingstone Daisy *(Aizoaceae).* This genus is a large one of succulent plants that come from the warmer parts of the world. In some species the flowers open late and close early (and in dull weather) and the name commemorates this – *Mesembria* 'midday', *Anthemon* 'flower'. In the South and West central areas of England *M. acinaciforme*, the Kaffir Fig, has become naturalised, and its evergreen mats hang down walls and cliffs in curtains, studded with large pink or yellow daisy flowers. It is easy to detach pieces of this but though they will grow in a cold greenhouse – and grow too large for comfort – they will not be happy away from the sea. The Livingstone Daisy is one of the jolliest of summer edging plants – low and flat with a continuous succession of bright daisies in shaded colours. Its flowers open only when the sun shines on them. Slugs adore the seedling plants.

M. acinaciforme syn. **Carpobrotus - Kaffir Fig** grows only 6in (15cm) high but forms hanging or spreading carpets of evergreen triangular succulent leaves with pink or yellow flowers in summer. Only suitable for cliff or seaside gardens.

M. criniflorum syn. **Dorotheanthus bellidiflorus - Livingstone Daisy** grows to 6in (15cm) high with shaded flowers of cream, yellow, pink, red, crimson and orange flowers from June to August. An annual plant from the Cape Province for edging sunny borders and paths, rockeries and walls.

Requirements: Livingstone Daisies will grow anywhere so long as there is full sunlight.

Cultivation: Sow seeds of Livingstone Daisies in flowering site in April and thin out later (protect from slugs) or sow under glass in a temperature of 15°C (59°F) and grow on in the usual way.

Seeds: of Livingstone Daisy, most seedsmen.

MIMULUS - Monkey flower *(Scrophulariaceae).* The plant's name from *Mimus* 'a mask', from its supposed resemblance to a monkey's face, and the common name is the same. All the genus would prefer to have permanent wet feet, but most do quite well in ordinary garden soil; *M. luteus* will live floating in water, or will climb out of the pond on the other side and settle down quite comfortably in a crack in a hot path, though it usually has designs on colonising the flower bed further over. *Mimulus moschatus* is the common musk, which was once so popular for its musky scent. It was grown in pots on cottage windowsills, often trained up small trellises, and was much loved; then suddenly all the plants lost their scent. It seems that this was a gradual occurrence all over the world and nobody has been able to explain it satisfactorily.

M. luteus - Monkey Flower, Monkey Musk (1826). Grows to variable heights from 4in (10cm) to 2ft (61cm) with yellow flowers from May to August. A gently invasive perennial from America for a sunny pond or bog garden.

M. moschatus - Musk (1826). Grows to 9in (23cm) with pale yellow flowers from June to September. A perennial from America for moist shady places.

M.L. luteus Grows to 9in (23cm) with yellow flowers spotted with red from May to August. For moist places in sun.

Requirements: Moist soil and sun or semi-shade according to type.

Cultivation: Divide and replant in spring or sow seeds in April or May in a cold frame. Grow on; plant out in nursery rows or individual pots.

Plants: Bees, Bennetts, Honeysome Aquatic Nursery, Scotts, Stapeley Water Gardens, St. Bridget, Waveney Fish Farm, Wildwoods.

Seeds: Chiltern, Kent County Nurseries.

MIRABILIS - Marvel of Peru *(Nyctaginaceae).* The plant takes its name from *Mirabilis,* 'wonderful'. This was much grown in former centuries, despite the difficulties of keeping it through the winter (Gerard kept his in a barrel of sand). It is an interesting plant often (but not always) producing flowers of different colours on the same plant. It is also called the Four o' Clock plant because its fragrant flowers open at that time and remain open all night, closing the following morning, though under English skies the plant gets confused, (especially in cool summer weather) and stays open all day. It was once thought to be the source of the medicinal drug Jalap, now known to come from *Ipomoea Purga,* the true Jalap of commerce). It is an interesting plant to grow, forming large roots that become dormant in winter and which can be treated like Dahlias. The plants grow well in a shaded greenhouse, in pots of John Innes No.2, though second-year plants will need larger pots. They can be grown outside and will do well in hot summers or in the south and west of the British Isles.

M. Jalapa - Marvel of Peru. Grows to 2ft (61cm) with flowers of pink, red, yellow, white and crimson that open at (about) 4 pm and fade the next day. (A good plant for a patio party) from July to September. A tender perennial grown as an annual or stored in a dormant state like Dahlia tubers.

Requirements: Light rich soil and a sheltered sunny position.

Cultivation: Sow seeds in a temperature of 18°C (64°F) and grow on under glass. Set out in pots when hardened off.

After flowering: Allow plant to die down, reducing watering.

Seeds: Thomas Butcher, Chiltern, Thompson and Morgan.

MOLUCCELLA - Bells of Ireland, Shell Flower *(Labiatae)*. Moluccella is so named because one of the species was supposed to come from the Moluccas. The whorled flowers are insignificant, though fragrant, and sit in the very conspicuous green calyxes and it is these that make the plant so unusual in flower arrangements. Sow seeds of *M. laevis* in a temperature of 15°C (59°F) barely covering with the seed compost. Grow on in the usual way and plant out in late May. Protect young plants from slugs.

M. laevis - Bells of Ireland, Shell Flower (1570). Grow to 18in (46cm) with whorls of fragrant white flowers in August. Distinctive green calyxes. An annual from W. Asia for the flower arranger's cutting border.

Requirements: Light rich soil and sun.

Cultivation: *See text.*

Uses: For flower arrangements and skeletonising.

Seeds: Most seedsmen.

MONARDA - Bergamot, Bee Balm, Oswego Tea *(Labiatae)*. Monarda is one of the few brightly flowered herb plants and it is most attractive to have in a small herb garden for this reason. There are pink, purple and white-flowered varieties as well but the red is the most characteristic. The species is named after Nicholas Monardes (1493-1588) a Spanish physician and botanist who, in 1571, produced a book about American plants called *Joyfull Newes out of the New Founde Worlde*. Bergamot has everything – it is a compact perennial, it has flowers of a most interesting form and colour, and the leaves have a delicious scent, the red-flowered sort being the strongest. Bergamot is used as a tea (it was first collected at Oswego on the shores of Lake Ontario) which has mildly febrifuge properties. It is much used in pot-pourris and herb pillows. Bees are very attracted to the flowers and it should be grown near garden hives. Even the roots have the same delicious scent, bringing summer memories flocking back in February when the border or herb garden is being tidied.

M. didyma - Bergamot (1656). Grows to 2ft (61cm) with scarlet (or pink, purple and white) flowers fom June to September. A perennial from N. America, it is a good choice for the scented or herb garden, or as a handsome edge-of-the-border plant.

Requirements: Needs moist soil and a sunny or semi-shaded position.

Cultivation: Seeds can be sown in boxes in a cold frame in March or April and grown on in the usual way. Named types do not always come true from seed. Specific varieties are best propagated by division.

Uses: For pot-pourris, herb pillows, sachets and as a fragrant tea to induce relaxation and sleep. As a waterside and border plant.

Plants: Most nurseries.

Seeds: Thomas Butcher, Chiltern, Thompson and Morgan.

MONTBRETIA *(Iridaceae)*. This plant is 'the easy one' with orange flowers in late summer. It was named after Antoine Francois Ernest Conquebert de Montbret (1781-1801), a French botanist, and even though most are now more properly called Crocosmias or Tritonia, old gardeners will still keep to the old name. The plants formerly known as Montbretias are the result of a cross between *Crocosmia aurea* and *C.Pottsii* and are hardier than both parents – they are also known as *C x Crocosmiiflora*. They are completely hardy (and almost unkillable) in the southern counties and need not be disturbed, though if you have a good form it is worth lifting and separating the corms every third year after the leaves have turned brown. The leaves can be clipped off when dead and the new shoots will be seen emerging in January. Montbretia is a belt and braces plant, it sets seed as well as producing offsets.
Requirements: Any soil, full sun.
Cultivation: *See text.*
Uses: As no-trouble late summer flowers for cutting. Zig-zag orange seed stems very attractive for arrangements.
Corms: Old forms of Montbretia are not easily obtained as they have been superseded by the various crosses. Most garden centres.

MORINA *(Dipsacaceae)*. Morinas were named after Louis Morin (1636-1715), a French botanist. They are handsome, if strange-looking plants with deceitfully weed-like thistly leaves and tall stems, with whorls of pink and white flowers that ought, at a casual glance, to belong to the nettle tribe. They are a trifle delicate, I have lost mine in hard winters, but replacement plants are fairly easy to get. The crowns of the plants should be heaped with litter for the winter, because like so many importations, they can't abide the wet, cold winters of N. Europe. They need good well drained soil but they are not too exact in their requirements. Do not attempt to move a well established clump, count your blessings – and the flower stems – and put that other plant somewhere else.
M. longifolia (1839) Grows to 2ft (61cm) with eyecatching spikes of white changing to pink flowers in June and July. A rather tender perennial from Nepal for a good, sheltered place in the garden.
Requirements: A rich sandy loam in sun is best.
Cultivation: Sever smaller side shoots with a root directly after flowering. This is not always possible and therefore seeds can be sown in March. Plant seedlings into individual pots and sink in the ground because they dislike disturbance.
Uses: Green stems after flowering for flower arrangements.
Plants: Robinsons, Beth Chatto, Hillier.
Seeds: Suttons, Thompson and Morgan.

MUSCARI - Grape Hyacinth *(Liliaceae)*. One of the easiest and best known of the spring bulbs. It is strange that the Elizabethans grew more of almost everything than we do today, as the old records clearly show. They were most observant "gardiners", greatly taken with the beauties or curiosities that were being discovered at the edges of their known world. Gerard described one species of Muscari (which one, we are not sure) as being "of a pleasant bright skie colour, verie little bottle-like flower set about the hollow entrance with small white spots, not easy to be perceived". Of the yellowish *M. moschatum* whose perfume is alluded to in the name *Moschos,* musk, that gives the species their name "They are kept and maintained in gardens for the pleasant smell of their flowers, but not for theire beautie, for that many stinking field flowers do in beautie far surpass them." It makes one look forward to seeing the flowers again so that one can bridge the centuries between. Parkinson did what many of us do, when he writes of *M. botryoides* as having "a very strong smell like unto starch when it is new made and hot ... it will quickly choke a ground if it be suffered long in it. For which cause, most men doe cast it unto some by-corner ... or cast it out of the garden quite."

M. armeniacum (1878) grows to 10in (25.5cm) with white-rimmed blue flowers in April and May. A bulb from N. E. Asia for the rockery or spring border in sun.

M. botryoides - Grape Hyacinth (1896) grows to 12in (30.5cm) with blue flowers from March to May. A European bulb for spring edging with tulips, as a tapestry with Aubrieta, Alyssum, Primulas, Iberis and other bulbs, and in pockets in the rockery. White form *M. botryoides album* is called Pearls of Spain. It must be remembered that the leaves last for many months and their presence can spoil later plantings, so put Muscari where other plants will grow up to hide the foliage. Do not knot or bunch them.

M. comosum - Tassel or Feather Hyacinth (1596) grows to 18in (46cm) with green and blue flowers in May and June. A European bulb for the rockery or border.

M. moschatum - Musk Hyacinth (1596) grows to 9in (23cm) with rather undistinguished green-yellow flowers in April and May. A bulb from Asia Minor to grow for its scent, plant it where you pass every day.

Requirements: Muscaris needs a sunny place or they will make too much leaf in proportion to flowers. Any soil suits them.

Cultivation: Lift and separate clumps when leaves turn yellow and replant immediately – the bulbs dry out quickly. Save seed and sow with bulbs or separately in boxes. Seedlings will take three or four years to grow to flowering size.

Bulbs: Avon, Broadleigh, Christian, Holden Clough, Ingwersen, Kelways, Orpington, Potterton and Martin, Stassen.

MYOSOTIS - Forget-me-not *(Boraginaceae).* There is a nice story about forget-me-nots, that began in about the year 1390. The Earl of Derby, who was at that time Henry of Lancaster, and afterwards Henry IV of England, took as one of his badges the little flower of the Forget-me-not, or as it was called then in the court-french, *Soveigne vous de moy.* From that time it appears in his household accounts – though not as the growing plant. Such items as '300 *Soveigne vous de moy'* in silver gilt, appeared, probably decorate his robes, and later a collar of linked S's with enamelled flowers hanging from it. 'S' meant *Soveignes* or *Souveraine,* and this collar or others like it was worn by Lancastrian sympathisers; a collar of linked S's was presented to the City of London in 1525 and is worn by the Lord Mayor on ceremonial occasions. I have not seen the collar so I cannot tell whether the flowers are stylised Forget-me-nots of Speedwells, as is possible, because in medieval continental herbals the name of *ne m'oubliez mye* and *vergiss-mein-nich* was sometimes given to the Speedwell – *Veronica chamaedrys.* Forget-me-nots are sometimes called Scorpion-grass from the resemblance of the flower-head to the curled Scorpion's tail. In the Doctrine of Signatures the plant was therefore expected to cure the scorpion's sting, even though there are no Scorpions in N. Europe.

M. alpestris grows to 6 in (15cm) with blue flowers from April to June. A short-lived European perennial for the rock garden.

M. scorpioides syn. **M. palustris - Water Forget-me-not** grows to 9in (23cm) generally trails into the water, with paler blue flowers from April to July. A European evergreen perennial for the waterside or damp margins.

Requirements: A sunny position and any soil for garden hybrids. As described for *M. scorpioides.*

Cultivation: Detach rooted portions of *M. scorpioides* and pot up until established. Sow seeds of garden varieties and hybrids thinly in boxes in July and August and grow on. Can be transplanted to nursery rows for the winter. Leave old plants to seed after flowering and line out seedlings for following year.

Plants: *M.scorpioides* Bennetts, Beth Chatto, Highlands Water Gardens, Holden Clough, Honeysome Aquatic Nursery, Stapeley Water Gardens, Waveney Fish Farm, Wildwoods.

Seeds: Most seedsmen for *M. alpestris* and modern hybrids.

NARCISSUS - Daffodil *(Amaryllidaceae)*. Daffodils and Narcissi are among the best loved flowers of spring. There is no botanical difference between them, though the varieties with long trumpets are more generally called 'Daffodils' and those with shorter trumpets and/or several flowers to each stem are known as 'Narcissus'. The ancient Egyptians knew them and used the flowers in their funeral wreaths, and it is fascinating to know that this particular species, *Narcissus tazetta,* is still being grown today.

The word 'Narcissism' has come to mean an extreme of personal vanity, from the legend of the Greek youth Narcissus, son of the river-god Cephisus. So beautiful was Narcissus that all the river nymphs vied with one another for his affection, though he was incapable of love for any woman. The nymph Echo was the most beautiful of the maidens, and, like most beautiful women was accustomed to having her own way. Because Narcissus rejected her advances she was piqued and she caused him to fall irrecoverably in love with his own reflection. Narcissus pined with longing for this beautiful youth, and the legend has it that as he pined away, so he changed into the flower that is named after him

Narcissi have been grown for many hundreds of years from species discovered in the wild. Gerard wrote in 1636 "But it is not greatly to our purpose, particularly to seeke out their places of growing wilde, seeing we have them all and everie one of them in our London gardens, in great abundance." It is known that Gerard had about 30 named varieties in his garden, most of which were imported from Holland. In the ensuing period gardening and the cultivation of imported treasures from foreign lands went into a decline until several decades had passed after the restoration of the Monarchy in 1660. It was not until around 1783 that 'Narcissuses and Jonquils' began to appear in the catalogues of the early nurserymen. Since those days they have become increasingly popular for their beauty, their variety of form, their early flowering and because they are so easy to grow. A recent international list contained over 8000 different named varieties, most of which have been bred in the last hundred years or so. The Royal Horticultural Society has grouped all the known varieties into eleven divisions as follows: 1. Trumpet daffodils 2. Large cupped Narcissi 3. Small cupped Narcissi 4. Double Narcissi 5. Triandrus Narcissi 6. Cyclamineus Narcissi 7. Jonquilla Narcissi 8. Tazetta Narcissi 9. Poeticus Narcissi 10. Species and wild forms and hybrids 11. Miscellaneous Narcissi.

Since everyone has their favourite type and colour from the noble old King Alfred to the tiniest of Hoop-petticoats, and much depends on area, soil and aspect, there would not be space to cover the subject properly here. Most (but not all) of the daffodils generally offered for sale belong to groups 1, 2, and 3 and again, most of these are fairly modern hybrids and are not the same as those grown in previous centuries. The wild species narcissi (daffodils) have not changed in appearance over the years though some hybridisation has been done and these bulbs are offered for sale as named types.

Narcissi can be grown for many purposes and in many ways. The sturdier types may be planted in the usual way and thereafter left in the ground to increase – this is called 'naturalising' and is suited to the less elaborate forms and varieties whose flowers look particularly beautiful when planted in drifts and sweeps all of one kind. The ground that they are to be planted in must have a good general fertiliser and further feeding every two years or so should be given; every three years the bulbs should be lifted and thinned out to prevent overcrowding. Other varieties of Narcissi are tiny in form and size, and very early-flowering, and are therefore more suited to an alpine house or prepared pockets in the rock garden.

The more familiar varieties are large-flowered and long-stemmed and these are planted so as to flower early (but not too early) in the year in borders or formal bedding. These bulbs are usually lifted and stored for replanting in autumn. To achieve a 'natural' appearance, where this is suitable, the bulbs should be broadcast in loose handfuls on the cleared ground, and then planted exactly where they fall. Each hole should be made either with a special bulb planter, or the smoothed-off end of an old spade handle can be used for smaller bulbs. The hole should be three times the depth of the bulb that is to be planted, and the holes must be flat at the bottom to accommodate the base of the bulb – no air space should ever be left underneath.

Cultivation: A good fertiliser containing potash and phosphate should be forked into the soil at planting time, and bulbs that are to be left in the ground in herbaceous borders should be planted more deeply so as to avoid damage from summer hoeing and weeding, when there is nothing above ground to indicate their presence. When the flowers are finished they should be dead-headed so as to preserve the bulb's strength unless seed for propagation is needed. It will take from four to seven years for bulbs to come to flowering from seed, but this is an inexpensive way of growing large quantities. The leaves should be allowed to die down naturally and as they often last until the end of June this fact should be taken into consideration when siting the bulbs. The leaves should *never* be plaited, twisted, knotted or tied into bunches with rubber bands, as this will affect their function of producing the food reserves that will be stored in the bulb.

If the bulbs are to be lifted and stored after flowering, wait until the leaves turn yellow. The bulbs should be carefully dug up and laid out in rows in a warm airy shed or outhouse until they have died off. After this the withered leaves, roots and the previous year's bulb-skin can be discarded as should any diseased or damaged bulbs. Narcissi should be planted in early September.

Requirements: *See text.*
Cultivation: *See text.*
Uses: *See text.*
After flowering: *See text.*
Bulbs: Reliable stockists of species Narcissi are Avon, Bees, Broadleigh, Christian, Ingwersen, Kelways, Orpington, Potterton and Martin, van Tubergen. Garden centres and catalogues should be consulted for general planting bulbs.

NEMESIA - Poor Man's Orchid *(Scrophulariaceae).* This bright little flower blooms without stopping to draw breath and is unaffected by bad weather. For the best effect it should be planted closely, and it looks good spilling out of tubs and containers – better almost than in the ground because the interesting form of the flowers is that much nearer eye-level. They are greedy little plants (because they work so hard) and it is worth while giving them fortnightly liquid feeds. If they are sheared off as their flowering season ends they will generally produce a second flush of bloom. They must not be allowed to dry out.

Nemesia strumosa (1892) grows to 2ft (61cm) with flowers in shades of yellow, cream, pink, orange, red, carmine and purple. Single colours can be obtained. An annual from S. Africa for a sunny border, patio, pots, troughs, and rockeries.

Requirements: Ordinary free-draining soil and a sunny position. Acid, sandy soil is ideal but not essential.

Cultivation: Sow seeds in a temperature of 15°C (59°F) and grow on and harden off in the usual way.
Seeds: Most seedsmen.
Plants: Christian.

NEPENTHES - Pitcher plant, Monkey Cups *(Nepenthaceae).* These are carnivorous plants, fascinating to grow and watch and possessing a slightly sinister character which is not to everyone's taste. They like moist places in their natural state where flies are abundant. The 'pitcher', which is formed from an extended leaf midrib, is brightly coloured in a way that is attractive to flies and other winged insects. It has sweet honey glands at the top as a further lure and inducement, and there is a lid which closes down in case the victims try to change their minds. Below the honey glands there is a slippery lining to the pitcher with water at the bottom in which the insects drown. There they decay and their juices nourish the plant that has evolved to capture them in this fascinating way. In addition, the plant produces flower spikes. Nepenthes need humid conditions and a temperature of 21 – 26°C (70 – 80°F) in summer and 17°C (65°F) in winter. They need a compost of two parts of brown peat fibre to one of Sphagnum, with some pieces of charcoal to keep the mixture sweet. Established plants need plenty of water in summer. They are best grown in baskets or Orchid pots. Propagation is by one year old shoots put through the hole in a 2-inch (5-cm) pot which is then put into Sphagnum in a closed, moist propagator set at 26°C (80°F). Roots will form and then the cuttings should be potted up in a mixture of chopped fibrous peat, moss, silver sand and some charcoal. Then they should be put back in the propagator. Do not over-water but do not allow to become dry.
N. Hookeriana (1847) has leathery leaves and red-spotted green pitchers that look rather like rucksacks. A carnivorous perennial from Borneo.
N. ventricosa (1898) has 6-inch (15-cm) green waisted pitchers with red rims. A perennial carnivorous plant from the Philippines.
Requirements: *See text.*
Cultivation: *See text.*
Plants: Marston Exotics.

NEPETA - Catmint *(Labiatae).* Catmint looks so 'right' when it is used to edge paths or a rose bed, or as a surround to a sundial or bird-bath. But it seems to be increasingly difficult to grow the plant unmolested by cats, who will eat it and roll so ecstatically in it that the neighbouring plants will be completely flattened. I have tried growing plants near it that I don't particularly care about, but this is not practical in a small garden because there is not room for anything that I don't love. Catmint is slightly tender, and the dead foliage should be left to cover the crown of the plant for the winter and early spring; it can be prevented from blowing away by being pegged down with canes or, more invisibly, with hairpins. The cats will start eating it as soon as the tight new leaves begin to form, and at this stage the plant is very vulnerable. Successive meals will kill it, and the answer to the problem is insurmountable. I have tried to cover it with wire netting – which the pussies just lie on, feeding daintily between the mesh: the mesh looks ugly, and in any case the plant will be consumed as soon as the netting is removed. This plant may be hard enough to protect but the old fashioned Nepta or Kattesmint was even more alluring to the feline population.
   Tournefort said that "when a Cat has smelt it (even before she has well seen it) hugg'd it and kiss'd it, wantonly running upon it and scouring away from it by turns, and has rub'd herself against it very much and long, using strange Postures and playing with it, she at last eats it up and devours it entirely". (This is *Nepeta cataria*).

There's an old saying ...
    If you set it, the cats will get it
    If you sow it, the cats won't know it.
I have tried both, and the last line, alas, is not true. Catmint is an
excellent plant to grow with white, pink, blue and darker purple flowers,
and as a foil to brighter colours that may need softening.
N. Cataria - Catmint, Catnip grows to 3ft (91.5cm) with greyish leaves and
undistinguished white flowers. This plant is the one that cats, particularly
tomcats, will destroy, and it will make them bad-tempered and scratchy. A
European perennial for the sunny herb garden and all cat-lovers.
N. mussinii - Catmint grows to 2ft (61cm) with blue-mauve flowers from June
to August. A perennial plant from Persia and the Caucasus (replaced now
by *N.* x *faassenii* which does not set seed).
Requirements: Any free draining soil and a sunny situation.
Cultivation: Divide established plants in spring. Sow seeds of *N. cataria* in March
and grow on in the usual way. Protect seedlings from cats.
Plants: Most nurseries.
Seeds: Thomas Butcher, Chiltern, Suttons, Thompson and Morgan.

NERINE *(Amaryllidaceae).*Nerines often flower in November and being the most
brilliant pink they seem almost tropical in their brightness – and, somehow,
a trifle unseasonal. The Nerine was originally thought to be a Japanese
flower because of the story of the cargo vessel that was wrecked on the coast
of Guernsey in the later part of the seventeenth century. The vessel had
come from Japan and it would seem that part of its cargo was flower bulbs
for Holland, because these were thrown up on the shore and covered by
sand. There they stayed for some years until, suddenly, the Guernsey people
were startled to find these pink flowers blooming by the sea shore. Of
course, the ship's manifest is not mentioned, though a copy must still exist,
and this might have told us that the bulbs were *Nerine sarniensis* from
South Africa, now called the Guernsey Lily. This Nerine was afterwards
'properly' discovered on Table Mountain by Francis Masson in 1773. This
is too tender a bulb to grow in the open in England, except in South
Cornwall and the Scillies, but *N. Bowdenii* will often succeed in warmer
parts of the country. This is the bright pink-flowered one whose leaves come
up in spring, leaving the flower to bloom alone on its naked stem.
N. Bowdenii (1889) grows to 18in (46cm) with pink flowers from September to
November and leaves in spring. A bulb from S. Africa for a warm, sunny
south-facing wall.
N. sarniensis - Guernsey Lily (1634) grows to 2½ft (76cm) with pink, salmon or
red flowers before the leaves in September to November. A bulb from S.
Africa for greenhouse or conservatory cultivation. Not suitable for growing
in the open in the U.K.
Requirements: Ordinary well drained soil for *N. Bowdenii*, Plant N. sarniensis in
6-in (15-cm) pots of John Innes No. 2, or a mixture of fibrous loam and
sharp sand, with necks of bulbs above soil surface. Do not water until flower
spikes turn yellow. Cease watering and leave them in their pots in a frame
with the glass light placed to protect them from rain, or in a sunny corner
with a cloche over them until it is time for them to flower again.
Cultivation: Nerines will produce offsets which should be grown in the same way
as the parent bulbs. Plant outdoor bulbs *(of N. Bowdenii)* 4in (10cm) deep.
Bulbs: Most nurseries.
Plants: Robinsons, Scotts, Sherrards, St. Bridget, Treasures of Tenbury.

NICANDRA - Shoo-fly, Apple of Peru *(Solaneaceae).* This is a curious annual
border plant which has a rather brooding air about it – perhaps because
there are more leaves than there are flowers, as if the plant were waiting for
something in order to begin work. Also, the flowers are only open for a few

hours in the middle of the day. But the fruit is interesting and can be dried for use in winter flower arrangements. It is poisonous, as are most of this family. Sow the seeds in a temperature of 15°C (59°F) and prick out the seedlings into individual pots because they will grow quickly. Plant out in May in a sunny part of the border, and in good soil there will be better flowers and better leaves. The plant is grown in America as a fly repellant.

Nicandra physalodes - Shoo Fly Plant (1759) grows to 3ft (91.5cm) with blue-violet flowers from July to September. An annual from Peru for a sunny place.

Requirements: *See text.*

Cultivation: *See text.*

Seeds: Thomas Butcher, Chiltern, Dobie, Suttons, Thompson and Morgan.

NICOTIANA - Tobacco Flower *(Solanaceae).* This genus was named after John Nicot (1530-1600). The flowers are sweetly scented in the evenings and at night and usually only half-open during the day, unless grown in shady places. The whole plant is sticky and therefore should not be planted in a dusty place such as a driveway or near the edge of a road. Tobacco flowers should be grown beside a garden seat, at the edge of a patio, or beneath windows that are usually open on warm summer evenings.

N. alata syn **N. affinis - Tobacco Flower** species grow to 2ft (61cm) with white flowers from June until September or even later. Other colours are cream, green, pink, red, crimson and yellow which are of more recent origin. A perennial from Brazil, grown as an annual. For warm places where the scent from the flowers can be enjoyed in the evenings.

Requirements: Good rich soil.

Cultivation: Sow seeds in March on the surface of the seed compost at a temperature of 18°C (64°F). Grow on in the usual way.

During flowering: Dead-head.

Seeds: Most seedsmen.

NIEREMBERGIA *(Solanaceae).* These are delightful and unusual plants with Campanula-like flowers for the rockery or alpine house. The genus was named after Eusebius Nieremberg, (1595-1658), a Spanish Jesuit who wrote a book on the marvels of the natural world. The low-growing hardy sorts are very good and unusual rockery plants. The perennial kinds are propagated by division in March and April and should be replanted immediately, and for those types that are grown as annuals, seed should be sown in a temperature of 15°C (59°F) and grown on in the usual way.

N. repens syn. **rivularis** (1866) forms a prostrate mat with white flowers in June and July. A perennial from Argentina for the damp, sunny rock garden. May do well in shade.

N. frutescens 1867 grows to 18in (46cm) with blue and white flowers from June to August. An annual from Chile for a semi-shaded place with rich, moisture-retentive soil.

Seeds: Dobies, Unwins.

Plants: Bressingham, Cunnington, Hillier, Ingwersen, Potterton and Martin, Robinsons, R.V. Roger Ltd.

NIGELLA - Love-in-a-Mist, Devil-in-a-Bush *(Ranunculaceae).* This innocent-looking, old-fashioned flower has been put to a variety of uses that are most interesting. The black seeds, from which it takes the name of Nigella, were used as a spice and in Egypt the seeds were scattered on bread and cakes as a decoration and seasoning. Egyptian ladies crunched them up like hundreds and thousands because they were considered to be fattening, and fatness was an attribute of beauty in Islamic nations. In the sixteenth century a gentleman who had the charming name of John Hollybush advised his readers to "Take the heads of herbe Sitt or Nigella and burn

them to ashes, put swynes grese thereto, and strake or kemme the heyres
therewyth, that dryveth away lyse and nittes". It had other, older names
like Love-entangle, Love-in-a-Puzzle and Jack-in-Prison.

N. damascena - Love-in-a-Mist (1570) grows to 2ft (61cm) with finely dissected
leaves and blue flowers in summer. An annual from the Mediterranean area
for summer bedding.

N. hispanica - Fennel Flower (1629) grows to 2ft (61cm) with deep blue flowers
and red stamens. An annual from Spain and S. France for summer borders.

Requirements: Ordinary soil and full sun.

Cultivation: Seeds can be sown in September or March where they are to flower,
and thinned out later. September is best.

Uses: As border and cut flowers and seed heads for decor, both green and dried.

Seeds: Most seedsmen.

NYMPHEA - Water Lily *(Nymphaeaceae)*. Water Lilies are quite specific in
their requirements but are so beautiful that they are worth pandering to,
especially as some of them are scented.

 Water lilies have a long history which goes back to Ancient Egypt. They
were revered as sacred flowers, and petals of two species found in funeral
wreaths have been precisely identified some three and a half thousand years
later. Representations of the flowers appear on walls, furniture, and pottery
and are clearly recognisable. The funeral rites were a very important part
of the Egyptian traditions – great families and even lesser ones in the social
scale set aside vast sums of money and made preparations throughout their
lives for the proper observances at the time of their deaths, and it is because
of this that we know so much about them today. It was the custom to lay
wreaths of a particular shape in rows down the sarcophagus of the deceased
personage, and sometimes these have lasted through the centuries in a
sufficiently good state of preservation so that botanists have been able to
identify the species of the flowers, which were usually water lilies.

 Most of the catalogues give planting depths, and this is very important
when choosing, or you may have a drowned infant, or (more usually) a lusty
plant that will spend its life trying to climb out of the pool, with long stalked
leaves and few flowers. Water lilies live a very long time and only need
attention every three years or so, though if planted on the bottom in a large
lake they will in time cover the surface of the water. They should be planted
in special water-lily baskets, in which a square of hessian has been placed
to prevent the soil sifting through. Plant the lily in ordinary loam and place
a layer of coarse gravel over the soil surface, especially if there are fish,
which being curious, will investigate the new mud and stir it up into clouds
in the water. If there are no fish the lilies can be placed at the correct depth
by means of a square of bricks under the baskets, with the water just
covering the crowns. (If there are fish make two 'walls' under each basket
so that a tunnel is achieved, and this will make a good hiding place for
them.) As the lilies grow the water level can be raised accordingly or the
bricks lowered. Water lilies need full sun. There are very many modern
hybrids with flowers in all colours – white, cream, pale pink, rose, deep
cerise, red and even blue, which is a tropical variety that needs to be kept
in a washing-up bowl in a warm greenhouse for the winter.

N. alba - White Water Lily with white flowers in summer. A strong growing
European perennial lily for large ponds and lakes.

N. odorata 1886 scented white flowers, tinged red. A lily from N. America.

 The following lilies were bred by M. Latour Marliac before 1911:- N.
'Marliacea Rosea' is medium to vigorous with pale pink flowers, 'Marliacea
Carnea' is medium to vigorous with many very pale pink flowers:
'Escarboucle' is of medium growth with bright red flowers: 'Sunrise' is
medium to small with large yellow flowers: 'Marliacea Albida' is of medium

size with white flowers and 'Marliacea Chromatella' is of medium size with a succession of large primrose-yellow flowers.

Requirements: *See text.*
Cultivation: *See text.*
Uses: *See text.*
Roots/Rhizomes/Tubers: Bennetts, Highlands Water Gardens, Honeysome, Stapeley, Waveney, Wildwoods.

OENOTHERA - Evening Primrose, Mississippi Primrose *(Onagraceae).* This genus is often despised or scorned because some of the species rather let the side down by being seen scrambling about on railway embankments. But, even if they are vigorous enough to survive this environment, they are still interesting plants whose flowers (usually scented) are of a particularly pleasing shade of lemon yellow, with no golden tones in it such as are seen on every side in late summer. The flowers open visibly at dusk, which is fascinating to watch. The flowers of *O. fruticosa* stay open all day and have the more suitable name of Sun-drops. This is an edible plant – the roots can be cooked and the leaves eaten either cooked or raw in salads, so there's an end to the worry of what to do with the surplus plants of the common variety. If several kinds are grown, seedlings will not come true.
O. biennis - Common Evening Primrose (17th century) grows to 3ft (91.5cm) with clear yellow flowers from June to September. A biennial from N. America for large borders and the wild garden in sun or semi-shade. Seed stems excellent in flower arrangements.
O. fruticosa - Sun Drops (1737) grows to 2ft (61cm) with deep yellow flowers from June to August. A perennial from N. America for the border.
O. missouriensis (1811) grows to 1ft (30.5cm) with yellow flowers (opening in the evening but lasting for several days) from June to August. A perennial from the S. United States for a sunny rockery.
Requirements: Any soil, and a sunny situation.
Cultivation: Sow seeds of all types in April and grow on in the usual way. Plant out in autumn because roots get large. Divide perennials in spring.
Uses: As rock, border, wild garden flowers: seed stems for decor.
Plants: Beth Chatto, Hillier, Holden Clough, Ingwersen, Notcutts, Scotts, Sherrards, Stassen, F. Toynbee Ltd.
Seeds: Thomas Butcher, Chiltern, Dobie, Thompson and Morgan.

OMPHALODES - Blue-eyed Mary, Navel-wort *(Boraginaceae).* The less pretty name of Navel-wort was given to it by our ancestors because of the seeds' resemblance to a navel. These blue spring flowers are very useful in the shady garden, if 'woodland' conditions exist – that is, leaf-mould and the shade of deciduous trees. Blue-eyed Mary, *O. verna* was a popular garden plant in the time of Charles I, as can be seen by the legacy of Stuart and Georgian paintings and embroideries where the flower is clearly recognisable. This is the easiest (but not that easy) of the species to grow, the others needing more care in their cultivation and often doing much better in an alpine house.
O. cappadocica grows to 9in (23cm) with azure-blue flowers from June to August. A perennial from Lazistan (Turkey) for the rock garden or dry wall.
O. Luciliae grows to 6in (15cm) with pale blue flowers from May to September. A perennial from Greece for the rock garden or dry wall.
O. verna - Blue-eyed Mary (1633) grows to 6in (15cm) with cobalt-blue flowers from February to May.
Requirements: *O. cappadocica* and *O. verna* need woodland conditions, *O. Luciliae* needs a sunny place with well-drained soil, with the addition of grit or mortar-rubble and a little bonemeal in spring.

Cultivation: Divide *O. cappadocica* and *O. verna* in spring, or after flowering. Divide *O. Luciliae* in July.

Plants: Broadwell, Peter Chappell, Beth Chatto, Hillier, Holden Clough, Ingwersen, Reginald Kaye, Notcutts, Robinsons, Scotts, Sherrards, F. Toynbee Ltd., Treasures of Tenbury.

ORCHIS - Orchid *(Orchidaceae)*. This is one of the largest plant families in the world, with about 750 genera and some 20,000 species, and even a single species is a specialists' affair. But there are several that can be grown in a conservatory or even indoors, providing they have the resting period that they need once a year. Orchids are (generally) either terrestrial or epiphytic – that is, living on trees, but in their natural habitat they obtain their food from the air, water or from humus that collects in the crevices. They have adapted themselves to this with the aid of specially long roots which is what you so often see dangling from the main bulb or rhizome. In some orchids such as *Calanthe*, and *Maxillaria* a swollen stem or pseudobulb arises, prodicing a fan of strap-shaped leaves. Others, such as *Cattleyea*, *Dendrobium* and *Epidendrum* have a stem-like pseudobulb with joints from each of which comes a single leaf. Another group called *Vanda*, have no pseudobulbs, merely an elongated stem with star-shaped leaves and dangling aerial roots.

Terrestrial orchids such as the wild British Orchids and *Cypripedium* have fleshy underground roots and/or tubers – in fact, the name *Orchis* comes from the Greek word for testicle because of the general shape and often paired form of these tubers. The leaves of these orchids are not so leathery as those of the epiphytic orchids, and many have purple or brown spots.

Orchid flowers are legendary for their lasting qualities – a month is an average period for some blooms – and their form, which, though made up of three petals and three sepals, is diverse and strange. The third petal has evolved into a lip which is usually larger than the other petals, and it can take the form of a tail, a spur, a pouch, a lobe or a keel. Orchids are either repellent to people or they have a strong fascination – nearly everyone either likes them or dislikes them and these emotions are quite powerful. They hybridise very easily, and this is why there are so many modern varieties.

Orchids, generally, are an expensive hobby because of the temperatures necessary for their welfare. They can be divided into three classes: cool house – min. winter temperature 7°C (45°F); warm or intermediate house – min. winter temperature 10°C (50°F); and hot-house – min. winter temperature 14°C (57°F). The minimum summer and night temperatures are 14°C (64°F) and 22°C (72°F) respectively.

Extra heat is all right, though temperatures above 11°C (52°F) must be controlled by ventilating the greenhouse, preferably with a fan so as to preclude stagnant, hot areas. The hot-house temperature can safely reach 32°C (90°F) providing the humidity level matches this. Orchids are shade-loving plants and therefore the greenhouse should be shaded, and there are several methods of doing this with the aid of slatted blinds, plastic netting or painted glass. The humidity factor is very important, and according to the type of house and the plants being grown, it will be found necessary to spray or damp down the greenhouse two or three times a day, according to the temperature.

Orchid composts vary quite widely and should always be used: each genus may differ from the next and precise requirements should be checked when purchasing the plants – most are very long lived indeed and increase dramatically in value with the years – and the care – of the owners. A description of the conditions necessary for Cymbidium, Pleione and Paphiopedilum will be found, as it is possible to grow these well in an ordinary greenhouse or conservatory in company with other plants. If you grow these successfully, and it is not difficult at all, you are very likely to become interested in other types and forms of Orchids. Beware! It is as addictive as any other vice, but nicer.

Requirements: *See text.*
Cultivation: *See text.*
Bulbs: Keith Andrew, Burnham Nurseries.

ORNITHOGALUM - Star of Bethlehem, Chincherinchee *(Liliaceae).* The Star of Bethlehem, *O. nutans* is a rare British wild flower, but fortunately its bulbs are easily obtainable. It is much appreciated by slugs, and as it is one of the early-flowering spring bulbs, coming out of the ground just at the time these pests begin to be active, in no time at all you can have none. Or so I have found.

This is an old garden flower, smelling of onions but beautiful nevertheless. It has names that are descriptive of its habits – Sleepy Dick, Ten o'clock Lady, Nap at Noon, Wake at Noon and Six o'clock Sleepers, though they do not agree as to when the plant really does go to bed. Mine close early in the afternoon and do not open in dull weather, but as the backs of the white petals are striped with green, and the green leaves have a central white stripe it is a pleasant thing to look at even when its eyes are shut. In addition, it prefers semi-shade. Chincherinchees, *O. thyrsoides,* are the exotic sisters from S. Africa, often seen in florists' shops lying in their boxes, having travelled all the way from their home country. The bulbs of *O. umbellatum* were formerly eaten as a vegetable in Palestine, Sweden and Italy and were much enjoyed. But recent analysis has shown that the bulbs are poisonous (except when thoroughly cooked) and they are quite dangerous for cattle – both leaves and bulbs together.

O. nutans - 'Bath Asparagus' grows to 18in (46cm) with panicles of green and white flowers in May and June. A hardy European bulb, the flower stalks of which were formerly eaten. For semi-shaded rockeries and borders.

O. thyrsoides - Chincherinchee (1757) grows to 18in (46cm) with white to cream long-lasting flowers in June. A bulb from S. Africa for the sunny rockery or border.

O. umbellatum - Star of Bethlehem grows to 12in (30.5cm) with green and white flowers in April and May. An oniony bulb and plant from Europe for the shady rockery or path edge.

Requirements: Plant the hardy European bulbs 2 – 3in (5 – 7cm) deep in shady corners of the rock garden or at the edge of the path, and leave undisturbed. Any soil suits them.

Cultivation: Lift congested clumps immediately after flowering and replant. Sow fresh seed into boxes of John Innes No. 1 seed compost and leave in a cold frame for two years. Keep weeded.

Bulbs: Avon, Bloms, Broadleigh, Thomas Butcher, de Jager, Holden Clough, Ingwersen, Potterton and Martin.

Seeds: Chambers, Chiltern.

OXALIS *(Oxalidaceae).* The Oxalis is an interesting genus because some of the early spring flowering species have a fail-proof method of fertilisation that does not depend on passing insects (as have some violas). The wild Wood Sorrel *Oxalis acetosella* has two sets of flowers – the first may or may not be visited by bees but the second set develops during the summer and never opens. The pollen grains actually germinate inside the closed petals and travel down the styles to fertilise the ovules. It is an independent sort of flower – this method of pollination is called cleistogamy.

The best known Oxalis is the pink-flowered cottage garden plant *O. floribunda* syn. *O. rubra,* whose blooms close quickly at the onset of rain; this useful habit was observed by cottagers who planted it beside their

doorsteps so that they could see what the day would do. It flourishes well –
all too well in light gravelly soils and may become invasive, though my own
clump has behaved well until now. I like to see it in the evening putting
itself to bed – the leaves close up so that they shed water or are less exposed
to the night air and they stay like that until the sun shines on them the
following day.

O. adenophylla (1905) grows to 6in (15cm) from a fibrous root with pink-lilac
flowers in summer. A perennial from Chile for the rockery.

O. enneaphylla (1876) grows only to 3in (7.5cm) with grey-green pleated leaves
and fragrant cream white flowers in summer. A tiny perennial plant from
the Falkland Islands and Patagonia for a trough or hot rockery.

O. floribunda syn. **O. rubra** grows to 8in (20.5cm) with pink flowers in summer.
An invasive perennial from S. Brazil.

Requirements: A well-drained soil with leaf-mould incorporated.

Cultivation: Divide carefully after flowering and replant immediately.

Plants: Broadwell, Bressingham, Cunnington, Hillier, Holden Clough,
Ingwersen, Reginald Kaye, Potterton and Martin, R. V. Roger Ltd.,
Sherrards, Alan C. Smith, F. Toynbee Ltd.

PAEONIA - Peony *Paeoniaceae* formerly *Ranunculaceae).* Peonies are among
the longest lived of all herbaceous plants – my two clumps of the old-
fashioned red *P. officinalis* have been there for 50 years, to my certain
knowledge. Most peonies need very little attention, once established. Their
strong leaves should be left on throughout the winter as a protection,
though if you must neaten the border totally, peg down some substantial
litter like bracken (and the peony leaves) to protect the tender pink buds
that begin to emerge in February. If these are caught by frosts, as they
surely will be, it is a set-back to the plant. Make sure the pegs do not go into
the thick roots. In the years that you remember, a mulch of well rotted
manure or good garden compost after flowering will repay you with even
finer flowers and healthier leaves. Bonemeal is excellent but is not necessary
every year. The leaves are so substantial and attractive that, even on their
own, they make a newish border look established. The one thing that
Peonies hate is disturbance, and if you must move them do it in a rain
shower and then they might not be so annoyed. Large established clumps
when divided (this is unnecessary except when more plants of the same kind
are wanted) will sulk, flowerless, for two or three years. They need to be
watered well in dry springs, and grow best in partial shade where it will be
noticed that the flowers last longer. In smaller gardens the purchase of
special 'peony rings' or plant supports is a good idea, because after flowering
the leaves grow larger and also outward, which makes it impossible to grow
anything else nearby. Spring bulbs can be planted near them in the certain
knowledge that their leaves will vanish under the vast crinoline of the Peony
leaves. Peonies are associated with a number of superstitions throughout the
world. A piece of root, worn round the neck, was a talisman against evil
spirits and beads were also made from Peony roots and strung as necklaces,
which were worn by children as an aid to painless teething and to prevent
convulsions. There is another nice legend about the roots which were used
to heal wounds in ancient Greece. (The plant was named after Paion, who
was a physician who used the roots to cure a wound given to Pluto). The
Peony had to be dug at dead of night, taking care that no woodpeckers were
about because they would furiously attack the digger in an attempt to peck
out his eyes. The hazards of medicine seem to have been very considerable
in those times.

Tudor names for Peonies were nice – they were popular garden flowers
and were called by such appellations as Hundred-bladed Rose, Chesses,
Marmaritin, Rose Royale, Pie Nanny and Nan Pie and, oddly, Sheep-
shearing Rose. There are single, semi-double and the traditional double

Peonies, and all of them are beautiful. The species are not easy to find (except *P. mlokosewitschii*) having been superseded by more modern hybrids.

P. emodi (1868) grows to 30in (76cm) with white flowers in March. A perennial from N.W. India needing winter protection – grow among shrubs, facing South West.

P. lactiflora (1784) grows to 2ft (61cm) with fragrant white flowers in June. A perennial from Siberia for the semi-shaded border. Parent of many of the modern peonies which have superseded the species.

P. officinalis - Peony (1548) grows to 2ft (61cm) with double crimson flowers in May. A European perennial plant for the semi-shaded border. Handsome leaves.

P. mlokosewitschii (1907) grows to 18in (46cm) with blue-green leaves and yellow flowers in April. A perennial from the Caucasus.

Requirements: Make their bed thoroughly before planting, adding well decayed manure or compost and bonemeal. Moist, well-drained soil suits them, site them so that they are not facing to the East, as early morning sun on frosted leaves or buds will damage them. Do not plant crown too deep – no more than 1in (2.5cm).

Cultivation: Divide only when absolutely necessary in September. Peonies will grow from seed, though named varieties do not come true. Sow ripe seed in September in individual pots in a cold frame. Germination may take some time but the seedlings can be set out in a nursery bed for two or three years.

Uses: As superb cut flowers. Foliage very handsome in the garden, and some varieties have beautiful seed heads.

Plants: Bees, Bloms, Bressingham, Beth Chatto, Hillier, Jackman's, Kelways, Notcutts, Scotts, Sherrards, St. Bridget.

PAPAVER - Poppy *(Papaveraceae).* Always beautiful and always interesting because of their creased-taffeta petals which, like a butterfly's wings, can never be re-packed. The Poppy is a historical flower, and according to mythology it was created by Somnus, god of Sleep, to give to Ceres who was exhausted with her labours. In her weariness the corn was being neglected. After her poppy-induced sleep she was refreshed and could care for all the crops once more, and that is why she is shown in statues and pictures as wearing a chaplet of corn intermixed with poppies. This is why corn and poppies were allowed to grow together for centuries because it was believed that the poppies were necessary for the health of the corn.

P. nudicaule (the Iceland Poppy) has delicate flowers in every shade (except blue) which are easily grown from seed. The alpine poppy looks particularly pleasing on a rockery, and though classed as a perennial it is best to have replacements ready every other year. *P. atlanticus* is a gentle plant with soft orange flowers that associate well with yellows or deeper, brighter oranges which can sometimes be too bright. It is a perennial plant, easily grown from seed but it is best to have some replacements ready. Since this poppy is always admired when in flower these may come in very conveniently in garden exchanges. One poppy in particular is of historical and medicinal interest, producing the opium which has alleviated man's pain for centuries; this is *P. somniferum*. It is an important plant in the east, more particularly for the production of narcotics but it is also grown for flavouring, as bird seed and as salad-oil.

P. alpinum grows to 10in (25.5cm) with white, yellow, apricot or pink flowers in summer. A short-lived perennial from the Carpathians for the sunny rock garden. Best in poor soil.

P. atlanticum (1890) grows to 18in (46cm) with soft orange flowers throughout the summer. A perennial from Morocco for sunny border or rock garden.

P. glaucum (1891) grows to 18in (46cm) with red flowers from May to July. An annual from Asia Minor for the sunny border.

P. nudicaule - Iceland Poppy (1759) grows to 12in (30.5cm) with white or yellow flowers (modern varieties are in almost every colour).

P. orientale - Oriental Poppy (1714) grows to 3ft (91.5cm) with red flowers in May and June. Dies back after flowering leaving an empty space, following year's leaves appear in autumn. A perennial from America for a large sunny border. Dislikes disturbance.

P. somniferum - Opium Poppy grows to 3ft (91.5cm) with pale lilac flowers in summer. (Many other colours – pink, purple, rose, white with single to very double flowers). An annual for the border – scatter seed before frosts. Do not move plants except when very tiny.

Requirements: Poppies will grow in almost any soil, though all need a sunny situation.

Cultivation: Sow seeds of annuals in flowering positions and thin out – most poppies have long roots and dislike disturbance. Divide roots of perennial types in early spring. Seeds may be sown of these but where a collection of poppies exists in the garden the progeny will not come true.

Seeds: Chiltern, Naturescape, Suttons, Thompson and Morgan.

Plants: Old types of oriental poppies are no longer available, they have been superseded by more modern hybrids, obtainable from most nurserymen.

PAPHIOPEDILUM - Slipper Orchid *(Orchidaceae)*. These orchids are terrestrial and can be grown in a conservatory or even indoors, though 'house' temperatures are usually too dry. They have leathery leaves that are sometimes mottled or spotted and these species require slightly different treatment and compost. They should be watered throughout the year as root activity is more or less continuous. Syringing is helpful in summer months and they should have a shaded place to live in throughout the year but may be brought into the house during the flowering season. A compost for the green-leaved species should be made up of three parts loam fibre, one part Sphagnum moss and one part of Osmunda fibre, with some finely broken crocks and a little charcoal. The mottled-leaved species should have double the quantity of Osmunda fibre and Sphagnum, and no loam. Winter night temperatures should be 18°C (65°F) for the mottled leaved species, and *P. insigne* is capable of enduring the much lower winter night temperatures of 13°C (55°F).

The very long-lasting flowers are waxy textured and very characteristic with a wide dorsal sepal, two large sometimes 'warted' petals and the large 'slipper' shaped lip. Colours vary from greenish yellow through bronze, brown, russet, violet, to crimson. All the species have been used to produce hybrids, but the genetic history of the hybrids is usually known. They have a strong constitution which is why they are so popular.

P. insigne syn. **Cypripedium insigne.** Height according to type, flowers in winter. Species very numerous, hybrids even more so.

Requirements: Allow one 6-in (15-cm) pot per plant and set in compost as described according to species. They will do best in greenhouses with high humidity, and they must be shaded during the summer months. Feed fortnightly with weak liquid manure from May to September and re-pot every other year after flowering.

Cultivation: Divide in May.

Uses: As very long-lasting cut flowers or pot plants.

Plants: Keith Andrew, Burnham.

PELARGONIUM - (wrongly but often called **Geranium)** *(Geraniaceae)*. A tender plant of cottage windowsills and Victorian bedding-out schemes of military exactness, the Pelargonium is much loved by its admirers. Most Pelargonium leaves are aromatic and there are many with specific scents which have rather inconspicuous flowers – one could go further and call them dull, but that would be unkind to the plant. There are many scents, some sweet, some tangy and some aromatic, but all these plants are tender and need greenhouse protection during the whole year.

Ivy-leaved geraniums – *P. peltatum* – are different in that they have (usually) a trailing habit and more leathery leaves. Some are very suitable for hanging baskets but others, such as 'Sussex Lace' and 'L' Elegante' must be given dry warmth in winter and shelter throughout the year. 'Zonal' Pelargoniums, sometimes called *P.* x *hortorum* are actually classed as shrubs but very seldom grown as such. These are the familiar 'Geraniums' which decorate balconies, window-boxes, troughs, tubs and street planting schemes. There are many foliage variations and these must be propagated vegetatively in order to stay true. 'Regal' Pelargoniums *P* x *domesticum* are ones with large, richly coloured edged and frilled flowers, often bi-coloured. These are greenhouse or conservatory dwellers at all times.

Some scented-leaved kinds are:- *P. graveolens* (Lemon), *P. crispum* (Citrus), *P. denticulatum* (Balsam), *P. fragrans* (Pine), *P. odoratissimum* (Apple), *P. tomentosum* (Peppermint) – and there are many more. These can be grown on a sunny windowsill, though not that of a kitchen because they do not like steam.

They have flowers of every colour (except blue) but in addition some have fascinating leaves such as the brilliant foliage of 'Mrs. Henry Cox' which is red, black, green and cream and really seems not to need its flowers at all – the leaves are far more eyecatching. 'Golden Harry Hieover' has yellow-green leaves, with a chestnut brown zone and 'Mountains of Snow' is an attractively variegated green and white plant with pink flowers. 'Freak of Nature' has apple green leaves with white butterfly markings and red flowers. The miniature 'Friesdorf' has a dark olive green leaf with a black-purple zone. Those that are grown for their flower-colour are easy and undemanding – except that they crave sun. If there is a wet summer the centre of the flower heads rots and turns brown, so it is as well to grow fancy-leaved kinds as well in the open so as to have some colour in bad weather. Tubs and pots can be pulled under cover and may escape the worst, but this becomes a nuisance if rain is of regular occurrence, which it most certainly is in these northern isles. Old-fashioned kinds of zonal Pelargoniums will not have survived, or if they have they are not easily obtained.

Requirements: Most greenhouse species should be grown in John Innes No. 2, and they need a mean winter temperature of 7 – 10°C (45 – 50°F). Reduce watering and keep the plants barely moist. Water well during growing and flowering, and open the door and ventilators or windows in hot spells. In prolonged hot spells this is essential and light shading should be given. Young plants for next year's planting out schemes can be kept in the greenhouse for the winter, also the old plants, which should be cut back. These will need regular checking to remove dead leaves which are the start of fungoid problems. Alternatively, zonal Pelargoniums can be kept growing through the winter, and should be re-potted each year in March unless they are to be planted out in the garden. Do not put out until late May or early June. They will benefit from fortnightly liquid feeds.

Cultivation: Take tip cuttings in March from the overwintered plants. Insert these in small pots of peat and sand, using a hormone rooting agent if liked. Cover with paper or otherwise shade for the first ten days and when rooted they will start to grow and can be potted on into potting compost. Pinch out the growing tips of the new plants to keep them bushy. Lift before the first frosts and reduce the size of the plants. Mixed varieties can be grown from seed in the usual way.

Uses: Excellent as cut flowers, but best in hanging baskets, pots, troughs, urns, window-boxes and in bedding out.

Plants: Blooms, Fibrex, Hortico, Thorpes, The Weald Herbary.

Seeds: Most seedsmen.

PELTIPHYLLUM - Umbrella plant *(Saxifragaceae)*. The name of the plant comes from *pelta,* shield, because of the shape of the leaf, which, if you have never seen Peltiphyllum is very like that of a gigantic nasturtium with scalloped edges. In the autumn these large round leaves – they can be as much as 1ft (30.5cm) across – turn to pleasing tones of pink and crimson. It prefers to live in damp soil by the water's edge where its huge roots will increase in size yearly, sending up naked stems of attractive pink flowers in spring (like a stalwart London Pride) that are eventually followed by the unfolding leaves. This is a really handsome plant to grow for its foliage which will do quite well in ordinary soil, providing it gets watered very regularly in summer. I have two clumps – one in the pond and one in a semi-shaded border, and there is little difference between them other than the drooping leaves of the border plant in hot afternoons which is quickly restored by a bucket of water.

P. peltatum (1873) grows to 2ft (61cm) with pink flowers before leaves in April. A handsome foliage perennial from California for a focal position.
Requirements: As text.
Cultivation: Divide huge rhizomes in spring or autumn.
Uses: Foliage for large arrangements.
Rhizomes: Bressingham, Peter Chappell, Beth Chatto, Hillier, Honeysome Aquatic Nursery, Jackamoor's, Sherrards, Stapeley Water Gardens, Treasure's of Tenbury.

PENSTEMON – Beard Tongue, Chelone *(Scrophulariaceae)*. This is a large genus with large herbaceous and tiny rock-dwellers among its members. They are never reliably hardy, so it is best to take cuttings of the favourites as well as covering their parents with litter for the winter. The flowers look very like Foxgloves, and their common name of 'Beard Tongue' is seldom used. The oldest species is *P. barbatus* which was introduced in 1794, then came *P. Hartwegii* which was later crossed with *P. cobaea* which produced the parents of most of the modern plants. Penstemons dislike wet and many are grown as annuals to avoid the necessity for yet more winter protection. The alpine species, which are so suitable for the rock garden, should be propagated from cuttings taken in August and inserted in pots of peat and sand in a cold frame. Take cuttings of non-flowering shoots from border Penstemons and insert in a compost of two parts loam, one part peat and one part sand. Put cuttings round the rim of a large clay pot, and when rooted pot on in individual pots for the winter and keep in the cold frame.
P. barbatus syn. **Chelone barbata** (1794) grows to 3ft (91.5cm) with pink-red flowers from June to August. A tender border plant from Colorado, United States of America.
P. diffusus (1826) grows to 18in (46cm) with pale purple flowers in September. A tender perennial from W. North America.
P. grandiflorus grows to 3ft (91.5cm) with lavender-purple flowers in August. A tender perennial from the E. United States.
P. heterophyllus (1834) grows to 18in (46cm) sometimes taller with pinkish-blue flowers in July. A tender perennial from California for a sunny border.
P. Roezlii grows to 9in (23cm) with blue flowers in July. A perennial from the W. United States for a sunny rockery.
P. Scouleri grows to 1ft (30.5cm) with rose-purple flowers in July. A perennial from N.W. America for the rock garden or sunny border.
Requirements: Full sun, a sheltered situation and free-draining soil. Protect in winter.
Cultivation: *As described.*
Plants: Bressingham, Broadwell, Hillier, Notcutts, Robinsons, St. Bridget.

PETUNIA *(Solanaceae)*. The first Petunia to be introduced to this country was the white-flowered *P. nyctaginiflora* which was discovered by a French expedition who sent the plant to Paris in 1823. There it was named Petunia, from the Brazilian word *Petun*, tobacco, to which it is closely related. Then a botanically minded Scotsman in Buenos Aires sent some seeds to his family, and these produced a purple flower. After several short stays in different genera it was named *Petunia violacea* and our present day flowers are the result of the crosses between *P. nyctaginiflora* and *P. integriflora*. *P. nyctaginiflora's* progeny are scented. The softly sticky leaves and calyxes of Petunias are great dust collectors and they should not be planted where there is traffic.

The plants are perennial, though never grown as such in this country. They are treated as half-hardy annuals, the tiny seeds being sown under glass in March at a temperature of 15°C (59°F). When large enough to handle, prick off into neat seed-boxfuls and grow on and harden off in the usual way. One-colour displays in urns and tubs are more telling than mixed collections, and it is possible to obtain seeds in single-colour packets.

Requirements: Full sun, ordinary soil. Do not feed.
Cultivation: *As text.*
During flowering: Dead-head.
Seeds: Most seedsmen.

PHACELIA *(Hydrophyllaceae).* One of the bluest of blue flowers and almost a rival to the Gentian. It is an annual, with bell-shaped flowers of varying widths according to type. The seeds should be sown thinly in the flowering site in April, only just covering them with sifted soil. Protect from cats with black cotton or wire netting and slugs with pellets or bran. The seeds can be sown in boxes in a cold frame, where it is much easier to keep an eye on them, though they do not really like being transplanted. Grow the low-growing kinds on a rockery for quick and vivid colour, while waiting for perennial plants to establish themselves.

P. campanularia - Phacelia (1882) grows to 9in (23cm) with brilliant blue flowers from June to September. An annual from S. California for rockery or border.

P. tanacetiflora (1832) grows to 30in (76cm) with a generally hairy appearance and lilac flowers in July. An unusual annual for the border and a good bee plant.

Requirements: Full sun, sandy well drained soil for *P. campanularia* and heavier soil for *P. tanacetiflora*.
Cultivation: *See text.*
Seeds: Thomas Butcher, Dobie, Chiltern, Suttons, Thompson and Morgan, Unwins.

PHLOMIS *(Labiatae).* This is an unusual and pleasing plant for a sunny part of the garden, with its wrinkled evergreen leaves and tall flower stems which have whorls of creamy-yellow flowers in May and June. After the flowers are over the green stems are most attractive in arrangements, and if they are left unplundered, the brown autumn stems will most certainly go off with the next avid arranger who visits the garden. *Phlomis Samia* is a good ground covering plant that even Ground Elder has difficulty in penetrating. It is easily propagated by detaching rooted rhizomes and replanting immediately. It does need sufficient space to grow in, but it is well worth an area of at least 5ft (1.5m) by 2ft (61cm) that is enough to show it off well, and it looks very good at the edge of stone paths. It prefers a neutral free draining soil.

P. Samia (1714) grows to 3ft (91.5cm) with evergreen leaves and yellow flowers in May and June. An excellent perennial from N. Africa throughout most of the year for a focal position in full sun.

Requirements: *See text.*
Cultivation: *See text.*

Plants: Beth Chatto, Hillier, Holden Clough, Ramparts.
Seeds: Thompson and Morgan, F. Toynbee Ltd.

PHLOX - Phlox drummondii *(Polemoniaceae).* Its name comes from ancient Greece, where Theophrastus used it for a flame-coloured flower. The name usually conjures up a picture of the late summer border and those fine garden plants *Phlox paniculata,* which came originally from N. America, so Theophrastus would not have known them. Many people grow and love the so-called 'Alpine' Phloxes in their rockeries, though some of these are miniature shrubs. They have flowers of a similar shape to *P. paniculata* – and its hybrid descendants – but are eminently suited to colourfully clothing the rocks. Some need acid or limy soils, and specific situations in part shade, so this should be checked before planting – but best before buying! The annual *Phlox drummondii* is a useful and pretty plant in the border because it is both low in height and very floriferous.

The tall border Phlox do best in rich soil in partial shade. They like a moist atmosphere and are good in wet summers. They should never be allowed to get dry whilst growing (their leaves droop when they are thirsty). If your collection of Phlox is in a prominent position, the weaker shoots can be taken off in spring so that all the strength of the plant goes into making good flower trusses. Phlox are amiable plants and can be moved easily, even in midsummer, before the flowers come. They should be well fed in April with a mulch of compost or well-decayed manure. In spring the large clumps can be divided up, taking only the outer edges and discarding the centre part of the plant. Root cuttings can be taken (see cultivation) rather than stem cuttings as this avoids carrying the dreaded eelworm – a pest of Phlox – into the new clump. With the little 'rock Phlox' or alpines, basal shoots can be inserted in sand and peat in a cold frame in July. When rotted and growing well they should be placed in individual pots of John Innes No. 1 and they can then continue growing in the frame until the following spring. *P. paniculata* has given rise to many modern varieties and the species plant is no longer found. Phlox is sweetly scented, especially in the evening. The shrubby 'alpine' species do not fall within the scope of this book, but there are some low-growing ones such as:-

P. amoena (1786) grows to 10in (25.5cm) with white to purple flowers in May and June. A perennial from S.E. United States for the front of the border or rockery in moist soil.
P. bifida grows to 8in (20.5cm) with violet purple to white flowers in April and May. Good soil and sun.
P. douglasii grows to 6in (15cm) with flowers of various colours (this has been much hybridised and is very popular). Species is a perennial from W.N. America suitable for the rock garden. Good soil and full sun.
Phlox drummondii (1835) grows to 18in (46cm) with flowers in almost every shade. An annual species from Texas and New Mexico for the sunny border or pots and containers of all kinds.
Requirements: Those for *P. paniculata* have been discussed. The alpine species need differing conditions as already listed. *P. drummondii* needs good well-drained soil.
Cultivation: For *P. paniculata,* take ½-in (1.3-cm) pieces of thick root and insert in boxes of peat and sand in a temperature of 13°C (55°F). When the shoots develop, transfer into John Innes No. 1 and put into a cold frame. Grow on and harden off.
Uses: As handsome border and rockery plants.
Plants: For Alpines – Bressingham, Broadwell, Beth Chatto, Hillier, Holden Clough, Ingwersen, Kelways.
Seeds: *P. drummondii:*– Most seedsmen.

PHYSALIS - Chinese Lantern *(Solanaceae).* Physalis or Chinese Lanterns are a familiar part of the late summer garden, with their uniquely shaped orange calyxes. The flowers are a grievous disappointment, if one happens to notice them at all, among all the other distractions of summer – very dull and exactly like those of a potato. Physalis will spread well when established (slugs are very partial to the new season's shoots) and this habit has always been recognised, because Parkinson said feelingly that it would "... runne undergrounde, and abide well enough ..." It can be grown among the vegetables in a small garden, unless there is a corner especially for autumn colour where the lanterns can have pride of place. Turner said "it hath the fruyte in little seed vesselles lyke unto bladders round and rede lyke golde ... whyche the garlande makers use in making of garlandes." Quite accidentally in the autumn garden, sometimes a skeletal lantern appears, with the berry enclosed in a cage of pale veins. Mrs. Loudon advised ladies to soak the lanterns six weeks in water so that the calyx would rot away and allow the berry to be seen. It is an old plant, easily recognisable in drawings, and the earliest known picture of it is in the year 512.

P. alkekengi - Chinese Lantern (1548) grows to 1ft (30.5cm) with undistinguished white flowers in July and August. Ripe calyx is orange-red, and encloses an edible berry. A perennial rhizome from Asia.

P. Franchettii grows to 18in (46cm) or more with white flowers in July and orange 'lanterns' in September.

Requirements: Any soil and a sunny position.

Cultivation: Purchased rhizomes can be planted in spring or divide the roots, which can be very invasive. Sow seeds in spring in a cold frame and grow on in nursery rows. Transplant in spring to flowering positions. Cut the stems when the lanterns change from green to orange and hang in bunches upside down to dry in an airy place. Pull off dead leaves when dry.

Uses: As very ornamental dried seed stems.

Plants: Most nurseries.

Seeds: Most seedsmen.

PHYSOSTEGIA - Obedient Plant *(Labiatae).* This rigid, stiff looking plant belies its appearance: push the flowers gently and you will see – they will stay there for quite a while. Phystostegia is most useful in the garden because it often flowers late, and its erect spikes make a usefully unusual accent in the border; there are two shades of pink and also a white variety.

It is increased by division in the spring and is very deep rooted, so if you should be moving the whole plant to a new place at that time, do not be surprised if it comes up several times in its old home in a dogged sort of way. It does in sun or semi-shade, and as one often has to ration the favoured sunny places to plants that really must have them, put it in one of the more shady positions, which it will brighten up in late summer. It is not fussy as to soil. Water well in dry spells.

P. virginiana syn **Dracocephalum virginianum** (1683) grows to 4ft (122cm) with pink, mauve or white flowers from July to September and sometimes later if grown in shade. Grows taller and bigger in richer soil, but is not generally fussy. A perennial from N. America.

Requirements: *See text.*

Cultivation: *See text.*

Uses: Late summer colour, amusing the children, and for flower arrangement at all stages of bloom.

Plants: Bees, Bloms, Bressingham, Beth Chatto, Hillier, Jackman's, Reginald Kaye, Kelways, Notcutts, Sherrards, St. Bridget.

PHYTOLACCA - Virginian Poke Weed, Pigeon-Berry, Red Ink Plant. *(Phytolaccaceae).* This is a large growing herbaceous plant with spikes of very dull-looking white flowers in summer that seem not to be worth the space that the plant is occupying. But – come September and October –

these undistinguished spikes will metamorphose into striking purple black berries that are the most eyecatching thing in the garden. Plant it for the berries then, with silver leaves behind, and put it in the middle of the border so as to be out of reach of little fingers – and the not so little acquisitive ones of the flower arrangers. The juice from the berries was once used for ink.

P. americana syn. **P. decandra** (1887) grows to 3ft (91.5cm) with enormous roots. Dull white flowers in summer and brilliantly beautiful red-black berries from August to October. A perennial from Florida for autumn effect. Roots and berries very poisonous.

Requirements: Sun, any soil.
Cultivation: Divide roots (if possible) in spring or sow seed in boxes in spring.
Uses: Superb arrangement material.
Plants: Beth Chatto.
Seeds: Chiltern.

PINGUICULA - Butterwort *(Lentibulariaceae)*. This pretty little plant that looks rather like a violet belies its innocent air. It is insectivorous, and in its native habitat of bogland it traps insects by means of a sticky secretion that is slowly exuded by glands in the leaves. The leaves are capable of slight movement, gradually cupping the victim in some cases, or very slowly rolling over it if the creature is trapped near the margin. The plant absorbs the digestible portions of the insects which provide it with essential nitrogen. One variety, *P. grandiflora* can be grown in the bog garden, but most of the others need alpine house conditions. The hardy kinds can be planted out, ideally, in sphagnum moss. These are propagated by dividing the crowns in April, or by sowing seeds thinly in autumn or spring, in pans of a compost made up of equal parts of chopped sphagnum moss and peat. Stand the pans in shallow water with a pane of glass over them in a temperature of 13°C (55°F). When the seedlings are large enough to handle, prick out into boxes of the same compost. When they are growing well transfer three or four of them into an 8-in (20.5-cm) pan which should be stood in shallow water during the summer. If they are to be planted out this should be done in March or April. If they are to remain in the alpine house, they should be lightly shaded during the brightest of the summer months, with good ventilation at all times, particularly when the temperature rises above 10°C (50°F).

P. grandiflora grows to 6in (15cm) with violet blue flowers from May to July. A European perennial for the sunny bog garden or alpine house.

P. gypsicola (1912) grows to 4in (10cm) with pink flowers from July to October. A perennial from Mexico for the alpine house.

Requirements: *See text.*
Cultivation: *See text.*
Plants: Reginald Kaye, Marston Exotics.
Seeds: Thompson and Morgan.

PLATYCODON - Balloon-Flower, Chinese Bell-Flower *(Campanulaceae)*. The buds of this flower are plumply parcelled into perfect little packages and it is this that makes it so memorable. These angular balloon-buds open to wide open bell-flowers which are very lovely. The species was discovered over two centuries ago – in 1782 – and it is only now becoming more popular. Mr Shirley Hibbard said of it that " ... the lover of hardy plants should give no rest to the soles of his feet or the palms of his hands till he has mastered every detail of their cultivation". It is not difficult to grow, though it may be a help to remember that slugs will nip off the purple asparagus-like spring growths before you even know that they are up, and that the plant vanishes without trace in the autumn and is therefore very easily damaged when tidying the bed during the winter or early spring. It is best propagated by seed because the established plants (though not always long lived) dislike disturbance and may not always survive division. Seeds should be sown in boxes of seed compost in March. Sow very thinly because the seedlings are fragile, and it is better to thin out than to prick out.

P. grandiflorus - Chinese Bell-Flower (1782) grows to 2ft (61cm) with purple blue flowers from June to August. A perennial from China and Japan for a sunny border. The species is not always grown, having been superseded by the following:

P. grandiflorus Mariesii (1885) which is less tall and has larger flowers.
Requirements: Good, free-draining garden soil.
Cultivation: *As text.*
Plants: Most nurseries.
Seeds: Thomas Butcher, Chiltern, Dobie, Thompson and Morgan.

PLEIONE *(Orchidaceae).* The plant takes its name from *Pleione,* the mother of the Pleiades. These are almost the easiest of Orchids to grow, needing simple growing conditions which can be easily supplied and in the mildest areas of the British Isles they are almost hardy.

The single flowers come in many colours and bi-colours – pink, cream, mauve, purple, yellow and ginger, with purple and maroon spots. They have an attractively fringed tubular labellum or lobe, which is often a different colour to the petals and sepals, and rise on short 6-in (15-cm) stems from the pseudobulbs – sometimes there are two flowers, but one is most usual. The leaves appear after the flowers. The pseudobulbs are usually 1 – 1½in (2.5 – 3.8cm) high, depending on the species, and they should be planted three to a 6-in (15-cm) pan, with only the bottom third of the pseudobulb set into the compost, which should be made up of two parts John Innes No. 1, and one part sphagnum moss. Plant these in April or May in a cool greenhouse or a conservatory. Shade the plants during the summer and give adequate ventilation except during cold and very wet weather. Give weak liquid feeds fortnightly from June to September, but take care not to overwater to begin with. Water well during their period of growth and flowering. Some Pleiones can be kept or planted outside in mild parts of southern England. When the foliage turns yellow the plants will become dormant and should be put, pot and all, in the ground in a shaded frame, watering only sufficiently to keep the pseudobulbs from shrivelling. When growing them outside, they should be planted in light rich soil mixed with leaf-mould, in a partially shaded place. Cover them with cloches from October until May for safety. When grown in pots they should be re-potted every year, or at the most, every two years immediately after flowering. The flowers, which are very large for the size of the plant, usually last for a fortnight; they are in bloom in winter and can be brought into the house for this period.

P. formosana syn. **P. bulbocodioides** grows to 6in (15cm) with 3-in (7.5-cm) wide flowers in many colours from January to May, out of doors, April and May. An orchid originally from Formosa, China and Tibet for greenhouse, conservatory and sheltered rock gardens in warm areas. (Slugs will be a hazard.)

P. Hookeriana (1877) has pink, white and yellow flowers in May. An Orchid from Sikkim.

P. humilis (1866) has flowers of various colours – pink, blush, white, mauve, on 4in (10cm) stems. An Orchid from Nepal.

Requirements: *See text.*
Cultivation: Offsets will be produced at the base of the pseudo-bulb; these should be detached at re-potting time and potted separately. The pseudobulb produces pseudobulbils at the top, which will drop off at the end of the plant's growing season. Collect them and put in pans of growing compost and grow on for two years in the same way as the parent pseudobulb.
Uses: As cool greenhouse, conservatory and houseplants. In mild areas as exotic rockery plants. As cut flowers.

Pseudobulbs: Amand, Avon, Bloms, Broadleigh, Burnham, Hillier, Holden Clough, Ingwersen, Reginald Kaye, Potterton and Martin.

POLEMONIUM - Jacob's Ladder, Greek Valerian, Charity *(Polemoniaceae).* Over the centuries it is only to be expected that names and plants would have become separated from each other, indeed, it is quite surprising that those long in cultivation have emerged at this end of a 2000-year-long tunnel of time with name and plant more or less the same and still together. 'Polemos' means war, and Pliny describes another plant (which could not be this one) as having clusters of berries and thick roots, and as being a herb of a thousand virtues. This plant was fought over by two princes who each wished to claim the honour of its discovery, but nothing fits, alas, and it has no real medicinal value, either. It is said that cats like it as they like the true Valerian *(Valeriana officinalis)* but my cats pass it by without a look on their way to what is left of the Catmint. But Jacob's Ladder has fine blue flowers when grown in the mass, and can be counted on as one of the easiest plants to grow in a sunny border.

P. coeruleum - Jacob's Ladder grows to 2ft (61cm) with blue flowers from May to July. There is a white variety. A short-lived European perennial for the sunny border in any soil.

Requirements: Totally undemanding.

Cultivation: Sow seeds in autumn or spring where they are to flower. Will sow itself. Separate clumps in spring.

Plants: Beth Chatto, Christian, Cunnington, Goatchers, Hillier, Ingwersen, Oak Cottage Herb Farm, Sherrards, Stoke Lacy Herb Garden, F. Toynbee Ltd., The Weald Herbary.

Seeds: Most seedsmen.

POLIANTHES - Tuberose *(Amaryllidaceae).* This plant – so seldom grown today – was a favourite of the Victorians because of its scent. It is a rhizomatous plant, and can be easily made to flower almost throughout the year if it is planted successively. The flower spike is handsome, unlike any other, and the perfume is legendary, though, oddly enough, the Tuberose does not appear in the Language of Flowers, even though it was used in floral arrangements and bouquets so extensively in former days. The Chinese used the flowers as just one ingredient in vegetable soup.

The rhizomes should be planted as soon as available in ordinary loam with some well-decayed manure mixed in, or moistened John Innes No. 1. Put one in a 5-in (12.5-cm) pot or three to a 7-in (18-cm) pot. Water carefully as soon as the leaves appear. To have them flowering successively, plant in pots as described and leave in a cold but frost free frame, and bring others on by putting them over bottom heat of 15 - 20°C (60 - 70°F). The bulbs should be discarded after flowering, and though they may produce offsets, these do not ripen properly in N. Europe.

P. tuberosa - Tuberose (1629) grows to 4ft (122cm) with a spike of very fragrant white flowers. A rhizome from Mexico for greenhouse or conservatory. The variety 'The Pearl' (1879) with double flowers is most generally obtainable.

Requirements: *As described.*

Cultivation: *See text.*

Rhizomes: Amand, de Jager.

POLYGONATUM - Solomon's Seal, Ladder-to-Heaven, David's Harp *(Liliaceae).* An easy and old-fashioned plant to grow, needing only to be left alone to increase and multiply, though to do this Solomon's Seal needs a peaceful place in semi-shade and plenty of humus-rich leaf-mould. Gerard thought that the roots of this plant, if pulverised and drunk in ale, would "... soddereth and gleweth togither the bones in very short space, and very strangely, yea although the bones be but slenderly and unhandsomely placed and wrapped up". This remedy was attributed to "the vulgar sort of people of Hampshire". The other more famous quotation about bruising is indicative of the unchanging attitude of the male-dominant world "... the roote of Solomon's Seale, stamped while it is fresh and greene, and applied, taketh away in one night or two at the most, any bruse, blacke or blew spots gotten by fals or women's wilfulness, in stumbling upon their hastie husband's fists, or such like".

The beautiful cool-looking flower-stems are often plagued by the grey-blue caterpillars of the sawfly which will make a nasty network of the leaves in a very short space of time. Examine your plants weekly for these pests, and if you find any, dust or spray with malathion, unless the plants are near water.

P. multiflorum syn. **P.x hybridum-Solomon's Seal** grows to 4ft (122cm) with green-edged white bells in June. Originally a European rhizomatous plant for a semi shaded place.

Requirements: Will do in any soil, but best is moisture retentive humus-rich soil.

Cultivation: Keep rhizomes just covered with soil. These can be lifted and divided when the leaves die down.

Uses: Superb for flower arrangements, graceful plant for the waterside and shady town garden.

Rhizomes: Most nurseries.

POLYGONUM *(Polygonaceae).* Most of this genus can be absolutely depended on to colonise a new garden with more rapidity than any other plant family. Nevertheless, most of them are attractive plants – they merely need a firm hand, especially if it is holding a pair of garden shears. They are close cousins to the Dock tribe, and though this may be as a bar sinister in their pedigrees, it indicates how vigorous they can be. There are several for different garden areas: *P. affine* is a delightful rock-dripper, no more than 9in (23cm) high, whose small two-tone pink pokers come out from July onwards, and in winter the dead, russet coloured leaves remain, much more pleasant than bare stems or a tracery of twigs. *P. amplexicaule atrosanguineum* (alas, it appears to have no common name) is taller – it grows to an angular 3ft (91.5cm) with a seemingly endless succession of rose-red spikes from August until October. These are most useful in the garden at this time of year. Its closest relative (in appearance) is *P. bistortum superbum,* and in winter it is impossible to tell these two apart. But at least it has a common name of sorts, though neither 'Bistort' nor 'Snakeweed' is particularly pleasing. It grows to the same height but has pale pink poker-spikes in May and June, with some after-thoughts later if the stems are dead-headed. Though the leaves of this pair are definitely Dock-like, their root system is so close that weeds can seldom penetrate and never flourish. *P. campanulatum* has most attractive leaves and grows to 3ft (91.5cm) with angular sprays of pink flowers from June to September. This is graceful among ferns in semi shade.

All like damp soil, but they will grow quite well in the ordinary border, though their leaves will tell you that they are unhappy on a hot afternoon.

P. affine (1822) grows to 9in (23cm) with hanging mats of flowers from July until September or October. A rhizomatous perennial from Nepal for the rockery, dry wall or front of the border.

P. amplexicaule atrosanguineum grows to 3ft (91.5cm) with rose-red flower spikes from August to October. A vigorous perennial from the Himalayas. Controllable in dry soil.

P. Bistorta - Bistort grows to 3ft (91.5cm) with pink flowers from June to September. Another vigorous perennial, but from Europe. Also controllable in dry soil.

P. campanulatum grows to 3ft (91.5cm) with sprays of pink flowers from June to September. A perennial from the Himalayas with rooting stems, for larger gardens.

P. vaccinifolium (1845) grows to 6in (15cm) with mats of small-leaved wiry stems and pink flower spikes in September and October. Likes to lurk behind rocks and drip down sunny walls. A perennial from the Himalayas for rock gardens.

Requirements: For more and even better flowers, grow the two larger plants in rich moist soil, but they will take up a great deal of space very quickly. *P. affine* is unfussy.

Cultivation: Divide all in spring and replant immediately.

Plants: Most nurseries.

POTENTILLA *(Rosaceae)*. There are only a few herbaceous members of the great Rose tribe, and the Potentilla is one of them, as are Alchemilla and Aruncus. *P. atrosanguineum* was formerly grown, but has been superseded by – I hate to say this – better hybrids, as is the case with *P. nepalensis. P. anserina* is the beautiful-leaved Silverweed, or as I prefer to call it, the aptly-named Midsummer Silver. This has delicate silver leaves like feathers, but is too dangerous to let loose in the garden, alas, except when firmly controlled in concrete corners from whence it cannot escape. It has one useful function – the roots are edible whether cooked or raw, though one needs a lot of them. There were many border varieties in former times, and they are so well described that we can picture them today. Their name is derived from *Potens,* powerful, because of the virtues, both magical and medicinal of that other member of the genus, the Cinquefoil, *P. repens* (Culpeper said of this plant "... some hold that one leaf cures a quotidian, three a tertian and four a quartan ague ...".

P. atrosanguineum var. **Gibson's Scarlet** (1909). This has brilliant red flowers, the species has purple ones from May to September. Grows to 2ft (61cm) with attractive leaves. A perennial for the sunny border.

P. nepalensis grows to 2ft (61cm) with purple or crimson flowers in July and August. A perennial from the W. Himalayas. The shorter-growing carmine flowered variety 'Miss Willmott' is generally offered.

P. recta (1648) grows to 18in (46cm) with yellow flowers in June and July. A perennial from S. Europe, Siberia and Algeria. The variety 'Warrenii' with yellows flowers is most usual.

Requirements: Ordinary well drained soil and full sun. Mulch with decayed manure and peat in March. Do not allow to dry out in hot weather.

Cultivation: Divide established clumps in autumn or spring, best in spring.

Uses: As cut and border flowers. Leaves attractive for flower arrangements.

Plants: Most nurseries.

PRIMULA - Primula, Primrose, Polyanthus, Oxlip, Cowslip, etc. *(Primulaceae)*. This huge and beautiful genus numbers over five hundred species, though many of these are not available. If they were they would be very difficult to grow, even in controlled alpine house situations. But there are very many species kinds, and the neat ruched leaves of the wild Primrose *P. vulgaris* are among the most welcome sights of winter. New leaves coming mean flowers soon, and they are in bloom from January onwards – the first flowers often seeming to be the best if the weather is kind. Our forefathers began experimenting with double kinds as early as the sixteenth century. These had one flower within another and were – and still are – called Hose-in-hose, Galligaskins, Jack-in-the-green and Jackanapes-on-Horseback. These all but died out in the craze for Victorian carpet-bedding and were only recently re-discovered in old Irish gardens. The Oxlip, *P. elatior,* is a rare wild plant that is distinctly different from a yellow-flowered Polyanthus or false Oxlip – its flowerscape falls to one side instead of evenly all round, the flowers are smaller and smell of apricots, and the leaves narrow abruptly and characteristically some distance from the root. These are easy plants to grow and will self-seed themselves when established. They should be kept well away from Polyanthus, Cowslips and Primroses or curious (though attractive) hybrids will result which will not be true Oxlips. Cowslips are becoming rare in England because of the ploughing-up of pasture land for the futile food mountains of Europe, and it is sad not to be able to pick them in glorious orange-scented bunches to make that most transient of playthings, a cowslip ball. To do such a thing today would make one feel like a criminal – so few are the plants in their pastures in comparison with those of forty years ago.

Polyanthus were known in previous centuries and were much grown in the seventeenth century, being called 'The English Primula' by continental gardeners of the time. Double varieties and flowers of every colour were grown, and sometimes these were called by their common name of Pug-in-a-pinner. So popular were they that they became Florists' flowers, with such telling names as 'Bang Europe'. The favourite flowers were the laced kind (see Auricula) and their colour was well described as tortoiseshell, being brown with gold edges. Fortunately these too have survived, though only just, and seeds of these lovely flowers can be obtained from Barnhaven.

The Asiatic primulas such as the 'Drumstick' and the 'Candelabra' types are very late introductions in comparison, not being discovered until late in the nineteenth century and during the first part of this, the twentieth. These are usually moisture-lovers, though this does not mean that they should be grown actually in the pond. They like to have plenty of moist soil during their growing and flowering period and afterwards can be much drier. They will grow quite well in ordinary humus rich soil as long as it is moisture retentive, and when settled in a garden will start to seed themselves about with liberality, so much so that I have found them coming up out of cracks in the path (where their roots are cool under the paving stones).

P. denticulata - the 'Drumstick' Primula (1840) Species not generally grown, very many hybrids now available with round flowerheads in many shades of mauve, pink, crimson or white. A perennial plant for damp pond margins in sun or partial shade

P. elatior - Oxlip grows to 10in (25.5cm) with gradually elongating stems and scented yellow flowers from March to May. A European and Asian perennial plant for a more sunny place and ordinary soil.

P. Juliae (1913) grows to 3in (7.5cm) with purple flowers in April. A well known old-fashioned hybrid variety is *P. Wanda* which often begins to flower in mid-winter, and which needs a well drained gritty soil with plenty of humus in sun or partial shade.

P. pulverulenta (1905) species grows to 3ft (91.5cm) with eye-catching tiers of whorls of crimson flowers with a purple eye in June. The stems may be farinose (silvery-mealy) which should not be touched or they will mark. Needs moist but not wet conditions in sun or partial shade.

P. veris - Cowslip grows to 8in (20.5cm) with scented yellow flowers in April and May. A European and Asian perennial, preferring full sun and calcareous soil.

P. vulgaris - Primrose grows to 5in (12.5cm) with distinctive pale yellow flowers from December until April. A native and European perennial for semi-shade in leafmould. (It will grow in full sun but this is not characteristic, just cussedness).

N.B. Polyanthus are of garden origin and it is difficult if not impossible to get the older kinds.

Requirements: Polyanthus and border types need good well drained soil with peat, well-decayed manure and bonemeal added before planting. In dry weather mulch with peat and do not allow to dry out. They are generally propagated from seed which does not come true in ordinary garden conditions. They can be easily grown in full sun in ordinary garden soil or in pots, troughs and window boxes.

Cultivation: All Primula seed should be sown as fresh as possible for best results though it is important to check whether the species that are being grown are likely to come true. Sow seeds thinly in boxes of seed compost and cover with a pane of glass to maintain humidity (even more important for the moisture loving types). Keep seedlings shaded. Divide species and hybrids of *P. denticulata* and *P. Juliae*. Grow on and plant out in nursery rows or individual pots, as appropriate. Take precautions against slugs.

Uses: Polyanthus types for all kinds of containers and as spring bedding plants which can be planted elsewhere after flowering and divided at this time. As waterside, bog garden and rockery plants. As wild garden subjects to grow in light woodland orchards and grassy banks.

Plants: Most nurseries.

Seeds: Barnhaven, Thomas Butcher, Chiltern, Naturescape.

PULMONARIA - Lungwort, Jesus, Joseph and Mary, Soldiers and Sailors *(Boraginaceae)*. Lungwort is so called, because according to the Doctrine of Signatures, the spotted leaves looked like diseased lungs and the plant was thought to be a cure for all pulmonary sickness. The plant produces its pink flowers (which turn blue as they age) very early in spring, with the flowers coming almost at the same time as the new season's leaves. These later enlarge and elongate and it is for these, as ground cover in moist sandy places, that the plant is grown. If the various species are grown together in the garden there is a great deal of promiscuity, and the resultant seedlings will not be true to either parent. Large clumps may be divided in early spring to ensure similar plants.

P. angustifolia - Blue Cowslip (before 1823) grows to 12in (30.5cm) with bristly dark green unspotted leaves and pink flowers later changing to blue. A European perennial for shady places.

P. officinalis - Lungwort, Spotted Dog (before 1597) grows to 12in (30.5cm) with bristly dark green leaves spotted with white, and pink and blue flowers in April and May. A European perennial for the shady border, shaded rockeries or pond side.

P. saccharata (before 1683) grows to 12in (30.5cm) with (usually) pink flowers in March and April. The bristly leaves are much more marked than any other variety and this is the best to grow for foliage contrast. A European perennial plant to grow for its leaves.

Requirements: Moist, humus rich soil and semi shade.

Cultivation: *As text.* Seeds can be sown in April but the resulting plants are seldom worth the effort of nurture.

Uses: Foliage plants in the garden – leaves do not last well in water.

Plants: Peter Chappell, Beth Chatto, Kelways, Hillier, Kaye.

PULSATILLA - Pasque Flower *(Ranunculaceae)*. The Pasque flower is a native British flower, though this may seem hard to believe. Its habitat was once the chalk downs that covered so much of the country, but now that many of these unique plant habitats have disappeared under the plough or the bulldozer the Pasque flower, with all its silky loveliness has gone too. But, fortunately, because it is so pretty and so easily propagated, there is little difficulty in acquiring plants. These should be grown in calcareous soil in the rockery, and it is worth importing some crushed quarry chalk or limestone grit which can be mixed with your own soil. The ferny leaves are also silky-hairy and after the purple flowers are over there are interesting whiskery seed heads.

The Pasque flower is still found in nursery catalogues under Anemone to which genus it formerly belonged, being called *Anemone pulsatilla*. (See Anemone.)

A. pulsatilla - Pasque flower grows to 8in (20.5cm) with silky hairy violet flowers in April. A European perennial for the rock garden in full sun.
Requirements: Chalky soil and full sun with plenty of humus. Do not allow to dry out in the growing season.
Cultivation: Obtain fresh seed where possible and sow in John Innes seed compost in boxes in a cold frame in July. When the seedlings are large enough transfer into individual pots and grow on, leaving them in the frame for the winter and the following summer. Plant in flowering positions in September.
Plants: Most nurseries.

PYRETHRUM - see **Chrysanthemum** *(Compositae)*.

RANUNCULUS *(Ranunculaceae)*. Once the Ranunculus was the most popular of all garden flowers, and an eighteenth century nurseryman, James Maddock, was able to list 800 different named kinds, with fifty thousand seedlings being grown annually for his eager customers. But by 1851 the demand had dwindled away to less than fifty, and now the nurseries that grow them are only able to list less than a dozen species.
  R. asiaticus is a beautiful 'garden' Ranunculus, reputedly brought back from the Middle East by King Louis IX of France as a present for his mother, Blanche of Castille. This was in the thirteenth century, and the flower increased in popularity until, during the sixteenth century, the corms were being imported as regularly as was practicable, though they often dried up on the long journey. There is a sad little note in the writings of Clusius, about a plant that survived in a fresh, green state but "which a domesticall theefe stole, foorth of his garden..." The Dutch began growing them and did very good business in the eighteenth century, though one English writer warned his readers, then as now, not to buy cheap imports. "The Dutchman is something like the Jew in his dealings; you must not expect great bargains for little money; he is very seldom charged, I believe, with sending us any of his best flowers among his common mixtures; his Pell Mells, as the florist calls them, are on the whole, very indifferent and not worth the amateur's notice ..."
R. aconitifolius - White Bachelor's Buttons (1598) grows to 2ft (61cm) with single white flowers in May and June. Var. *flore-pleno* has double flowers and is called 'Fair Maids of France', and *R. aconitifolius grandiflorus* with larger flowers is 'Fair Maids of Kent'. Perennials from Europe for moist soil in partial shade.
R. asiaticus - Garden Ranunculus (1596) grows to 15in (38cm) with flowers in every colour except blue. A perennial from the Orient, flowering in May and June. This needs special cultivation, as follows: Prepare special beds by removing the soil to a depth of 2ft (61cm) and putting in small stones at the bottom of the trench to act as drainage material. The trench should then be filled up to a level that is higher than the path, with a compost consisting of two parts loam to one part leaf-mould with plenty of well rotted cow manure and some sharp sand. The roots of this Ranunculus have small claws and these should be planted 2in (5cm) deep with the claws downwards in February, if the weather is suitable. When the flowers begin to open it was at one time customary to shade them with an awning, and fruit netting would be suitable to stretch over them. Watering should be done carefully in the evening, and the soil should never be allowed to become dry enough for the soil to crack. After flowering, when the leaves have turned yellow, the roots should be lifted and stored in a dry, airy place.
R. lingua - Greater Spearwort grows to 3ft (91.5cm) with large shining yellow buttercups from June to August. A good plant for large ponds, but it is invasive in small ones. Trap it in lily baskets or large pots, though it must

Plate 9

Liliaceae:
Fritillaria imperialis,
Polygonatum multiflorum,
Hyacinthoides non-scriptus,
Lilium candidum.

Plate 10

Malvaceae:
Althaea rosea,
Lavatera trimestris,
Sidalcea malviflora.

Plate 11

Onagraceae:
Clarkia elegans,
Gaura Lindheimerin,
Godetia grandiflora,
Oenothera erythrosepala.

Plate 12

Papaveraceae:
Eschscholzia californica,
Papaver somniferum,
Macleaya (Bocconia) cordata,
Papaver orientale.

Plate 13

Primulaceae:
Primula vulgaris,
Polyanthus,
Cyclamen coum,
Lysimachia nummularia,
Primula japonica.

Plate 14

Ranunculaceae:
Aconitum anglicum,
Aquilegia vulgaris,
Eranthis hyemalis,
Helleborus niger,
Helleborus orientalis,
Anemone blanda.

Plate 15

Scrophulariaceae:
Digitalis purpurea,
Antirrhinum majus,
Mimulus guttatus.

Plate 16

Violaceae:
Viola odorata,
Viola 'Irish Molly',
Viola tricolor,
Viola x *wittrockiana.*

have sufficient depth to prevent it from falling over. It has submerged leaves
throughout the winter. A vigorous European perennial for the pond.
Requirements: *As text.*
Cultivation: *As text for R. asiaticus.* Divide roots of *R. lingua* in spring.
Plants: Bennetts, Peter Chappell, Cunnington, Hillier, Honeysome Aquatic
Nursery, Notcutts, Rock Garden Nursery, Stassen, Waveney, Wildwoods.
Corms: Amand, Bloms, Hortico, Ingwersen, Kelways, Unwins.

RESEDA - Mignonette, Frenchman's Darling *(Resedaceae).* Such an undistinguished flower – but such a scent! Mignonette is as old-fashioned as
bonnet-strings but fortunately the hybridisers have (more or less) left it
alone. Oddly enough, it comes from Egypt, where in the past centuries it
was used in the burial ceremonies to decorate the catafalques. It was grown
in France before being introduced to England, but it became so popular so
quickly that people wanted it everywhere, and they planted it in their
window-boxes so that some London streets were perfumed for weeks. It has
always been associated with France, possibly because Napoleon noticed it
while he was in Egypt and sent seeds of it to Josephine for her garden at
Malmaison. The French *haut monde* loved all perfumed flowers, indeed,
French people were quite obsessional about scented flowers, and they grew
Mignonette in pots to perfume their grand apartments. Flowers have always
been a French industry, and Mignonette was grown by the acre in southern
France to supply the florists' shops.
     There is an old belief that a lover who rolls three times in a bed of
Mignonette will be attended by success. I have all kinds of mental images of
this and would love to participate in some field tests – I'll grow the
Mignonette. A group of well-grown plants are quite sculptural, and might
be placed at the edge of a patio, where their scent can be easily enjoyed.
Since their flowers are in tones of greenish yellow this colour looks pleasing
against dark hedges, brick or stone walls or with other green-flowered
plants.
Reseda odorata - Mignonette (1752) grows to 2½ft (76cm) with sweetly scented
greenish flower spikes from June to October. An annual from N. Africa for
a sunny border.
Requirements: Sun, any soil.
Cultivation: Sow seeds in March and grow on in the usual way.
Uses: As cut and arrangement flowers and as suggested in text.
Seeds: Most seedsmen.

RUDBECKIA - Coneflower *(Compositae).* All this genus are welcome in the
garden, flowering as they do at summer's end. They are named after Olaf
Rudbeck (1660-1740) and also his son of the same name, who were both
professors of Botany at Uppsala. Their flowers are of a very defined daisy-
shape, and are almost always yellow with, usually, as in *R. laciniata* and *R.
hirta,* prominent cone-shaped centres.
     Olaf Rudbeck *père* started a botanical garden and managed to grow a
surprising number of newly discovered plants, in spite of the Swedish
climate which is even worse that that of the British Isles. He started a life-
work called the *Campi Elysii* which was to contain illustrations of all the
then known plants of the world. This mighty project was proceeding well,
with two volumes completed, when a fire occurred in 1702 which consumed
all the manuscripts and some 10,000 woodcuts which were for the
remaining work. Only three copies were saved from this disaster and Olaf
Rudbeck himself died later in the same year, probably of a broken heart.
The taxonomists do not appear to agree about the nomenclature for this
genus.
R. fulgida (1760) grows to 3ft (91.5cm) (variable according to type) with dark-
centred golden yellow flowers from July to September. A perennial from the

S.E. United States for the late summer border. Species not generally available, *R. fulgida* 'Deamii' and 'Goldsturm' having replaced the older plant.

R. hirta - Black-eyed Susan (1714) grows to 3ft (91.5cm) with yellow flowers with brown-purple centres. A short lived perennial from N. America.

R. laciniata - Coneflower (1640) grows to 7ft (2.1m) with yellow flowers and pointed green central discs. A perennial from Canada and the United States for a good corner, with moist soil and sun.

R. nitida very similar to *R. laciniata* but shorter, the variety 'Herbstonne' is most usually obtainable.

R. speciosa syn. **R. Newmannii** See *R. fulgida*

Requirements: Full sun or partial shade, any soil. Taller species will need support because of autumn gales.

Cultivation: Divide established clumps in March and replant.

Uses: As garden and cut flowers in late summer.

Plants: Beth Chatto, Goatchers, Highfield, Hillier, Notcutts, Scotts.

Seeds: Thomas Butcher.

SAINTPAULIA - African Violet *(Gesneriaceae)*. When one sees these tropical plants – for tropical they are – in a florist's shop, they look so perfect in form and colour with their neat velvety leaves surrounding the posy of flowers, that they are instantly desirable. The trouble starts when you get them home. Grown as house plants, naturally, they must have their requirements met – they are pernickety plants needing four specifics. They should have good light, but never direct sunshine during the summer as their flowers will be scorched. They should be kept on a bright, not sunny, windowsill – north-facing during the summer months. They need good light so that their flowers retain their rich colours and so that new flower buds will continue to form. When grown commercially they live in a constant temperature of 22°C (72°F) though they will survive temperatures as low as 10°C (50°F) but they will not be happy. They are best kept in the warmest room in the house during the winter, but move them away from the cold window glass each night. That gap between the window and the curtains is fatal for many house plants. When it comes to watering, the pot should be stood in a bowl of tepid water that rises to a height of 1in (2.5cm) up the sides of the African Violet's pot. Leave them to soak this up for about two hours, then leave to drain and then return to its home on the windowsill. They should never be left permanently standing in water, and should only be watered thus when the compost becomes dry. They will need feeding to produce the successions of flowers that they are capable of, and they need assistance in the form of a house-plant food of your choice, reading the instructions most carefully. Liquid plant food can be added to their drinking water at the correct intervals which will vary according to the kind used.

  Curiously enough, they are quite easy to propagate. Take two or three healthy leaves with about 1in (2.5cm) of stem from good plants (label the pots). Snip them carefully and handle as little as possible. Stick them upright in a 3-in (7.5-cm) pot containing a soilless compost, which has been moistened from below. The pot or pots should be put in a light place (but not in sunlight) with a minimum temperature of 13°C (55°F), though warmer is better.

S. ionantha - African Violet (1893) grows to 4in (10cm) with (in species) blue-violet flowers almost continuously. The species is seldom seen, having been superseded by the very many modern varieties and hybrids.

Requirements: *As text.*

Cultivation: *As text.*

Plants: Tony Clements, Floralands, Leeslane.

SALPIGLOSSIS - Salpiglossis, Painted Tongue *(Solanaceae).* The name comes from *Salpinx,* 'trumpet', *glossa,* 'tongue' from the tongue-like protruding style at the base of the corolla. Closely related to the Tobaccos, this annual plant has very beautiful flowers that are strongly veined in self, toning or contrasting colours; the permutations seem to be endless. These rather delicate plants need twiggy support so that the beauty and variety of their colouration can be seen. Seeds should be sown under glass in February or March at a temperature of 18°C (64°F) and grown in the usual way. In sheltered, southern areas the seed can be sown in the open ground in April and the seedlings thinned out later, allowing about 8in (20.5cm) between plants. They make very beautiful pot plants under glass in the winter, more particularly because there is more time to examine and enjoy the richness of their colouring, and little else of this nature can be produced so easily. For winter flowers in the greenhouse, sow seeds in September and thereafter keep the temperature at a minimum of 61-64°F (16-18°C). As there is no close season for aphids, a careful watch should be kept for these pests which can ruin the plant.

S. sinuata - Salpiglossis grows to 2ft (61cm) with flowers in all colours except blue from July to September. A tender annual from Chile for the sunny border or for picking. Species no longer grown, being replaced by modern hybrids.

Requirements: Rich soil and a sunny, open position.
Cultivation: *As text.*
Uses: As cut and border flowers.
During and after flowering: Dead-head.
Seeds: Most seedsmen.

SALVIA - Sage, etc. *(Labiatae).* The name was given to the genus by Pliny from *salvus,* safe/healthy, and throughout history species of this genus have been associated with traditional medicine. The culinary sages, being shrubs, do not come into this book so it is the annual and herbaceous species that are dealt with here.

The design of the chanuka, the ceremonial branched candlestick that is the signal for the commencement of the orthodox Jewish Sabbath is said to have derived from a middle eastern plant, *Salvia judaica.*

The bright red *Salvia splendens,* without which no park bedding scheme or urban roundabout would be complete, is actually a perennial in its native home of Brazil, though always grown as an annual in Northern Europe. It has its place in the summer border, in pots or window boxes, but a little of that scarlet, a soundless scream that almost pains the ears as well as the eyes, is more than sufficient, except to celebrate Royal occasions in company with blue Lobelia and white Alyssum. Then we can forget good taste and delicate combinations and go all out for loyal support for the monarchy, and it's all great fun. In its native home it is pollinated by small birds who are attracted by its brilliant colour – insects leave it alone. I would disagree with Ruskin's opinion of the exquisitely pure blue of *S. patens* which must be one of the bluest of true-blue flowers. Ruskin said "The exotic sages have no moderation in their hues ... the velvety violent blue of the one and scarlet of the other, seem to have no gradation and no shade. There's no colour that gives one such an idea of violence – a sort of rough, angry scream – as that shade of blue, ungradated. In the gentian it is touched with green, in the cornflower with red ... but in the salvia it is simply blue cloth."

Transfer all that animosity of feeling to *S. splendens* and I would, as I previously said, agree.

S. Horminum (1596) grows to 18in (46cm) with purple flowers and enlarged coloured bracts from June to August. An annual from S. Europe for a sunny border and flower arrangements.

S. patens (1838) grows to 2ft (61cm) with blue flowers from August - September.

A perennial from Mexico, this plant is usually grown as an annual for a sunny border.

S. splendens - Scarlet Salvia (1822) grows to 15in (38cm), species 3ft (91.5cm) with very red flowers from July until the frosts. A popular bedding plant from Brazil for borders, pots, windowboxes and anywhere that bright permanent colour is needed – bad weather seems not to affect it. Any soil, full sun.

S x superba syn. **S. virgata nemorosa** (about 1900) grows to 2ft (61cm) with spikes of purple blue flowers from July - September. A rather tender perennial for a sunny border.

S. argentea (1759) grows to 18in (46cm) with silver-green felted leaves and pinkish flowers in July and August. A perennial, grown as a biennial from the Mediterranean region; this is a pleasingly soft-coloured foliage plant as a foil to brighter border flowers.

Requirements: Ordinary soil and full sun. Protect *S. x superba* from winter wet with a pane of glass or a cloche.

Cultivation: Sow seeds of annuals in March under glass in boxes of seed compost at a temperature of 18°C (64°F) and grow on. Harden off before planting out and pinch out growing tips to encourage bushiness. Divide *S. x superba* in the spring – it is late coming into leaf. Sow seeds of tender perennials in April and grow on in nursery rows. Keep *S. patens* in a frame for the winter. *S. argentea* can be propagated from cuttings or its lateral shoots, which are often rooted. Replant immediately.

Uses: As border, container, cut and 'effect' plants.

Plants: Bees, Bressingham, Beth Chatto, Cunnington, Goatchers, Hillier, Holden Clough, Notcutts, Scotts. Any garden centre for *S. splendens*.

Seeds: Thomas Butcher, Chiltern, Dobie, Thompson and Morgan.

SANGUINARIA - Bloodroot *(Papaveraceae)*. This was an unusual garden plant in Gerard's time and it still is, which is strange because it is attractive, historically interesting and not difficult to grow. As may be guessed from its name, the plant is full of red sap, with which the Red Indian tribes used to paint their faces. They also believed that the juice of the plant would cure the bite of rattlesnakes, but this latter use is seldom needed in the British Isles. The Victorians knew and grew it because their Language of Flowers gives the plant the rather sad meaning of 'Early Fading Beauty'.

S. canadensis grows well in sandy soil, or almost anywhere, seeming not to mind whether it is in sun or semi-shade. It produces its white flowers in early spring and is valuable in the garden because of this. The flowers emerge in a hurry, before the leaves have completely expanded, and an earlier description of it accepts that it cannot "... be considered a showy plant, yet it has few equals in point of delicacy and singularity; there is something to admire from the time its leaves emerge from the ground and embosom the infant blossom ..." This would have been the single variety and the double kind, more often seen now, looks as opulent as a water-lily come ashore.

S. canadensis grows to 9in (23cm) with white flowers in April. A perennial plant from E. North America for deciduous shaded areas.

Requirements: Any soil not waterlogged.

Cultivation: Divide carefully after leaves die down, in January.

Plants: Avon, Broadleigh, Holden Clough, Jackamoor's, Reginald Kaye, Potterton and Martin, Treasures of Tenbury.

SAPONARIA - Lady-by-the-Gate, Bouncing Bet, Soapwort, Farewell to Summer, Goodbye to Summer *(Caryophyllaceae)*. Bouncing Bet is a most appropriate name for this jolly plant which certainly lives up to it. *Saponaria officinalis*, the Soapwort or Bouncing Bet, comes in two forms, single or double, with flowers of a pleasant pale pink – the double form is blousier-looking and seems to be more vigorous. The plant takes a little while to settle, and life in the border proceeds calmly, and then suddenly Bouncing Bet kicks up her heels and lives up to her name. In late summer long leafy stems of pink flowers grow longer and longer. Being of a lax habit they get tired quickly and Bouncing Bet stops her bouncing and lies down – all over everything else nearby, which she flattens in the process. This laziness has to be attended to without spoiling the character of the plant or the shape of the neighbouring ones, and so if *S. officinalis* is grown in poor soil she will not grow quite so vigorously. On the other hand, this guaranteed flopping habit of hers is very useful – she can be grown behind such plants as Oriental Poppies and Eremurus which vanish in midsummer leaving empty spaces. The long leafy flowering stems can be positively encouraged to grow long, and can then be artfully pulled forwards to conceal the gaps. The single-flowered *S. officinalis* has slightly better manners. Both are disappointingly scentless. The roots of *S. officinalis* contain a useful washing agent so mild that is is used to clean antique embroideries and lace. *S. ocymoides* is a charmer of a different sort. This one grows neatly but profusely, making pleasant flower-covered hummocks in the rockery, or they can be planted to spill over a raised bed or down a dry wall.

S. ocymoides (1768) grows to 6in (15cm) forming pleasant green mats of leaves with pink, white or carmine flowers from July to September. A useful and very attractive Alpine plant for dry walls, troughs, raised beds, and rockeries or path-edges.

S. officinalis - Bouncing Bet etc. grows to a lax 4ft (122cm) with light green leaves, and pink flowers from later July to September. A lusty European plant for the wild garden or large border, or to flop down a wall. The single form is the oldest kind.

Requirements: Any soil, full sun.

Cultivation: Divide clumps in spring. Restrain roots of *S. officinalis* by cutting round plant with a spade in winter and discarding the questing runners.

Plants: Most nurseries.

SAXIFRAGA - Saxifrage *(Saxifragaceae)*. This is a huge genus, containing plants for every soil, situation and gardening interest. The comfortable and easy ones are the familiar old London Pride – *S. umbrosa* which makes such a pleasing strip of evergreen embroidery along a shady path. The name comes from *saxum*, rock, *frangere*, to break for either of two reasons: in former times some species were used medicinally to break down stones in the bladder, and because the plants in their native habitat grow out of rock crevices it was thought that their roots were strong enough to split them. There is a Russian belief that the plant could release unhappy spirits from their graves.

A very good plant for shady gardens is *S. Fortunei* which has a cloud of delicate white flowers in October, most unexpected and precious at this time of the year. The leaves are jellified by the frosts but the plant always seems to recover. It might be kinder to pop a cloche over it for the coldest part of the winter, but, on the other hand, the late spring frosts are even more devastating than the expected ones of the winter. Plant S. Fortunei in as sheltered a place as possible, but where the flowers can be easily seen in their season. Saxifrages are (mostly) rock dwellers and prefer to sit on stones, where their rosettes look more pleasing in any case, because of the contrasts of form and colour than just sitting on soil. The genus has been divided into 16 sections, of which only a few are generally grown, though there are very many hybrids. The sections are as follows, with those most popular marked by an *: 1. *Boraphila*, needing cool, damp, acid growing conditions. 2. *Hirculus* These species need bog or damp screes. 3. *Robertsonia* Needing damp, shady situations; *S. umbrosa* belongs to this section. Most of these can be easily grown. 4. *Miscopetalum* Mostly white flowers. These also like shade. 5. *Cymbalaria* Mostly annuals, liking walls and crevices. 6. *Tridactylites* Not generally grown horticulturally. 7. *Nephrophyllum* Not often grown, though the native *S. granulata* 'Pretty Maids' is the exception, with the variety *plena* being readily obtainable. 8. *Dactyloides** This section contains all the familiar 'mossy' saxifrages. There are many hydrids — they cross pollinate with happy abandon. Most flower in spring, with flowers in white and many shades of pink, red and crimson. 9. *Trachyphyllum* Not generally grown horticulturally. 10. *Xanthizoon* This contains the many types and forms of *S. aiziodes*. Yellow and orange flowers, sometimes purple. This section prefers damp shingle. 11. *Euaizoonia** These are the broad-leaved 'silver' encrusted or lime-encrusted Saxifrages, forming neat rosettes or cushions. If groups of these charming plants are grown together the resulting progeny will not come true. They are propagated from offsets. Most appreciate lime-rubble and full sun, though a few do better in semi-shade. 12. *Kabschia** This group contains the most beautiful of the genus, with very many hybrids. Most are best grown in the alpine house. 13. *Engleria* Most flower in early spring and are therefore best in an alpine house. Most need a free draining limy compost. 14. *Porphryion* Not generally grown horticulturally. 15. *Tetrameridium* Not generally grown — one species only. 16. *Diptera* sometimes Ligularia. Mostly tender plants, not generally grown except for *S. Fortunei*.

A few easy-to-grow plants are here listed. Success with these will inspire you to pick about in the catalogues, though a visit to a specialist grower to see for yourself the various shapes and forms of these delightful plants is by far the best thing to do. You will get invaluable cultural advice which will enable you to grow your new plants well, and then — you will be hooked!

S. Aizoon (2). Height according to type. Mostly white or cream flowers in June. Perennial plants from Europe and N. America for a crevice in the rock garden, needing sun or partial shade and very good drainage.

S. Burseriana (1826) (12). Grows to 2in (5cm) or according to variety. Large (usually) white flowers in February/March. A perennial from the E. Alps for the rock garden or best in an alpine house. Needs shade in mid-summer, gritty, limy soil and humus.

S. cochlearis (1883) (11). Grows to 6in (15cm) with silver-encrusted hummocks and white flowers in June. A plant from the Maritime Alps for crevices in the rock garden.

S. decipiens (8). Height according to variety. This is the 'mossy' Saxifrage that is seen in the spring with flowers in all shades of pink, red and crimson, and it has many hybrid forms. Its mats of green may become brown in the middle in time. Good soil and a partly shaded position.

S. Fortunei (1863) (16) Grows to 18in (45cm) with panicles of delicate white flowers from October to November. Handsome leaves which can be blackened by frost but which always grow again. Needs a sheltered situation. A perennial from China and Japan for shady paths or large rockeries.

S. longifolia (11). Grows to 18in (46cm) with a shower of white flowers in June after about 3-5 years. Monocarpic. A plant from the Pyrenees for a sunny steep rock garden — leave room for the eventual cascade of flowers.

S. moschata (8). 'Mossy' saxifrages. Height according to variety. Yellow, orange, red, crimson and pink flowers, mostly April to May according to variety. A perennial from the Pyrenees to the Caucasus. Partial shade.

S. stolonifera (1815) (16) - **Hen-and-Chickens, Mother-of-thousands, Roving Sailor, Strawberry Geranium.** Grows to 12in (30.5cm) with delicate sprays of white orchid-like flowers in July and August. Attractive rounded, hairy, veined dark green leaves. Offsets produced on stolons, easily replanted. Usually grown as a house plant but does well in a shady sheltered place in southern counties. A perennial from China and Japan.

S. umbrosa (formerly **S x urbicum**) (3) - **London Pride, London's Pride.** Grows to 12in (30.5cm) with stems of dainty pink flowers in May. Does well in shaded walks, a good evergreen plant for edging. Originally a European wild flower.

Requirements: Saxifrages belonging to the encrusted or Euaizoonia section (11) need extra good drainage, plenty of grit and lime in the soil. In southern counties they do best in partial shade, facing east or west. In northern counties they need sun.

Those belonging to the Dactyloides (8) section will grow in any good garden soil in semi-shade.

The Saxifrages in the Kabschia and Engleria sections (12 and 13) need limy, gritty soil and require shading from the sun at mid-day.

Cultivation: All these Saxifrages, except *S. longifolia,,* can be divided after flowering and replanted immediately, or non-flowering rosettes can be removed in May or June. Take off the lower leaves and put each rosette in a separate pot of peat and sand (equal parts). Stand the pot in water until the soil is wet, allow to drain and then put into a cold frame for the winter. Leave the lights open in cold weather, and water very little until the spring then water more freely, re-pot the plants in an appropriate compost in September and leave in frame until the following spring when they may be planted out.

Uses: As the most delightful and interesting 'small garden' plants for town and roof gardens, balconies, sinks, troughs and containers of all kinds. (Do not use concrete tubs for acid-loving plants).

Plants: Bressingham, Broadwell, Hilliers, Holden Clough, Ingwersen, Kaye, Waterperry.

SCABIOSA - Scabious, Pincushion Flower *(Dipsacaceae).* What a pretty flower this is, so easily recognisable among all the other shapes and colours in the border because there is nothing else like it. But its name of Scabious came from Scabies — the itch, which the ordinary wild plant, the closely related *Knautia arvensis* was said to cure. Its virtues were exactly described by Mathiolus "The decoction of the roots taken for forty daies together, or a dram of the Powder of them taken at a time in Whey, doth wonderfully help those that are troubled with running or spreading scabs, Tetters, Ring Worms, yea, though they proceed from the French Pox." The most generally grown garden plant is *S. caucasica* with larger flowers (and less pins) than the wild variety. The annual Sweet Scabious, *S. atropurpurea* has many old names like Mournful Widow, Egyptian Rose, Pincushion Flower or Soldier's Buttons. This is a compact, cushiony flower, again with less pins than the wild plant, but very colourful in today's shades of red, purple, pink, rose, crimson, cherry, salmon and lavender. The flowers of the original species plant were much used for funeral wreaths in Latin countries.

S. atropurpurea - Sweet Scabious (1629) grows to 3ft (91.5cm) with crimson flowers from July to September. An annual from S. W. Europe for the sunny border (will need twiggy pea sticks to support it).

S. caucasica - Scabious grows to 18in (46cm) with lavender-mauve flowers from June to September. A perennial from the Caucasus for the sunny border.

Requirements: Any good soil and sun.

Cultivation: Sow seeds of annual kinds in flowering position in autumn or spring and thin out. Divide established perennials in spring.

Uses: As cut and border flowers.

Seeds: Thomas Butcher, Chiltern, Thompson and Morgan.

Plants: Bressingham, Hillier, Goatchers, Notcutts, St. Bridget.

SCHIZANTHUS - Butterfly flower, Poor Man's Orchid *(Solanaceae).* These are very colourful annuals that can be grown as border plants or as pot plants under glass, to flower in early spring. Their markings suggest those of the orchid, and are so interesting that they are best grown at eye level so that all the intricacies of the flowers can be better seen. Schizanthus means the 'cut flowers' from *Schizein*, to cut and *anthos*, flower, meaning that the corolla is deeply indented.

For border and tub flowers, the seeds should be sown either in the open ground in April, with subsequent thinning out, or under glass in March. The seeds are tiny and should barely be covered, and the soil that they are to grow in should have been manured in early spring and then raked to a fine tilth. In the greenhouse the seedlings can be grown on in the usual way, hardened off, and planted out in May: they will need twiggy sticks for support. For early spring flowers in pots, sow seeds in John Innes seed compost in August or September, at a temperature of 16°C (61°F) until germination takes place. When large enough to handle prick out into individual pots, and pot on as necessary ending with John Innes No. 2. Pinch out the growing tips at 3in (7.5cm) and continue doing this to encourage bushiness. Water well as growth increases but do not overwater.
S. pinnatus (1822) grows to 2ft (61cm) with brightly coloured and patterned flowers in summer. A variable annual from Chile for the sunny border or growing under glass.
Requirements: *As text.*
Cultivation: *As text.*
Uses: As cut, pot and border flowers.
Seeds: Most seedsmen.

SCHIZOSTYLIS - Kaffir Lily *(Iridaceae).* The star-like flowers of Kaffir Lilies come at a quiet time in the garden, and as they are such elegant-looking flowers as well they are doubly welcome. They need a sheltered site but do not crave full sun, doing just as well in semi-shade. Remembering that they came originally from S. Africa, I took pity on my clump and re-planted it in a much better situation, or so I thought, in the south-facing border. The Kaffir Lilies didn't agree, dwindled away and never reappeared after their annual rest. But in their old home, the green spikes appeared here and there – the rhizomes that I had missed were growing well, and they were better than ever in a rather doubtful corner behind a conifer, enjoying very little direct sunlight even at mid-summer. But it was a sheltered corner, and the clump has gradually moved about 2ft (61cm) to where it wants to be and is exceptionally floriferous in October. If they are happy they will increase well and smother their neighbours.
S. coccinea - Kaffir Lily grows to 3ft (91.5cm) with red flowers (or pink) in October and November. A rhizomatous perennial from S. Africa for a sheltered part of the garden.
Requirements: A sheltered position and good soil with peat and leaf-mould added.
Cultivation: Kaffir Lilies have a resting period in summer and vanish for a while. Divide the clumps in spring and re-space if they are getting too congested and are ceasing to flower, otherwise leave them alone and be grateful.
Uses: As late garden colour and as cut flowers.
Rhizomes: Most nurseries.

SCILLA - Squill *(Liliaceae).* Scillas have been grown for hundreds of years and were observed and commented on by Gerard who said of *S. bifolia*, that it "... has small blew flowers consisting of sixe little leaves spread abrode like a star. The seed is contained in small round bullets, which are so ponderous or heavie, that they lie trailing upon the ground". *Scilla bifolia* is still resting its "ponderous or heavie" seed heads on the ground some 400 years later, but this is partly because the stiff little flower stems, their task completed, have lost their rigidity. This Scilla flowers almost a fortnight earlier than *S. sibirica* which was not introduced until some two hundred years afterwards. *S. nutans* was the proper name of the Bluebell but this has now been moved into a different genus to satisfy the taxonomists (see Endymion).

The whole genus took its name from the former *Scilla maritima* (now renamed *Urginea maritius*). This plant is the source of 'syrup of squills' which has been used in medicine since the time of Pliny as a diuretic. It is still used to alleviate chronic bronchitis, catarrh and asthma in conjunction with other constituents. In excess it is poisonous, causing nausea, vomiting, abdominal pains, and then stupor, convulsions, a drop in body temperature, slowed circulation and in some cases death. A potent plant, indeed. Mark the place where the bulbs are planted. They are large bulbs and can be easily damaged as they are out of sight for a long time.

S. bifolia grows to 6in (15cm) with blue flowers from February to March. A European bulb to increase well in sun or semi-shade.

S. siberica - Siberian Squill (1796) grows to 6in (15cm) with brilliant blue flowers in March that will eclipse all other blues in the garden. Plant away from these, in sun or semi-shade.

Requirements: A well-drained but reasonably moisture-retentive soil.

Cultivation: Plant bulbs 3in (7.5cm) deep as early as they can be obtained. Seeds can be saved from seed-heads if they ripen, plant in pans and when large enough the small bulbs can be planted out in nursery rows.

Bulbs: Avon, Bees, Bloms, Broadleigh, Christian, Holden Clough, Ingwersen, Kelways, Potterton and Martin, Orpington, van Tubergen.

SCUTELLARIA - Skull-cap *(Labiatae)*. The plant takes its name from *Scutella*, drinking bowl, because of the shape of the ripening calyx. Scutellarias are not often grown, and when they are they are not always recognised, being rather easily confused with some other members of the great Labiatae family. Many Scutellarias are short enough – and interesting enough – to live in the rock garden, and, needing good drainage as they do, they usually do well in such situations.

Hardy varieties should be propagated by division in spring or by seed sown in March in a cold greenhouse or frame. Grow on into boxes and then into pots. Keep in the frame for the winter in most areas except the most southern counties. Established plants may be cut back in February to 3 or 4in (7.5 - 10cm) of the ground, and the tips of the young plants can be stopped once or twice to encourage bushiness.

S. alpina - Alpine Skull-cap (1752) grows to 9in (23cm) with blue-purple flowers in August. The white variety is *S. alpina* 'alba'. A perennial plant from Europe and Central Asia for the front of a border or a well drained rockery.

S. scordiifolia grows to 6in (15cm) with blue flowers from July to August. A perennial plant from Asia for a sunny rock garden.

Requirements: A compost of loam, leaf-mould or well rotted manure with a little sharp sand suits them well.

Cultivation: *As text.*

Plants: Beth Chatto, Cunnington, Hillier, Holden Clough, Robinsons.

Seeds: Chiltern.

SEDUM - Stonecrop *(Crassulaceae)*. This is another large genus of very amiable plants, whose name of Sedum, meaning 'Plant-that-sits', indicates their characteristic habit. They belong in rockeries or at the edge of stone paths, where their plump leaves and interesting foliage colours contrast and soften the hard edges most pleasingly. In fact, I like the easy-tempered *S. spectabile* so well because it looks so good when sitting on my Purbeck stone rocks that I have to restrain myself most firmly or I would have it everywhere. This is a plant that looks pleasing from early spring onwards, with its stems of light-coloured leaves that increase tidily in size and stature until the flat green heads form. The pink or crimson flowers are most attractive, being much favoured by the late butterflies. My only thought, when surveying a happy crowd of drunken Tortoiseshells is to wince at the colour-clash – the pink of the flowers is not the best background for the orange-tawny colour of the butterflies' wings. *S. maximum purpureum* is a taller version of this, with exciting black-red leaves and stems that make a powerful feature of a mature plant. This Sedum takes longer to establish itself and is more tender, so do not take its presence for granted. Keep a little offset or two in a cold frame as insurance. *Sedum acre*, with its sheets of clinging yellow is the Wall Pepper or Stonecrop, which in some gardens is impossible to get rid of and in some cannot be coaxed to stay. *Sedum album* syn. *S. anglicum* is a laxer, looser plant to *S. acre* but otherwise very similar, with equally invasive habits. In a dry situation on top of a wall, its leaves and stems turn red, contrasting pleasingly with the white flowers. *S. spurium* is another invasive wall-plant, useful for cracks and crevices and to cover large areas of dry, poor soil, where it will flourish. However, when you find that you need some of its territory you will have to fight to get it back, and for a time *S. spurium* will keep coming back like a song. It has very attractive crimson flowers and is most useful even in semi-shade, though here it seldom flowers. *S. roseum* is the Rose-root, whose dried roots smell of roses. Dried and grated, it was used in pot-pourris. It is a most attractive member of this large genus, with large heads of yellow flowers. *S. rupestre* syn. *S. forsteranum* is the very common west-country plant that is seen on cottage walls and in gardens. It is given as part of a starter kit to new garden owners, who virtuously do the same thing with it when their turn comes to pass on their surplus. It, too, is useful because it does well on dry walls, sending up yellow flowers in plenty in July. *S. telephium* is a native woodland plant, unusual in the sedum family. It has an astonishing capacity for endurance, and was once used as a good-luck charm, being hung from the ceiling of a room on Midsummer Day. It would remain green until Christmas, and was called 'Midsummer Men'. It is a pleasant and usefully different plant for shaded parts of the garden.

S. acre - Wall Pepper, Biting Stonecrop grows to 2in (5cm) with mats of bright yellow flowers in June and July. A native, European, Asian and N. African perennial for a hot, dry position, doing best on limestone walls. Can be invasive.

S. album grows to 6in (15cm) with green, turning to red, stems and leaves. White flowers in July. A native, European and Asian perennial for poor, dry, sunny situations. Also invasive, but gentle.

S. roseum syn. **rhodiola - Rose-Root** grows to 12in (30.5cm) with glaucous leaves and cymes of yellow flowers in May and June. A perennial of the N. Hemisphere for a sunny corner or the large rock garden.

S. spathulifolium grows to 4in (10cm) with grey-green or reddish purple leaves. Cymes of yellow flowers in June. The variety 'Capa Blanca' with grey-white spathulate leaves is very attractive.

S. spurium grows to 4in (10cm) with mats of evergreen leaves; cymes of crimson flowers in July and August. A creeping perennial from the N. Caucasus and Persia for poor dry situations. Can be very invasive.

S. spectabile grows to 18in (46cm) with pale green glaucous leaves and deep rose-pink flower heads in September. These deepen to red and crimson and finally to brown, remaining all winter unless picked. An invaluable perennial of sculptural appearance from China for any sunny situation, best among stonework and in a focal position.

S. Telephium - Midsummer Men, Orpine, Live-Long grows to 18in (46cm) with rose-purple flowers in August and September. A native and European plant for woodland conditions – the only Sedum that is happy in semi-shade.

Requirements: Ordinary well-drained soil. *S. Telephium* needs moisture retentive soil and more humus.
Cultivation: Divide these species in autumn or spring, this is the only time to move most Sedums. Though named varieties do not come true from seed, seeds of species varieties will. Sow thinly in boxes of gritty compost in spring, and when large enough to handle transfer to individual pots of John Innes No. 1. Plunge outside in a partly shaded place until the young plants are large enough to plant out. Slugs will menace all the fleshy-leaved kinds.
Plants: Most nurseries.
Seeds: Chiltern, Thompson and Morgan.

SEMPERVIVUM - Houseleek, Singreen *(Crassulaceae)*. These are the rosette-shaped plants whose rigid cushions look so pleasing in rockeries, troughs and on all kinds of stonework. Tubs of all one kind can look most interesting throughout the year, because most species change colour slightly with the seasons. An established collection of Sempervivums is beautiful – they can look as precious as jewellery. Because many are so small it is better to raise the troughs or sinks so that one can the more easily see them. They are very easy to grow, though newly-planted specimens may need some protection from birds which often peck about and disturb them, leaving them uprooted and upside-down. When they have got a real grip on their surroundings this would be all right – but the birds, such is the perversity of life, then leave them alone.
     Once upon a time it was believed that Houseleeks on the roof meant good luck and certain protection from lightning. They had elaborate old names like Thunder-Plant and Welcome-home-husband-however-drunk-you-be (this was often indiscriminately applied to the commoner Sedums like *S. acre* and *S. album*) and Jupiter's Beard, (Jove's Beard – the medieval Latin is *Jovis barba* and some species are now being regarded by taxonomists as belonging to a separate genus, *Jovibarba*, which at least is a most appropriate name). Singreen is from the OE word for 'evergreen', and the plant (usually the familiar *S. tectorum*) has always been used as a cooling poultice for ulcers, swellings and scalds.
S. arachnoideum - Cobweb Houseleek (1699). Height 1in (2.5cm), has 'cobwebbed' rosettes and pink flowers in July. For a sunny trough or sink garden. Protect in winter.
S. tectorum - Houseleek Green rosettes, sometimes as much as 6in (15cm) wide, may be more or less crimson-tipped. Pink flowers in July. For a sunny rockery. Spreads well when established.
S. sobolifera syns. **S. soboliferum, Jovibarba sobolifera - Hen and chickens, Houseleek.** Has green and red rosettes and globular offsets which root themselves eventually unless helped. Yellow flowers in July. An interesting species from N. Europe and Asia for a trough, large pot or sink-garden.
Requirements: Ordinary well-drained soil and sun.
Cultivation: Offsets are produced when the plants have settled down. Allow to root and then gently detach and replant.
Uses: In small gardens, and for sinks, troughs, pots and windowboxes.
Plants: Bressingham, Hillier, Holden Clough, Ingwersen, Reginald Kaye, Oak Cottage Herb Farm, R.V. Roger Ltd, Alan C. Smith, F. Toynbee Ltd.

SENECIO *(Compositae)*. The Cineraria has been dealt with earlier though it more properly belongs here as *S. cruentus*. There are several shrubby Senecios which have no place in this book, alas, though they do in my garden. However – there is a very striking member of the genus for a sunny, damp border or by the pond side. This is *Senecio Przewalskii*, though it has now been classified as *Ligularia*. I am sorry about this but I would rather be correct, so please refer to Ligularia, which at least is easier to spell and pronounce.

SHORTIA *(Diapensiaceae)* Exquisite plants that are hardy enough to be grown in cool, damp, but well-drained rock gardens, though they are more often seen in alpine houses. Shortias dislike disturbance and need a great deal of special care in establishing them in a new home. The genus was named after Dr. Charles W. Short, 1794–1863, a botanist of Kentucky, United States of America.

These plants need a peaty soil with sand and leaf-mould, and semi-shade. Propagation is by carefully lifting and dividing after the flowers are over. With such difficult plants as these it is worth attempting to take a small amount of the plant away in one place only, leaving the main portion of it undisturbed. These flowers are for alpine enthusiasts and those gardeners with green fingers.

S. galacifolia grows to 6in (15cm) with delicate white to pink flowers in April and May. A perennial from North Carolina for the shady rock garden and woodland conditions.

S. uniflora grows to 4in (10cm) with delicated frilled pink flowers in April and May. A perennial from Japan for the shady rock garden and woodland conditions.

Requirements: *As text.*
Cultivation: *As text.*
Plants: Hillier, Holden Clough, Reginald Kaye, Potterton and Martin.

SIDALCEA - Prairie Mallow, Wild Hollyhock (in U.S.) **Greek Mallow** *(Malvaceae)*. This is a long-lived herbaceous plant that grows lustily when established. It has little temperament and will grow in any good soil, preferring full sun but tolerating partial shade. It is best not to move really well established plants as they resent disturbance, becoming set in their ways. The graceful spires of shiny flowers in various shades of pink and red are very colourful. The plants will grow into fine 'bushes' each year and may need a little support, like a spare peony ring, because of the later summer storms that can so easily spoil the herbaceous border. Twiggy branches are usually sufficient and are not as intrusive visually as canes or string.

The plants should be cut to about 14in (35.5cm) after flowering and the lateral flower stems will usually produce a second show of bloom.

S. malvaeflora - Sidalcea (1838) grows to 4½ft (137cm) with pink, rose or red flowers from June to September. A showy perennial from California for a sheltered garden site.

Requirements: Any soil that does not dry out. Mound plants with litter in the winter in cold areas.
Cultivation: Lift and divide plants in spring, discarding centre of crown. Sow seeds in spring in the usual way. Plants do not always come true.
Plants: Bees, Bloms, Bressingham, Cunnington, Highfield, Hillier, Kelways, Notcutts, Scotts.
Seeds: Thomas Butcher, Chiltern, Dobie, Thompson and Morgan.

SILENE - Campion *(Caryophyllaceae)*. These plants are not grown as often as they once were, perhaps because some of them need very specific garden conditions – e.g. *S. acaulis* flowers best on a moraine. However, the annual *S. pendula* is an easy, pretty plant whose flowers look like a more restrained wild Campion: they are all closely related in any case. *S. armeria* is another annual which will grow quickly, forming interesting and different-looking border plants with a long flowering season.

S. Coeli-rosa or Viscaria – the Rose of Heaven – produces primrose shaped flowers from June to August in shades of purple, blue, lilac, pink, red and white. This is a most attractive plant when grown in mixed colours, though one-colour seed packets are available.

S. maritima is the wild Sea Campion whose mats of grey leaves drip down the sea cliffs of the British Isles. This is not grown as a garden plant – though it is attractive when in full flower – but the variety *S. m.* 'Flore pleno' is most pleasing, with flowers that resemble small cream carnations. The perennial species dislike disturbance once established.

S. acaulis - Moss Campion only 2in (5cm) high with cushion-like green leaves and pink or white flowers from June to August. Needs light soil and full sun, but is best on a scree or moraine. A perennial from the mountains of Europe for the rock garden enthusiast.

S. Armeria grows to 18in (46cm) with purple, pink or white flowers from May to September. A European annual for the border.

S. Coeli-rosa syn. **Viscaria elegans - Rose of Heaven** (1713) grows to 18in (46cm) with flowers of lilac, lavender, blue, pink, red, carmine and white from June to August. An unusual annual from the Canaries and the Mediterranean area for a sunny place.

S. maritima - Sea Campion Species not usually grown but *S.m.* 'Flore-pleno' has very double creamy flowers and the same cascading habit. For a sunny rockery or dry wall.

S. pendula grows to 9in (23cm) with silvery-hairy leaves and pink flowers from May to September. An annual from S. Europe for the sunny rock garden.

Requirements: Well-drained soil and a sunny position.

Cultivation: Sow seeds of *S. armeria* and *S. pendula* in September *in situ* or in boxes, grow on and thin out as required, or sow in spring. Do both, and have four months of flowers. Propagate perennial kinds by taking basal shoots from *S. acaulis* in July or August and from *S. maritima* 'Flore-pleno' in April. Insert round the edge of clay pots in a compost of equal parts of peat and sand until rooted; keep in a cold frame and then transfer into pots of John Innes No. 1.

Uses: As wall, rockery, border, edging and cut flowers.

Plants: Broadwell, Cunnington, Hillier, Holden Clough, Reginald Kaye, Notcutts, Potterton and Martin, Southcombe Garden.

Seeds: Chiltern, Dobie, Thompson and Morgan.

SINNINGIA - Gloxinia *(Gesneriaceae).* The genus was named after Wilhelm Sinning 1794-1874 who was head gardener at Bonn University. Gloxinias are luscious-looking flowers and need greenhouse or conservatory conditions, though they can be brought into the house when in flower (but not for long) for all to enjoy. At one time the cultivation of Gloxinias (now more properly called Sinningias) took some time, and it was often nearly two years before the new plants (grown from divisions and offsets) were ready to flower well. But labour and coal were cheap and people were then not in so much of a hurry. In the wild state, *S. speciosa* (the Gloxinia) was originally a plant of the Brazilian jungles, enjoying rich moist soil and a warm humid atmosphere. This must be remembered and the conditions emulated as far as possible.

In February the tubers should be started into growth in boxes of moist peat at a temperature of 21°C (70°F). When the new shoots are 2in (5cm) high they can be carefully potted into 6-in (15-cm) pots of John Innes No. 2. The tops of the tubers should be at soil level. The greenhouse needs to be shaded throughout the summer, and the plants can be grown on in a temperature of 18°C (64°F) with regular liquid feeds at ten-day intervals. The pots should be kept moist throughout this time, but should never be watered from the top. When they cease to flower (about August) the leaves will gradually turn yellow and watering can slowly cease. Take off dead leaves and stems and when the plants are dormant the tubers can be stored in a dry, airy place with a minimum temperature of 12-16°C (54-61°F). Seed can be sown in January or February in an appropriate seed compost at the same temperature – 21°C (70°F). When the seedlings are large enough they can be planted into 2-in (5-cm) pots of growing compost, and when they have got over the move the temperature can be lowered to 18°C (64°F). Many plants will flower in their first year, and after three or four years the tubers should be discarded. A succession of flowers throughout the year may be had by starting the tubers into growth at regular intervals, or flowers can be planned for a special occasion like a wedding or an anniversary. Though plenty of water should be given during the growing and flowering season, take great care not to over-water. There is a perfect middle point to aim for, remembering that even fish can be drowned. Another method of propagation is from leaf-cuttings. In July, take a healthy leaf and cut into the secondary veins on the underside near the central vein. Put the leaves, cut side down, on to pans of peat and sand in a propagator, at a temperature of 21°C (70°F). New plants will come up from the cuts and will root there, and the remains of the leaf can be cleared away when these are safely established.

S. speciosa - Gloxinia (1815). The species (seldom grown except in botanical gardens) has purple foxglove-like flowers in September. A tuberous plant from tropical Brazil for a heated greenhouse or conservatory. The large-flowered plants that are grown today are the only ones generally available.

Tubers: Amand, Blackmore and Langdon, Dobie and garden centres.
Seeds: Thomas Butcher, Chiltern, Dobie, Thompson and Morgan, Unwins.

SISYRINCHIUM - Satin Flower *(Iridaceae). Sisyrinchium striatum,* the Satin Flower, is a rather special-looking member of the Iris tribe, though if you give it special treatment to match it will die on you. It likes the poorest, hottest soil available, and thrives in neglected gravel drives and in gardens of empty seaside bungalows. In the West Country it is regarded as something of a nuisance, about on a par with Red Valerian. I have learned my lesson. My clump lives in hot, thin soil under the Eucalyptus, which must obviously take all the nourishment thereabouts. The Sisyrinchiums seem very happy here, and their characteristic leaves are slowly increasing, and though I would rather have them somewhere else where their flat fans of leaves and creamy flower-stems would be really eyecatching, I'll let them be.

The other little chap – *S. brachypus* is more accommodating. Start this off beside the path and it will gradually creep into it and furnish the cracks, giving the paving that established, happy look that old gardens of the nicest sort always have. This Sisyrinchium is only 6in (15cm) high in midsummer, with miniature iris-like leaves and flat yellow star-flowers ¾in (2cm) across that keep coming from June until the weather turns cold in October.

S. angustifolium - Blue-eyed grass grows to 6in (15cm) with blue flowers from May to October. A perennial from N. America for the sunny rock garden, trough or low border.

S. striatum - Satin Flower (1788) grows to 18in (46cm) with cream-yellow flowers irregularly up the flowering stem. A perennial from Chile for a hot dry place and poor soil.

Requirements: All need situations in full sun, *S. augustifolium* and *S. brachypus* do well in good garden soil with leaf-mould added. *S. striatum's* needs have been discussed.

Cultivation: *S. striatum* will self sow into cracks in the path, otherwise collect the ripened seed and sow in September into a pan or box of sandy soil in a cold frame. Leave soil undisturbed near the other two and seedlings will appear in due course, or collect ripened seed and sow in the same way.

Plants: Most nurseries.
Seeds: Thompson and Morgan.

SMILACINA False Solomon's Seal *(Liliaceae).* What a happy name for a plant to have, though its more common one of False Solomon's Seal or False Spikenard completely spoils the image. Smilacina has rather similar leaves

to those of Solomon's Seal, but instead of the hanging bells there are scented panicles of creamy flowers, rather like a more solid Aruncus. The plant likes woodland conditions and will increase slowly over the years, forming a handsome clump of long-lasting flowers in early summer. After flowering the plant packs itself up and slowly disappears, leaving the ground quite bare and its place in the shady border should be marked or remembered.
S. racemosa (1690) grows to 3ft (91.5cm) with scented, creamy flowers in May and June. A perennial from N. America for the shaded border.
Requirements: Woodland conditions.
Cultivation: Lift and divide in October or best in spring.
Plants: Broadleigh, Peter Chappell, Beth Chatto, Hillier, Jackamoor's, Kelways, Scotts, Sherrards, Treasure's of Tenbury.

SOLDANELLA *(Primulaceae).* These pretty little plants have the most charmingly fringed bell-shaped flowers, quite different from any others. Soldanellas take their name from the Italian *soldo*, 'a coin', because their leaves are almost round.
They do not care for our winters much, and a well placed pane of glass will help them to survive. In their mountain homes they are often seen – and painted – when growing up through melting snow but that kind of cold is quite different to the damp cold of the British winter. Soldanellas do not like trees over them, they need free draining but moisture-retentive soil (add peat and leaf-mould) and a collar of grit with more spread about – this will discourage the slugs that will eat the flower buds which often form very early in the year. Most like a sunny position. They are often grown in alpine houses where they are not subjected to all the hazards of the British winters. Gardeners have been trying to grow them for centuries.
S. alpina (1656) grows to 4in (10cm) with blue flowers in April. A perennial alpine plant from the mountainous areas of Europe for a sheltered rockery.
S. montana (1816) grows to 4in (10cm) with blue or lavender flowers in April. A perennial alpine from the mountains of Eastern Europe for the rockery or alpine house.
Requirements: *As text.*
Cultivation: Divide after flowering time and replant. The divided plants may do better if potted up in John Innes No. 1 with extra peat, then plunged in a cold frame.
Plants: Ingwersen.

SOLIDAGO - Golden Rod *(Compositae).* How opinions change! Once Golden Rod was revered and respected as a wound herb, being imported from N. America for this purpose. One reads much of wound herbs, and therefore it must be remembered that there was as much violence in those days as there is today, which is a sobering thought, and of course, all corn and grass-cutting was done with scythes and sickles, often by exhausted and ill-fed labourers so accidents would have been more prevalent. But to return to Solidago; the plant itself was introduced from America and took to our herbaceous borders as a duck does to water, much to the astonishment of American visitors who regarded it then (and still do) as a weed. There was a very early belief that he who holds Golden Rod in the hand will have hidden treasures revealed unto him. The earlier kinds, usually *S. virgaurea* or *S. canadensis* were grown for many years, being very easy of cultivation. They were known to get mildew in late summer, as they still do, and much effort went into breeding new species (enthusiastically helped by Solidago itself which hybridises with incestuous ease while you stand and watch it happen – bees and insects absolutely love the plant).
Being something of an old-fashioned gardener, to match this book and most of my plants, I have to say that I like the tall old kinds – usually a naturally-occurring cross between *S. canadensis* and anything of the same

genus that happens to be nearby. My Solidagos (inherited with this old garden) rise up into a golden fountain of flowers in late summer, and as they have an isolated bed to themselves they are very striking and visitors always comment. They probably do get mildewed in some years, but I try to remember to spray both them, the roses and the Michaelmas Daisies from June onwards and this usually does the trick.

S. canadensis - Golden Rod (1648) grows to 6ft (1.85m) with golden yellow flowers from August to October. A perennial from E. N. America for the large wild or old-fashioned garden.

S. brachystachys syn. **S. Virgaurea** grows from 6in-2ft (15-61cm) with several named varieties. Flowers from July to October. A European plant for border or rockery according to height.

N.B. There are very many named hybrid forms, all of them attractive. The species is seldom offered.

Requirements: Sun or partial shade and good moisture retentive soil. A peony-ring as a support – stems are stiff enough if helped a little. Cut down stems in late autumn, and feed in spring.

Cultivation: Divide plants in Spring.

Plants: Bloms, Bressingham, Goatchers, Hillier, Robinsons, Scotts, St Bridget, F. Toynbee Ltd.

SPARAXIS *(Iridaceae).* These are rather special flowers to grow – either in the open (though in a sheltered corner) or in a frost-free greenhouse or conservatory for the rest of us. Sparaxis are grown from corms set 3-4in (7.5-10cm) deep and planted in the open in November. If they are to be grown in pots the corms can be planted in August or September, about 5 or 6 to a 6-in (15-cm) pot in John Innes potting compost No. 2. Soak the pots thoroughly and allow to drain, then give no more water until the leaves appear, then water carefully as needed. Sparaxis need no feeding – the compost is rich enough for them. After the flowers are over the leaves will start to turn yellow: at this stage gradually decrease watering until the bulbs are dormant. Re-pot in August or September, detaching the offsets which will have formed – these will reach flowering size in two years. The greenhouse or conservatory should be frost-proof, so a cold house is not safe enough for Sparaxis.

S. tricolor - Harlequin Flower (1789) grows to 2ft (61cm) with flowers in brilliant shades of red, yellow and purple and white all in one flower – hence the name. A tender corm from S. Africa mainly for a frost-free greenhouse or conservatory.

Requirements: *As text.*

Cultivation: *As text.*

Corms: Amand, Bees, Bloms, Hortico, Ingwersen, van Tubergen.

STACHYS - Flannel Flower, Lamb's Tongue, Donkey's Ears, etc. *(Labiatae).* The most well known of this genus is the friendly-feeling silver-furred *S. lanata,* whose soft white leaves are so eminently strokable. Oddly enough, though most gardeners take this plant for granted, it is not always stout-hearted enough to withstand the cold, wet British winters, and, come the spring, *S. lanata* will often be among the casualties. If your stocks of this plant are getting less instead of more, then it is time to take steps, because it is such a superb contrast in colour and texture to almost everything else in the garden and, really, one cannot do without its pleasant presence. Divide the roots in spring and grow them on in separate pots in a cold frame, where you can keep an eye on them. This can be done in late summer – Aesop knew mankind well when he wrote the fable about the ant and the grasshopper – winter always comes and it is better to be prepared. Try to grow *S. lanata* in a place where the leaves do not lie on the ground in winter – even a very large pot with cuttings of the plant all round the edge and hanging over the sides will be better than where the furry leaves will blot up all the wet, and it is happy hanging down walls. (There is an excellent 'modern' variety called 'Silver Carpet' which does not flower, but this is less hardy, needing the care I have described.) These Stachys are excellent as edging for summer bedding schemes or as 'contrast' plants.

S. lanata - Lamb's Lugs (1782) grows to 18in (46cm) with mauve flowers in July. A perennial from the Caucasus for edging, rockeries, walls, as contrast and as ground cover in sunny places. Not happy in shade.

S. macrantha syn. **Betonica grandiflora** (1800) grows to 18in (46cm) with pink or violet flowers from May to July. A lusty perennial from the Caucasus for a sunny border.

Requirements: Any free draining soil where rainwater does not collect.

Cultivation: Divide in autumn or spring.

Uses: The flowering variety *(S. lanata)* is interesting texturally in flower arrangements, and for mass planting with a dark-leaved background, or with brick walls and paving.

Plants: Most nurseries.

STERNBERGIA *(Amaryllidaceae).* The flower was named after Count Kaspar Moritz von Sternberg (1761-1838) a botanist of Prague. Of the three kinds generally available (two flower in the autumn and one in the spring) the autumn-flowering *S. lutea* is perhaps the most beautiful, and is an unexpected shape and colour at this time of year. The leaves appear with the flowers, and continue growing after these are over, reaching their full size of some 12in (30.5cm) long by spring. The Turks called this flower *Lale* (meaning Lily) and it is one of the flowers that may have been the origin of the Biblical 'Lily of the Field'. Sternbergias need rather exact growing conditions and should never be disturbed once established – count your blessings along with the blooms. The bulbs need to be well baked in the summer, so plant in a hot, well-drained spot.

S. clusiana grows to 4in (10cm) with yellow flowers in September and October. A bulb from Asia Minor for the same conditions.

S. Fischeriana (1868) grows to 6in (15cm) with longer leaves. Yellow crocus-like flowers in March. A bulb from the Caucasus for a hot sheltered corner with good drainage.

S. lutea (1599) grows to 6in (15cm) with longer leaves. Golden crocus-like flowers in September and October. A European bulb for the same conditions.

Requirements: *As text.*

Cultivation: When – and if – the clump or clumps become congested, lift in August and separate the bulbs and offsets. Replant immediately.

Bulbs: Amand, Avon, Broadleigh, Christian, van Tubergen.

STRELITZIA - Bird of Paradise Flower, Crane Flower *(Musaceae).* The Strelitzia was named after Charlotte of Mecklenburg-Strelitz (1744-1818), who was Queen to George III of England. These interesting flowers are cousins of the Banana, and *S. reginae* is the only one that is generally obtainable for the greenhouse or conservatory. The plant makes a fine sight when in full flower, and is not difficult to grow. In its native home it is pollinated by bird's feet, and in season it is often seen in florist's shops. The plants are best grown in a warm greenhouse border, though if this is not possible, extra large pots should be used. Set small plants out in John Innes No. 1, pot on as necessary into larger pots, using John Innes No. 2 for the first change and John Innes No. 3 for the next.

Grow on in a temperature that does not descend below a winter mean of 10°C (50°F) and water sparingly during the winter months. In spring and summer water well, giving a liquid feed at 14-day intervals. Water less from September onwards. In the summer the greenhouse or conservatory should be well ventilated when the temperature rises above 10-20°C

(64-70°F) and some shading should be given or the leaves will scorch. The plants should be re-potted every two years, when rooted shoots may be detached to form new plants, to be grown on in the same way. It may be easier to obtain seed, which should be soaked in rainwater for 48 hours and sown in seed compost in spring at a temperature of 18-21°C (64-70°F). (Germination may take six months.) When large enough the seedlings may be pricked out into individual pots of John Innes No. 1 and grown on in the same way.

S. Reginae - **Bird of Paradise Flower** (1773) grows to 5ft (1.52cm) with amazing flowers resembling an exotic bird's head, in April. A perennial plant from S. Africa for the warm greenhouse or conservatory.

Requirements: *As text.*
Cultivation: *As text.*
Plants: Hortico, Kent County Nurseries.
Seeds: Thomas Butcher, Chiltern, Dobie, Holtzhausen, Kent County Nurseries, Unwins.

STREPTOCARPUS - Cape Primrose *(Gesneriaceae)*. These tender greenhouse plants are most interesting, because some of them have to manage with one leaf only throughout their lives, though this leaf can sometimes be as much as 5ft (1.52m) long. I always think that they are hard-done by, but they seem to manage very well, having no special need of my sympathy or of any one else's. The leaves develop in the normal manner from a pair of cotyledons but one shrivels early on, leaving the plant with the other which develops normally. These single-leaved plants are monocarpic. All can be grown from seed sown in John Innes seed compost at a temperature of 18°C (64°F) which can be grown on until large enough to prick out into boxes and then into individual pots of John Innes No. 2. They can be potted on into successively large pots, watering freely and feeding fortnightly during the summer months and keeping the plants shaded. The greenhouse or conservatory should be well ventilated during hot periods. The growing temperature should be 13°C (55°F) during the summer which must be maintained or the plants will not flower well. Reduce watering from autumn until March, and the temperature should be 10°C (50°F). The species seeds are seldom available except in 'mixture' packets. Modern named hydrids are obtainable from most seedsmen.

Requirements: *See text.*
Cultivation: *See text.*
Seeds: Thomas Butcher, Chiltern, Dobie, Unwins.

SYMPHYTUM - Comfrey, Knitbone, Boneset *(Boraginaceae)*. Comfrey was the medieval medicine-chest. It cured almost everything, inside and out, and is still an important plant in homoeopathy. Taken internally it was used as a cure for quinsy, whooping cough and similar pulmonary complaints, and also for diarrhoea and dysentery. Used externally in the form of fomentations it eased the pains of sprains, strains, swellings and gout, and as a poultice it healed cuts, wounds, burns and promoted the suppuration of boils, abscesses and external ulcers. Its main use was to reduce the swellings in the region of fractured bones, thereby promoting their union. Gerard extolled its virtues as follows "The slimie substance of the roote made in a posset of ale, and given to drinke against the paine in the backe, gotten by any violent motion, as wrestling, or over much use of women, doth in fower or five daies perfectly cure the same, although the involuntaire flowing of the seed in men be gotten thereby."

Comfrey is a good plant for the wild garden or when large areas of semi-shaded ground need to be filled with something trouble-free and vigorous. It will grow in either damp or dry ground, once it has taken hold, and there are several kinds to choose from, of varying degrees of vigour and tenacity.

The trouble will come when, and if, you decide that you have better or different things that you would like to plant where the Comfrey grows, and this is when you will find that it is a determined plant. Every piece of broken root will grow, so plant it with circumspection. The Russian Comfrey, *S. caucasicum* has good blue flowers and is not as vigorous as the native *S. officinale*, which has flowers in shades of cream, pink, crimson, blue and purple as well as white.

S. caucasicum - Russian Comfrey (1820) grows to 2ft (61cm) with pink changing to blue flowers from April to June. A perennial from the Caucasus for semi-shade, and the large rock or wild garden.

S. grandiflorum (1900) grows to 8in (20.5cm) with red buds and cream flowers in April and May. A perennial from the Caucasus for ground-cover in semi-shade.

S. officinale - Comfrey grows to 4ft (122cm) with pink, cream, crimson, blue maroon, purple or white flowers from April to July. This is the old herbal plant, too vigorous a native perennial for the small garden, but interesting historically and useful among the herbs.

Requirements: In damp rich soil they will be uncontrollable – so be cruel and keep them on the dry side.

Cultivation: Plant in autumn or spring. Seed can be sown in autumn or spring and grown on in the usual way. Seeds can be slow to germinate.

Uses: As ground cover, as shady garden plants, for herbal remedies, to eat as a vegetable or as fritters, but never for picking as the stems will wilt instantly.

After flowering: Cut down plants which will re-furnish themselves with new leaves that will look fresh for the rest of the year.

Plants: Bressingham, Beth Chatto, Hillier, Parkinson Herbs, Scotts, Sherrards.

Seeds: John Chambers, Thompson and Morgan.

TAGETES - French or **African Marigold** *(Compositae)*. Despite their name, both kinds of Tagetes come from Mexico which is why they are so excellent in summer bedding schemes – that is, when there is a real summer in Northern Europe. The taller kind – *T. erecta* – the 'African' Marigold, arrived here via Spain early in the sixteenth century and became very popular in Europe, being called 'Rose of the Indies'. It also took to the North African coastal areas and became naturalised there, so much so that it was thought to be a local plant, and was named as such. Parkinson and Gerard grew them both, and commented on their aromatic scent – which is a polite term; Henry Lyte dispensed with such niceties, saying more forthrightly that both kinds has a "naughtie, strong and unpleasant savour". Many varieties were grown with single, double, orange and yellow kinds, and like retired seafaring men, the eighteenth century gardeners went in for size, producing huge plants (which must have been *T. erecta)* some 5ft (1.52m) in height.

The smaller *T. patula*, called the French Marigold, was brought to England by the Huguenot refugees in the sixteenth century. It is known that there are symbiotic associations between *T. patula* and certain vegetables, and it has long been the custom in France to edge the vegetable beds with a border of *T. patula*, which in some mysterious way seems to keep the vegetables healthier and more free of pests, though slugs will destroy a newly set row overnight, rather like felling trees.

T. erecta - African Marigold grows to 3ft (91.5cm) with yellow and orange flowers from July until the frosts. A half-hardy annual from Mexico for borders and edging.

T. patula - French Marigold (1573) grows to 18in (46cm) (shorter varieties are the most popular) with flowers in shades of yellow, orange, bronze, red and brown and mixtures of these). A half-hardy annual from Mexico for edging, borders, pots and troughs. Good even in bad weather.

Requirements: Full sun, any soil.

Cultivation: Sow seeds in March at a temperature of 18°C (64°F) in John Innes seed compost. Grow on and harden off and plant out after the last frosts.
Uses: As reliable border and edging plants, for pots and containers or anywhere that solid colour is wanted. As cut flowers, though they still smell as strongly as they did in the sixteenth century.
During and after flowering: Dead-head.
Seeds: Most seedsmen.
Plants: Most garden centres.

THALICTRUM - Rue *(Ranunculaceae).* Though this delicate plant is a rue it is not the same as Ruta, which is also called rue and which is a small shrub, generally used for culinary purposes; *Ruta graveolens* 'Jackman's Blue' is the ornamental blue-leaved foliage plant. Thalictrums would be beautiful even if they had no flowers, because their leaves, often blue-toned, look like a taller and more diffuse Maidenhair fern. The tiny flowers are most attractive, in various shades of mauve, purple, pink and yellow, and the leaves of the variety *T. dipterocarpum* earn its place in the border even more by turning completely yellow in autumn. The plant was used as a plague-cure in Europe in former days, and has always been grown in gardens, even by the Romans. It is not at all difficult to grow and should be seen more often, though a good-sized plant takes some three or four years to come to maturity.
T. aquilegiifolium (Before 1731). Grows to 3ft (91.5m) with ferny leaves and mauve-purple flowers from May to July. A European perennial for the border.
T. dipterocarpum (1908) grows to 5ft (1.52cm) with ferny leaves and sprays of tiny mauve flowers from June to August. (There is a white form.) A perennial from Europe and N. Asia for the sunny or partly shaded border.
Requirements: Ordinary garden soil and sun or part shade.
Cultivation: Divide established plants in the spring as soon as growth can be seen. Sow seeds in John Innes seed compost in March in a cold frame. Grow on in the usual way and set out in a nursery bed. Plant in final position in autumn or spring.
Plants: Bloms, Broadleigh, Beth Chatto, Goatchers, Great Dixter, Kelways, Notcutts, Scotts, Sherrards, St. Bridget, F. Toynbee Ltd.
Seeds: Thomas Butcher, Chiltern, Thompson and Morgan.

THUNBERGIA - Black-eyed Susan *(Acanthaceae).* Thunbergias were named after Dr. Karl Pehr Thunberg (1743 - 1822), a botanist who travelled in the far East, afterwards becoming Professor of Botany at Uppsala. Most of this genus are climbers, the remainder being herbaceous species or shrubs. The most familiar is Black-eyed Susan, an annual climber having orange-yellow flowers with dark brown centres. All Thunbergias are more or less tender, coming as they do from S. and E. Africa, Asia and Madagascar, and need warm greenhouse conditions, where it is difficult to keep these beautiful but strong growing plants under some sort of control – they are apt to grow only too well in the right situation. *T. alata* has flowers in colours of white, orange and several shades of yellow, but it is generally the deep yellow kind that is offered. Though it grows well outside (in hot summers) it grows even better in the shelter of a conservatory.
T. alata - Black-eyed Susan grows to 10ft (3.05m) having dark-centred yellow, orange or white flowers from June to September. An annual twiner from S. Africa for the greenhouse, or warm walls, trellis and pergolas outside in the southern counties.
Requirements: Ordinary soil, appreciates feeding.
Cultivation: Sow seeds in March in a temperature of 16 - 18°C (61 - 64°F). When large enough, prick out into individual pots and harden off before planting out in early June. Or grow in the greenhouse border, or in 8-in

(20.5-cm) pots of John Innes No. 2 if the plants are to be kept under glass. Provide a trellis or strings for them to climb, and give fortnightly feeds of weak liquid manure.
Seeds: Most seedsmen.

TIARELLA - Foamflower *(Saxifragaceae).* The name of the genus is taken from Tiara, a Persian diadem or ornament, because of the shape of the seeds. The plants have foamy flower-spikes in summer in shades of creamy-white or pale pink, and as they are evergreen they are most useful for permanent edging, ground cover or in the rockery. Most are quite happy in semi-shade, though they need a moist situation. These are elegant plants with quiet-toned blossom and they should be carefully placed where their understated charm is not eclipsed by brighter coloured flowers. *T. cordifolia* is used as a gentle medicinal plant in America.
T. cordifolia - Foamflower (1731) grows to 9in (23cm) with attractive evergreen leaves and spikes of small creamy flowers in May and June. A stoloniferous perennial from E. North America for ground cover, rockeries and edging in semi-shade or moisture retentive soil.
Requirements: *As text*
Cultivation: Take off outside growths in autumn, or best in spring.
Plants: Broadwell, Bressingham, Peter Chappell, Beth Chatto, Hillier, Ingwersen, Holden Clough.

TIGRIDIA - Tiger Flower, Peacock Flower *(Iridaceae).* These exotic-looking flowers are not difficult to grow, though they should be sited carefully, because their strange beauty needs to be somewhat set apart – perhaps by interesting foliage – from the more familiar flowers of the summer garden. Tigridias apparently have three large petals, rather like many water plants, Tradescantias, and Libertias. In reality, they have six petals: three large ones are brilliantly coloured (or white) with a yellow zone separating the solid colour from the central cup-shaped area with its orchidaceous spots. The small petals match or tone with the patterned area and the whole flower is fascinating to see, particularly as each bloom only lasts for one day. Tigridias were known about in the sixteenth century but not really believed in – Gerard discounted their existence, having only seen a second or third copy of a drawing originally made in Mexico, probably by Francisco Hernandez, who was physician to Philip II of Spain. Hernandez had been sent to study the herbal plants of Mexico, especially those used by the Indians. The Tigridia was grown by the Aztecs, who believed that it had medicinal properties, and later on they used it as a food plant.
Tigridias are not really hardy except in favoured places in the south-west corners of the British Isles; the bulbs should be planted 3 - 4in (7.5 - 10cm) deep in April in well-drained soil enriched with well-decayed manure in a warm south-facing corner, though they should not be allowed to dry at the roots. (In their native country they grow on river banks.) They should be lifted before the frosts and taken into a warm, airy shed where the corms can finish drying. These can then be stored in dry sand or peat until planting time the following year. In warm areas where they can be left in the ground, they need only be lifted every three or four years to divide the corms and cormlets which are generally produced each year.
T. pavonia - Peacock Flower, Tiger Flower (and even 'Peacock Tiger Flower') 1796. Grows to 2ft (61cm) with exotically dappled flowers in shades of red, yellow, pink and white (there is also a pure white variety without spots) from July to September. A corm from Mexico for a warm and sheltered place in the border.
Requirements: A light, rich, sandy soil, adequate water during growing season. Protect from mice.

Cultivation: *As described.* 'Cormlets' form annually if plant is happy. These can be grown on and will flower in two years.
Uses: As spectacular flowers for a focal position.
Corms: Amand, Bloms, de Jager, Hortico.

TRADESCANTIA - Spider-Wort, Flower-of-a-day, Trinity Flower, Moses in the Bulrushes, Widow's tears *(Commelinaceae).* There is much history to this interesting and rather unusual flower which has only three petals. It was discovered in America by John Tradescant the Elder who became gardener to Charles I in 1629. Tradescant had travelled widely in search of plants, visiting America, North Africa, Europe and Russia. His son John Tradescant inherited his father's interest in plants and went to North America to see what he could discover in the New World. He brought back very many plants and natural curiosities to add to the collections begun by his father, who had died whilst he was in Virginia. This collection of traveller's treasures, which included a stuffed dodo and what were said to be feathers from the legendary 'Phoenix Tayle' was left to John Tradescant the younger, and he in turn bequeathed it to his friend Elias Ashmole who founded the Ashmolean Museum in Oxford, where some of Tradescant's collection of oddities may still be seen.

The 'Spider-Wort' was believed to cure the bite of the Phalangium spider and was therefore burdened with the ponderous name of *Phalangium ephemerum virginiana joanna tradescantium.* Thankfully, it was reclassified and its name shortened to honour the Tradescants, father and son. The first plants had the familiar dark blue flowers (described rather uncharitably in 1659 as being of "... a deepe fowle blew colour" though red, purple, white, light blue and a blush colour were being grown by that time, also double flowers. This is a plant to handle with care, because the sap can cause irritation to the skin. When the flower itself dies the petals dissolve into a dark-coloured puddle of moisture – hence the name of Widow's Tears. Tradescantias hybridise all too readily, and are therefore best propagated vegetatively if named varieties are desired, though mixed seed is available and can be sown in spring and grown on in the usual way.
T. virginiana syn. **T x andersoniana, Spider-Wort** etc. (1629) grows to 2ft (61cm) with blue, violet, purple, lilac, pale blue, rose and white 3-petalled flowers from June to September. A perennial from the E. United States for the border, in sun or semi-shade.
Requirements: Ordinary well-drained soil. Water well in hot weather.
Cultivation: Divide in spring or sow seeds. The seedlings may not come true.
Plants: Most nurseries
Seeds: Chiltern, Thompson and Morgan.

TRILLIUM - Wood Lily, Trinity Flower *(Trilliaceae* syn. *Liliaceae).* The Trillium is most properly named, everything about it comes in threes – the petals, the sepals and the leaves, all of which makes for a very harmonious arrangement. When the plant is in bloom, the solitary flowers perch at the top of the stem where the three leaves meet. The flowers are like no others, though *T. grandiflorum* looks a little like a larger pale pink Tradescantia in shape, except for the most characteristic ovate leaves. *T. sessile* looks a little like a very sombre-coloured 3-petalled tulip, except for the un-Tulip-like leaves. The roots were used medicinally by the Red Indian Tribes and are still used in American herbal medicine.
T. grandiflorum - Wake Robin (1799) grows to 18in (46cm) with a single stem, 3 leaves and a solitary white, changing to pink flower from April to June. A perennial rhizomatous plant from E. North America for woodland conditions.
T. sessile (1759) grows to 12in (30.5cm) with (usually) two stems together and

reddish-purple flowers in March and April. A rhizomatous plant from the United States for woodland conditions.

T. undulatum - Painted Wood Lily (1811) grows to 12in (30.5cm) with white and purple flowers in April and May. A rhizomatous perennial from E. North America for woodland conditions.

Requirements: *As described.*

Cultivation: Plant rhizomes 3 - 4in (7.5 - 10cm) deep in natural groupings in August or September. It is essential to increase stock, lift and divide the rhizomes when the leaves die down in late summer. Make sure that each new piece has a growing tip; leave them alone thereafter, as they dislike disturbance in any case. Protect emerging shoots from slugs.

Rhizomes: Avon, Broadleigh, Peter Chappell, Hillier, Holden Clough, Ingwersen, Reginald Kaye, Potterton and Martin.

TROLLIUS - Globe Flower, Locker gowlan *(Ranunculaceae).* Globe flowers are quite easily recognised, even by those who have never seen them, because of their almost spherical shape. They like damp sunny situations, and will increase well beside a pond where the soil is permanently moist, or in a bog garden. They are native British flowers, though not seen so often today as in former times. The older Scottish name of 'Locker gowlan' is a literal description of the flower shape – 'Locker' meaning locked-in or closed in, and 'gowlan' meaning yellow. Northern British and Scandinavian people used the flowers for garlands and for decorating their houses at festival times, and there was a certain amount of superstitition about the plant. Some sources say that the trolls used to 'unlock' the flowers at night in order to drop poison in to dispose of the milkmaids and herd-boys. But one can believe anything of a troll – nasty, spiteful Scandinavian dwarfs that they are, with never a good deed to their names. Trollius are easy plants to grow as they still retain their native sturdiness.

T. europaeus - Globe Flower grows to 2ft (61cm) with lemon-yellow globular flowers from June to August. A European perennial for damp sunny places; they will grow in semi-shade if there is moisture, though they are shorter and sturdier in sun.

Requirements: Damp, heavy soil and sun or partial shade.

Cultivation: Divide roots in autumn, but best in spring, or sow ripe seeds. These may take two years to germinate if seed is stale. Sow seed in spring and wait. Grow on in the usual way, eventually.

Uses: As unusual waterside and cut flowers.

Plants: Bees, Bloms, Peter Chappell, Beth Chatto, Highfield, Hillier, Notcutts, Robinsons.

Seeds: John Chambers.

TROPAEOLUM-Nasturtium, Indian Cress *(Tropaeolaceae).* The Nasturtium is a favourite old garden flower, beloved since Elizabethan days and it does best on poorish soil where it will produce more flowers. If the soil is rich and good, so will the growth of leaves be, with fewer flowers which (in the older kinds) usually lurk underneath them. The name Nasturtium was given to it when it was first introduced into England because the leaves tasted like that other Nasturtium, *N. officinale* the Watercress plant, though nothing else about the plants is similar and they belong to completely different families. Nasturtium seeds were first sent to Spain and from there the plant went to botanists in Holland, France and England. Its common name in Elizabethan times was 'Yellow Larke's Heels' and Parkinson called it 'Yellow Larkes Spurr'. This plant was *Tropaeolum minus*, and there is a dried specimen of it, dated 1585, in the herbarium at Genoa. This is not grown today because *T. majus*, the plant that was introduced a century later in 1686, has much finer flowers. There are two main sorts of Nasturtium – the climbing kind (which is really a lank and floppy trailer) and the

ordinary border plant which does not ramble about, though these are of a
much later date. Nasturtium leaves are exceedingly nutritious in salads,
containing much more vitamin C than lettuce. The seeds are interesting to
eat and have been used as substitute capers, though they are even nicer to
eat in the raw state.

The Canary Creeper is another tender plant from Peru that has thinner
stems and is therefore better equipped to twine up and through more
substantial plants, from where its small fringed yellow flowers will suddenly
peep out in the most charming way.

T. majus - Nasturtium (1686) grows either to 8ft (2.44m) when assisted to
climb, or trails to an even greater length. The others grow to 15in (38cm)
with a spread of 18in (46cm) or the miniature 'Tom Thumb' varieties grow
only to 10in (25.5cm) or less. All have round leaves and flowers in yellow,
cream, red, orange, crimson and salmon pink, with single or semi-double
flowers, some varieties of which are scented, though most have the
characteristic 'Nasturtium' smell when crushed. A tender annual from Peru
with flowers from June until the first frost. Best in poor soil.

T. peregrinum - Canary Creeper (1810) grows to 12ft (3.66m) with small
yellow flowers from July to October or the frosts. A tender perennial, grown
as an annual, from Peru. Needs better soil.

Requirements: Full sun and something to climb up, which should be substantial
for *T. majus* which is heavy when wet.

Cultivation: Sow seeds in the open in May where intended to flower, or start the
seeds off in a warm greenhouse in individual pots in March. Leaves of *T.
majus* much favoured by the caterpillars of the Cabbage White butterfly.

Uses: *T. majus* for cut flowers and as a climbing plant for patios, terraces,
pergolas and trellis. Leaves, seeds and flowers in salads. 'Tom Thumb'
varieties for pots and containers. *T. peregrinum* as an attractive and
delicate climber or trailer.

Seeds: Most seedsmen.

TULIPA - Tulip *(Liliaceae).* Tulips came originally from Turkey where they
were prized as garden flowers for centuries. The culture of the Tulip was
very important in Turkey in those far-off times. In 1728 Sheikh Mohammed
Lalizali, Tulip grower to the Grand Vizier Ibrahim Pasha, wrote two
manuscripts (and probably very many more, but these two only have
survived and are in Berlin). The manuscripts listed 1323 different varieties
of Tulip, and seventy-four of them were exactly described. The Turks
preferred their Tulips to have pointed petals of one colour – they liked them
to resemble a dagger or a needle, (whereas in Europe the petals had to be
rounded). Stylized paintings of these early Tulips are still to be seen in tiled
rooms and tombs and on pottery and surviving textiles. The first tulips were
brought back to Vienna by the Ambassador Ogier Ghiselin de Busbecq when
he returned from the court of Suleiman the Magnificent. Then the bulbs
were taken to Holland by Clusius when he went to the Netherlands to take
up an appointment as Professor of Botany at Leiden. The bulbs were
precious, and therefore expensive, and an enterprising villian (who must
have been something of a gardener) stole them and grew them on for the
seeds. Thus began the craze that was known as Tulipomania. Gambling and
speculation in the bulbs escalated, brief fortunes were made and as quickly
lost, until the government brought in legislation to limit the price of any one
bulb to £400. This was in about the year 1637, so today's exact value would
be, in this year of 1984, the astonishing sum of £16,323 – for one bulb only,
remember. It is recorded that the sum of £370 (then 5500 Dutch florins)
was paid for a bulb of 'Semper Augustus' which was a very beautiful red
and white flower with rose-coloured flamings and pointed petals, so the
Turks would have approved of the shape if not the colouration and the price

would have been no deterrant. After the bottom fell out of the market things settled down a little, and most people sensibly grew them for their beauty. Parkinson listed names such as Gingeline, Testamount Brancion, a Crimson Foole's Coat and to go with it, a Greene Swisser. A little later on, in 1754, there was a minor craze for huge flowers, which were larger than anything that we have today. There was a Tulip called the Baguet Rigaude that had flowers so large that they were capable of holding 'an English pint of wine' or so the description goes. In the nineteenth century Tulip culture was taken up by the Northern weavers and factory workers who loved the flowers almost as dearly as they loved their Pinks and their Auriculas. There was a poor fellow in Dulwich who had a few prized Tulips that he was cherishing. One frosty night he covered the flowers with the thin blankets from his own bed. Then he caught pneumonia and died – a poor reward for such selfless devotion.

The reason for all this passionate interest was a virus transmitted by aphids which was the cause of the 'breaking' (or feathering, or flaming) as it was then called. These were the 'Florists' Tulips' which were exceedingly popular from about 1830 until 1870, with shows and a fancier's language all to themselves, and in their opulent symmetry they were entirely suited to the Victorian garden schemes.

But of course, there are the other Tulips, so different in their habit and yet of course, so similar. These are the species tulips that grace our rockeries and that still grow wild in certain parts of Europe and Asia Minor. There are many kinds of these, and most flower much earlier than the 'Garden' Tulip. The Royal Dutch Bulb Growers' Society, in collaboration with the Royal Horticultural Society, has now classified all known tulips into 15 categories as follows; most of the titles are self-explanatory:

Division 1: Single Early. Division 2: Double Early. Division 3: Mendel – raised from crosses between Single Early and Darwin. Division 4: Triumph – from crosses between Single Early and late flowering. Division 5: Darwin hybrids – containing the largest and most brilliantly coloured flowers, these are from crosses between Darwin tulips and *T. fosteriana*. Division 6: Darwin. Division 7: Lily-flowered – with 'waisted' flowers having pointed petals. Division 8: Cottage – a very old group. Division 9: Rembrandt – famous for their broken colours. Division 10: Parrot – having twisted and/or fringed petals. Division 11: Double Late. Division 12: *T. Kaufmanniana* and similar kinds. Division 13: *T. fosteriana* and derivations. Division 14: *T. greigii* and derivations. Division 15: Species.

Some examples are as follows: 'Kaizerskroon' (Division 1) had red and yellow flowers and blooms in April. This is a very old variety indeed. 12 – 15in (30.5 – 38cm). 'Triumphator' (Division 2) is deep pink and flowers in April. 15in (38cm). 'Athleet' (Division 3) is white and flowers in April and early May. 15 – 20in (38 – 51cm). 'Orange Wonder' (Division 4) is shining orange with a scarlet glow and flowers in April. 18in (46cm). 'Gudoshnik' (Division 5) yellow, flushed and spotted with red, flowers in April and May. 2ft (61cm). 'La Tulipe Noir' (Division 6) has very dark crimson flowers in May. 2ft – 2ft 6in (61 – 76cm). 'Arkadia' (Division 7) has yellow flowers in April. 18in (46cm). 'Artist' (Division 8) has green petals edged with red in April and May. 2ft (61cm). 'Absalon' (Division 9) has yellow petals with crimson-brown 'breaks'. 2ft – 2ft 6in (61 – 76cm). 'Black Parrot' (Division 10) has large dark purple flowers in April and May. 18in – 2ft (46 – 61cm). 'Brilliant Fire' (Division 11) has scented scarlet double flowers in April. 18in – 2ft (46 – 61cm). 'Shakespeare' (Division 12) has yellow and red flowers opening flat in April. 6in (15cm). 'Purissima' (Division 13) has creamy-yellow flowers in April. 9in (23cm). 'Red Riding Hood' (Division 14) has red flowers in April with striking maroon-veined leaves. 8in (20.5cm).

The species tulips (Division 15) because they open early may need protection from the elements, and more particularly, from slugs. Some charmers for a sunny rockery are:

T. Clusiana - Lady Tulip grows to 12in (30.5cm), has flat white flowers with a central purple blotch in April and May. From Afghanistan, Persia and Iraq.

T. Fosteriana grows to 8in (20.5cm), has flat scarlet flowers in March. From Samarkand.

T. Kaufmanniana-Water-Lily Tulip grows to 8in (20.5cm), has flat white, cream or pale yellow flowers in March. From Turkestan.

T. Pulchella (1877) grows to 6in (15cm) high with purple flowers with white margined deep blue blotch, in March. From Asia Minor.

T. sylvestris grows to 12in (30.5cm) with fragant yellow flowers tinged green and red in April. A European flower, rare in Britain.

Requirements: Tulips need to be planted in a sunny position in free-draining alkaline soil. (In acid soil, apply 3 – 4oz of powdered limestone per sq. yd.)

Cultivation: Plant the bulbs in October or November, they should not be put in too early. Plant deeply if they are to be left in the ground, 9 – 12in (23 – 30.5cm) or 6in (15cm) as a general guide, and no deeper than 6in (15cm) in heavy clay soil. Species tulips come true from seed but the garden tulips do not, these must be propagated from their offsets which are almost always the same as the parent.

Bulbs: Species Tulips: Amand, Avon, Bees, Broadleigh, Ingwersen, Kelways, Potterton and Martin, Stassen, van Tubergen. Garden Tulips: Bees, Bloms, Christian, Kelways, Orpington, Spalding, Stassen, van Tubergen and garden centres.

UVULARIA *(Liliaceae)*. These unusual, graceful little flowers are a charming addition to a shady border, having nodding yellow flowers rather like a Trillium with twisted petals. Some gardening sources say that they need peat and others that they thrive in a light sandy soil. Buy enough of the rhizomes to try in both situations.

U. grandiflora - Merry Bells (1802) grows to 9in (23cm) with pendular yellow flowers in spring. A rhizomatous perennial from N. America for a shady border.

Requirements: Good soil and partial shade.

Propagation: Divide in spring.

Rhizomes: Broadleigh, Peter Chappell, Christian, Holden Clough, Ingwersen, Jackamoor's, Potterton and Martin.

Plants: Robinsons.

VERATRUM - False Helleborine, Black (and wrongly) **White Helleborine** *(Liliaceae)*. The name of the plant comes from *Vere*, 'truly', and *Ater*, 'black', because of the dark-coloured root. Veratrums are handsome-leaved and distinguished looking plants that are not often seen; they have been cultivated for centuries for medicinal purposes, though their powerfully poisonous and dangerous nature has always been known. In earliest times they were grown for these poisonous qualities, being used to tip arrows, spears and daggers. Later, extracts of the plant were used in attempts to alleviate epilepsy, various manias and gout, in spite of the violence of its action. It was used externally to cure scabies and lice and was still used until recently as an Errhine (a medicine to be sniffed up the nose to increase the natural secretions and provoke sneezing) for chronic cases of mental disorder. It is a tall plant with large, pleated leaves which make it a fine, focal subject, though Veratrums should be grown as a group of one kind as a single plant looks odd. They are as caviar to slugs which will spoil the fine leaves very quickly unless all possible precautions are taken.

V. album - Langwort, White Hellebore, White Helleborine grows to 4ft (122cm) with green-white flowers in July. A perennial from N. Africa and Siberia for the partly shaded border.

V. nigrum - Black Helleborine (1596) grows to 4ft (122cm) with purplish-black flowers in June. A perennial from S. Europe and Siberia for the partly shaded border.
Requirements: Rich light soil, partial shade. Moisture during growing season, mulch with peat in dry springs.
Cultivation: Divide roots in autumn or spring, or sow ripe seed in October. Grow on in a nursery bed. The plants will take about four years to come to flowering.
Warning: All parts of these plants are poisonous, particularly the roots.
Plants: Broadleigh, Cunnington, Hillier, Treasure's of Tenbury.
Seeds: Chiltern, Thompson and Morgan.

VERBASCUM - Mullein *(Scrophulariaceae)*. The wild and woolly-leaved Mullein is a familiar sight in the country in late summer, but it would have been banished from most gardens as a weed until the advent of William Robinson (born 1838) who was a prime advocate of 'wild' gardening. Later Gertrude Jekyll and Vita Sackville-West used this plant to such good effect that they set the seal of good gardening approval on it, to such purpose that it and all its relatives are welcome inside the garden boundaries. One should always remember that the imported plants that we admire so much (and pay to match) are often the wild flowers of other countries. Our native Mullein *(V. thapsus)* has a history of usefulness, the 'wool' from its furry leaves was once used for lamp-wicks, and its many common names reflect this and its comfortably soft appearance. It was called Adam's Flannel, Beggar's Blanket, Flannel Petticoats, Hag's Taper and The Virgin Mary's Candle. It was used as a candle or torch by the poorer folk, and Parkinson wrote of it "Candela regia and Candelaria, because the elder age used the stalks dipped in suet to burne, whether at funeralls or otherwise". It was appropriately called 'Aaron's Rod' which was "... budded, and brought forth buds and bloomed blossoms" (Numbers XVII, v.8) which is exactly what the flower stems do, opening haphazardly and unevenly up the stalk. Mulleins of all kinds thrive in limestone areas and look well when grown on old dry-stone walls, where they will generally seed themselves about in a most attractive way.

The native Mullein has some spectacular cousins such as *V. olympicum* (taller and whiter) and a group of these plants is a fine sight, especially when grown against something dark such as a hedge, some conifers or a wall. In addition it is sometimes very long-lived for a Verbascum. Other members of the genus have greener, though still furry, leaves, and very large panicles of (generally) yellow flowers, though there are white, pink, orange and apricot flowered species.
V. Chaixii (1821) grows to 5ft (152cm) with yellow flowers in July and August. A perennial from South and Central Europe for the back of a large border.
V. olympicum (1883) grows to 6ft (185cm) with silver-white leaves and stems and bright yellow flowers opening unevenly from June to September. A handsome (usually) perennial plant from Bithynia for the back of the larger border or in a good focal position.
V. thapsus - Mullein grows to 4ft (122cm) with woolly grey leaves and yellow flowers from June to August. A European biennial for a sunny place. Grow in an open position to avoid mildew.
Requirements: Any soil, a hot sunny position, does well on dry-stone walls and in paving.
Cultivation: Sow seeds in April in boxes in a cold frame. Prick out seedings into pots in the case of *V. thapsus* and nursery rows for the others. Set out in flowering positions as soon as large enough – the plants dislike disturbance and may die if moved when well established. Examine plants regularly for caterpillars, which ruin the leaves.
Plants: Beth Chatto, Ramparts, Stoke Lacy Herb Garden, The Weald Herbary.

Seeds: Thomas Butcher, Chambers, Chiltern, Stoke Lacy Herb Garden.

VERBENA *(Verbenaceae).* In the Language of Flowers, white Verbena meant 'Pray for me', pink meant 'Family union' and red meant 'Unite against evil' or 'Church unity'. From this one can see that the Verbena was a very proper kind of plant for the respectable Victorian flower garden.

Verbena is not grown very much today, for several reasons. It is somewhat tender, and therefore either has to be wintered under glass or some other form of protection given, except in Cornwall or the Isles of Scilly. It was much used as a bedding-out plant in Victorian times until the advent of 'Verbena disease'. This was so serious that the cultivation of the plant was discontinued and as a result of this the plant was almost forgotten. But such is the way of things, when the Verbena ceased to be cultivated on the grand scale as it had been, so it seemed to recover, and it is thought that the sickness was due to the wrong cultural methods that were then employed. It used to be crowded into warm greenhouses for the winter and kept too starved of space and nourishment, so that when it came to be planted out for the summer it had not made sufficient root. Verbena likes plenty of room and deep rich soil to grow in. Vegetative propagation was widely practised.

V x hydrida (syn. **V. hortensis) - Garden Verbena** (1837) grows to 18in (46cm) with flower clusters in shades of pink, magenta, red, purple, lilac, blue and white from June onwards. A perennial (grown as an annual) of garden origin for the sunny border.

V. peruviana syn. **V. chamaedrifolia** (1827) grows to 4in (10cm) with a trailing habit and scarlet flowers from June onwards. A perennial from S. America for a sheltered sunny rockery, needs winter protection such as a cloche.

V. rigida syn. **V. venosa** grows to 2ft (61cm) with purple or magenta flowers (there is a white variety also) from June until October. A tuberous-rooted perennial from S. America for a sheltered, sunny border. Tubers should be treated like Dahlias, or covered with mounded litter or sand in the warmer counties.

Requirements: Deep rich moisture-retentive soil and full sun. Do not allow roots to dry out in hot weather. Give weak liquid feeds.

Cultivation: Sow seeds in January or March at a temperature of 18 – 21°C (64 – 70°F) and cover very lightly with seed compost. Germination may take a month and is often erratic. Grow on in the usual way, harden off and plant out in late May.

During flowering: Dead-head.

Uses: As very floriferous border colour.

Seeds: Thomas Butcher, Chiltern, Dobie, Thompson and Morgan, Unwins and most seedsmen.

Plants: Robinsons.

VERONICA - Speedwell *(Scrophulariaceae).* Most of the Speedwells are blue (that most restful of flower colours) and a good true blue at that. The species has a confused lineage, with several changes of name (see Forget-me-not) and the rare Spiked Speedwell, *V. spicata* was once called the Blew Willow Herb. In Europe certain types of Veronica, usually *V. officinalis* though sometimes *V. spicata,* were dried and used instead of tea; this brew was called *Thé de l'Europe.*

V. filiformis is a delightful mat-forming perennial plant that will make a spreading carpet of purest blue. It has a territorial nature, but once established it is easily – if ruthlessly – controlled by the half-moon edger. It is a good plant for new, bare rockeries or dry walls, but do not let it escape.

V. filiformis grows only to 1in (2.5cm) but spreads several feet. Blue flowers from April to July. A mat-forming perennial from Asia Minor for a sunny corner or dry wall.

V. incana (1759) grows to 15in (38cm) with spikes of blue, pink or white flowers from June to August. A European perennial for the border.

V. prostrata grows to 6in (15cm) or less according to type, with blue, pink or white flowers from May to July. A perennial for the rock garden (many kinds under this name).

V. spicata grows to 18in (46cm) or more according to type with blue, white or pink flower-spikes from June to August. A European perennial for the border.

V. Teucrium (1596) grows from 6 – 36in (15 – 91.5cm) according to type with blue flower spikes from June to August. A perennial from S. Europe and N. Asia for sunny rockery or border, according to height.

Requirements: The alpine varieties of Veronica need full sun and ordinary free draining soil; the herbaceous kinds need slightly better conditions and a little well-decayed manure or other fertiliser.

Cultivation: Divide in spring.

Plants: Broadwells, Beth Chatto, Hillier, Holden Clough, Reginald Kaye, Kelways, Notcutts, Robinsons, Scotts, Southcombe.

VINCA - Periwinkle *(Apocyanaceae).* The Periwinkle is classed as a sub-shrub but always thought of by gardeners as a perennial. It is a very old garden flower indeed, often mentioned in fourteenth-century poetry and manuscript. It was a flower of myth and meaning even then, and was used in many a magic spell. In the days of public executions, some criminals would have a garland of Periwinkles placed on their heads in mockery as they went on their last journey on earth to the gibbet.

"Crowned one with Laurer, hye on his head set other with Pervink, made for the gibet."

The flower was once called 'Joy of the Ground' though this charming name has not been used for some five centuries. Interestingly, this flower and not the Dianthus is the origin of the saying 'Pink of Perfection' which is derived from its earlier name of Pervenke; the phase 'Pervenke of Prowess' or the Parvink of Perfection became abbreviated to 'the pink of perfection'. The Periwinkle or Vinca is a rather scorned plant because of its invasiveness, but it is easily controlled with shears, and it is a fine evergreen, quite unscathed by the worst of winter weather. Indeed, in mild winters and in the southern counties it often begins to open its amethystine-coloured flowers in November, continuing without a break until the following May. I grow it to scramble up through evergreen shrubs such as *Cistus ladanifer* and Escallonia, which it decorates with unexpected flowers through most winters. It can be used as ground cover in shade, but it will not flower so consistently. *Vinca major* 'Elegantissima' is the cream-and-green leaved variety, which has the same scrambling habit though it is less vigorous. This looks pleasing when growing up through evergreen or dark-leaved shrubs; if these are in a sunny position the Vinca will flower more, but even in the shade and flowerless it will light up dark, dull corners and do well. The smaller kind, *V. minor*, has several pleasing varieties with white, deep purple, wine-red and double flowers, but these do need more care and a reasonably good position in the garden.

V. major - Band-plant, Periwinkle grows to 12in (30.5cm) though stems will climb up to 3 or 4ft (91.5 – 122cm) through shrubs. Blue-mauve flowers from April to June and from November onwards in mild winters. A vigorous trailing evergreen perennial, useful for clothing difficult corners. Does well in any soil. Var. 'Elegantissima' has cream and green leaves, paler flowers and is less vigorous.

V. minor grows to 4in (10cm) spread 3 – 4ft (91.5 – 122cm) with darker green leaves and purple, white, blue or wine red flowers from March to July and intermittently throughout the year, A European perennial for better soil and situation than *V. major*.

Requirements: More flowers are produced in sunny situations, though *V. major* will grow almost anywhere. Grow variegated sorts of *V. minor* in choice positions.

Cultivation: *V. major* roots at the tips and nodes of the trailing stems. Allow these to get settled, then sever the umbilical stem and transfer new rooted plant. *V. minor* needs to be pegged down over a pot of seed compost to root. Shear over the vigorous kinds when too exuberant.

Uses: As ground cover plants for walls, banks, hedge bottoms, woodland in light shade or full sun.

Plants: St. Bridget, Hillier, Highfield, Beth Chatto, Peter Chappell, Kelways, Southcombe, Scotts, Ingwersen, Notcutts, Robinsons, Holden Clough.

VIOLA - Violet, Violetta, Pansy *(Violaceae).* Botanically, Violas, Violets, Violettas and Pansies are all Violas. Over the centuries their paths have divided a little, aided by man or his bees. Pansies evolved into 'Florists' flowers which have an interesting history. They are botanically named *V. x Wittrockiana,* after Professor Wittrock, a Swedish botanist who wrote a treatise on them in 1896. These sumptuous flowers began to be developed early in the nineteenth century from crosses between *V. tricolor* (Hearts-ease), *V. lutea* and, probably, *V. altaica.* Their story is said to have begun in the garden of the discredited Lord Gambier (who was discharged with igominy from the Royal Navy at the beginning of the nineteenth century). He took up gardening as a therapy in order to forget his past, but it is his gardener, a Mr. T. Thompson, who did all the actual work. From 1816 onwards Mr. Thompson raised so many varieties that the flower was taken up by the Florists, who formed the first society for the flower – called the Hammersmith Heart's-ease Society, with its first show in 1841. There would have been about 400 named kinds at that time, with flowers that, initially, had to conform to the 'Show Pansy' type, with its almost circular, flat flowers that had to have a yellow or white ground and a clearly marked border of colour on the lower petals, with the two upper petals in the same shade and a small but definite blotch in the centre of the flower. This must have been exceedingly limiting. The European growers were producing flowers of a different kind, with brighter colours and the large (usually dark) blotch in the centre that is so familiar today. These were called 'Fancy' Pansies, and even though they had richer colours they were not immediately successful, though eventually they became more popular than the old 'Show Pansy' which must by now have almost vanished.

The flower became popular in the industrial areas, much as the Pinks and Auriculas had, in spite of the fact that Pansies need pure air to grow in. But such was the craving for beauty in those grim surroundings that people grew Pansies, and grew them well, in spite of their bleak and grimy surroundings. In 1889 a James Simkins wrote about the importance of the Pansy in working-class gardens. He said "It is inexpensive, it is easily managed and it is beautiful, and beauty is a thing more needed by the poor, than by the rich". The wisdom of his words is perennial, even though the flowers that he wrote about are not. Most Pansies are annual or biennial plants, with a rather sprawling and open habit of growth.

Violas are more or less perennial plants with a more compact habit of growth and smaller flowers. They are a race of garden flowers that came from crosses between 'Show Pansies' and the species *V. cornuta* and *V. lutea,* and they came into cultivation round about 1863, being raised by James Grieve (of apple fame). They are sometimes called Tufted Pansies and they have longer spurs and the flowers are often self-coloured. There are several old varieties such as 'Irish Molly' which have most unusual colourations and these must be propagated vegetatively. Violas are botanically named V. x *williamsii.*

The Violet has changed the least, and the perfumed Sweet Violet, *V.*

odorata is still much the same as it was when being grown by the ancient Greeks, whose gardeners were so knowledgeable that they could have plants in bloom throughout the year. Napoleon was no gardener, but he liked the flowers, perhaps because Josephine wore them on their wedding day. He sent her violets on each anniversary, and the flowers became a symbol of loyalty to the Napoleonic cause when he was banished to Elba. When he escaped and returned to Paris in the spring, as he had promised, his friends and supporters greeted him wearing the flowers or violet-coloured cloaks and gowns. The Violets were grown (probably in frames) by that rather tetchy-tempered critic and poet, Walter Savage Landor who, in a fit of fury, threw his cook out of the window; rushing back to look out he cried "Good God, I forgot the Violets!". The Parma Violet has a legendary perfume, though its parentage is not known: it is thought to have been brought to Europe from the Middle East, and it needs frame cultivation in Northern Europe.

Almost everyone is sentimental about Violets – and even non-gardeners can recognise the ordinary kind. One interesting fact about the scent is that the more you sniff the less scent there appears to be – it seems to disappear in some odd way. This is because it is so strong that it has a gently numbing effect on the olfactory system. Wait a little for your nose to recover and sniff again – the scent will still be there as strong as ever. The Heartsease, or *V. tricolor* had a number of common names such as Cat's Face, Jack-behind-the-garden-gate, Leap-up-and-kiss-me, Kitty-run-the-street, Love-in-idleness, Stepmothers, Three-faces-under-a-hood, Tittle-my-fancy, and very many more.

In 1887 a Scottish viola grower called Dr. Charles Stuart found a single seedling among his plants that had rayless white flowers; this was the first Violetta.

V. altaica (1805) grows to 5in (12.5cm) with yellow (occasionally violet) flowers from March to June. A rhizomatous perennial from the Crimea and Turkestan for the rockery. Probably one of the parents of *V.* x *Wittrockiana*.

V. cornuta (1776) grows to 12in (30.5cm) with mauve or purple flowers in June and July. ('Alba' is the white-flowered variety). A rhizomatous perennial from the Pyrenees for the rockery.

V. labradorica grows to 3in (7.5cm) with purple leaves and small dog-violet size mauve flowers in April and May. A perennial from Greenland and N. America for sun or semi-shade. (Probably a variety of *V. adunca minor*, a N. American species).

V. odorata - Sweet Violet grows to 6ins (15cm) with scented purple, lilac or white flowers from February to April. A rhizomatous perennial from E. Asia, N. Africa and Europe for semi-woodland conditions, with some decayed manure incorporated. Top-dressings every year will be of benefit.

V. tricolor - Heart's-ease grows to 6in (15cm) with yellow, purple, blue, cream and white flowers from May to September. A short-lived freely seeding perennial, probable ancestor of *V.* x *wittrockiana*.

V. Williamsii The group name for Violas, Tufted Pansies and Violettas.

V. x **wittrockiana** syns. **V. tricolor hortensis, V. t. maxima - Garden Pansy** grows up to 12in (30.5cm) with flowers of almost every colour from pure white to almost black and every shade in between. Summer-flowering kinds in bloom from May to September. Winter-flowering kinds bloom throughout the winter in mild districts. Many Pansies have characteristic masks or faces.

Requirements: Plant out Violas in autumn or spring, according to type, in any good garden soil. Protect young plants from slugs.

Cultivation: Sow seeds of hybrid summer-flowering kinds in July in boxes of seed compost in a cold frame or a dampish shady corner. Grow on in the usual way and prick out into more boxes or nursery rows. It is best to keep the young plants in a cold frame for the winter. Garden Pansies do not come true from seed grown in ordinary garden conditions, therefore if stocks of certain colours are wanted, take basal cuttings of non-flowering shoots in July, insert in a mix of soil and peat and keep in a cold frame until rooted. Transfer into pots of John Innes No. 1 when well rooted.

Violets need heavy soil with well-decayed cow manure. The better kinds of scented violet can be grown in frames to prevent the weather spoiling the flowers. For top quality blooms the method is as follows: make up a bed of leaves to 3ft (91.5cm) and tread firmly down. Set the frame on this and put the prepared soil in to a depth of 10in (25.5cm). This should be three parts of light loam to one of leaf mould. To increase the stock divide the plants after flowering, making sure that each new plant has two or three 'crowns'. Violet seed can be sown in early autumn and covered with a light sifting of soil. The boxes should be kept in a well ventilated cold frame and the small plants can be pricked out in spring.

During flowering: Dead-head regularly.
Plants: Most nurseries.
Seeds: Most seedsmen.

ZANTEDESCHIA - Arum Lily, Lily of the Nile, (wrongly) **Calla** *(Araceae)*.
This genus was named after Giovanni Zantedesch, (1773 – 1846) an Italian botanist and physician. The Arum Lily is not hardy in the British Isles except in some southern counties, though being a moisture lover it can be grown in a large pot in the garden pond, so long as there is at least 9in (23cm) of water over it during the winter. The blooms are much used for church decoration and for funerals and have been clearly recognisable in formal design for centuries. People either like them or hate them – there seems to be no half-way house about these beautiful flowers, formerly called *Richardia aethiopica*. It can be grown in several ways – out of doors against a warm south-facing wall, with plenty of water in early spring and during the summer, and a good heaping of litter over the leaves in the winter which would be handsomely evergreen were it not for the frosts. They can be put in a large pot which should be stood permanently in its own pan of water, the whole can go outside for the summer, never letting the plant get too dry. It will make a fine patio subject when grown in this way, but should not be be put out until late May and should be brought inside in September to spend the winter in a frost-free conservatory or greenhouse or even indoors in a good light. It can be put into a pond to grow up into the sun with 9 – 12in (23 – 30.5cm) over the crown, and it may be left there all the year round. It may be grown as a large houseplant, and should be given liquid feeds and it will reward you with enormous and perfect flowers, or it can be grown in the greenhouse where it can be given manure-water to drink, and being a greedy plant it will thrive and grow very large, and the flowers will match.

Z. aethiopica - Arum Lily (1731) grows to 2½ft (76cm) with creamy-white spathes from March to June. A rhizomatous perennial from S. Africa for the conservatory, greenhouse, pond, sheltered garden in Cornwall and Devon and as a large houseplant.

Requirements: Frost-free conditions, enriched soil or compost, sun and plenty of water during the growing season, weekly feeds of liquid manure.

Propagation: Divide after flowering or at re-potting time, which is October or November. Plants can be allowed to rest in winter by gradually withholding water after flowering until leaves turn yellow and die down. Re-pot into John Innes No. 2.

After flowering: Cut down flower stems.
Rhizomes: Most nurseries.

ZEPHYRANTHES - Flower(s) of the Western Wind, Zephyr Lilies

(Amaryllidaceae). The genus is named from *Zephyros*, the West Wind, and *anthos*, flower, because the plants are American and therefore came to Europe from the West. They are not hardy except in Cornwall and parts of Devon, and if it is wished to grow them in the garden a certain amount of juggling will be necessary. The flowers are rather like a large crocus and as *Z. candida* blooms in the autumn it is worth taking a little trouble.

The bulbs should be planted in spring or as soon as purchased, according to type, and the best site for them is against the south wall of a warm greenhouse. However, this is not an ideal world and if no such site is available they can be planted in pots in a compost of two parts turfy loam to one part of coarse sand and one part of leafmould or peat. Worms can be a problem with these bulbs, so sterilised soil (or a John Innes compost) should be used. They can be left in their pots for several years, as they usually flower better when they are crowded. In cold areas the pots can be kept in a just-warm greenhouse or conservatory, and can be planted, pot and all, into the ground in late May. There are several species such as *Z. candida*, the hardiest, and *Z. grandiflora* with rose pink flowers in summer.

Z. candida - Flower of the Western Wind (1822) grows to 8in (20.5cm) with evergreen leaves and white flowers in September and October. A bulb from S. America for a hot sheltered border in warm counties.

Z. grandiflora (1824) grows to 8in (20.5cm) with rose-pink flowers in June and July. A tender bulb from Guatemala and the W. Indies. Best in a cold greenhouse, or can be grown in large pots to be 'planted' in the open in summer.

Requirements: *See text.*
Cultivation: From offsets which can be separated when re-potting. This should not be done too often.
Bulbs: Amand, Avon, Broadleigh, de Jager, Holden Clough, Potterton and Martin.
Plants: Robinsons.

ZINNIA - Mexican Marigold, Youth and Age *(Compositae).* The flowers were named after Gottfried Zinn (1727-59) a Professor of Botany at Gottingen who died at the early age of 32. At one time Zinnias were grown with a certain amount of care, the seeds being sown on a hotbed – the early equivalent of a propagator. Even the soil into which the seedlings were ultimately planted was carefully prepared, and of course the resulting flowers were spectacular, as they had been grown without any check.

These stiffly handsome flowers, which must have suited the Victorian bedding-out schemes so well, came originally from Mexico. The Aztecs were a race of gardeners, even though it must seem from history that their gardens were soaked in blood. The gardeners used to prick their ears so that blood would fall on each new species that was planted. It is known that Montezuma's gardens contained specimens of all the known species of the times and the gardeners must have dreaded the advent of a new flower or tree. Dahlias, Tigridias and Sunflowers were there and the Zinnia would have been a most important flower, though it was not introduced into Europe until the end of the eighteenth century with the lesser-known species *Z. pauciflora* coming first, some 43 years before the introduction of the familiar *Z. elegans*. The Europeans fell in love with the Zinnias, and it was cultivated by many nurserymen who had begun to breed the double-flowered sorts by 1856. One bloom was said to have had 586 petals – truly a football of a flower. Zinnias lent themselves most obligingly to hybridization and giant flowers were bred, though curiously enough for the times, dwarf forms were very popular. Zinnias are true to their heritage and do best in dry hot summers.

Z. elegans - Zinnia (1796) grows to 2½ft (76cm) with dahlia-like flowers in every colour except blue, throughout the summer. A half-hardy annual from Mexico for bedding schemes.

Requirements: Rich, light soil.

Cultivation: Sow seeds in March at a temperature of 16 – 18°C (61 – 64°F) and when large enough prick out into individual pots of John Innes No. 1 as they dislike being moved. Harden off and plant out without disturbing roots. Pinch out growing tips to encourage bushy plants.

During flowering: Dead-head with scissors.

Seeds: Most seedsmen.

Biographical Notes

CLUSIUS - Jules Charles de L'Ecluse (1526-1609) – born in what was Flanders, at Arras. A botanist who spoke eight languages. Met Sir Frances Drake and through him obtained some of the first American plants. One of the founders of the bulb-growing industry in the Netherlands.

NICHOLAS CULPEPER (1616-54) – an apothecary and a Puritan who fought in the Civil War, where he was severely wounded. In spite of his faith he believed in the powers of astrology, linked to plants that were governed by the planets. He wrote *The English Physician Enlarged* (published in 1653) which was very popular.

DIOSCORIDES - Pedianos Dioskurides – (*circa* AD40 to *circa* AD90). His most important work was *De Materia Medica* which was about the identification and use of medicinal plants. This was still in use over 1000 years later. A manuscript copy (dated AD 512) is in Vienna.

REGINALD FARRER (1880-1920) – was a great gardener, traveller and plant collector, visiting Japan, the Himalayas and Burma. His most famous book is *The English Rock-Garden* though this is, of course, outside the time scale of this book. His name is commemorated in all the plant varieties named 'Farreri'.

ROBERT FORTUNE (1812-80) – became a 'botanical collector' to the Royal Horticultural Society in 1842. He went to China in 1843 where he discovered many plants and flowers that bear his name (Fortunei). He returned to a post as curator to the Chelsea Physic Garden and began writing his books, but returned to China as an employee of the East India Company and found many more plant species.

JOHN GERARD (1545-1612) – born in Cheshire, England. Became a Barber-Surgeon in 1569 and was a garden-planner. His book, the *Herball or Historie of Plantes* (1597) was 'borrowed' from Dodoens. Important because of the list of his own garden plants that he made in 1596 and 1599.

WILLIAM HANBURY (1725-78) – became rector of Church Langton in Leicestershire in 1753. Was famous for his extensive tree plantations, his garden and his writings on gardening. He wrote *The Complete Body of Planting and Gardening* a fortnightly publication that sold at 6d. a copy. This ran from 1769-73.

GERTRUDE JEKYLL (1843-1932) – 'Artist - Gardener - Craftswoman' – these words on her memorial stone sum up her abilities. She wrote many books about plants and gardening and is famous for her herbaceous borders and beautiful planting schemes.

LINNAEUS - Carl von Linne (1707-78) – the Swedish botanist who is famous for the plant classification system and the binomial method of nomenclature that is still in use today. Though most of his work was with plants he also classified insects, birds and animals.

JOHN CLAUDIUS LOUDON (1783-1842), **JANE LOUDON** (1803-58) – John Loudon was a landscape gardener who wrote many gardening books, in spite of the fact that he had the partial use of his left arm only – his right had been amputated in 1825. Jane Loudon knew nothing of gardening when she met her husband but studied so that she might understand his work and help him as much as possible. She wrote several books for learner-gardeners.

They lived in Bayswater Terrace in London, and had only a moderate-sized garden.

HENRY LYTE (1529-1607) – born in Somerset, England. He wrote *A Nievve Herball* in 1578 which was a translation from Clusius. He was married three times and had a large family of 13.

PHILIP MILLER (1692-1771) – had a small nursery-garden in London. Was the protégé of Sir Hans Sloane who later made him the first curator of the Chelsea Physic Garden. He wrote several books, the most important being *The Gardener's Dictionary* (published 1731). He employed only Scottish gardeners.

JOHN PARKINSON (1567-1650) – an apothecary, becoming the Warden of the Society of Apothecaries in 1617. His famous garden was in Long Acre. Wrote *Paradisi in Sole, Paradisus Terrestris*, an illustrated book on plants whose title was a pun on his name – 'Park in Sun'. Became Botanist to King Charles I.

PLINY the Elder - Gaius Plinius Secundus – born in AD23 at Como, died in AD79. His death was attributed to the sulphurous atmosphere during a great eruption of Vesuvius. He held many public offices and was a most industrious man, spending each day in writing and learning throughout his life.

WILLIAM ROBINSON (1838-1935) – a rather violent Irishman who left his first employer under dubious circumstances. His second job was in London, where he was put in charge of a collection of English wild flowers. These so influenced him that he pioneered the 'Wild Garden' or more natural form of gardening. He was a contemporary and friend of Gertrude Jekyll. His name is commemorated in the many plants named after his house, Gravetye Manor. He designed and promoted rock gardens that looked like natural rock-strata. He detested the formal Victorian form of gardening and in particular he hated 'carpet-bedding'.

THEOPHRASTUS (Greek) – born at Lesbos in about 370 B.C. Said to have lived to the age of 107. A friend of Alexander the Great. Wrote several books including the earliest still-surviving botanical work *Enquiry into Plants*.

JOHN TRADESCANT (the elder) (d. 1638) – began a 'career' as a gardener, first to the Earl of Salisbury, then to Lord Wotton, the Duke of Buckingham and finally to King Charles I. He went with Sir Dudley Digges to Russia in 1618, and afterwards travelled to Algeria to fight the Corsairs. He began an extensive collection of natural curiosities which was the foundation collection of the Ashmolean Museum.

J. PITTON DE TOURNEFORT (1656-1708) – his father wished him to enter the Church but he became Professor of Botany at the Jardin du Roi. Louis XIV sent him on an expedition to discover new plants in 1700, and he visited Crete, many of the Greek Islands, the Black Sea coast, Tiflis, Erzerum and Smyrna (accompanied by the artist Charles Aubriet – see Aubrieta). He was a great botanist of his day.

WILLIAM TURNER (c. 1508-68) – a student at Cambridge where he began to classify British flora, the nomenclature of which was in a state of confusion. Exiled (twice) voluntarily because of his religious beliefs, he utilised the time abroad to take his degree in Medicine at Bologna. Published first part of *A New Herbal* in 1551 and the second part in 1562. Finally became Dean of Wells.

NURSERIES, SEEDSMEN AND BULB MERCHANTS

The species and varieties described in the book are all obtainable from the nurseries, bulb merchants and seedsmen listed here. But it should be remembered that nurseries are not garden centres – they actually grow what they sell and may not be geared for visitors. Some of them are mail-orders only, whereas others sell plants in containers to visitors on certain days (usually at weekends). Some sell only to visitors and do no mail orders at all. So it is as well to write (enclosing an S.A.E.) or telephone first to find out how they do things. All of them produce catalogues, which can cost from 30p to about £1.50p, plus postage. If seeking particular plants, it is essential to peruse the catalogues before ordering or visiting as not all the nurseries have all the plants.

The smaller nurseries (often with the most interesting plants) operate with minimum staff, so do not be surprised if the telephone bell goes unanswered at first. Just keep on trying, and choose a different time of day to make your next call. Nurseries are run by fascinating individuals who are in themselves collectors' items. If you are genuinely interested in their plants they will be most helpful. Many British nurseries are licensed to export their plants or bulbs, but as each country of destination has different agricultural import rules, it is as well to check. Many nurseries, bulb-merchants and seedsmen exhibit at the Royal Horticultural Society shows, where you can see the standard of their plants. Go early – they always run out of catalogues.

NURSERY AND SEEDSMEN DIRECTORY

Abbey Brook Cactus Nursery – Old Hackney Lane, Matlock, Derbys. Tel: Matlock (0629) 55360.

Allwood Brothers (Hassocks) Ltd – Clayton Nursery, Hassocks, West Sussex BH6 9LX. Tel: Hassocks (079 18) 4229/2115.

Amand – Beethoven Street, London W10 4LG. Tel: 01 969 9797.

Keith Andrew Orchids Ltd – Plush, Dorchester, Dorset DT2 7RH. Tel: Piddletrenthide (03004) 375.

P.H. Artiss – Hill Rise Nursery, 295 Bath Road, Slough SL1 5PR. Tel: Burnham 61220.

Avon Bulbs – Bathford, Bath BA1 8ED. Tel: Bath (0225) 859495.

Helen Ballard – Old Country, Mathon, Malvern, Worcs.

Barnhaven – Brigsteer, Kendal LA8 8AU. Tel: Crosthwaite 386.

Bees (Sealand Nurseries Ltd) – Sealand, Chester CH1 6BA. Tel: Saughall (024 458) 501.

Bennetts' Water Lily Farm – Chickerell, Weymouth, Dorset DT3 4AF. Tel: Weymouth (0305) 785150.

Penny Black – Treskewes Cottage, Trewithen Moor, Stithians, Truro, Cornwall. Tel: (0209) 860312.

Blackmore and Langdon – Pensford, Bristol. Tel: Chew Magna (0275) 89230.

Walter Blom & Son Ltd – Coomblands Nurseries, Leavesden, Watford, Herts WD2 7BH. Tel: Garston (092 73) 72071.

Robert Bolton and Son – Birdbrook, Halstead, Essex CO9 4BQ. Tel: Ridgewell (044 085) 246.

Bressingham Gardens – Diss, Norfolk IP22 2AB. Tel: Bressingham (037 988) 464.

Broadleigh Gardens – Barr House, Bishops Hull, Taunton, Somerset TA4 1AE. Tel: Taunton (0823) 86231.

Broadwell Nursery – Broadwell, Nr Moreton-in-Marsh, Gloucestershire GL56 0TL. Tel: Cotswold (0451) 30549.

Burnham Nurseries Ltd – Orchid Avenue, Kingsteignton, Newton Abbot, Devon TQ12 3HG. Tel: (0626) 2233.

Thomas Butcher Limited – 60 Wickham Road, Shirley, Croydon, Surrey CR9 8AG. Tel: 01 654 3720/4254.

Richard G.M. Cawthorne – 28 Trigon Road, London SW8 1NH. (Visit by written appt. only).

John Chambers – 15 Westleigh Road, Barton Seagrave, Kettering, Northants NN15 5AJ. Tel: Kettering (0536) 513748 (evenings).

Peter Chappell – Spinners, Boldre, Lymington, Hants. Tel: Lymington (0590) 73347.

Beth Chatto – White Barn House, Elmstead Market, Colchester, Essex. Tel: Wivenhoe 2007.

Chiltern Seeds – Bortree Stile, Ulverston, Cumbria LA12 7PB. Tel: Ulverston (0229) 56946.

P.J. and J.W. Christian – Pentre Cottages, Minera, Wrexham, Clwyd, North Wales. Tel: 051 733 9889 evenings.

T. Clements – see Lynn Houseplants.

Collinwood Nurseries – Mottram St Andrew, Macclesfield, Cheshire SK10 4QR.

W. Cunningham and Sons (Heacham) Ltd – Dewdrop Nurseries, Heacham, Kings Lynn, Norfolk PE31 7DA. Tel: Heacham (0485) 70262.

J. Cunnington, Engelberg Nursery – Bulls Lane, Brookmans Park, Hatfield, Herts AL9 7AZ. Tel: Potters Bar (0707) 58161.

P. de Jager and Sons Ltd – The Nurseries, Marden, Kent TN12 9BP. Tel: Maidstone (0622) 831235.

Samuel Dobie and Son Ltd – Upper Dee Mills, Llangollen, Clwyd LL20 8SD. Tel: Clwyd (0978) 860119.

Joe Elliot – see Broadwell.

Fibrex Nurseries Ltd & Greybridge Geraniums – Harvey Road, Evesham, Worcs. Tel: Evesham (0386) 6190.

A Goatcher and Son – The Nurseries, Washington, Sussex. Tel: Ashington (0903) 892626.

Great Dixter Nurseries – Northiam, Sussex. Tel: Northiam (079 74) 3107.

C.W. Groves and Son – The Nurseries, West Bay Road, Bridport, Dorset DT6 4BA. Tel: Bridport (0308) 22654.

Highfield Nurseries – Whitminster, Gloucester GL2 7PL. Tel: Gloucester (0452) 740266.

Highlands Water Gardens Nurseries – Solesbridge Lane, Chorleywood, Herts WD3 5SZ. Tel: Chorleywood (092 78) 4135.

Hillier Nurseries (Winchester) Ltd – Ampfield House, Ampfield, Romsey, Hants SO5 9PA. Tel: Braishfield (0794) 68733.

Hill Rise Nursery – see Artiss.

Holden Clough Nurseries – Bolton-by-Bowland, Nr Clitheroe, Lancs BB7 4PF. Tel: Bolton-by-Bowland (02007) 615.

M. Holtzhausen – 14 High Cross Street, St Austell, Cornwall. Tel: St. Austell (0726) 4737.

Honeysome Aquatic Nursery – The Row, Sutton, Nr Ely, Cambs CB6 2PF. Tel: Ely (0353) 778 889.

Hortico (UK) Ltd – The Chestnuts, Spalding, Lincs PE12 6EB. Tel: (0775) 5936.

W.E.Th. Ingwersen Ltd – Birch Farm Nursery, Gravetye, E Grinstead, West Sussex RH19 4LE. Tel: Sharpthorne (0342) 810236.

Jackamoor's Hardy Plant Farm – Theobald's Park Road, Enfield, Middlesex EN2 9BG. Tel: 01 363 4278.

Jackman's Nurseries Ltd – Woking, Surrey. Tel: Woking (048 62) 4861/2.

Reginald Kaye Ltd – Waithman Nurseries, Silverdale, Carnforth, Lancs LA5 0TY. Tel: Carnforth (0524) 701252.

Keeper's Hill Nursery – Stapehill, Wimborne, Dorset BH21 7NE. Tel: Ferndown (0202) 873140.

Kelways Nurseries – Langport, Somerset TA10 9SL. Tel: Langport (0458) 250521.

Kent County Nurseries Ltd – Challock, Nr Ashford, Kent TN25 4DG. Tel: Challock (023 374) 256.

Lynn Houseplants Ltd – African Violet Nurseries, Station Road, Terrington St. Clements, King's Lynn, Norfolk PE34 4PL. Tel: King's Lynn (0553) 828374.

Marston Exotics – Marston Mill, Spring Gardens, Frome, Somerset BA11 2NZ. Tel: Street (0458) 42192.

Naturescape – Little Orchard, Whatton in the Vale, Nottingham NG13 9EP. Tel: Kinoulton (09497) 527.

Notcutts Nurseries Ltd – Woodbridge, Suffolk IP12 4AF. Tel: Woodbridge (039 43) 3344.

Oak Cottage Herb Farm – Nesscliffe, Nr Shrewsbury, Shropshire SY4 1DB. Tel: Nesscliffe (074381) 262.

The Orpington Nurseries – Rocky Lane, Gatton Park, Reigate, Surrey RH2 0TA. Tel: Merstham (0703 34) 2221.

Parkinson Herbs – Barras Moor Farm, Perran-ar-Worthal, Truro, Cornwall. Tel: Devoran (0872) 864380.

Potterton and Martin – The Cottage Nursery, Moortown Road, Nettleton, Caistor, Lincs LN7 6HX. Tel: Caistor (0472) 851792.

Ramparts Nursery – Bakers Lane, Colchester, Essex CO4 5BB. Tel: (0206) 852050.

Rileys Chrysanthemums – Alfreton Nurseries, Woolley Moor, Derby DE5 6FF.

Robinsons Hardy Plants – Greencourt Nurseries, Crockenhill, Swanley, Kent. Tel: Swanley (0322) 63819.

Thomas Rochfords & Sons Ltd – Forest Road, Cotebrook, Nr Tarporley, Cheshire. Tel: Little Budworth (082 921) 485.

The Rock Garden Nursery – Balbithan House, Kintore, Inverurie, Aberdeenshire AB5 0UQ. Tel: Kintore 2282.

R.V. Roger Limited – The Nurseries, Pickering, North Yorkshire YO18 7HG. Tel: Pickering (0751) 7226.

Scotts Nurseries (Merriott) Ltd – Merriott, Somerset. Tel: Crewkerne (0460) 72306.

Sherrards – Wantage Road, Donnington, Newbury RG16 9BE. Tel: 0635 47845.

Alan C. Smith – 127 Leaves Green Road, Keston, Kent BR2 6DG. Tel: Biggin Hill (095 94) 72531.

Southcombe Gardens Plant Nursery – Widecombe-in-the-Moor, Newton Abbot, Devon TQ13 7TU. Tel: Widecombe (036 42) 214.

Spalding Bulb Company Ltd – Spalding, Lincs PE11 1NA. Tel: Spalding (0775) 4436.

Spinners – see Peter Chappell.

Stassen – Spalding, Lincs PE11 2BQ. Tel: (0775) 2452.

St Bridget Nurseries – Old Rydon Lane, Exeter EX2 7JY. Tel: Topsham (039 287) 3672/3/4.

Stapeley Water Gardens Ltd – Stapeley, Nantwich, Cheshire CW5 7LH. Tel: (0270) 623868.

Stoke Lacy Herb Garden – Bromyard, Herefordshire. Tel: Burley Gate (043 278) 232.

Suttons Seeds Ltd – Hele Road, Torquay, Devon TQ2 7QJ. Tel: Torquay (0803) 62011.

Thompson and Morgan Ltd – London Road, Ipswich IP2 0BA. Tel: Ipswich (0473) 214226.

Thorp's Geraniums – 257 Finchampstead Road, Wokingham, Berks RH11 3JT. Tel: Wokingham (0734) 781181.

F. Toynbee Ltd – Toynbee's Nurseries, Barnham, Nr. Bognor Regis, Sussex. Tel: Yapton (0243) 552121.

Treasure's of Tenbury Ltd – Burford House Gardens, Tenbury Wells, Hereford and Worcester. Tel: Tenbury Wells (0584) 810777.

Mark and Elaine Trenear – Southview Nurseries, Chequers Lane, Eversley Cross, Hants RG27 0NT. Tel: Eversley (0734) 732300 or 732206 evenings.

Unwins Seeds Limited – Histon, Cambridgeshire, Tel: Histon (022 023) 2270.

van Tubergen – Oldfield Lane, Wisbech, Cambridge PE13 2HW. Tel: Wisbech (0945) 64949.

Harold Walker – Oakfield Nurseries, Huntingdon, Chester CH3 6EA.

Washfield Nursery – Horns Road, Hawkhurst, Kent. Tel: Hawkhurst (05805) 2522.

Waterperry Horticultural Centre – Nr Wheatley, Oxfordshire, OX9 1JZ. Tel: Ickford (084 47) 226.

Waveney Fish Farm – Park Road, Diss, Norfolk. Tel: Diss (0379) 2697.

The Weald Herbary – Park Cottage, Frittenden, Cranbrook, Kent, TN17 2AU. Tel: Frittenden (058080) 226.

Whitestone Gardens Ltd – Sutton under Whitestonecliffe, Thirsk, North Yorkshire YO7 2PZ. Tel: Thirsk (0845) 597467.

Wildwoods Water Gardens Ltd – Theobalds Park Road, Crews Hill, Enfield, Middlesex EN2 9BW. Tel: 01 366 0243/4.

HORTICULTURAL SOCIETIES DIRECTORY

ALPINES – E.M. Upward, Secretary, **Alpine Garden Society,** Lye End Link, St John's, Woking, Surrey. Tel: Woking (048 62) 69327.

AURICULA – R.G. Archer, Secretary, **National Auricula & Primula Society,** 128 Oxford Road, Old Marston, Oxford OX3 0RE.

BEGONIA – E. Catterall, Secretary, **The National Begonia Society,** 3 Gladstone Road, Dorridge, Knowle, Warwickshire.
J.A. Todd, Secretary, **Scottish Begonia Society,** 126 Sheephouse Hill, Fauldhouse, West Lothian, Tel: Fauldhouse (050 17) 265.

CARNATION – Mrs G.F. How, Secretary, **British National Carnation Society,** 56 Kingston Road, Romford, Essex. Tel: Romford (0708) 41552.
A.J. Langford, Secretary, **Lancashire & Cheshire Carnation Society,** 258 Mosley Common Road, Worsley, Manchester. Tel: 061 790 8462.

CARNIVOROUS – Alistair J. Mackie, Secretary, **The Carnivorous Plant Society,** Arnecote Park, Bicester, Oxon OX6 0NT. Tel: Bicester (086 92) 42126.

CHRYSANTHEMUM – S.G. Gosling, Secretary, **National Chrysanthemum Society,** 65 St Margaret's Avenue, Whetstone, London N20 9HT.

CYCLAMEN – Miss Gay Nightingale, Secretary, **Cyclamen Society,** Lavender House, 47 Lechmere Avenue, Chigwell, Essex.

DAFFODIL – D.J. Pearce, Hon Secretary, **The Daffodil Society,** 1 Noak's Cross Cottages, Great Braxted, Witham, Essex. Tel: Maldon (0621) 891495.

DAHLIA – Philip Damp, General Secretary, **National Dahlia Society,** 26 Burns Road, Lillington, Leamington Spa, Warwicks CV32 7ER.

DELPHINIUM – C.R. Edwards, Secretary, **The Delphinium Society,** 11 Long Grove, Seer Green, Bucks HP9 2YN. Tel: Beaconsfield (049 46) 6315.

GERANIUM – Arthur Biggin, Hon. Secretary, **British and European Geranium Society,** 'Morval', The Hills, Bradwell, Sheffield S30 2HZ. Tel: Hope Valley (0433) 20459.
Miss J.Y. Baynham, Secretary, **The Midland Geranium, Glasshouse & Garden Society,** 179 Poplar Avenue, Edgbaston, Birmingham B17 8EJ. Tel: 021 429 1947.

GLADIOLUS – Mrs M. Rowley, Secretary, **The British Gladiolus Society,** 10 Sandbach Road, Thurlwood, Rode Heath, Stoke-on-Trent ST7 3RN.
E.C. Robinson MBE, Secretary, **Gladiolus Breeders Association,** 13 Chelsea Avenue, Southend on Sea, Essex SS1 2YL.
W.F. Murray, Secretary, **Scottish Gladiolus Society,** 63 Gardiner Road, Edinburgh EH4 3RL. Tel: (031 332) 3681.

HARDY PLANTS – Miss Barbara White, Secretary, **The Hardy Plant Society,** 10 St. Barnabas Road, Emmer Green, Caversham, Reading, Berks RG4 8RA.

HERB – Ms Elaine M. Hackney, Secretary, **The Herb Society,** 34 Boscobel Place, London SW1. Tel: 01 235 1530.

IRIS – Mrs. T.A. Blanco White, Secretary, **The British Iris Society,** 72 South Hill Park, London NW3 2SN. Tel: (01 435) 2700.

LILY – E.M. Rix, Secretary, **The Lily Group of the RHS,** RHS Gardens, Wisley, Ripley, Woking, Surrey. Tel: Ripley (048 643) 2235.

NERINE – C.A. Norris, Secretary, **The Nerine Society,** Brookend House, Welland, Malvern, Worcs.

ORCHID – P. Seaton, Secretary, **The Central Orchid Society,** 8 Church View, Bewdley, Worcs. Tel: Bewdley (0299) 402731.
L.E. Bowen, Secretary, **The Orchid Society of Great Britain,** 28 Felday Road, Lewisham, London SE13 7HJ. Tel: 01 690 4519.

PANSY – Hugh Campbell OBE, Sec & Treasurer, **Scottish Pansy & Viola Association,** 34 Berkeley St, Glasgow, Scotland.

PELARGONIUM – Henry J. Wood, Secretary, **British Pelargonium & Geranium Society,** 129 Aylesford Avenue, Beckenham, Kent BR3 3RX.

SAINTPAULIA – Miss. N. Tamburn, Secretary, **Saintpaulia & Houseplant Society,** 82 Rossmore Court, Park Road, London NW1 6XY.

SEMPERVIVUM – Peter J. Mitchell, Secretary, **The Sempervivum Society,** 11 Wingle Tye Road, Burgess Hill, Sussex RH15 9HR. Tel: Burgess Hill (044 46) 6848.

SWEET PEA – L.H.O. Williams, Secretary, **The National Sweet Pea Society,** Corderoys, Upton, Didcot, Oxon OX11 9JH. Tel: Blewbury (0235) 850261.

Bibliography

Aphrodisiacs and Love Stimulants – John Davenport, Luxor Press, 1965.
Aphrodisiacs in your Garden – Charles Connell, Arthur Barker, 1965.
Art of Botanical Illustration, The – Wilfrid Blunt, Collins, 1971.
Atlas of the British Flora – Ed. by F.H. Perring and S.M. Walters, Thomas Nelson, 1962.
Botanic Garden, The – B. Maund F.L.S., Simpkin and Marshall, 1825-6.
Cinquefoil: Herbs to Quicken the Five Senses – Mrs C.F. Leyel, Faber and Faber, 1957.
Colour Schemes for the Flower Garden – Gertrude Jekyll, Antique Collectors Club, 1983.
Compassionate Herbs – Mrs C.F. Leyel, Faber and Faber, 1946.
Complete Herbal – Nicholas Culpeper M.D., Thomas Kelly, 1828.
Complete Naturalist, The
A Life of Linnaeus – Wilfrid Blunt, Collins, 1971.
Concise British Flora in Colour, The – W. Keble Martin, George Rainbird 1969.
Dictionary of Garden Plants, The – Roy Hay and Patrick M. Synge, Ebury Press and Michael Joseph in collaboration with the Royal Horticultural Society, 1969.
Dwarf Bulbs – Brian Mathew, Batsford, 1973.
Early Gardening Catalogues – John Harvey, Phillimore, 1972.
Early Nurserymen – John Harvey, Phillimore, 1974.
Elixirs of Life – Mrs C.F. Leyel, Stuart and Watkins, 1970.
Englishman's Flora, The – Geoffrey Grigson, Paladin, 1975.
Familiar Garden Flowers – Figured by F. Edward Hulme, F.L.S., F.S.A. and Described by Shirley Hibberd, Cassell.
Fantastic Garlands: An Anthology of Flowers and Plants from Shakespeare – Lys de Bray, Blandford Press, 1982.
Flora of the British Isles – A.R. Clapham, T.G. Tutin and E.F. Warburg, Cambridge University Press, 1962.
Flowers and their Histories – Alice M. Coats, Adam and Charles Black, 1968.
Flowers of the World – Frances Perry, Illustrated by Leslie Greenwood, Hamlyn, in collaboration with the Royal Horitcultural Society, 1972.
Folk-Lore of Shakespeare – Rev. T.F. Thiselton Dyer M.A. Oxon, Griffith and Farran, 1883.
Frederick Sander: The Orchid King – Arthur Swinson, Hodder and Stoughton, 1970.
Garden, The, An Illustrated History – Julia S. Berrall, Penguin Books, 1978.
Georgian Gardens – David C. Stuart, Robert Hale, 1979.
Gerard's Herball – The Essence thereof distilled by Marcus Woodward from the Edition of T.H. Johnson, 1636, Gerald Howe, 1927.
Grandmother's Secrets: Her Green Guide to Health from Plants – Jean Palaiseul, Barrie and Jenkins, 1973.
Herbaceous Garden Flora – F.K. Maskins M.A., F.L.S., J.M. Dent and Sons, 1957.
Herb-Garden, The – Frances A. Bardswell, Adam and Charles Black, 1911.
History of England – G.M. Trevelyan, Longman, 1981.
Holy Bible, The – Collins, 1954.
Illustrated Herbal Handbook, The – Juliette de Baïracli Levy, Faber and Faber, 1974.
Language and Sentiment of Flowers – Compiled and Edited by L.V., Frederick Warne, 1866.
Living Tradition in the Garden – R. Gorer, 1974.

Miss Jekyll: Portrait of a Great Gardener – Betty Massingham, David and Charles, 1982.
Modern Herbal, A – Mrs M. Grieve F.R.H.S., Jonathan Cape, 1974.
My Garden in Autumn and Winter – E.A. Bowles M.A., David and Charles, 1972.
My Garden in Summer – E.A. Bowles M.A., David and Charles, 1972.
New Illustrated Gardening Encyclopaedia, The – Ed. by Richard Sudell F.I.L.A., A.R.H.S., Odhams Press.
New Larousse Encyclopedia of Mythology – Introduction by Robert Graves, Hamlyn, 1978.
Old Fashioned Flowers – Sacheverell Sitwell, Illustrated by John Farleigh, Country Life, 1948.
Pelargoniums – Derek Clifford, Blandford Press, 1958.
Perennial Garden Plants, or the Modern Florilegium – Graham Stuart Thomas, J.M. Dent and Sons, 1982.
Plants for Shade – Allen Paterson, J.M. Dent and Sons, 1981.
Pot-Pourri from a Surrey Garden – Mrs C.W. Earle, Smith, Elder and Co., 1900.
Potter's Cyclopaedia of Botanical Drugs and Preparations – R.C. Wren, Potter and Clark.
Power of Plants, The – Brendan Lehane, John Murray, 1977.
Quest for Plants: A History of the Horticultural Explorers – Alice M. Coats, Studio Vista, 1969.
Reader's Digest Encyclopaedia of Garden Plants and Flowers – Reader's Digest Association, 1975.
Reader's Encyclopaedia – William Rose Benét, A. C. Black, 1972.
Royal Horticultural Society Dictionary of Gardening – Ed. by Fred J. Chittenden, O.B.E., F.L.S., V.M.H. and Patrrick M. Synge M.A., F.L.S., Oxford University Press, 1977.
Scented Garden, The – Eleanour Sinclair Rohde, Medici Society.
Sentiment of Flowers, The – Robert Tyas F.R.B.S., Houlston and Stoneman, 1844.
Simon and Schuster's Complete Guide to Plants and Flowers – Ed. by Frances Perry, Simon and Schuster.
Victorian Flower Garden, The – Geoffrey Taylor, Skeffington, 1952.
Wild Flowers of the World – Barbara Everard and Brian D. Morley, Octopus Books, 1974.
Wild Garden, The – William Robinson, Century Publishing, 1983.
Wood and Garden – Gertrude Jekyll, Antique Collectors' Club, 1981.

Index